POLITICAL PARTIES, PARTY MANIFESTOS AND ELECTIONS IN INDIA, 1909–2014

In the parliamentary system of government, manifestos constitute and represent an important aspect of the democratic electoral politics as statements of a party's ideology, response and policy. This book offers an examination of election manifestos of different political parties in India at the national level. It explores the manifesto as an input to these policy process and presents a comparative perspective and understanding on the issues and approaches of the national political parties on key affairs.

The book traces the evolution of the electoral system, political parties and party manifestos in India as they emerged and developed over time. It looks at the Statutes of 1909, 1919 and 1935 along with the party manifestos and elections until 1945–1946. The author further analyses Constituent Assembly debates on the electoral system and the stances of political parties on national reconstruction through documents from parties, including the Indian National Congress, the Communist Party of India, the Socialist Party, Jana Sangh and the All India Scheduled Castes Federation.

Covering manifestos of sixteen Lok Sabha Elections (from the first general election of 1952 to 2014), this book provides a comprehensive overview of how major political parties think on significant social, economic, political, foreign and defence-related issues. It will be useful to scholars and researchers of political science, election studies, modern Indian history, public administration, law and governance, sociology, media and journalism and also to legislators and policymakers.

R. K. Tiwari is former Professor of Public Administration and former Honorary Consultant at the Indian Institute of Public Administration, New Delhi, India. He also worked as Senior Consultant, Centre for Public Policy and Governance, Institute of Applied Manpower Research and was Senior Fellow at the Indian Council of Social Science Research (ICSSR). His books include *Rural Employment Programmes in India: The Implementation Process* (1990); *Human Rights and Law: Bonded Labour in India* (2011); and *Reflections on Indian Administration*, 2 volumes (2017, co-edited). In 2013, he was conferred the Paul H. Appleby Award for rendering outstanding services in the field of Public Administration.

POLITICAL PARTIES, PARTY MANIFESTOS AND ELECTIONS IN INDIA, 1909–2014

R. K. Tiwari

Routledge
Taylor & Francis Group
LONDON AND NEW YORK

First published 2019 by Routledge

2 Park Square, Milton Park, Abingdon, Oxon, OX14 4RN
605 Third Avenue, New York, NY 10017

Routledge is an imprint of the Taylor & Francis Group, an informa business

First issued in paperback 2020

British Library Cataloguing-in-Publication Data
A catalogue record for this book is available from the British Library

Library of Congress Cataloging-in-Publication Data
A catalog record for this book has been requested

ISBN: 978-1-138-57529-5 (hbk)
ISBN: 978-0-367-73333-9 (pbk)

Typeset in Sabon
by Apex CoVantage, LLC

FOR SHREE DEVIKA, AGASTYA AND ROHAN

CONTENTS

TABLES

TABLES

FOREWORD

Party manifestos constitute the most important source of a political party's aim and object as well as its approach to bring about social, political and economic change. Party manifestos deal with complex societal issues. In a way, the manifestos represent what has been generally attributed to the definition of ideology, i.e. 'ideas about society'. In the Indian context, one has to look into the history of the period relating to the Renaissance and freedom struggle to understand the evolution of ideas on nation-building and economic modernization.

In India, the debate and discussion on the question of polity, economy and society commenced with the emergence of political associations and interest groups in the early 1840s much before the founding of the Indian National Congress (INC). However, the annual conferences of the INC brought to the forefront in a more intense manner the main social, political and economic issues confronting the country. In a way, these conferences summed up the problems of the social and economic backwardness of the country. This was voiced in party resolutions and protests that were mostly non-violent, but were sometimes violent also.

The constitutional reforms brought by the British in the Statutes of 1909, 1919 and 1935 introduced albeit slowly and gradually reform in the system of representation. The elections were conducted on the basis of classes and interests. However, the electoral politics since the first election of 1909–1910 contained all the trappings of a parliamentary system. This process of parliamentary system became more refined with each successive constitutional reform.

Since the beginning, party manifestos formed an important part of electoral politics in India. In this context, the manifesto of Congress Democratic Party (1920), prepared by Bal Gangadhar Tilak, is a landmark document. It is very fascinating to know that, nearly a century ago, Tilak thought of modernizing the Indian economy on the western lines, on the one hand, and on the other also pleaded for Swadeshism. In the social sphere, emphasis was given to the need for sanitation, industrial and technical education as well as compulsory and free education, etc. Similarly, we also get a glimpse of political programmes of the Swaraj Party manifesto (1923 and 1926), the Justice Party manifesto (1923, 1926 and 1930) and the National Unionist Party manifesto (1923 and 1926). It is equally interesting to know the intense debate between the right-wing and the left-wing of the Indian National Congress on economic modernization from 1928 to 1937. It eventually culminated in the election manifesto prepared by Jawaharlal Nehru for the 1937 elections. In the context of 1937 elections, besides INC, other regional parties (Krishak Praja Party, National Unionist Party, Justice Party, National Agriculturalist Party) also expressed their approach on all the major issues. In retrospect, since 1919 upto independence, most of the initiatives regarding social and economic development in the provinces came from the party manifestos. From this perspective, these manifestos have a historical significance.

The development in the field of representation also includes changes brought out in the electoral machinery and procedures. It also deals with the emergence of political parties and elections. This monograph also provides a brief sidelight on the electoral behaviour, methodology of election campaigns, selection of candidates, funding pattern and organizational issues of political parties, etc.

The second phase in the development of party manifestos commenced after Independence. A period which saw not only the emergence of new political parties, but also the Constitution providing along with the machinery for governance, a vision of social and economic change. To concretize this vision, the Planning Commission was set up in March 1950 (now replaced by the Niti Aayog). Immediately after Independence and before the first general election 1951–1952, the national political parties engaged themselves in the preparation of their approach to the reconstruction of the Indian society. This resulted in the publication of the following party documents: Indian National Congress – Report of Economic Programme Committee (January 1948); the Communist Party of India – Draft Programme (October 1951); the Socialist Party – Programme (October 1947); All India Scheduled Castes Federation– Draft Manifesto (October 1951); Jana Sangh (BJP) – Party Manifesto (October 1951). The Swatantra party came with their approach – Statement of Principles (August 1959). These documents are an important source of the initial approach of these political parties on various issues. Besides, the author has made a very fine effort in analysing the party manifestos of national political parties in a comparative manner. This comparison provides an overview of the approach of political parties on a large number of complex problems and also helps in identifying the similarities and differences on various facets.

So far, in the study of Indian politics, party manifestos have remained a neglected area. I hope that this monograph will generate interest in the study of party manifestos from multiple perspectives. In this context, I am of the view that there is a need for a volume devoted to the compilation (on selective basis) of the party manifestos of all elections conducted before and after independence. This will provide an important source of information on the approach of the political parties and also help in relating manifestos with other parameters of governance. Another area which I feel needs to be explored relates to the implementation of party manifestos. It is generally assumed that, by and large, the party which forms the government fulfills their electoral promises. However, there is a need to systematically examine how far different political parties which formed the government at the Centre (1952–2014) were able to implement their manifesto.

We established a parliamentary democracy in which the political parties play a pivotal role and provide, through the manifestos, their vision for reconstructing society. From this perspective, I feel that this monograph is an important contribution to Indian politics.

T. N. Chaturvedi
Chairman, Indian Institute of Public
Administration, New Delhi, India

ACKNOWLEDGEMENTS

I am grateful to the Indian Council of Social Science Research for awarding me a Senior Fellowship from 2010 to 2012, to pursue the study on *Political Parties, Party Manifestos and Elections in India*. Most of the research and writing of this study was carried at the Indian Institute of Public Administration (IIPA). At the IIPA, I am particularly thankful to the late Dr P. L. Sanjeeva Reddy, Dr. B. S. Baswan and the late Dr. Rakesh Hooja, the former Directors and to the present Director, Dr. Tishyarakshit Chatterjee, for extending all the facilities to conduct this study.

I am grateful to Dr. Ajit M. Banerjee, formerly of the United Nations, New York, for his encouragement and professional help. I am also grateful to Professor C. P. Bhambri, formerly of the Jawaharlal Nehru University, for reading and commenting on the manuscript.

I am also thankful to the following friends both for professional and personal help: Professors Jaideep Singh, S. N. Mishra, Aasha Kapur Mehta, Dolly Arora, Sujata Singh, S. N. Singh and Dr. M. K. Narian.

In the completion of the study, I am grateful to many librarians and their professional staff, who dealt with my numerous requests with patience. I am particularly thankful to A. K. Nath, Meena Mishra and H. C. Yadav at the IIPA Library; Hemlata Yadav, Kanchan Nagpal and Rajiv Mishra at the India International Centre Library; Shashi Kumar and Geeta Yadav at the Nehru Memorial Museum and Library; Dr. Sulekh Chand at the Election Commission of India Library; Dr. Jyotsana Arora at the Indian Council of Historical Research Library; Dr. G. C. K. Rai at the Indian Council of World Affairs (Sapru House); Dr. Avinash Jha, Centre for the Study of Developing Societies and Sudhir Hilsayan, Editor, Dr. Ambedkar Foundation, Ministry of Social Justice and Empowerment, Government of India.

Most of the material on the manifestos was taken from secondary sources. Due acknowledgments have been made at appropriate places.

Besides, I am thankful to the headquarters of the following national political parties for readily providing some of their recent manifestos and other relevant literature: Indian National Congress, Bharatiya Janata Party, Communist Party of India and Communist Party of India (M).

I am extremely thankful to Taruna Rani, Research Associate, for providing excellent research support. Her able assistance has been of great value. She showed a remarkable sense of responsibility and sincerity in the completion of the study. I am also thankful to Devinder Soni and Komal Hadhaly of COMPUTEC, New Delhi, for assisting me in all computer-related matters.

I am thankful to my daughter, Anushree Tiwari Sharma, for professionally assisting me in this study and performing related tasks with great skill.

I am indebted to my wife, Dr. Neera for her constant understanding, encouragement and unstinted support without which I could not have completed the study.

R. K. Tiwari
Indian Institute of
Public Administration

ABBREVIATIONS

ABLTC	Akhil Bharatiya LokTantrik Congress
AC	Arunachal Congress
AD	Akali Dal
AGP	Asom Gana Parishad
AI	Anglo-Indians
AIADMK	All-India Anna Dravida Munnetra Kazhagam
AIFB	All India Forward Bloc
AICC	All India Congress Committee
AIMIM	All India Majlis-E-Ittehadul Muslimeen
ASDC	Autonomous State Demand Committee
BJD	Biju Janata Dal
BJP	Bharatiya Janata Party
BJS	Bharatiya Jana Sangh
BSMC	Bodoland State Movement Committee
CCF	Citizens Front Common
Cong(I)	Congress Indira
CPI	Communist Party of India
CPI(M)	Communist Party of India (Marxist)
DBSM	Democrartic Bahujan Samaj Morcha
DMK	Dravida Munnetra Kazhagam
HLD(R)	Haryana Lok Dal (Rashtriya)
HVC	Himachal Vikas Congress
HVP	Haryana Vikas Party
INC	Indian National Congress
INC(I)	Indian National Congress(I)
INC(O)	Indian National Congress (O)
IND	Independent
INLD	Indian National Lok Dal
IUML	Indian Union Muslim League

JD	Janata Dal
JD(A)	Janata Dal Ajit
JD(S)	Janata Dal (Secular)
JP(U)	Janata Party (United)
JKNC	Jammu and Kashmir National Conference
JM	Jan Morcha
JMM	Jharkhand Mukti Morcha
JNP	Janata Party
KCM	Kerala Congress (Mani)
KMPP	Kisan Mozdoor Praja Party
LD	Lok Dal
LK	Lok Shakti
LJSP	Lok Janashakti Party
LKS	Lok Shakti
MADMK	MGR Anna Dravida Munnetra Kazhagam
MDMK	Marumalarchi Deravida Munnetra Kazhagam
MGR-ADMK	MGR Anna Dravida Munnetra Kazhagam
MSCP	Manipur State Congress Party
MUL	Muslim League
NC	National Conference
NCP	Nationalist Congress Party
PDP	People's Democratic Party
PDS	Public Distribution Scheme/Party for Democratic Socialism
PMK	Pattali Makkal Katchi
PRBP	People's Republican Party
RLD	Rashtriya Lok Dal
RPI	Republican Party of India
RPI(A)	Republican Party of India (Athavale)
RJD	Rashtriya Janata Dal
RJP	Rashtriya Janata Party (Anand Mohan)
RSP	Revolutionary Socialist Party
SAD	Shiromani Akali Dal
SCF	Scheduled Castes Federation
SDF	Sikkim Democratic Front
SMT	Samata Party
SP	Samajwadi Party
SHS	Shiva Sena
SOC	Socialist Party
SWA	Swantantra Party
TC	Trinamool Congress

TDP	Telugu Desam Party
TMC	Tamil Maanila Congress
TRC	Tamizhaga Rajiv Congress
TRS	Telangana Rashtrya Samiti
VCK	Viduthalai Chiruthaigal Katchi

GLOSSARY

Aadhaar serves as a proof of identity and address, anywhere in India.
Adivasis refers to some tribes and forest people in India.
Anna one-sixteenth of a rupee.
Arya Samaj Modern Hindu sect, founded by Dayanand Saraswati (1824–1883), based mainly on *Vedas* and opposed to idolatry.
Ayurveda the traditional Hindu system of medicine.
Babri Masjid a mosque, built as far back as the sixteenth century by a general of the Mughal emperor Babar (1483–1520).
Bande Mataram ('Hail to the Mother'): a hymn written by Bankim Chandra Chatterjee (1838–1894) in his novel *Anandmath;* it became the national anthem of the Indian freedom movement.
Bhagvad Gita one of the most popular sacred texts of Hinduism.
Brahma Samaj Hindu sect formed by Raja Rammohan Roy (1772–1833) in early nineteenth century, worshipping not idols but formless divinity; flourished in Bengal.
Brahmin the highest Hindu caste.
Crore ten million.
Dalit the term is used for Scheduled Castes. The earlier term 'harijan' has been in disuse since the seventies.
Devadasi the official name of the girls who are devoted to dancing in the idol-temples of Southern India.
Doordarshan the Indian Public Service Broadcaster, is one of the largest television networks in the world.
Gram Panchayat village tribunal or 'council of five'.
Gram Sabha a body consisting of persons registered in the electoral rolls relating to a village comprised within the area of Panchayat at the village level.
Indira Mahila Yojana a scheme for the welfare of women for pursuing micro enterprises.

Jagirdari holder of a royal grant of land and its rental.
Khadi hand-spun cloth.
Khal it's a Bengali word meaning canals.
Kisan peasant.
Lok Pal the institutional framework recommended for fighting corruption by the first Administrative Reforms Commission.
Lok Sabha lower house of the Indian Parliament.
Mandal a sub-taluka unit of revenue administration.
Maryada code of conduct.
Mussalman Muslim.
Nyaya Panchayat institutions for dispensation of justice at the local rural level.
Panch a member of panchayat.
Panchayat originally a caste of village council (from panch, Hindi for five); later used for officially constituted organs of local government.
Panchayati Raj 'rule by panchayats'; name given to new form of local government in the 1950s.
Pandit title given to a learned man or teacher, especially a Brahmin.
Praja public.
Prarthana Samaj Prayer Society modelled after the Brahma Samaj. M.G. Ranade (1842–1901) was one of the early members of the Samaj. Under Ranade's judicious guidance, the Prarthana Samaj did not cut itself off from the rest of Hindu society, but strove gradually to bring the orthodox around to its position.
Prasar Bharati an autonomous body appointed by the Government of India, which manages the Doordarshan and the All India Radio.
Ramakrishna Mission The Ramakrishna Mission was founded by Swami Vivekananda (1863–1902). There are numerous centres, located in different parts of India, devoted to social service and educational work. The Mission has its own hospitals, dispensaries, high schools, industrial and agricultural schools, colleges, libraries and publishing houses. It has been consistently active in relieving the victims of earthquakes, floods, famines and epidemics.
Ram Janmabhoomi Ram Janmabhoomi is the name given to the site that many Hindus believe to be the birthplace of Rama. The Ram Janmabhoomi – Babri Masjid issue relate to the belief that the Ram Janmabhoomi was located at the site of the Babri Masjid.
Rajya Sabha upper house of the Indian Parliament.
Rashtriya Swasthya Bima Yojana National Health Insurance Scheme.

Rashtriya Uchhatar Shiksha higher education.

Rath Yatra Rath Yatra is a Hindu festival associated with Lord Jagannath at Puri, Orissa.

Ryot a peasant cultivator.

Samachar The independent news agencies, the United News of India (UNI) and the Press Trust of India (PTI), were amalgamated with two lesser agencies into a single state-controlled news service called Samachar.

Sarva Shiksha Abhiyan programme to educate all.

Swadeshi Indian made.

Swaraj independence.

Taluq a sub-division of a district.

Tehsil a revenue-collecting sub-district.

Thana a police station.

Theosophical Society The Theosophical Society was founded in 1875 by Russian Madame Blavatsky and the American Colonel Olcott. This Society hold reincarnation, Karma ('the sum of a person's actions in this and previous states of existence, viewed as affecting their future fate; the sum of good or bad luck, viewed as resulting from one's actions' – *The Oxford Dictionary*) and other Hindu or Buddhist conceptions as central doctrines. In 1882, the headquarters of the Society was moved to Adyar, Madras.

Unani a system of medicine practiced in parts of India, thought to be derived via mediaeval Muslim physicians.

Van Bandhu Kalyan Yojana a welfare scheme for the forest dwellers.

Vidya Mandir Scheme Mahatma Gandhi's views on education are contained in *Hind Swaraj*. He was of the view that 'we have enslaved the nation by receiving English education'. In the context of the Vidya Mandir scheme, he emphasized the following: ethical education, education through craft, and not merely through books, and the mother tongue as a medium of education. In the 1937 manifesto of the Congress Party, the Vidya Mandir scheme was an important component in the sphere of education. It was introduced after the victory of the Congress Party in Bihar, Orissa, UP and Central Provinces at the elementary level.

Wakf The Supreme Court of India in a Judgement of January 28, 1998 observed the following about *wakf* 'a permanent dedication of property for purposes recognized by Muslim law as pious, religious or charitable and the property having been found as *wakf* would always retain its character as a *wakf*'.

Yoga one of six systems of Hindu philosophy; practice of concentration (including physical) to control the mind.

Zamindari land held by a *zamindar*.

Zamindars landholder, often with a considerable holding.

Zila Parishad local self-government at district level.

INTRODUCTION

In the parliamentary system of government, manifestos constitute and represent an important aspect of electoral politics. Cecil S. Emden in his classic book *The People and The Constitution*, delves deeply into this aspect and provide a historical account of the people's influence in British Government. This influence commenced after the passing of the Great Reform Bill of 1832.[1] The people's influence not only gave rise to consultation with the electorate, i.e. 'making submissions of proposed items of policy to the electorate', but also impacted 'reorganization of political parties; methods of conducting general election campaigns', etc.

The further widening of franchise in Britain in 1867 and 1884 produced 'a radical change in the constitutional balance'. This change led to demand for social reform, which compelled the political parties, to include in their manifestos 'some proposal of social amelioration'.[2] The inclusion of 'social amelioration' measures became more prominent and pronounced after the extension of the franchise in 1918. In this context, the British Labour Party gave a new 'orientation' to the manifesto by putting before the electorate 'with the set of concrete proposal which if successful, it is thereby mandated to put into practice'. One important corollary, which emerged from the influence of the people resulted, as has been observed by Richard Crossman, that in Britain since 1920s 'We have moved from . . . an unchanging established order . . ., to a Government of planned change and welfare economics'.[3] In the context of manifesto, another aspect which Crossman emphasized relate to its implementation 'the pace at which it is implemented, and whether anything else is implemented, is a matter completely and absolutely at the discretion of the Parliamentary Party'.[4]

In a major study on party manifestos in European democracies, it has been observed that manifesto represents party policy at a given point in time.[5] A number of studies have been conducted in the context of British political system, whereby it has been demonstrated that contents of the manifesto are 'well reflected in post-election priorities' And as such the British party 'can be assumed to carry through most of the election priority into government'.[6] In the background of the meaning and place of manifesto in the British political system, it is not only interesting but also revealing to emphasize the place of British Labour Party manifesto of 1945, 'which transformed British society for the better through the welfare state'.[7]

Indian political system and manifesto

It is proposed to provide an overview of the role, function and place of party manifesto in the Indian political system. After the revolt of the 1857, the power was transferred from the East India Company to the Crown by the Government of India Act, 1858. The Government of India also started to nominate both to its central and provincial councils selected Indians, for the purpose of consultation on matters of governance. The number of such non-officials was increased in 1892, and along with nomination a process of consultation commenced with such representative bodies as municipalities, universities, landholder's associations and chambers of commerce. The Indian Councils Act 1909 further introduced non-official majorities in the Councils. And it also provided at the provincial level for the direct election by secret ballot of more than half of the non-official members. This process was further strengthened by the Government of India Act 1919. The Act committed the government to an extension of parliamentary government and to a radical devolution of legislative and financial powers from the Centre to the Provinces. At the Centre, the consultative pattern remained as mentioned previously. The Act of 1935 provided for an All India Federation with division of power between the centre and the units. The Act also provided for dyarchy at the centre. The Federal Legislature was to be bicameral. It is evident that the British introduced, in the provincial and central legislative councils, electoral politics, both on the basis of 'classes and interests' as well as upon 'group and community' lines. Party manifestos constituted an important aspect in the elections conducted between 1909 and 1946.

In the context of the aforementioned background, the Union Constitution Committee of the Constituent Assembly (1946–1950) under the Chairmanship of Jawaharlal Nehru recommended the parliamentary type of government based on the English model. Regarding the suitability of the parliamentary system of government, K.M. Munshi observed that 'For the last thirty or forty years, some kind of responsibility has been introduced in the governance of the country. Our Constitutional traditions have become parliamentary and we have now all our provinces functioning more or less on the British model'.[8]

On the other hand, Mahavir Tyagi highlighted the importance of the political parties their manifestos and the mandate of the people. He observed that 'The Cabinet . . . has to be loyal to the majority party which has the mandate of the people to run the government on their behalf. The administration shall be run on the lines of the manifesto which has been approved by the general electorate'.[9]

The object of analysing party manifestos in the Indian context, is to understand the ideology as well as responses of national political parties on various complex issues. Party manifestos are taken as an indicator of the party's policy positions. Policy/programmatic statements are central features of political parties. In party programmes, the political ideas and goals of parties are put on record. Manifestos offer several things important in a parliamentary democracy: 'one, a standard of performance against which subsequent achievements can be measured: two, authoritative statement of the party's clarity on policy; three, articulation of the popular consensus on major themes'.[10]

India can rightly claim to have a most extensive experience of conducting democratic elections amongst all the developing countries of the world. India can also claim to be world's largest democracy. Democratic systems are based on periodic elections to give a choice to the people to elect their representatives. Since 1952, India has held sixteen general elections for the Lok Sabha. Millions of Indian voters went to the polls to cast their votes on each occasion.

On the eve of elections, each party issues its manifesto, outlining its basic beliefs, assessment of situation and approach to different problems and issues. It is imperative for each political party to identify the problems in the first place, to set before itself certain objectives with a view to solve those problems and to decide a certain strategy of means by which to attain those objectives. In doing so, each political party articulates its overall perception of its environment and the role it envisages for itself in the same. In other words, each party spells out its distinct ideology. Manifestos are statements of party policy on various issues. The political parties in India and elsewhere also try to get the electoral support not only through their image but also through the articulation of concrete policy proposals.

Besides, the political parties in India have been regarded as playing an important role in directing the policies of government. Most of these policies and programmes are part of each party's election manifesto, and they promise to carry them out, if elected. However, in the literature on political parties in India, little attention has been given to the manifesto both as an input to the policy process as well as comparative perspective on the issues and approach of different national political parties. This study does not examine the methodology of the preparation of manifestos by different political parties.

In the Indian context, it is also true that the Prime Ministers regularly report back to their annual party conferences on the promises fulfilled as delineated in the party manifesto. Recently the Prime Minister Narendra Modi asked his Cabinet colleagues 'to treat the BJP's poll manifesto as a sacred document like the *Bhagvad Gita* and read it every day to assess the amount of work they have done so far to fulfill the promises'.[11] As a matter of fact, each manifesto is considered a bench-mark against which the progress of a government may be measured. In fact, a manifesto is regarded as a means of judging the faithfulness of a government in carrying through its intentions. Without the manifestos, the voter has no criteria for judging the government. To the party which forms the government, the manifesto provided the 'mandate' for the government actions.

Scope of the study

The party government model assumes, firstly, that there should be important policy choices between parties. Analysis of manifestos do show that there are clear differences between the parties on many policies. A second assumption is that the replacement of one party by another in government will have different consequences. In the general sense of term, manifestos are accurate guides to what a party will do in government, and as and when the promises can be cast in the form of parliamentary legislation.

From 1952 to 1991, for the Lok Sabha elections, the manifestos were issued by all the contesting political parties. However, from 1996 to 2004, party manifestos were issued by the alliance partners. The first such manifesto was issued in 1996 termed as 'Common Minimum Programme' (CMP) by the National Front parties. Such an experiment was also attempted by the National Democratic Alliance (NDA) 1999 and by United Progressive Alliance (UPA) in the Lok Sabha Elections 2004. These manifestos contained concrete and considered policies of the alliance partners and were based on common consensus.

In the context of Indian democracy, political parties have attracted enormous attention. There have been studies dealing with the growth and functioning of political parties; contemporary overview of political parties; society and democratic structures; and the organization of political support (around caste and community), communal politics, coalition politics, etc. There have also been a large number of studies on elections with a special focus on primary data relating to Constituency-wise and State-wise Lok Sabha results. Besides, survey-based studies on elections have also been conducted. However, party manifestos since the first general elections of 1952 have not been given any prominence. In the absence of such studies, it is difficult to compare manifestos of political parties, understand the changing party ideologies as well as generalize about the way political parties shape their appeals.[12] On the other hand, since the Post World War period, in the western democracies, party manifestos have been an important subject of study.

The framework of study

This study will focus attention only for the Lok Sabha elections from 1952 to 2014 by the following national political parties: Indian National Congress (INC), Communist Party of India (CPI) and Communist Party of India Marxist (CPI(M)), Socialist Party (SP)/Samyukta Socialist Party (SSP) and Jana Sangh/Bharatiya Janata Party (BJP). Even those national parties which are now defunct (Swatantra Party (SWP) and Praja Socialist Party (PSP)), etc. also have been analysed. This study covers almost all the issues as delineated by and large in the manifestos of these parties.

The information has been collected from the party manifestos of these national parties. For the objective and systematic description of the content of the written communication, the party manifestos are analysed by the content analysis method. This analysis is derived from the question as to what ideas, issues and concerns political parties advocate in their manifestos. Myron Weiner's observation, in the context of the politics of modernization in India, rightly emphasizes the need for

> 'research and analysis of both the orientation and political position of various groups supporting and opposing new changes, as well as the political patterns emerging, would not only provide greater understanding of the ways in which Indian politics now functions, but might give us additional insight into the direction of change'.[13]

Outline of the book

Keeping the aforementioned perspective, the study has been divided in four chapters. The first chapter deals with the evolution of ideas on nation-building and modernization. The purpose of this chapter is to analyse and provide the essence of ideas on nation-building commencing from the Indian Renaissance. It briefly describes the ideas of Raja Rammohan Roy, Dadabhai Naroji, Mahadev Govind Ranade, Romesh Chandra Dutt, Gopal Krishna Gokhale and others on social and economic modernization. It also briefly covers the political philosophy of Mahatma Gandhi, as contained in his first pamphlet, the *Hind Swaraj*.

The other significant aspect relates to the report of the National Planning Committee (1938), which laid down the basic purpose of planning. It was the first attempt on national basis to coordinate the manifold activities of the nation. This chapter also contains very briefly the ideas on economic planning in the Bombay Plan (1944), People's Plan (1944) and the Gandhian Plan (1944). It also contains 'Mahatma Gandhi's Constructive Programme' and the views of Jawaharlal Nehru, primarily from *The Discovery of India*.

Chapter 2 of the volume has undertaken an overview of the growth of electoral system, emergence of political parties, party manifestos and general elections before Independence. The purpose of this chapter is to analyse the constitutional reforms undertaken by the British Government in India, primarily for providing political representation to the people. The political representation of the people significantly impacted the emergence of political parties, electoral system and party manifestos before Independence.

It also deals with the beginning of elections in India: Lord Ripon's Resolution of 1882, Indian Councils Act of 1892, Morley-Minto Reforms of 1909, the emergence of political parties, the electoral system under the Act of 1909, the elections conducted under the Act, the shortcomings noticed under the elections and the Lucknow Pact of 1916

This chapter also deals with the Montague-Chelmsford Report and the Act of 1919, the changes brought out in the franchise as recommended by Lord Southborough and the composition of Legislative Council. It also provides the information regarding the eight provinces and the composition of urban and rural electors; the electoral system under the Act of 1919; a brief outline of the Muddiman of Enquiry Committee of 1924 and some significant aspects of the general elections of 1920, 1923, 1926 and 1930.

It also contains the significant constitutional development like the Simon Commission Report, the Communal Award, the Poona Pact and the Government of India Act of 1935 (with reference to the significant changes made in the electoral system and the composition of electors). Besides, it covers the election manifestos of Congress Party, Muslim League, Krishak Praja Party, National Agriculturist Party, National Unionist Party, etc., and also provide an overview of the significant aspects of 1937 elections and the implementation of election manifestos of different political parties which formed ministries in the eleven provinces under the Act of 1935. It also briefly covers the development after October 1939 like: August Offer 1940, the Cripps Proposals 1942, Quit India Resolution 1942. Besides, it discusses the elections of 1945–1946 including the manifestos of INC, Muslim League and Communist Party along with the composition of Provincial Assemblies. It also discusses the Cabinet Mission 1946, the Interim Government of 1946 and the Indian Independence Act 1947.

Chapter 3 broadly consist of the growth of the electoral system and general elections since independence. It is followed by the Constituent Assembly Debates on Constitutional provisions of the electoral system, discussing the distinction between the national party and state party and the significant aspects of the Indian Elections to the Lok Sabha from 1952 to 2014. To this end, it provides briefly some major aspects of elections from 1952 to 1984 and also analyses the era of coalition governments from 1989 to 2014, specifically in terms of pre electoral and post electoral alliances among the constituent parties.

Chapter 4 broadly contains some important initiatives on the question of nation-building and modernization taken by the Indian Constitution, the Government of India and the political parties between 1947 and 1952. The initiative from the Constitution came through the Directive Principles of state Policy which serves as 'mandates of the community to its organized representatives'. The Government of India established a Planning Commission as an institution and mechanism to bring modernization and development in the country. Since January 2015, it has been replaced by the Niti Aayog. All the political parties immediately after independence devoted their time to formulating their basic approach to the problems of nation-building of the country.

Chapter 4 also provides a comparative analysis of the election manifestos of the major national political parties (1952–2014). The comparison has been made broadly on the following issues: economic, financial, human and social development, infrastructure and foreign policy including defence.

Notes

1 In this context, Robert Peel's manifesto of 1834 announced at Tamworth was the first 'recognised party manifesto': "Upon his unexpected appointment as Prime Minister, after the dismissal of Melbourne in 1834 and while Parliament was not sitting, he saw that he could have no hope of obtaining a majority unless he found some means of laying his policy before the country. He could not explain his programme in Parliament; and he and his colleagues decided that the best way of effecting a similar result was to outline the policy of the Ministry in a manifesto nominally addressed by him to his own constituents at Tamworth, but actually addressed to the electorate at large" in Cecil S. Emden, *The People and the Constitution: Being a History of the People's influence in British Government*, Second Edition, London: Oxford University Press, 1956, p. 203.

2 See, for example, Disraeli's (1868) proposal of some social amelioration; Gladstone's (1874) proposal for the repeal of income tax as well as the Liberals (1906) increase in legislation conferring social benefits ibid., pp. 244–265 and see Cecil S. Emden, Parties and the People's Mandate, *Parliamentary Affairs*, Vol. V, No. 1 (1951), pp. 158–159. Along with some modicum of social measures between 1832 and 1918, in Britain during the nineteenth century mostly elections were dominated by one single issue like in 1831 on the question of reform of the parliamentary system; in 1868 regarding the disestablishing the Irish Church, in 1906 concerning free trade versus protection and in 1910 (elections were conducted twice) rejection by the Lords of the Government's 1909 budget and by the proposal to curtail the powers of the House of Lords. See A.H. Birch, *Representative and Responsible Government: An Essay on the British Constitution*, London: George Allen and Unwin Ltd, 1964, p. 116.

3 Richard Crossman, *Inside View: Three Lectures on Prime Ministerial Government*, London: Jonanath Cape, 1972, p. 86. See also Herbert Morrison, *Government and Parliament: Survey from the Inside*, Third Edition, London: University Press, 1964, pp. 151–156.

4 Ibid., p. 92. In this context, Herbert Morrison observed the following: "first, political parties should not make promises unless they have reasonable grounds for believing that they can fulfil them; secondly, having made promises, they ought to carry them out unless it is proved, on closer investigation, that to do so would be contrary to the public interest'. See Herbert Morrison, et al., *Vitality in Administration*, London: George Allen & Unwin Ltd, 1957, p. 13.

5 Ian Budge, David Robertson and Derek Hearl, eds., *Ideology, Strategy and Party Chang: Spatial Analyses of Post-War Election Programmes in 19 Democracies,* Cambridge: Cambridge University Press, 1987, p. 18. See also Richard Rose, *Do Parties Make a Difference*, London: The Macmillan Press Ltd, 1980; F.W.S. Craig, ed., *British General Election Manifestos 1900–1974*, London: The Macmillan Press Ltd, 1975; Dennis Kavanagh, The Politics of Manifestos, *Parliamentary Affairs*, Vol. XXXIV, No. 1 (1981).

6 Richard I. Hofferbert and Ian Budge, The Party Mandate and the Westminster Model: Election Programmes and Government Spending in Britain, 1948–85, *British Journal of Political Science*, Vol. 22 (1992),

pp. 151–181. See also Terry J. Royed, Testing the Mandate Model in Britain and the United States: Evidence from the Reagan and Thatcher Eras, *British Journal of Political Science*, Vol. 26 (1996), pp. 45–80 and Lucy Mansergh and Robert Thomson, Election Pledges, Party Competition, and Policymaking, *Comparative Politics*, Vol. 39, No. 3 (2007), pp. 311–330. For an overview of British Politics from 1979 to 2005, see Joel Krieger, Britain in Mark Kesselman, Joel Krieger and William A. Joseph, *Introduction to Comparative Politics*, Fourth Edition, New York: Houghton Mifflin Company, 2007, pp. 81–86.

7 See the Labour Party Manifesto 1945, in full, in F.W.S. Craig, compiled and edited, *British General Election Manifestos, 1900–1974*, London: The Macmillan Press Ltd, 1975, pp. 123–131 and see also Diane Abbott, The Q & A in *New Statesman*, Collector's Edition, Vol. 2 (1913–2013), p. 138.

8 K.M. Munshi, *Constituent Assembly Debates: Official Report*, Vol. VII, New Delhi: Lok Sabha Secretariat, Second Reprint, 1989, pp. 984–985.

9 Ibid., p. 1154.

10 Polarisation and Consensus in *Economic and Political Weekly* (August 1999), p. 2367.

11 *The Times of India* (October 22, 2014).

12 V.M. Sirsikar, Studies of Political Parties and Pressure Groups in Indian Council of Social Science Research in *A Survey of Research in Political Science*, Vol. 1, Political System, New Delhi: Allied Publishers Private Limited, 1979, pp. 69–98 and Ramashray Roy, Electoral Politics: A Trend Report, in Indian Council of Social Science Research in *A Survey of Research in Political Science*, Vol. 2, Political Process, New Delhi: Allied Publishers Private Limited, 1981, pp. 165–180.

13 Myron Weiner, Some Hypothesis on the Politics of Modernization in India in Richard L. Park and Irene Tinker, eds., *Leadership in Political Institutions in India*, Princeton, NJ: Princeton University Press, 1959, p. 38.

1

EVOLUTION OF IDEAS ON NATION-BUILDING AND ECONOMIC MODERNIZATION

The purpose of this chapter is to provide an outline of the essence of ideas on nation-building and economic modernization as developed during the freedom movement. Indian nationalism before independence provides 'various shades of visions' for transformation and restructuring the Indian society. The development of ideas on various aspects of nation-building has a considerable bearing on the present-day ideologies (political programmes) of national political parties.

This process commenced in the middle of the nineteenth century, when India developed 'a westernized native class to interpret and mediate the new ideas and institutions'.[1] In this context, Majumdar observed that

> 'A new ideology suddenly burst forth upon the static life, moulded for centuries by fixed sets of religious ideas and social conventions. It gave birth to a critical attitude towards religion and a spirit of enquiry into the origin of state and society with a view to determining their proper scope and function'.[2]

The reasons for the emergence of 'modern consciousness' are the following: English education, liberal ideas of the West, critical outlook on the past and new aspirations for the future.[3] The modern consciousness helped in inculcating the spirit of questioning on the basic issues concerning state, society and religion.

It is proposed to provide the views and observations of some prominent nationalist leaders as well as important committees on nation-building during this period.

I

Raja Rammohan Roy 1772–1833

Raja Rammohan Roy was the chief proponent of the 'new spirit'. He exhibited it by undertaking a number of social issues for the reform and enlightenment of his fellowmen. Some of the significant social issues relate to the establishment of the *Brahma Samaj,* the reforming of social abuses of Hindu society, the establishment of English language schools and newspapers, the champion of the liberty of the Press, etc.[4] For his contributions relating to Hindu society and religion, Raja Rammohan Roy has been rightly called 'The Father of Modern India'.

He was also conversant with the economic problems of the country. He was of the view that poverty was not only due to the landlords and dealers but also due to the appropriation of revenue from agriculture produce by the government.[5] He also observed that the 'comparative freedom of trade after 1813 had created an illusion of prosperity'. He advocated agricultural and industrial modernization of the country 'with the aid of western technique, western capital and western enterprise'.[6] He believed 'that economic modernization must involve the masses of the population, the impoverished tillers of the soil and that it should not merely benefit the new Indian middle class working in alliance with the new European middle class'.[7] He was in favour of continuance of the Permanent Settlement with 'necessary reforms to alleviate the pressing miseries of the *ryots*'.[8] He was in favour of the modification, of the ancient laws of inheritance, of free trade, of the 'elimination of the remaining monopolistic privileges of the East India Company' and of the entry of foreign capital and land revenue reforms to help the process of building more wealth and prosperity.[9]

The new awakening

The period between1858–1905 has been described as the emergence of new India. Some of the contributing factors were these: the rapid growth of education, and the establishment of the Brahma Samaj, the Prarthana Samaj, the Arya Samaj, the Ramakrishna Mission and the Theosophical Society. These movements were brought out by 'the impact of new ideas and beliefs'. These movements in a significant manner encouraged the growth of individual and organized efforts for social reform.[10]

The emergence of the Indian National Congress (INC) in 1885 has been the most significant event in the growth and development of the national consciousness and awakening. The INC served as a platform for debate and discussion on political, social and economic reforms.

It is proposed to provide a brief account of the significant features of the socio-economic and political vision of the INC leadership. This vision was comprehended by a small fraction of the society.[11] This period is generally characterized as the years signifying the 'gradual development . . . of the nationalist understanding of the economic basis and policies of British imperialism in India and the evolution of an alternative nationalist programme for the development of an independent national economy'.[12] Some of the most outstanding leaders of the Indian Nationalist Movement, who contributed in a significant manner on the theme of nation-building, are these: Dadabhai Naoroji, Mahadev Govind Ranade, Romesh Chunder Dutt, Gopal Krishna Gokhale, Mahatma Gandhi, Subhash Chandra Bose and Jawaharlal Nehru.

Dadabhai Naoroji 1825–1917

The exploitative nature of British rule in India, which was first analysed by Raja Rammohan Roy, came under bitter attack in the speeches and writings of Dadabhai Naoroji. This exploitative nature he explored with his famous theory of "the drain" of India's wealth to Britain. Naoroji's work *Poverty and Un-British Rule in India* (1901) provides a comprehensive exposition of the 'drain theory'. Some of the important forms of the economic exploitation were the following: the direct political rule; the heavy civil and military expenditure (with exclusive British employment); the investing in transport and communication to control India; an unrequited export of Indian commodities and bullions; the investment of British capital with guarantee of returns by the state; the private remittances; the payment of annual tributes; the post-retirement migration of men of liberal professions to England; the converting public finance into an instrument of exploitation through regressive taxation on items of basic mass consumption like salt, kerosene and cotton and the manipulation of the pound-rupee exchange rates to the disadvantage of India.[13]

Dadabhai Naoroji not only provided the analysis of poverty in India but also underlined the economic reforms necessary for the prosperity of Indian people. Self-government or '*Swaraj*' was the first precondition of the reform in India for the prosperity of the country. He advocated the use of capital in productive channels, as India had both natural resources and an abundant supply of labour. He also suggested the steps necessary to reverse the process of 'economic drain'.

Naoroji in his economic reforms suggested a positive role to the state, encouragement to private enterprise both Indian and foreign, moderate taxes, advantageous land tenure and improved technology for raising productivity, etc. He also recognized the importance of economic overheads like irrigation and cheap communications and speeding up the process of public works. He also favoured a system of mixed economy: 'association of government and private enterprise in which government control is necessary, so that each takes its risk and profits according to its shares'.[14] He advocated political independence for the development of a country 'As long as the people of a country have no share in its administration the powerful stimulus of patriotism and self-interest cannot come into action'.[15]

Mahadev Govind Ranade 1842–1901

Justice Mahadev Govind Ranade is often hailed 'as the Father of Modern Indian Economics'. His monograph *Indian Political Economy* (1892) is considered as the 'cornerstone of the economic theory which underlies the present Five Year Plans'.[16] He believed that 'national development is an integrated process to which economic development was, no doubt, an important, but only one, dimension'.[17] He was a rationalist and his contribution was largely in the area of social and economic reforms.[18]

Justice Ranade's twelve essays on Indian Economics, many delivered between 1890 and 1893, cover a large number of issues: credit organizations, state encouragement of agriculture and industry, emigration, local self-government, emancipation and relief of the agricultural classes and the alienation of land. Analysing the prevalence of poverty, Justice Ranade observed 'we are a people of little resources. Many millions among us scarcely earn a couple of annas a day, many millions more are always underfed, and live on the borderland of Famine and slow Death, into which the failure of a single Monsoon precipitates them'.[19]

While describing the whole economic situation of the country, he observed 'we are standing on the edge of precipice, and the slightest push down will drive into the abyss below of unmixed and absolute helplessness'.[20] In this context, while discussing the functions and the role of the state in economic development, Ranade advocated that 'The State . . . as the National Organ for taking care of National needs, and the duty of the State is not simply maintaining peace and order, but also such functions as Education, both Liberal and Technical, Post and Telegraphs, Railway and Canal Communications, the pioneering of new enterprise, the insurance of risky undertakings'.[21]

The reorganization of rural credit in India was another issue addressed by Ranade in the following terms:

> No fact in the economic condition of this Country arrests attention more forcibly than the contrast presented by the hoards of unused Capital, stored up in the vaults of the Presidency and other Exchange Banks, and the high Premium Government Securities command on one side, and, on the other, the utter paralysis of industry in rural India, due to the poverty of the resources of the Classes engaged in the production of Wealth.[22]

These words 're-echoed in 1969 when the demand for the nationalization of banks came up before the Parliament of free India'.[23] He pleaded for the reorganization of credit on some sound and progressive basis which would help in the promotion of national well-being and provide assistance not to agriculturalist classes, but to 'Spinners and Weavers, Carpenters, Smiths, Dyers, Potters, Brass and Copper, Silk and Embroidery workers, Shopkeepers, Carriers, and all the Trades and Professions that are now practised in this Country'.[24]

In order to reclaim India 'from the ancient bondage of Feudalism and Status', Justice Ranade advocated 'encouragement of New Industries in the Country by means of advances, or subsidies, or guarantees according as circumstances require'.[25] Besides the financial incentives, he also suggested a change in the mind-set in bringing about industrial development:

> It pre-supposes a change of habits, it postulates the previous growth of Culture and a spirit of enterprise, an alertness of mind, an elasticity of temper, a readiness to meet and conquer opposition, a facility of organization, social ambition and aspiration, a mobile and restless condition of Capital and Labour, all which qualities and changes are the slow growth of Centuries of Freedom and Progress.[26]

Ranade also observed that, for manufacturing on a large scale, a large number of concessions are needed: terms of lease must be long, government should allow the Company to float its debentures, Companies should get lands free, no royalties and fines in the beginnings, guaranteed demand for that produce and a separate Department of Commerce and Manufactures to devote itself to this work.

In order to come out of extreme poverty, Ranade also pleaded for agricultural development. For this purpose, he suggested the need for the creation of peasant proprietorship and periodical assessment of land tax first in kind, and then commuted into money.[27]

Romesh Chunder Dutt 1848–1909

Romesh Chunder Dutt made a very impressive contribution to the study of Indian Economics, primarily through his works like *England and India* (1897), *Famines in India* (1900) and *The Economic History of India*, vol. 1 (1902) and *The Economic History of India*, vol. 2 (1904). His experience as a civil servant provided him insights into the problems of India's agrarian system, poverty, famines and other related issues.

Discussing about the real causes of famines in India, Dutt pointed out the following factors: heavy land assessment, decline of village industries, dependence of cultivators on agriculture, etc. Talking about the cause of the poverty in India under the British Rule, he pointed out that military expenditure as the main source of economic drain.[28]

He provided policy prescription on a large number of economic problems. He criticized the decline of the Indian industries due to the 'commercial policy of East India Company'. As a result of this, he pointed out that agriculture was left as the only industry of the people. He further articulated his views on this problem by stating that 'Little was done to foster new industries after the Crown assumed administration of India in 1858'.[29] In the context of solving the economic problem of the country, he emphasized the need

> in relieving agriculture from excessive and uncertain taxation; in fostering those indigenous industries in which millions of Indian artisans find employment in their villages; and in helping those nascent manufactures which the people are starting with their own capital in towns.[30]

On the question of irrigation and railways, he suggested the need

> to protect Indian revenue from undue expenditure, railway lines on the guarantee system should not be undertaken in India except on the ground of absolute political necessity; that all other lines should be left entirely to private enterprise; and

> that canals were more suited to the needs of India, both as a means of cheap transit to the people and as a protection against droughts and famines.[31]

Gopal Krishna Gokhale 1866–1915

The contribution of Gopal Krishan Gokhale, has to be seen from the perspective, that he 'exhibited most clearly and effectively the practical application of the ideas of his predecessors to economic problems'.[32] His speeches as member of the Bombay Legislative Council (1900–1902) and the Imperial Legislative Council (1902–1913) as well as written and oral evidence before the Welby Commission (1897) and Commission on Decentralization (1908) and his address as President of INC at Banaras Session (1905) constitute his most significant observations on the problems of the country.

The problem of poverty had been the most pressing problem which Gokhale addressed in his first Budget speech of 1902. He stated it as a 'deep and deepening' poverty of the country. He rebutted the claim of the government by pointing out that

> the attempt to determine the average income per head for a given population is useful only for the purpose of obtaining a statistical view of the economic condition of that people. . . . But when these calculations are used for taking a dynamical view of the economic situation, the method is open to serious objection, as the necessarily conjectural character of many of the data renders them of little value for such a purpose.[33]

In this context, he spelled out some important indications: 'rising annual death-rate (independently of famine and plague)', 'increasing proportion of the population underfed', 'decrease of the net cropped area', 'the indebtedness of the agricultural population', 'shrinkage of the area under superior crops', 'wages of labourers in proportion to the rise in prices remain unchanged etc.'[34]

The other major issues on which he voiced concern, relate to the budget surpluses. He pointed out that it constitutes a 'double wrong to the community' because they exist and, secondly, they 'lend themselves to easy misinterpretation'. This problem exists because there has been a tendency 'to fix the taxation of the country at a level far above the actual needs of the situation'.[35] Gokhale suggested for reduction in taxation through reduction of salt duty raising the exemption limit on the income tax, and abolition of the excise duty on cotton.[36]

Gokhale also discussed at length the question of 'Increase in Public Expenditure' by surveying the trends for a period of about thirty-five years, i.e. between 1875 and 1911. To contain the increase in public expenditure, he suggested 'a spirit of economy' in place of 'spirit of expenditure', substantial reduction of military expenditure, larger employment of Indians in public services and provision for independent audit, etc.

Discussing about the *Swadeshi* movement, Gokhale described it as both a 'patriotic and an economic movement'. As a patriotic movement it instils in the people the idea of sacrifice 'to take an intelligent interest in economic development' and inculcates the spirit of co-operation with one another for a national end.[37] He also described the economic aspect of the movement by stating that

> to ensure a ready consumption of such articles as are produced in the country and to furnish a perpetual stimulus to production by keeping the demand for indigenous things largely in excess of the supply, the difficulties that surround the question economically are so great that they require the co-operation of every available agency to surmount them.[38]

In the Banaras Congress Session 1905, he talked about the 'idea of a United India'. He was the aware of the arduous character of the struggle, and the immense sacrifices it requires. 'The goal of the Congress is that India should be governed in the interests of the Indians themselves, and that, in course of time, a form of Government should be attained in this country similar to what exists in the Self-Governing Colonies of the British Empire'.[39]

In his budget speech of 1903, Gokhale provided a comprehensive view for the 'industrial and educational advancement of the people'. For this purpose, he suggested the need for

> a large and comprehensive scheme for the moral and material well-being of the people should be chalked out with patient care and foresight, and then it should be firmly and steadily adhered to, and the progress made examined almost from year to year.[40]

Gokhale also took up the question in the Imperial Legislative Council of the indentured labour but also pointed out that this system is 'really border on the servile' because of the helplessness in all matters of life. He not only pleaded for its abolition altogether but also legislation with strong penal provisions.[41]

Agriculture was another sector which Gokhale discussed in detail, particularly the problem of agricultural indebtedness and suggested special tribunal with sufficient legal power to look into this problem. He suggested to strengthen the co-operative credit societies for this purpose. He especially pleaded for the 'promotion of agricultural prosperity in India'. He suggested 'Irrigation and Scientific Agriculture'. He suggested the promotion of industrial and technical education as an urgent necessity as a remedy for the extreme poverty of our people. He advocated the need for primary education 'free in all schools throughout the country' and also suggested need of works of sanitary improvement such as 'good water supply and drainage'. In short, he wanted 'moral and material advancement of the mass of our people'.[42]

Gokhale was highly critical of the India's industrial domination by England. Gokhale expressed that due to this dominance, the results have been disastrous because 'When hand-made goods are exposed to the competition of machine-made goods, it is inevitable that the former should perish'.[43] 'The object aimed at by the East India Company was to reduce India to the level of the merely agricultural country producing raw material only, without factories to manufacture the same'.[44] This, according to Gokhale, was the first stage in our industrial decay. He also pointed out that the 'free trade policies' has been responsible for killing all our industries. He pleaded for the protection and utilizations of Indian raw materials. He also added that 'Home Charges, railway construction and regressive taxation were the forms of drain of wealth form India to England'.

As explained in the proceeding section from 1885 to 1905, i.e. a period of twenty years, the moderates dominated the Congress movement. The chief characteristic of this movement were the gradual development of the country towards self-government under the British dispensation. For this purpose, demand was made and resolutions were passed to bring constitutional reform of Supreme and Local Legislative Council both in terms of making them representative by inclusion of some members from representative institutions like local bodies, institutions and the chamber of commerce, etc. Besides there was also demand for the Indianization of services, a separation of the judiciary and more representation of Indians in the army at a higher level. These leaders were also critical of the backwardness of Hindu society as well as 'against the traditional institutions of the Indian system of social order'.[45] In this context, they were of the view to bring social reforms through the governmental system. They were also concerned with the poverty of the people, and suggested measures for bringing out economic modernization. It has been said that the Moderate leaders tended to be anglicized in their personal life and highly successful men in their professions and 'Politics remained for the bulk of the Moderates very much a part- time affair'.[46] The methodology adopted by the moderates leaders to bring grievances to the attention of the British administration was through resolutions, party speeches and articles. In the context of their anglicized nature 'they removed themselves from emotional rapport with the bulk of the population- the illiterate, poverty-stricken, and devoutly Hindu and Muslim peasant'.[47]

Mahatma Gandhi 1869–1948

Mahatma Gandhi's *Hind Swaraj* has been called his seminal work by Mahadev Desai. It is considered as the 'Gandhi Manifesto'. It was originally written in Gujarati on Mahatma Gandhi return journey from London to South Africa during November 13–22, 1909. A number of publications have interpreted and analysed Mahatma Gandhi's thinking as expounded in *Hind Swaraj*.[48] It is one of the few booklets which have been translated into English by Mahatma Gandhi himself. The book is written in the form of dialogue between a newspaper Editor and Reader.

Regarding both the background and significance of *Hind Swaraj*, Mahatma Gandhi, in 'A Message' to the 1938 Edition, observed, 'I might change the language here and there, if I had to rewrite the booklet. But after the stormy thirty years through which I have since passed, I have seen nothing to make me alter the views expounded in it'.[49]

Anthony Parel, while analysing the intellectual content of Hind Swaraj observed that by 1909, Mahatma Gandhi integrated and 'acquired a definite philosophical vision' from the East and the West,

> to assess the relative significance of things that concerned him – the problem of the self, of the Indian *praja*, the nature of Indian nationalism, the modern industrial civilization, colonialism, the extreme selfishness of the Indian middle class, racialism, the spectre of rising violence in India and the legiti mation of terroristic violence by extreme nationalists.[50]

Parel has identified the two strands: historical reflections and philosophical reflections in the structure and argument of *Hind Swaraj*.[51] The first aspect discusses the contributions of the Indian National Congress, particularly those of Naroaji, Hume, Wedderburn, Gokhale and Tyebji in 'bringing together Indians from different parts of India and enthused us with the idea of nationality'. The second aspect deal with the partition of Bengal and Mahatma Gandhi observed that 'the partition has caused an awakening and Our leaders are divided into two parties: the Moderates and the Extremists'. The third aspect discusses 'the causes and consequences of British rule in India'. The argument provided by Mahatma Gandhi in this context relates to the point 'that we keep the English in India for our base self- interest' and in the process 'The English have not taken India; we have given it to them. They are not in India because of their strength, but because we keep them'. For this attitude, Mahatma Gandhi was critical of the modern civilization because men are 'enslaved by temptation of money and of the luxuries that money can buy'. Mahatma Gandhi further observed that the modern civilization 'takes note neither of morality nor of religion' and 'immorality is often taught in the name of morality'. Mahatma Gandhi elaborated his views on civilization in the context of India by stating that 'India is being ground down, not under the English heel, but under that of modern civilization'. Mahatma Gandhi further mentioned that 'We are turning away from God'. Mahtama Gandhi attributed this decline to the parliament, the railways and called them as the 'most dangerous institution'. Further, he even included the machinery and professionals like lawyers and doctors responsible for enslaving India. To come out of the present condition, Mahatma Gandhi suggested 'to cling to the old Indian civilization'.

After analysing the factors responsible for the moral decline of the country, Mahatma Gandhi analyses the nature of *Swaraj* and the means to obtain *Swaraj*, 'It is *Swaraj* when we learn to rule ourselves'. Mahatma Gandhi vision provides lot of significance to civilization, which he defined as 'Civilization is that mode of conduct which points out to man the path of duty'. Mahatma Gandhi further elaborated this argument by emphasizing that 'The tendency of the Indian civilization is to elevate the moral being that of the Western civilization is to propagate immorality'. In the context of Swaraj, Mahatma Gandhi emphasized the need not to use 'brute force'. For this purpose, he suggested 'the remedy of passive resistance' i.e. 'soul-force'. Mahatma Gandhi further pointed out that the Extremists are advocates of brute force. Mahatma Gandhi explained further that Swaraj is possible only 'where passive resistance is the guiding force of the people'.

According to Mahatma Gandhi's vision, in order to attain Independence, educational reforms and the use of machinery constitute two important aspects. Mahatma Gandhi believed that the English and 'The foundation that Macaulay laid of education has enslaved us'. In education reforms, Mahatma Gandhi pleaded for the inclusion of character building, ethical education, provincial language and in addition a second Indian language. Mahatma Gandhi also advocated Hindi should be a universal language for India. Besides, he felt that 'machinery has impoverished India'. For this purpose 'it is necessary to realize that machinery is bad. We shall then be able gradually to do away with it'. However, Mahatma Gandhi's views on machinery has to be seen in the context of *Swadeshi*, which he defined as 'reliance on our own strength'. Mahatma Gandhi further elaborated this aspect by emphasizing 'Pure swadeshi is not at all opposed to machinery'.[52] 'Opposition of mills or machinery is not the point. What suits our country most is the point. I am not opposed to the movement of manufacturing machines in the country, nor to making improvements in machinery. I am only concerned with what these machines are meant for'.[53]

Mahatma Gandhi repeated in concluding the *Hind Swaraj* with the following propositions 1) 'Real home-rule is self-rule or self-control. 2) The way to it is passive resistance: that is soul-force or love-force. 3) In order to exert this force, *Swadeshi* in every sense is necessary 4). . . . I bear no enmity towards the English but I do towards their civilization'.[54]

Subhash Chandra Bose 1897–1945

Subhash Chandra Bose was interested in propagating socialist ideas and bringing the youth in the mainstream of the nationalist movement. Bose as a politician had a plan both for India's freedom as well as for the post-independence scenario.

His presidential address at the 51st Haripura Congress of 1938 gave attention to the question of 'social reconstruction' of the country. He felt that the national problems of the country like poverty, illiteracy, disease, scientific production and distribution, 'can be effectively tackled only along socialistic lines'. He suggested for this purpose the establishment of a commission for 'drawing up a comprehensive plan of reconstruction'.[55] He had very definite ideas about planning. He suggested that such a plan of reconstruction will have two parts 'an immediate programme and a long-period programme'. In the preparation of the immediate programme, the factors to be observed will be threefold – 'firstly, to prepare the country for self-sacrifice; secondly, to unify India; and thirdly, to give scope for local and cultural autonomy'. He also pleaded for educational policy 'to foster a common spirit among the entire, population'. He was one of the few national leaders to discuss the problem of increasing population. He suggested for this purpose 'to restrict our population until we are able to, feed, cloth and educate those who already exist'.

He also suggested for eradication of poverty: 'a radical reform of our land system', the 'abolition of landlordism', a 'cheap credit for the rural population', an 'extension of the cooperative movement' and the cultivation of scientific agriculture. Similarly, to solve the economic problem, he suggested a comprehensive scheme of industrial development under state ownership and state control. However, in the context of industrialization, he also suggested

> to devise means to minimise its evils and at the same time explore the possibilities of reviving cottage industries where there is a possibility of their surviving the inevitable competition of factories. In a country like India, there will be plenty of room for cottage industries, especially in the case of industries including hand-spinning and hand-weaving allied to agriculture.[56]

He even advocated for the adoption of a comprehensive scheme 'gradually socializing our entire agricultural and industrial system in the spheres of both production and appropriation'. For this purpose, he suggested mobilization of capital through 'internal or external loans or through inflation'. He also suggested an active foreign trade policy to be drawn up 'in a comprehensive manner so as to coordinate India's economic development with its export trade on one hand and its external obligation on the other'.

Bose in his book *The Indian Struggle*, Part Two, visualized that 'the future of India ultimately lies with a party with a clear ideology, programme and plan of action'.[57] Some of the important aspects provided on nation-building and economic modernization are the following: the Party will stand for the interests of the masses; 'complete political and economic liberation of the Indian people'; for 'a strong Central Government'; for 'believe in a sound system of state-planning for the reorganisation of the agricultural and industrial life of the country'; 'to establish a new monetary and credit system; to abolish landlordism and introduce a uniform land-tenure system for the whole of India' in order 'to build up a new social structure, . . . ruled by the village "Panch", . . . to break down the existing social barriers like caste', etc.[58]

National Planning Committee

One very significant development in the national planning relates to the setting up of the National Planning Committee (NPC) in October 1938 by Subhash Chandra Bose, under the Chairmanship of

Jawaharlal Nehru. Its composition was very broad based; it consisted of congressmen, scientists, industrialists, economists and businessmen, including persons drawn from organizations representing village industries and labour.

The NPC issued a comprehensive questionnaire to collect data and suggestions for the plan of the country. It also appointed thirty subcommittees consisting of eminent and distinguished experts in various fields of national activities on various aspects of economic regeneration of the country.

The NPC identified that the basic purpose of planning as a whole was as 'atleast double the present standard of living, including not only the absolute necessaries but also the amenities of civilized existence, to be achieved in a definite period of five (or 10) years at most'.[59] It was made clear that 'the Plan must be a comprehensive programme of national development, each part fitting into the other'.[60]

From the very beginning specially after the setting up of the subcommittees of NPC during the second session in June 1939 conflict started between 'the claims of cottage industries and large-scale industries'.[61] The Jawaharlal Nehru contention was that 'Without industrialization no country can have political or economic freedom, and even cottage industries cannot develop to any large extent if economic freedom is absent'. Nehru was of the view that the problem 'is one of co-ordinated growth in both directions'.[62]

The NPC also provided certain objectives of planning: improvement of nutrition from 2,400 to 2,800 units, improvement of clothing from fifteen yards to thirty yards per capita per income, diminution of unemployment, increase in per capita income, increase in public utility service, one health unit for 1,000 population and increase in the average expectation of life.[63]

In connection with the final report of NPC, it is important to mention that, due to Jawaharlal Nehru's arrest, the NPC from August 1940 to June 1945 had 'formal existence only'. The final session was held on March 26, 1949.[64] The work of National Planning Committee had impacted in the drawing up of a number of plans from 1943 onward. Bombay Plan 1944, People's Plan 1944 and Gandhian Plan 1944. Besides it also resulted in setting up, by the Government of India, a department of planning.[65]

Bombay Plan

'A Plan of Economic Development for India', popularly known as the Bombay Plan, was prepared by eight industrialists.[66] It aimed to bring about a doubling of present per capita income within a period of fifteen years. It also proposed to raise the net output of agriculture to a little over twice and that of industry to about five times the present output.

The planning period was limited to fifteen years. This period was divided into three plans each covering a period of five years. The total expenditure to be incurred was to the tune of Rs 10,000 crore. The Bombay Plan was brought out in two parts: Part I (January 1944) and Part II (January 1945). Part I elaborated on the theme of requirements of minimum standard in terms of diet, clothing, housing, health, water supply, minimum education, minimum cost of living and minimum income, etc. Besides, it also consisted of economic plan which look into the questions relating to agriculture, industries, irrigation, transport and communication, education and health, sources of finance and stages of development, etc.

The Part II of the Bombay Plan dealt in a comprehensive manner the issues like distribution of national income and state and economic organization looking into such aspects like states intervention, planning and democracy, role of the state, methods of intervention, state control and state ownership, etc.[67]

People's Plan

According to the 'People's Plan', the object of the plan was the satisfaction of the immediate and the basic needs of the people. M.N. Roy was the guiding force behind the People's Plan. The member of the people's Plan were B.N. Banerji, G.D. Parekh and V.M. Tarkunde (Convener). The People's Plan Committee underlined that it is important first to discover the real nature of our problem so as to understand 'the economic reality of our country'. This type of exercise will open up the prospects of an increasingly gainful employment for our people and thus to bring about the improvement in their standard of living. The report emphasized that agricultural should form the foundation of planning for India. Similarly, it advocated for the more productive employment of labour and natural resources for increasing the national income and industrialization. The People's Plan was against 'unrestricted private ownership'. It advocated employment or relief as a right of citizenship.

The People's plan estimated that agricultural output will increase by 400 percent and industrial production by 600 percent involving a capital expenditure of Rs 15, 000 crores within a period of ten years. This plan also emphasized the need regarding 'the problems of number' and hoped that improvements in the standards of living and the growth of the secular outlook will be an effective check on population growth. It also provided for unemployment insurance, old age pensions, etc. as well as network of social services in respect of health, housing and education.[68]

Gandhian Plan

Shriman Narayan compiled a monograph on *Principles of Gandhian Planning*. Mahatma Gandhi, in the foreword of the 'Gandhian Plan' (1944), observed that the compiler 'has not misrepresented me in any place'.[69] The Gandhian Plan emphasized that planning should be based on the indigenous culture and civilization of the country, the least amount of state control and coercion and that each citizen has a right to work.

Simplicity is the first principle of Gandhism. Mahatma Gandhi believed that 'a progressive economic system should lead to greater simplicity though fuller life. My views on national planning differ from the prevailing ones. I do not want it along the industrial lines. I want to prevent our villages from catching the infection of industrialism'.[70] Mahatma Gandhi emphasized the need for decentralization and localization of industries and was critical of all kinds of centralization. The second basic principle of Gandhi thought is non-violence. Mahatma Gandhi was against the use of force and coercion for bringing 'economic equality'. He also believed 'lop-sided mechanization and large-scale production responsible for the present world catastrophe'. The third principle of Gandhian economy's thought is dignity and sanctity of manual labour. The fourth fundamental principle of Gandhian planning is a change in the standard of values.

In the context of decentralization, Mahatma Gandhi emphasized advocating for the revival of ancient village communities with their prosperous agriculture, artistic and decentralized industries and small-scale co-operative organization. Gandhi disliked mechanized, large-scale and centralized production which tends to reduce men to mere cog-wheels and drains out their finer human feelings; Gandhi's attitude towards machinery and its use is directed to the 'craze for machinery' and its 'indiscriminate multiplication'. Besides, he was also not against scientific invention and improvement in machinery;[71] Gandhi believed that in the Indian conditions, due to paucity of capital and abundance of labour, there is need to provide employment opportunity to a large number of people. For this reason, Mahatma Gandhi was of the view that plans for the industrialization of India 'on Western lines cannot solve the problem of unemployment'; 'Instead of mass production on a large-scale basis Gandhi desired production by masses on a small-scale and decentralized basis'. Gandhi was of the view 'Distribution can be equalized when production is localized'. Mahatma Gandhi believed that 'from the stand point of defence and foreign aggression, decentralization and ruralization of industries is a vital necessity'. As the centralization of industries makes the country more 'vulnerable but also throws the whole economic life of the country completely out of gear', the Gandhian plan also advocated that 'large-scale production', whether state controlled or privately managed, inevitably leads to participation in the frantic race for 'foreign markets', which has been the root cause of the present as of the last World War, is this unfettered greed for profits.'That is why Gandhiji has been against the present international economy'.[72]

The core of Gandhian Plan is based on decentralization and cottage industrialism and it also advocated that 'India must evolve a Plan of economic organization which shall be congenial to her genius and culture'.

Mahatma Gandhi's Constructive Programme

This Programme is an important development in the evolution of ideas relating to nation-building. It was written by Gandhi on the train while travelling from Sevagram to Bardoli on December 8, 1941. This programme represents the practical aspect of Mahatma Gandhi's philosophy as enunciated in Hind Swaraj.[73] The thirteen items of the constructive programme are as follows:

1 Communal unity: Mahatma Gandhi emphasized that the communal unity does not mean 'political unity', 'It does however, mean an unbreakable heart unity'. For achieving communal unity, he suggested that every Congressman 'will cultivate personal friendship with persons representing faiths other than his own'.
2 Removal of untouchability: Mahatma Gandhi regarded the removal of untouchability as 'something indispensable'. This problem should be approached in a 'spirit of friendliness'. Mahatma Gandhi was critical 'of their awful isolation' and emphasized that for the task of nation-building removal of untouchability is necessary.
3 Prohibition: Gandhi was concerned about the people 'under the curse of drink and drugs' and suggested that 'medical men can make effective contribution towards the removal of this evil'. He

also suggested that 'women and students have special opportunity in advancing this reform'.

4 Khadi: In advocating the cause of khadi, Gandhi believed that 'It means a wholesale swadeshi mentality, a determination to find all the necessaries of life in India and that too through the labour and intellect of the villagers'. He was of the view that 'This needs a revolutionary change in the mentality and tastes of many'. He regarded khadi as the 'symbol of unity of the Indian humanity, of its economic freedom and equality'. He also defined the 'khadi mentality' as 'the decentralization of the production and the distribution of the necessaries of life'. He also elaborated his views on heavy industries by observing that 'Heavy industries will necessarily be centralized and nationalized. But they will occupy the least part of the vast national activity in the villages'.

5 Other village industries: Mahatma Gandhi regarded the following village industries: hand-grinding, hand-pounding, soap making, paper-making, match-making, tanning, oil-pressing, etc., as a part of village economy. In the context of village-made products, he was of the view that 'we will develop a true national taste in keeping with the vision of a new India in which pauperism, starvation and idleness will be unknown'.

6 Village sanitation: Gandhi attributed 'Divorce between intelligence and labour has resulted in criminal negligence of the villages. And so, instead of having graceful hamlets dotting the land, we have dung-heaps'. He was critical of the un-sanitary condition of the villages. 'Regarding dirtying the well or tank or river', Gandhi observed 'I regard this defect as a great vice which is responsible for the disgraceful state of our villages and the sacred banks of the sacred rivers and for diseases that spring from insanitation'. Gandhi pleaded to 'make our villages models of cleanliness in every sense of the word' and for this purpose, he suggested that it is the duty of congressmen 'to identify themselves with the villagers in their daily lives'. There is a need to develop 'a sense of national or social sanitation'.

7 New or Basic Education: Mahatma Gandhi believed that basic education 'links the children, whether of the cities or the villages, to all that is best and lasting in India. It develops both the body and the mind, keeps the child rooted to the soil with a glorious vision of the future'. This education is meant to the transform of village children into model villagers.

8 Adult education: Mahatma Gandhi was critical of the fact that the adult education has been neglected and suggested that the process

of this type of education 'should begin with opening the minds of the adult pupils to the greatness and vastness of their country'. Mahatma Gandhi defined adult education as 'first true political education of the adult by word of mouth'. He was of the view that along with this type of education there is also need for literary education of the adults.

9 Uplift of women: Mahatma Gandhi categorically believed, that 'Woman has been suppressed under custom and law for which man was responsible and in the shaping of which she had no hand . . . woman has as much right to shape her own destiny as man has to shape his'. Mahatma Gandhi for this purpose pleaded the need to frame 'rules of social conduct . . . by mutual co-operation and consultation. They can never be imposed from outside'. Regarding the women in the villages, Mahatma Gandhi observed that 'the legal and customary status of woman is bad enough throughout and demands radical alteration'.

10 Education in health and hygiene: Gandhi was of the view that the fundamental laws of health and of hygiene are 'simple and easily learnt'. Mahatma Gandhi further pointed out that 'ignorance and neglect of the laws of health and hygiene are responsible for the majority of diseases to which mankind is heir'. Mahatma Gandhi was of the view that the high death rate 'could be mitigated if the people were properly educated about health and hygiene'.

11 National language: Mahatma Gandhi criticized that 'Our love of the English language in preference to our own mother tongue has caused a deep chasm between the educated and the politically minded classes and the masses'. Mahatma Gandhi supported the case of Hindi as 'India's national language'.

12 Provincial Languages: For the cultural regeneration of the country, Mahatma Gandhi advocated the importance of 'India's provincial languages'.

13 Working for economic equality: By the phrase 'working for economic equality', Mahatma Gandhi meant 'abolishing the eternal conflict between capital and labour'. Mahatma Gandhi further elaborated this phrase by observing that it means 'the leveling down of the few rich in whose hands is concentrated the bulk of the nation's wealth on the one hand, and leveling up of the semi-starved naked millions on the other'. Mahatma Gandhi was aware of the fact that 'A non-violent system of government is clearly an impossibility so long as the wide gulf between the rich and the hungry millions persists'. For this purpose, Mahatma Gandhi suggested the need for his 'doctrine of trusteeship'.[74]

Jawaharlal Nehru 1889–1964

Jawaharlal Nehru's *The Discovery of India*[75] was published in 1946 and was written during his five months imprisonment in Ahmadnagar Fort (April to September 1944). His earlier two books – '*An Autobiography*' (1936) and '*Glimpses of World History*' (1936–1937) were also written in jail. *The Discovery of India* provides the quintessence of Nehru's views on a large number of issues concerning nation-building and economic modernization. This book came out approximately one and a half years before independence. During the time of his writing the book, he was not only actively associated with the freedom movement but was also a top rung leader and heir to Mahatma Gandhi. He was the President of the Indian Congress (Lahore, December 1929, Lucknow April 1936 and Faizpur December 1936). In these sessions some very important resolutions dealing with the political and economic aspects were discussed and passed. Needless to write, before independence he initiated a process and prepared a framework of change after the coming of independence. For an understanding of his vision of the transformation of the country, *The Discovery of India* is very important. Discussing about the past and its relation to the present Nehru observed, 'The roots of that present lay in the past and so I made voyages of discovery into the past, ever seeking a clue in it, if any such existed, to the understanding of the present'.[76] In the context of Indian history, Nehru observed that it provided him 'that vision of five thousand years gave me a new perspective'.[77]

Within the overall context of the Indian history, he was of the view that 'National progress can, therefore, neither lie in a repetition of the past nor in its denial. New patterns must inevitably be adopted but they must be integrated with the old'.[78] He pointed out that Indian history shows adaptation of old ideas of changing environment. He was of the view that every kind of development necessitates the contact with life itself and with social needs. Lack of this contact leads to 'stagnation and carelessness'. He advocated that we should move away from 'narrowing religious outlook' and inculcate the scientific outlook and temper.

The Discovery of India concludes on the theme 'The Importance of the National Idea: Changes Necessary in India'.[79] Nehru emphasized the need of synthesis, which is making the whole world our field of study. This emphasis will take the country and individual 'to grow out of the narrow grooves of thought and action'[80] and help in building integrated perspectives, generating a capacity to understand and compete with the peoples of other countries and, above all, 'drawing sustenance from the rich treasures that humanity has accumulated, adding to them, and applying them in building for the future'.[81]

Nehru was critical of the division of Hindu society into castes. He was of the view that in the present context, caste has no place. He advocated the need for adopting merit as a criterion for individuals development and opportunities provided to everybody. Then the system of caste will lose it significance. He was aware of the fact that caste has only provided 'suppression of certain groups' as well as a 'separation of theoretical and scholastic learning from craftsmanship, and a divorce of philosophy from actual life and its problems'.[82]

He regarded the backwardness of any group is not due to 'inherent failings' but due to lack of opportunities and domination by other groups. He was in favour of providing equal opportunities for all and no political economic and social barriers should come in the way to achieve this kind of opportunity. He was of the view that equal opportunity should be provided to each and every group so as to give them a chance to advance in life. For the backward communities, especially he was in favour of providing special opportunities for educational, economic and cultural growth to enable them to move forward.

Nehru felt the need for an economic system which will not only provide equality of opportunities but will also sustain this type of equality. Economic goal for this purpose needs a 'democratically and planned collectivism', by which he meant public ownership of the basic and major industries, co-operative or collective control of the land as well as cooperatively controlled small and village industries. It requires a 'careful and continuous planning and adaptation to the changing needs of the people'.[83] The goal of such planning, he observed, is three-fold: expansion of the productive capacity of the nation, absorbing labour power and preventing unemployment. He was aware of the fact that this will not bring an 'equalization of income', but it will lead to 'equitable sharing and some kind of equalization'. In totality, it will contribute to eliminating the glaring differences in income and class distinctions.

To bring about this fundamental change in 'acquisitive society based primarily on the profit motive', he was aware of the fact that the system will also simultaneously lead to disturbance in the present day. In this context, he pointed out that though the profit motive will continue, but the dominant urge and emphasis which is displayed, for it should go. From this perspective, he was of the opinion that emphasis will be laid on things for the public good.

Further elaborating on the theme of collectivism, he pointed out that the British rule destroyed and injured to a large extent the Indian social conceptions which were based 'on the idea of the group'. It is in this context that he advocated the need of co-operative concerns in land and small industry. He was of the view that it is difficult to make the village a self-contained economic unit but, in the present context, it can become easily a governmental and electoral unit. The purpose behind this unit is to be a part of the larger political framework of the country and looking after essential needs of the village. Besides this political function at the village level, he also favoured and advocated strongly 'direct representation of the collectives and co-operatives on the land and in industry'.[84]

He envisaged the 'democratic organization of the state will consist of both functional and territorial representatives' and further stated that it will be 'completely in harmony with the India's past as well as with her present requirements'.[85]

In the overall context of the economic modernization and development he emphasized the need for planning. The purpose of planning is 'the well-being and advancement of the people as a whole'.[86] In the context of planning, he specifically pointed out that 'old established privileges and vested interest should not be allowed' to come in the way of any scheme designed to further the well-being of the community as a whole. He further pointed out that it must have a definite aim and social objective. The aim of planning, he was of the view is 'to ensure an adequate standard of living for the masses . . ., to get rid of the appalling poverty of the people'.[87] Nehru favoured attainment of national self-sufficiency. He viewed international trade, 'to avoid being drawn into the whirlpool of economic imperialism'.[88] In this context, he favoured, in the beginning, producing to meet the domestic needs of the country in all the sectors of economy.

Within this broad perspective of planning, he viewed the function of planning so as to bring about a large 'measure of regulation and co-ordination'. He did not rule out the private enterprise but he restricted its scope. Similarly, with regard to the defence industries, he was of the opinion that they must be owned and controlled by the state. This was also his view regarding key industries and public utilities.

Regarding land policy, he favoured the 'exploitation of land by developing collective and co-operative farms'. The idea was to start collective farms immediately on the culturable waste land and co-operative farming could be combined either with individual or joint ownership. Similarly, he also discussed about the desirability of evolving a 'socialized system of credit'. The whole purpose was to bring under the control of the state some regulation of capital and credit. He was in favour of some state control even for export and import trade.

Notes

1 Myron Weiner, Some Hypotheses on the Politics of Modernization in India, in Richard L. Park and Irene Tinker, eds., *Leadership and Political Institutions in India*, p. 18. See also Edward A. Shils, The Intellectuals, Public Opinion and Economic Development, *Economic Development and Culture Change*, Vol. VI, No. I (October 1957), p. 55.
2 R.C. Majumdar., H.C. Raychaudhari and Kalikinkar Darra, *An Advanced History of India*, London: The Macmillan Press Ltd, 1950, p. 812. See also K.N. Panikkar, The Intellectual History of Colonial India: Some Historiographical and Conceptual Questions, in Sabyasachi Bhattacharya and Romila Thapar, eds., *Situating Indian History for Sarevepalli Gopal*, New Delhi: Oxford University Press, 1986, pp. 403–432; Ramachandra Guha, ed., *Makers of Modern India*, New Delhi: Penguin, 2010, pp. 1–20.
3 Majumdar, Raychaudhari and Darra, *An Advanced History of India*, p. 812. See also R.C. Majumdar, ed., *The History and Culture of India*, Vol. 10, *British Paramountcy and Indian Renaissance*, Part II Bombay: Bharitya Vidya Bhavan, 1965, p. 92.
4 Wm. Theodore de Bary (complied by) *Sources of Indian Tradition*, New York: Columbia University Press, 1958, Third Printing, 1960, p. 572. See also Asok Sen, The Bengal Economy and Rammohun Roy in V.C. Joshi, ed., *Rammohun Roy: And the Process of Modernization in India*, New Delhi: Vikas Publishing House Pvt. Ltd, 1975, pp. 103–135 and Rachel Fell McDermott and others, eds., *Sources of Indian Traditions*, Third Edition, Vol. 2, Modern India, Pakistan and Bangladesh, London: Penguin Books Ltd, 2014, pp. 72–78.
5 B.N. Ganguli, *Indian Economic Thought: Nineteenth Century Perspectives*, New Delhi: Tata McGraw-Hill Publishing Co. Ltd, 1977, p. 38.
6 Ibid., p. 38.
7 Ibid., p. 47.
8 Joshi, ed., *Rammohun Roy*, p. 109, 122 and see also Amiya P. Sen, *Rammohun Roy: A Critical Biography*, New Delhi: Penguin, First Published, 2012, pp. 118–201.
9 Ibid., pp. 128–129.
10 Majumdar, Raychaudhari and Darra, *An Advanced History of India*, pp. 876–887.
11 Bipan Chandra, *The Rise and Growth of Economic Nationalism in India*, New Delhi: Anamika Publishers and Distributors (P) Ltd. First Published, 1966, Revised Edition, 2004, p. 9.
12 Ibid., p. 9.
13 V.B. Singh, *From Naoroji to Nehru: Six Essays in Indian Economic Thought*, New Delhi: Macmillan India Limited, n.d., p. 8. See also Ganguli, *Indian Economic Thought*, pp. 126–153 and Chandra, *The Rise and Growth of Economic Nationalism in India*, pp. 303–551.
14 B.N. Ganguli, *Dadabhai Naoroji and the Drain Theory*, Bombay: Asia Publishing House, 1965, pp. 79–80.
15 Ibid., p. 145.
16 Bary (complied by), *Sources of Indian Tradition*, p. 690.
17 Ganguli, *Indian Economic Thought*, p. 164.

18 Aparna Devare, *History and the Making of a Modern Hindu Self*, New Delhi: Routledge, 2011, pp. 93–152.
19 Mahadev Govind Ranade, *Essays on Indian Economics: A Collection of Essays and Speeches*, Second Edition, Madras: G.A. Natesan, 1906, p. 195.
20 Ibid., p. 199.
21 Ibid., p. 34.
22 Ibid., p. 43.
23 Singh, *From Naoroji to Nehru*, p. 52.
24 Ranade, *Essays on Indian Economics*, p. 65.
25 Ibid., p. 102.
26 Ibid., p. 131.
27 Singh, *From Naoroji to Nehru*, p. 62.
28 A.M. Zaidi, ed., *Congress Presidential Addresses*, Vol. 1, 1885–1900, New Delhi: Publication Department, Indian Institute of Applied Political Research, 1985, p. 466.
29 Romesh Dutt, *The Economic History of India in the Victorian Age*, Seventh Edition, Vol. 2, London: Routledge & Kegan Paul Ltd, 1950.
30 Ibid., Vol. 2, p. 528 and see also Meenakshi Mukherjee, *An Indian for All Seasons: The Many Lives of R.C. Dutt*, New Delhi: Allen Lane Penguin Books, 2009, pp. 171–194 and pp. 195–214.
31 Ibid., pp. 177–178.
32 D.R. Gadgil, Gokhale as an Economist in C.P. Ramaswamy Aiyar, et al. *Gokhale: The Man and His Mission*, Bombay: Asia Publishing House, 1966, p. 42.
33 R.P. Patwardhan, ed., *Speeches and Writings of Gopal Krishna Gokhale*, Bombay: Asia Publishing House, 1962, Vol. 1 (Economic) p. 12. See also B.N. Ganguli, Gopal Krishna Gokhale: His Economic Thinking in Aiyar, et al., *Gokhale: The Man and His Mission*, pp. 72–73.
34 Ibid., pp. 38–39.
35 Ibid., p. 4.
36 Ibid., pp. 6–9.
37 Ibid., Vol. 2, p. 196.
38 Ibid., pp. 196–197.
39 Ibid., p. 201.
40 Ibid., Vol. 1, pp. 49–50.
41 Ibid., pp. 352–357.
42 Ibid., Vol. 2, p. 107.
43 Ibid, p. 227.
44 Ibid., Vol. 1, p. 266.
45 Theodore L. Shay, *The Legacy of the Lokmanya: The Political Philosophy of Bal Gangadhar Tilak*, Geoffrey Cumberlege: Oxford University Press, 1956, p. 48.
46 Sumit Sarkar, *Modern India 1885–1947*, Madras: Macmillan India Limited, First Published 1983, Reprint 1985, p. 91.
47 Bary (complied by), *Sources of Indian Tradition*, p. 662.
48 Aryan Path – Special Hind Swaraj Number (September 1938); in the Preface to the 1938 edition of *Hind Swaraj*, Mahadev Desai provides the views of Professor Soddy, G.D.H. Cole, C. Delisle Burns, John Middleton

Murry, J.D. Beresford, Hugh Fausset, Claude Houghton, Gerald Heard and Irene Rathbone in M.K. Gandhi, *Hind Swaraj or Indian Home Rule*, Ahmedabad: Navajivan Publishing House, 1938, Twentieth Reprint-November 2008, pp. 5–12; see also *Gandhi Marg*, Special Number, Vol. 17 (October 1973); Nageshwar Prasad, ed., *Hind Swaraj: A Fresh Look*, New Delhi: Gandhi Peace Foundation, 1985; Raghavan Iyer, ed., *The Moral and Political Writings of Mahatma Gandhi*, Vol. I, *Civilization, Politics, and Religion*, Oxford: Clarendon Press, 1986-This volume not only contains the text of *Hind Swaraj* but also Mahatma Gandhi's observations on it mainly in the form of letters and prefaces to various editions of the booklet from (March 1910–October 1945), pp. 271–287; Anthony J. Parel, ed., M.K. Gandhi, *Hind Swaraj and Other Writings*, Cambridge: Cambridge University Press, 1997. See also Bhikhu Parekh, *Gandhi*, New York: Oxford University Press, 1997, pp. 63–74 and pp. 75–91.

49 Gandhi, *Hind Swaraj or Indian Home Rule*, p. 14.

50 Parel, ed., and Gandhi. *Hind Swaraj and Other Writings*, p. l.

51 All quotations are from Gandhi, *Hind Swaraj or Indian Home Rule.*

52 New Year (G.), *Indian Opinion* (January 2, 1909), quoted in Iyer, ed., *The Moral and Political Writings of Mahatma Gandhi*, Vol. 3, 1987, p. 326.

53 Swadeshi Machinery, *Young India*(September17, 1919), quoted in Iyer, ed., *The Moral and Political Writings of Mahatma Gandhi*, Vol. 3, 1987, p. 352.

54 Ghanshyam Shah, ed., *Re-reading Hind Swaraj: Modernity and Subalterns*, London: Routledge, 2013.

55 A.M. Zaidi, ed., *Congress Presidential Addresses*, Vol.4, 1921–1939, New Delhi: Publication Department, Indian Institute of Applied Political Research, 1988, pp. 471–499. See also Sugata Bose, *His Majesty's Opponent: Subhas Chandra Bose and India's Struggle against Empire*, New Delhi: Allen Lane Penguin Books, 2011, pp. 141–146.

56 Ibid., pp. 485–486.

57 Subhas Chandra Bose, *Netaji's Life and Writings*, Part Two: The Indian Struggle1920–1934, First Indian Edition, Calcutta: Thacker, Spink and Co. (1933) Ltd, 1948, pp. 424–443.

58 Ibid.

59 K.T. Shah, *National Planning Committee: Being an abstract of Proceedings and other particulars relating to the National Planning Committee*, Honorary General Secretary, Bombay: National Planning Committee, n.d., p. 16.

60 Ibid., p. 75.

61 Ibid., p. 78.

62 Ibid.

63 Ibid., p. 80.

64 A.H. Hanson, *The Process of Planning: A Study of India's Five-Year Plans 1950–1964*, London: Oxford University Press, 1966, p. 35.

65 Sarvepalli Gopal, *Jawaharlal Nehru: A Biography Volume One 1889–1947*, Bombay: Oxford University Press, 1976, p. 248.

66 Sir Purushotamdas Thakurdas, J.R.D. Tata, G.D. Birla, Sir Ardeshir Dalal, Sir Shri Ram, Kasturbhai Lalbhai, A.D. Shroff and John Matthai, Ardeshir Dalal. See Purshotamdas Thakurdas and others, A Plan of Economic Development for India (1944) Part I.

67 Ibid and Purshotamdas Thakurdas and others, A Plan of Economic Development for India (1945) Part II Distribution – Role of the State (Sir Ardeshir Dalal, who was a signatory of Part I of the Plan, was unable to sign Part II of the Plan due to his appointment as Member for Planning and Development in the Government of India).
68 B.N. Banerjee and others, *People's Plan for Economic Development of India, being the Report of the Post-War Reconstruction Committee of the Indian Federation of Labour*, New Delhi: A. K. Mukerjee, 1944.
69 Shriman Narayan, *Principles of Gandhian Planning*, First Edition, Allahabad: Kitab Mahal, 1960, p. 1.
70 Ibid., quoted in, p. 17.
71 Ibid., p. 34.
72 Ibid., p. 43.
73 D. G. Tendulkar, *Mahatma: Life of Mohandas Karamchand Gandhi*, Vol. 6, Bombay: Vithalbhai K. Jhaveri, 1940–1945, p. 21.
74 Ibid., pp. 21–40 and Parel, ed., and Gandhi, *Hind Swaraj and Other Writings*, pp. 170–181; see also: Foreword to *Constructive Programme – Its Meaning and Place in The Collected Works of Mahatma Gandhi*, Vol. LXXXII, pp. 66–68.
75 Jawaharlal Nehru, *The Discovery of India. Jawaharlal Nehru Memorial Fund*, New Delhi: Oxford University Press, Seventeenth Impression, 1997.
76 Ibid., p. 23.
77 Ibid., p. 52.
78 Ibid., p. 517.
79 Ibid., p. 515.
80 Ibid., p. 519.
81 Ibid.
82 Ibid., p. 520.
83 Ibid., p. 522.
84 Ibid., p. 523.
85 Ibid.
86 Ibid., p. 501.
87 Ibid., p. 397.
88 Ibid., pp. 397–398.

2

CONSTITUTIONAL REFORMS, ELECTORAL SYSTEM, POLITICAL PARTIES AND ELECTIONS BEFORE INDEPENDENCE

Chapter-3

The question of representation to Indians in the affairs of the administration of India was raised ever since the passing of the Government of India Act 1858, which transferred the power from the East India Company to the Crown. The Indian Councils Act of 1861 was the first statute which enabled the Governor-General to associate the people with the work of legislation as well as providing powers to the provincial governments for the institution of legislative councils. The provincial legislative councils were set up in Madras (1861), Bombay (1861) and Bengal (1862); in North-Western Province (1886) and the Punjab (1897)

It is proposed to discuss the question of representation in the context of the constitutional reforms in India since 1892 up to independence.[1] The main question which surrounded the problem of representation relates to the 'territorial representation' versus 'separate representation'. As a matter of fact, this was the main issue both in the Indian Councils Act of 1892, and Morley-Minto Reforms of 1909 and even subsequent constitutional reforms.

While dealing with the problem relating to constitutional reforms, the emphasis is on the developments relating to representation. This includes the following: composition of electorates, electoral processes and procedures, conduct of elections, emergence of political parties and party manifestos and the growth and development of parliamentary experience

I

Indian Councils Act of 1892

The Indian Councils Act, 1892, for the first time made a limited and indirect provision of election, as against pure nominations for filling some non-official seats in the provincial councils as well as central legislative council. The object of this Act was to widen the basis and expand the functions of the Government of India and provinces so as to provide further opportunities to the non-official element in Indian society regarding right to ask questions and discuss the budget.

Lord Curzon (then Under Secretary of State for India) while introducing the Bill expressed that there was 'illiteracy' and 'absence of political consciousness' in the country. He was of the view that elective principles 'might be at least premature and unwise'.[2] The word 'election' was never used in the statute; the process was described as a nomination made on the recommendation of certain bodies. In the case of the Indian legislative council, five more 'additional' members were recommended by the non-official members of each of the four provincial councils, and one by the Calcutta Chamber of Commerce. In the case of the provincial councils, the majority of the non-official seats were filled by the recommending bodies, i.e. municipalities and district boards.

II

Morley-Minto Reforms 1909

The period between 1905 and 1909 was one of restlessness and discontent. The discontent was due to a number of factors: the partition of Bengal, the demand for the constitutional reforms, the Russo-Japanese war of 1904–1905, the criticism of the Universities Act of 1904, the agrarian grievances of the people of Punjab and the many front-ranking leaders 'denouncing' the British Raj, etc. All these factors led in generating impulses for the reform.

The names of Lord Morley and Lord Minto are associated with further advance regarding the constitutional reforms. Minto in November 1905 had replaced Curzon as Viceroy, and in December 1905, Morley, became Secretary of State for India. To consider increase of the representative element in the Indian and provincial legislative councils, was a priority issue before Morley. He was also interested in increasing 'the representative element'.[3] Morley advised Minto 'we must persevere with liberal and substantial reforms, perhaps wider than those in your original sketch'.[4] However, Minto was against 'territorial representation' and proposed representation of 'landed proprietors and of communities'.

On August 16, 1906, Minto appointed the Committee of the Executive Council to consider the need for reforms.[5] A good deal to work regarding constitutional reforms was undertaken by Herbert Risley. He had intimate knowledge of the Indian social structure and its intricacies. He was of the view that in India the caste system 'favour[s] particularist rather than nationalist tendencies'. Besides, he viewed 'religious differences create distinct types within a nation and tend to perpetuate separate and antagonistic interests'.[6] In the context of caste and nationality, Risley observed that 'it must not be forgotten that caste would provide the party in power, the party that had spoils to divide, with – a "machine" surpassing in efficiency the wildest dream of the most ingenious wire-puller'.[7] He further observed:

> These are some of the blessings which popular government, controlled and directed by caste organization, would confer upon the subjects committed to its charge. Whatever future centuries may have in store for the people of India, it may be hoped that they will be spared the misfortune of government by social ostracism.[8]

He observed that as a consequence 'the growth of national sentiment either do not exist at all in India, or tend to produce separation rather than cohesion'.[9] In the context of electoral system, Risley suggested separate representation in the legislative councils and attacked the idea of territorial representation advocated by Morley.

In the meanwhile, a delegation led by Sir Aga Khan, presented its address to the Viceroy Minto on October 1, 1906. The address primarily asserted the 'separatist communal consciousness' and a 'fair share' of any representation, for the Muslim community. Minto's reply was as follows 'I make no attempt to indicate by what means the representation of communities can be obtained . . ., but I am as firmly convinced as I believe you to be that any electoral representation in India would be doomed to mischievous failure which aimed at granting a personal enfranchisement regardless of the beliefs and traditions of the communities composing the population of this continent'.[10]

In the constitution of legislative councils, Morley agreed with the suggestion of representation by 'classes and interests' and the 'impossibility of applying any uniform system throughout'. However, Morley suggested 'the principle of Electoral Colleges'. The purpose was that 'minorities would be protected against exclusion by majorities and all large and important sections of the population would have the opportunity of returning members in proportion to their ratio to the total population'.[11] The electoral system suggested by the committee consisted of the principles of minority and class representation along with communal representation.

Provisions of the Act of 1909

The following are the some of the significant provisions of the Indian Councils Act of 1909 – the size of the councils was enlarged, the additional members of the Governor General's Council were increased up to a maximum of sixty, the Act did not provide for any official majority in the provincial legislative councils, there was representation by the classes and interests and there were separate legislative constituencies for Muhammadans along with their to right to vote in the general constituencies.

The functions of the councils were increased. The members were given the right to ask questions and move resolutions in the councils. The system of election was indirect. The people elected members of local bodies and they in turn elected a member of an Electoral College. The Electoral College elected the members of the Provincial Legislatures. They in turn elected members of Imperial legislature. It is important to emphasize that the Act of 1909 gave a legal recognition to the principle of election 'which involved the imposition of legal disqualifications for election'.

The Government of India, on November 15, 1909, issued the Regulations for giving effect to the Indian Councils Act 1909. The composition of the Indian Legislative Councils (Table 2.1), as reconstituted under the Indian Councils Act of 1909, consisted of Imperial Legislative Council and the Provincial Legislative Councils of Madras, Bombay, Bengal, Bihar, United Provinces, the Punjab, Burma and Assam. As is evident from the table, these Councils had non-official majorities, with a large proportion of elected members.[12]

In the context of legislative councils, Broomfield observed that 'Morley . . . recognized that although Bengal had only a Lieutenant-Governor, its administrative problems demanded that, unlike other Lieutenant Governors' provinces, it should not be denied an Executive Council'.[13] In the legislative reforms of 1909, Bengal's superior political maturity was acknowledged by the provision of Representative Government. No other province was given this privilege.[14]

Table 2.1 Strength of the Councils (Imperial Legislative Council and the Provincial Legislative Councils) under the Indian Councils Act, 1909.

Province	*Ex-officio*	*Elected*	*Officials*	*Non-officials*	*Experts*	*Total*
India	8	27	28	5	--	68
Madras	4	21	17	5	2	49
Bombay	4	21	15	7	2	49
Bengal	4	28	16	4	2	54
Bihar	4	21	15	4	1	45
U.P.	1	21	20	6	2	50
Punjab	1	8	10	6	2	27
Burma	1	1	6	8	2	18
Assam	1	11	9	4	1	26

Source: A. Rangaswami Iyengar, *The Indian Constitution Study: An Introductory Study*, Madras: G.C. Loganadham Bros, 1913, p. cxvii.

After the Act of 1909, the development of political parties tended to be more on communal than on political lines. The explanation of the communal origins of the political parties is attributed to the fact that the constitutional reforms recognized the existence of the communal groups in the electoral system and reserved seats according to the population percentage and some others extraneous factors. Except for the INC, which was established in December 1885 with the objective of attainment of self-government, the other political parties in India were founded on communal basis. The emergence of these parties had a definite co-relation with the principle of election as put in operation by the Indian Councils Act 1909. It generated communal impulses. It is important to mention that the Indian Councils Act 1909 provided separate representation to the Muslims not only to according to the ratio of population but also looking at their importance in the overall context of the country. Although even during the period of 1906 to 1909, i.e. (before the announcement of the Act), a number of communal groups Sikhs, Christians and non-Brahmins formed Madras and requested for seat reservation for their communities. However, expect the Muslims, no such organization was favoured (Table 2.2).

The INC in its Lahore session 1909 and Allahabad session 1910 disapproved the creation of separate electorates on the basis of religion. It urged the government for modifying the regulations framed under the Indian Councils Act 1909. In its Benares session, it made a Resolution to make legislative councils truly representative of the people so as to provide 'real voice', in the governance of the country.

Table 2.2 Composition of Bengal and Eastern Bengal and Assam Legislative Councils under Indian Councils Act, 1909.

Bengal	
Ex officio members:	
Lieutenant-governor	1
Executive councilors	2
Nominated members:	
Officials, maximum	17
Indian commerce	1
Planters	1
Experts	2
Others, minimum	3
Elected members:	
Corporation of Calcutta	1
Calcutta University	1
Municipalities	6
District boards	6
Landholders	5
Muhammadans	4
Bengal Chamber of Commerce	2
Calcutta Trades Association	1
Eastern Bengal and Assam	
Ex officio member:	
Lieutenant-governor	1
Nominated members:	
Officials, maximum	17
Indian commerce	1
Experts	2
Others, minimum	2
Elected members:	
Chittagong Port Commission	1
Municipalities	3
District and local boards	5
Landholders	2
Muhammadans	4
Tea interest	2
Jute interest	1

Source: PP, 1910, [Cd. 4987], vol. LXVII, p. 883 and 1021 quoted in J.H. Broomfield, *Elite Conflict in a Plural Society: Twentieth-Century Bengal*, Bombay: University of California Press, 1968, p. 38.

Electoral System under the Act of 1909

The Regulations provided certain qualifications for the Members of the council, 'no person shall be eligible for election' if such person – (1) is not a British subject, or (2) is an official, or (3) is a female, or

(4) is of unsound mind or (5) is under twenty-five years of age, or (6) is bankrupt or (7) dismissed from the government service, etc.

In the context of an election, these Regulations also explained corrupt practices. A corrupt practice usually related to the following: inducement to any voter, offers money or valuable consideration, any promise of individual profit or any threat of injury. An election shall be invalid if the candidate elected committed any corrupt practices.[15]

These Regulations also provided a detailed categorization of the members (1) Ex-Officio Members, (2) Nominated Members – Officials, (3) Nominated Members – Non-Officials, (4) Experts and (5) Elected Members. The distribution of elective seats in India in respect of the various Legislative Councils was based, only to a limited extent, on the principle of territorial division and largely on principles of minority, class representation and communal representation.[16] The electorates of the various Legislative Councils in India were divided under three heads: (1) general electorates; (2) class electorates comprising of Landed Interests and Muhamadans; (3) special electorates comprising of the Presidency Corporations, the Universities, Commerce, Trade, Planting, Port Trusts and other Interests.

The qualifications were prescribed separately for landholders' constituencies and Muslim electorates. The landholders' constituencies qualifications varied for the Imperial and the provincial councils for the Muslim and the Hindu voters and from province to province. For the Mohammedan electorates, qualifications also varied for the Imperial and provincial councils and from province to province as well.

Provisions were also made for the preparation and publication of an electoral roll containing the names of all persons qualified to vote as well as electoral machinery of different kinds according to the nature of the constituencies. In all cases, votes were allowed to be recorded before the Returning Officers, in some cases, votes were recorded before Attesting Officers who were to attest the votes recorded and transmitted the same to the Returning Officers.

Elections under the Act of 1909

As has been pointed out earlier, the councilors were given the power to discuss 'any matter of general public interest and move resolutions on the budget'. In a way, 'the system of electoral politics' was introduced in India. Wolpert has mentioned that India's first nationwide elections 'were conducted between November 15, 1909 (when these regulations were officially announced) and the first meeting of new legislative councils on January 25, 1910'.[17] Besides, elections were also conducted from December 1912 to January 1913 and in June 1916. Thereafter the life of legislative councils was increased by an executive order in anticipation of the reforms. Studies on the provincial elections of 1912 and subsequent elections are very few.[18] It is important to emphasize that both the Extremist and Moderate wings of the Congress in Bengal 'refused to enter the reformed legislatures as a protest against the British failure to reunify the province'.[19]

Broomfield's study in the context of Bengal is one of the very few studies which have analysed the elections conducted between December 1912 and January 1913. Broomfield identified a number of shortcomings in the political parties contesting these elections: 'the absence of a satisfactory organization' for the conduct of an election campaign; the 'absence of a campaign fund'; an 'inability to speak the new language of electoral politics'; and 'the electors were primarily concerned with questions of their personal obligation to the candidates, or with the acquisition of local, communal, and personal advantages'.[20]

Broomfield further observed that 'what mattered most at an election was not a candidate's political beliefs or experience of public affairs, but the length of his rent roll, his local prestige, his religion, caste, and family, his connections, his wealth, and his benefactions'.[21] This study also identified 'a number of distinct levels of politics, and, for a politician. . . . He had to talk the language of local influence and community to the electors, and the language of nationalism to his fellow legislative councillors'.[22]

Regarding elections of 1912–1913, Broomfield's study mentions some other noteworthy issues relating to the political parties: 'no formal party structure nor discipline'; 'disorganization and confusion at the polls'; 'personality and local influence . . . counted for considerably more than political allegiance'.[23] Broomfield has further provided a point of fundamental importance by stating that

> The grant of the vote introduced a new form of power to Indian society. From the British viewpoint this was one stage (some thought an advanced stage) in the development of representative institutions; from the Indian angle it was the chance for a person, community, or political group to gain power and increased status at the expense of other sections of society.[24]

Regarding the electoral system and procedures, Broomfield observed that 'the electoral regulations were badly framed' and that 'electoral registers were inaccurate which encouraged malpractice'. He further provides some more fundamental reasons

> The franchise was novel and exotic. It was introduced to an illiterate and poverty-stricken society, which was politically inexperienced and for which representative institutions certainly had no intrinsic value. These disadvantages were tempered, to a degree, by the restriction of the vote to a minute fraction of the population (1 in 4650) but the result was small electorates in which a handful of votes could determine contests – and a handful of votes can often be bought.[25]

One interesting aspect of 1912–1913 elections relates to the existence of election manifesto of Moderates (Banerjea group). Broomfield refers to an election manifesto prepared by Abdul Rasul, a member of Calcutta High Court Bar, emphasizing the importance of exercising the right to vote as well as the importance of legislative bodies:

> To the people of India has been granted the right of increasing participation in the work of framing laws for themselves, and to prove ourselves worthy of this right we must return the best of our men. Laws that are passed in the Legislative Councils affect the interests of all. . . . Great responsibilities we have before us and if we do not exercise our votes in favour of the best man, the 'Hon'ble' members who may go to the Council will not be the sufferers, but we alone shall be left to suffer. Our interests will remain uncared for the three years to come.[26]

Besides, one important development with regard to electorates relate to the Lucknow Pact of 1916. In this Pact, the INC and the Muslim League jointly took steps towards self-government for India. Some of the significant aspects of this scheme which is known as 'The Congress- League Scheme of Reform' contains the following important provisions: (1) representation to Mahomedans through special electorates on the Provincial legislative councils and Imperial legislative council; (2) full authority to the Provincial council to deal with all matters affecting the internal administration of the province; (3) 'no Bill nor a resolution . . . affecting one or the other community, shall be proceeded with, if three-fourths of the members of that community in the particular Council, Imperial or provincial, oppose to Bill or any clause thereof, or the resolution'; (4) besides, Muslims were granted weightage in the provinces in which they were in minority.[27]

The growth and development of parliamentary experience

The Report on Indian Constitutional Reforms made some significant observations on the work carried out in the Indian legislative council as well as the Provincial councils from 1909 to 1917.[28] The Report observed that during this period the Indian Legislative Council passed 131 laws out of which 77 or 59 percent were passed without any discussion. The most important reason for the lack of discussion was 'the Government policy of avoiding opposition as far as possible'. The Committee further observed that 'in spite of the official majority', the non-official members had 'in many cases been able to make their weight felt'. The Report also refers that during this period five private Bills were also passed by the Imperial Legislative Council. The Report further observed that the non-officials members exercised 'influence' on the work of administration by means of questions and resolutions. The Report pointed out that the right of interrogation was not abused. Similarly the right to move resolutions on matters of general importance and of the financial statement was given in 1909. This right was the most important of all the changes made in the Legislative system: 'In all 168 resolutions were moved in the council up till the end of the year 1917; of these 24 were accepted by government, 68 were withdrawn, and 76 were rejected either with or without a division'. The Report also analysed in detail the work carried out in the provincial legislative councils specifically with reference to their contribution on legislation, the use of the right of interrogation and the use of resolutions, etc.

III

Montague-Chelmsford reforms

The announcement to bring constitutional reforms was made in the wake of political agitation, political violence and political consciousness in the country as a whole. The First World War and the British problem with Turkey were two other factors responsible for this change. The Secretary of State for India, on August 20, 1917, announced in the House of Commons the need 'of the increasing association of Indians in every branch of the administration and gradual development of self-governing institutions with a view to the progressive realization of responsible government in India'. The Montague-Chelmsford Report[29] recommended the appointment of two committees known as the Franchise Committee and the Functions Committee. The Franchise Committee was to determine the issues related to the franchise and strength of the Councils. The Functions Committee to advise regarding the departments that were to be 'reserved' and those that were to be 'transferred'.

Some of the important recommendations of Montague-Chelmsford Reforms are as follows: to establish a Council of State and a Legislative Assembly; the Council of State to consist of fifty members (twenty-one to be elected and twenty-nine nominated by the Governor-General); the Legislative Assembly to consist of about 100 members of whom (two-thirds to be elected and one-third nominated); the composition of each Legislative Council based on a substantial elected Majority members, elected on 'as broad a franchise as possible and nominated composed of official, non-official and Ex-officio members'.

The duration in the case of the Council of State was five years and that of the Legislative Assembly was three years. General elections were to be held after the expiration of the aforementioned duration. It is interesting to point out that the Franchise Committee recommended a system of indirect elections to the Central Assembly. However the Government of India decided direct elections for both Houses of the Central Legislature. The franchise was very much restricted. In 1920, the total number of votes for the Council of State was 17,364 and for the Central Assembly was 9,09,874.

The Government of India Act, 1919, provided for two lists of subjects: Central List and Provincial List. The items included in the Central List were defence, foreign and political relations, public debt, tariffs and customs, posts and telegraphs, patents and copyright, currency and coinage, communications, commerce and shipping civil and criminal law and procedure, major ports, etc.

Dyarchy was introduced in the provinces. The subjects given in the Provincial List were divided into two parts, reserved and transferred subjects. The reserved subjects were to be administered by the Governor as before with the help of the Executive Council. Some of the reserved subjects were the administration of justice, police, irrigation, land revenue administration, land improvement and agricultural loans, famine relief, etc. On the other hand, the transferred subjects were to be dealt with by the Governor in the future with the help of his ministers. While the members of the Executive Council were nominated by the Governor, the ministers were chosen by him from the members of the legislature. Some of the important transferred subjects were local self-government, public health, sanitation and medical administration, medical education, education public works (including roads, bridges and municipal tramways) and the development of industries (including industrial research and technical education). The Governor was given special responsibilities. He was given the authority to overrule his ministers and the members of the Executive Council if that was considered necessary for the discharge of his responsibilities. The Governor was expected to encourage joint deliberations between the ministers and the members of the Executive Council.

Electoral system

The Montague-Chelmsford Report and the Act of 1919 added a new dimension in the electoral system in India. The Report also provided a background for the rise of new political organizations on communal basis in many parts of the country. It is proposed to analyse the various political organizations/parties which came into existence along with the constitutional reforms provided under the Act of 1919. However, the Government of India Act 1919 provided communal representation not only to the Muslims (on the basis of the Lucknow Pact), but to Sikhs in the Punjab, the non-Brahmans in Madras, the Indian Christians, the Anglo-Indians, the Europeans and the Lingayat community in Bombay.

The franchise and the composition of the Legislative Council was determined by regulations to be made on the advice of a special committee appointed for this purpose under the Presidentship of Lord Southborough. The recommendations of the 'Franchise Committee' covered the following issues: problem of franchise, distribution of seats, qualification of candidates, nomination and official representation, etc. In these recommendations, the 'Franchise Committee' was guided by the principles laid down that the franchise should be as broad as possible.

In prescribing the electoral qualification in the popular constituencies in the provinces, the Franchise Committee 'was guided in deciding the minimum property qualification' and discarded as options the 'literacy test' and 'uniformity in the standard of property qualification'. The Committee observed that the 'qualifications adopted by us will result in enfranchising a substantially higher proportion of the urban than of the rural population, a result which we believe to be justified by the higher standard of wealth and intelligence in the towns'.[30] The general proposals for the franchise were based up on the principle of residence and the possession of certain property qualifications (payment of land revenue or municipal rates and income tax). Besides, the Committee also recommended the enfranchisement of all retired and pensioned officers both commissioned and non-commissioned of the

Indian Army. These recommendations were considered by the Joint Select Committee of Parliament. Afterwards these recommendations were approved by the authorities and subsequently contained in Electoral Rules made under a section of the Act of 1919.

Table 2.3 gives the province-wise strength of urban and rural electors against the total population of each province, based on the criteria suggested by the Franchise Committee.

The electoral system provided not only the legislative basis but also the constituencies (general constituencies, Muhammadan constituencies and constituencies in the special category), as well as provisions for franchise and the electorate; candidates; nominating procedures, agents and expenses; polling; election petitions; bye-elections and new general elections.[31]

Under the new scheme, the composition of the Legislative Assembly (Table 2.4), the Council of State (Table 2.5), and the Provincial Legislative Councils (Table 2.6) is as follows in these tables.

Due to the unequal distribution of population and wealth, the Report on Indian Constitutional Reforms, stressed the necessity to differentiate the qualifications for a vote between provinces, as well as between different parts of the same province. The Report also pointed the limitations of the franchise with reference to 'practical difficulties': the problems involved in the maintenance of an electoral roll, the attendance of voters at a polling centre, the danger of impersonation and the subsequent adjudication of electoral petitions.[32]

Table 2.3 Urban and rural electors in the Provinces.

Province	*Total population*	*Urban electors*	*Rural electors*	*Total electors*
Madras	39,827,885	32,000	510,000	542,000
Bombay	19,580,312	149,000	504,000	653,000
Bengal	45,063,697	106,000	1,122,000	1,228,000
United Provinces	47,182,044	64,500	1,419,000	1,483,500
Punjab	19,565,013	77,000	160,000	237,000
Bihar and Orissa	32,446,461	58,500	517,500	576,000
Central Provinces	12,269,638	39,500	120,000	159,500
Assam	6,000,000	–	–	300,000
Total				5,179,000

Source: W.A.J. Archbold, *Outlines of Indian Constitutional History [British Period]*. London: Curzon Press, first published 1926 and New Impression 1973, p. 187.

Table 2.4 Legislative Assembly.

Province	*Nominated*		*Elected*						*Total*
	Officials	*Non-officials*	*Non-Muhammdan*	*Muhammadan*	*Sikh*	*European*	*Landholders*	*Indian commerce*	
Government of India	14	5	–	–	–	–	–	–	19
Madras	2	–	10	3	–	1	1	1	18
Bombay	2	1	7	4	–	2	1	2	19
Bengal	2	2	6	6	–	3	1	1	20
United Provinces	1	2	8	6	–	1	1	–	19
Punjab	1	2	3	6	2	–	1	–	15
Bihar and Orissa	1	1	8	3	–	–	1	–	14
Central Provinces and Berar	1	1	3	1	–	–	1	–	07
Assam	1	–	2	1	–	1	–	–	05
Burma	1	–	3	–	–	1	–	–	05
Delhi	–	–	1	–	–	–	–	–	01
AjmerMerwara	–	–	1	–	–	–	–	–	01
N.W. Frontier Province	–	1	–	–	–	–	–	–	01
Total	26	15	52	30	2	9	7	4	145

Source: Indian Statutory Commission. *Report of the Indian Statutory Commission*, Volume 1: Survey Calcutta: Government of India, Central Publication Branch 1930, p. 168.

Table 2.5 Council of State.

Province	*Nominated*		*Elected*					*Total*
	Officials	*Non-officials*	*Non-Muhammdan*	*Muhammadan*	*Sikh*	*Non-communal*	*European commerce*	
Government of India	11	–	–	–	–	–	–	11
Madras	1	1	4	1	–	–	–	7
Bombay	1	1	3	2	–	–	1	8
Bengal	1	1	3	2	–	–	1	8
United Provinces	1	1	3	2	–	–	–	7
Punjab	1	3	1	2	1	–	–	8
Bihar and Orissa	1	–	2	1	–	–	–	4
Central Provinces and Berar	–	2	–	–	–	1	–	3
Assam	–	–	–	1	–	–	–	1
Burma	–	–	–	–	–	1	1	2
N.W. Frontier Province	–	1	–	–	–	–	–	1
Total	17	10	16	11	1	2	3	60

Source: Indian Statutory Commission: *Report of the Indian Statutory Commission*, Volume I: Survey Calcutta: Government of India, Central Publication Branch, 1930, p. 167.

Table 2.6 Provincial Legislative Councils.

Provinces	*Total (ex-officio, nominated and elected)*	*Nominated*																	
						By special electorates				*By communal electorates*						*By General Electorates*			
											Rural	*Urban*						*Rural*	*Urban*
		Total (nominated and ex-officio)	*Officials (nominated and ex-officio)*	*Non-officials*	*Total (elected)*	*Total*	*University*	*Landholders*	*Commerce and Industry, including Mining and Planting*	*Total*	*Mohammedans*	*Mohammedans*	*Europeans*	*Anglo-Indians*	*Indian Christians*	*Sikhs*	*Total*	*Non-Mohammedans*	*Non-Mohammedans*
Madras	127	29	23	6	98	13	1	6	6	20	11	2	1	1	5	--	65	56	9
Bombay	111	25	20	5	86	11	1	3	7	29	22	5	2	--	--	--	46	35	11
Bengal	139	26	20	6	113	21	1	5	15	46	33	6	5	2	--	--	46	35	11
United Provinces	123	23	18	5	100	10	1	6	3	30	25	4	1	--	--	--	60	52	8
Punjab	93	22	16	6	71	7	1	4	2	44	27	5	--	--	--	12	20	13	7
Bihar and Orissa	103	27	20	7	76	9	1	5	3	19	15	3	1	--	--	--	48	42	6
Central Provinces	70	16	10	6	5439	7	1	3	3	7	6	1	--	--	--	--	40	31	9
Assam	53	14	9	5		6	--	--	6	12	12	--	--	--	--	---	21	20	1

Source: W.A. J. Archbold, *Outlines of Indian Constitutional History [British Period]*, London: Curzon Press, p. 195.

The Electoral Rules under the Government of India Act, 1919, were made by the Governor-General in Council with the sanction of the Secretary of State in Council. These rules provided detailed qualifications for membership of the Indian Legislatures. Besides, it also provided detailed norms and qualifications for the following: the electoral roll; electors for the Council of State; electors for the Legislative Assembly and electoral procedure and membership.

The Electoral Rules regarding the qualifications for candidates mentioned that 'no person will be eligible for election as a Member of a Council, if such person is not a British subject or a subject of any State in India. Besides, the general disqualification excluded the following: women, persons of unsound mind, persons under twenty-one years of age and subjects of any foreign state'.[33] The total electors were 5,179,000, i.e. less than 2.5 percent of the total population of the electoral areas. There were also special qualifications necessary for election to the different legislative bodies. These qualifications varied from province to province.

In the case of the Council of State, the qualifications of an elector for a general constituency were based on the following: residence, landholding, payment of income tax, past or present tenure of office on a local authority, University distinction, the tenure of office in a co-operative banking society or the holding of a title conferred for literary merit. In the case of the Legislative Assembly and Provincial Legislative Council, the qualifications of an elector are based on community, residence, and the ownership or occupation of a building; or payment of municipal taxes or local cesses, or payment of income tax; the holding of land or membership of a local body.

Every Provincial Government was required to make regulations for electoral machinery providing for the electoral roll and the constitution and the appointment of Revising Authorities to dispose of claims and objections on the electoral roll, etc. The franchise qualifications for the Council of State varied from province to province and from one part of a province to another according to the variation in local circumstances.

Under the 1919 Act, the electoral rules known as the 'Electoral Procedure and Membership' were common to all legislative bodies in India. According to these rules the Governor-General, in the case of elections to the Indian Legislature, or the Governor, in the case of elections to a Legislative Council, called upon the constituencies concerned to elect members in accordance with the Electoral Rules. These rules dealt with the following: nomination of candidates, deposit on nomination, procedure at election, election agents, return of election expenses, election offences, bribery, undue influence and personation.

Besides, the government of each province was empowered to make regulations regarding the conduct of elections providing (1) for the scrutiny of nominations; (2) for the appointment in each constituency of a Returning Officer and for his powers and duties; (3) in the case of general constituencies, for the division of the constituencies into polling areas for the convenience of electors; (4) for the creation of polling stations; (5) for the appointment of officers to preside at polling stations; (6) for the checking of voters by reference to the electoral roll; (7) for the manner in which votes are to be given; in particular, (8) for the case of illiterate voter or voters under physical or other disability; (9) for the procedure to be followed when persons represent themselves to be electors after other persons have voted as such electors and (10) for such other purposes connected with the conduct of elections as it thinks necessary.[34]

The attitude of political parties towards the reforms and their manifestos

It is proposed to analyse the attitude and the approach of the political parties towards the reforms. Like the Surat spilt of 1906–1907, the Montague-Chelmsford Reforms also created a division in the ranks of Indian political parties.

The National Liberal Federation of India

On the question of the Montague-Chelmsford Reforms, the Liberals broke away from Congress in 1918. They formed a party of their own – the Moderate Party, under the leadership of Surendranath Banerjea. Its name was changed to National Liberal Federation of India in December 1919.[35]

This Party never announced its manifesto in the formal sense of the term, but followed certain objectives. The following are some of its objectives: to work for the success of the constitutional reforms; to follow a policy of co-operation with the government; to follow in its working 'a higher standard of rational efficiency by means of administrative reforms'; to advocate the need for the spread of education and the improvement of public health and to ensure economic development and amelioration of the condition of the backward classes.[36] The Party advocated the need to build up the strength of the nation and promote unity among its component parts by means of education, social reform and economic development.[37] It also advocated for the need for complete self-government in India's internal affairs and absolute equality with the Dominions in inter-imperial and international relations.

It is these liberals who formed the 'ministries' in various provinces during the period of its operation. Regarding the Liberal Ministries, it has been pointed out that 'They were generally chosen by the Governors on personal grounds and not on grounds of party. None of them had sought election as a party candidate'.[38]

Congress Party

The Congress Party boycotted the elections and resolved that 'Swaraj' must be attained 'within one year' by means of 'non-violent non-cooperation'. Gandhiji maintained that a programme of total non-cooperation would make Council entry 'ethically impossible'. The Congress passed resolutions at the Delhi Congress Session in December 1918 and dubbed the Reforms Act as 'inadequate, unsatisfactory, disappointing'.

As the government failed to do justice in the matters of the Khilaphat and the Punjab, the Indian National Congress (INC) in September 1920 adopted the resolution on non-cooperation and boycott of the Reformed Councils. This resolution was moved by Mahatma Gandhi. The INC also advised for the 'withdrawal by candidates of their candidature for election to the Reformed Councils, and refusal on the part of the voters to vote for any candidate'.[39]

Congress Democratic Party

Tilak disagreed with Mahatma Gandhi on the question of 'Council entry'. Tilak's approach was to enter the Councils and work for non-cooperation both within the government and outside it. Tilak was of the view that this would help in making the British Raj 'not only . . . aware of the injustice of their actions but would also be made to realize that the 1919 reforms were inadequate'.

To contest the elections to the legislatures, Tilak had set up the Congress Democratic Party and issued its manifesto in April 1920.[40] This manifesto enunciates Tilak's vision for India's future with particular reference to nation-building and economic modernization.[41] The manifesto is divided in two parts Part I refers to the responsibilities and initiatives assigned to the Imperial (Centre) and Part II refers to those issues to be dealt by the Provincial.

Imperial

1 Repeal of all repressive legislation.
2 Securing for the labouring classes a minimum wage, establishing the relationship between capital and labour on an equitable basis and promoting organizations suitable for the purpose.
3 Control of the export of foodstuffs and other necessaries of life by tariff or by other methods, with a view to reducing the prices thereof and conserving supplies.
4 Promotion of Swadeshism and development of industries by all recognized methods, including state subsidies and protective tariff.
5 Nationalization of railways and regulation of railway tariffs by legislation.
6 Taxation when imperative or desirable, but taxation graduated according to the capacity of various classes – corporations or individuals.
7 Creation of a Citizen Army, officered by Indians; naval, aerial and military education; commissions for Indians in all military services without racial discrimination.
8 Recruitment of all services by open competitive examination in India.
9 Promotion of national unity by such means as the establishment of a *lingua franca* for all India, betterment of relations between followers of different religions, and especially a Hindu-Muslim *Entente*.
10 Re-adjustment of Provinces on linguistic basis.

Provincial

1 Immediately securing full popular autonomy for the Provinces.
2 Permanent Ryotwari settlement on the basis of an equitable assessment.
3 Village control over reserved and protected forests in regard to pasturage, fuel, dealwood and use of minor products.
4 Absolute prohibition of *Veth, Begar* and *Sarbarai* (forms of agrarian bondage prevailing in some parts of India).
5 Education through the vernacular.
6 Free and compulsory education without distinction of sex, with special contributions and increased grants-in-aid from State Funds to Municipalities and Local Boards to carry out this object immediately.
7 Restoration of Village Panchayats with administrative and judicial powers.

8 Prohibition.
9 Extension of the franchise without sex distinction.
10 Sanitation on a systematic basis under a Minister of Health.
11 Carrying out of departmental reforms, e.g. agricultural development, extension of irrigation, the co-operative movement, industrial and technical education suitable to the needs of the country, organized medical relief, and encouragement to indigenous system of medicine.

The manifesto reflected the initiatives to be taken for the nation-building activities and modernization of the country. It is appropriate to call it the first most comprehensive enunciation of the vision for the transformation of the country. The manifesto covered almost all the aspects necessary to bring about change: constitutional, legal, social, political and economic. It has been a very forward-looking manifesto which took care of analysing all the complex social, economic and cultural problems of the country. Tilak had gone into each problem of the country with a large degree of thoroughness and it shows deeper understanding of the problems of the country in all walks of life. In a way, it was precursor of the fundamental rights which Congress adopted in 1931. Most of the aspects which the fundamental rights covered were part and parcel of Tilak's manifesto in one way or the other.[42]

Swaraj Party

To enquire into the slackening of the Non-cooperation movement, the All India Congress Committee appointed the Civil Disobedience Enquiry Committee in 1923.[43] This Committee gave a comprehensive report on the status of the Non-cooperation movement. The Report was unanimous with regard to the Civil Disobedience movement. However there was no unanimity amongst the members of the Committee on the question of desirability of boycotting the legislatures. At the Special Congress Session, which met in Delhi in September 1923 under the Presidentship of Maulana Abdul Kalam Azad, a compromise was made which permitted those 'who had no conscientious objection' to take part in elections to the Provincial and Central Legislatures. This resulted in the emergence of the Swaraj Party within the fold of the INC.

The elections of 1923 saw the entry of the Swarjists Party within the intention of 'destroying the constitution from within'. One important highlight of this election relates to the Swaraj Party manifesto under the heading 'Councils entry', which was issued under the signature of Motilal Nehru and mainly focused and spelled the political demand for the transfer of responsibility.[44] The party emphasized that the immediate objective of the party was the speedy attainment of Dominion status, which was further explained to mean 'the right to frame a Constitution and adopting such machinery and system as are more suited to the conditions of the country and to the genius of the people'. Within this broad perspective, the Swaraj Party declared to contest the elections so as 'to secure such effective control'.

Except when referring to the betterment of agriculturist of India, the manifesto did not touch upon any other social or economic aspect for the modernization of the country. Even on the problem of the agriculturist, the manifesto did not suggest any measures to contain the suffering of the tenant. On the other hand it assured the land-owning classes that it would do nothing to 'undermine the very foundations of society by trying to eliminate an important an influential class from it'. The manifesto further pointed out that the Party stands 'for justice to the tenant'. However, it balanced the statement by pointing out that 'but poor indeed will be the quality of their justice if it involve[s] any injustice to the landlord'. The Party further emphasized 'that it is only by serving the true interests of both that it can find a solid base for Swaraj and is pledged to stand by the one as firmly as by the other in its hour of need'. The manifesto also pointed out that 'It welcomed nationalist Zamindars who intend contesting the election'.

In the 1923 general elections, the Swaraj Party gained a clear majority in the Legislative Councils of Bombay, Central Provinces and United Provinces. It is interesting to point out that in the manifesto, Motilal Nehru made a provision for the formation of a coalition by including those nationalists 'who are in sympathy with the Party programme so far as it relates to Councils, it is open to them if they sign the Congress creed to join the Council section of the Party without identifying themselves with the activities of non-co-operators outside the Councils'. The coalition consisted of 70 members with Motilal Nehru as its Chairman and it included the Swarjists, Nationalists and the Independents. This was the first Legislative Assembly in India organized on the basis of Montagu Chelmsford Reforms. It has been observed that 'For the first time the party system was noticeable in a much more developed form'.[45]

The Swaraj Party in 1924 also approved a 'policy and programme' of the party with the guiding principle of the partybeing 'self-reliance in all activities which make for the healthy growth of the nation'. To give effect to this principle, the party resolved to adopt the following programme for the Legislative bodies: to 'refuse supplies and throw out Budgets unless and until the system of government is altered in recognition of our rights or as a matter of settlement between the Parliament and the people of India'; to throw out all proposals for legislative enactments by which the bureaucracy proposes to consolidate its powers; to move for resolutions and introduce and support measures and Bills which are necessary for the healthy growth of national life and the consequent displacement of the bureaucracy; to help the constructive programme of the INC; to follow a definite economic policy to prevent the drain of the public wealth from India by checking all activities leading to exploitation and to advance the national, economical, industrial and commercial interests of the country; to protect rights of labour, agricultural and industrial and to adjust the relations between landlords and tenants, capitalists and workmen.[46]

The Responsivist Cooperation Party

The Responsivist Cooperation Party (a Party within the Congress) emerged in 1926 to contest the elections to the Legislative Assembly and the Bengal Legislative Council. The Party claimed that 'none but members of the Indian National Congress are eligible to become its members'. The aim of the Party was the attainment of the Swaraj by peaceful and legitimate means. Some of the important leaders of the Party were M.R. Jayakar, J. Baptista, N.C. Kelkar, M.S. Aney, B.S. Moonje and S.V. Kelkar. The Party also claimed Bal Gangadhar Tilak as their leader. It is significant to note that the political programme of the Party was on the lines laid down in the Congress Democratic Party Manifesto.[47] The manifesto of the Party was released at its conference at Akola on 14–15 February 1926.[48]

Justice Party

The Act of 1919 provided separate electorates not only to Muhammadan community but also for Sikhs, Indian Christians, Anglo-Indians and Europeans. It also provided separate representation in a modified form to non-Brahmins in Madras Presidency. Irschick identified the factors which gave rise to this kind of representation.[49] He outlined the linguistic, cultural and social difference between Brahmans and non-Brahmans. The non-Brahman movement in South India is important because it illustrates a drive for separatism extraordinarily well. The announcement of August 1917 intensified the political interest in Madras between Brahmans and non-Brahmans. It was argued that the non-Brahmans in the Madras Presidency 'could not hope to attain political influence without special privileges'.

At the time of its emergence in December 1916, the Justice Party issued its 'non-Brahmin Manifesto'. The Justice Party Manifesto, in the true sense of the term, is the first of its kind. It became a major public pronouncement of the Party. From 1920 onwards, it also served as the Justice Party's election manifesto. It is important to provide an overview of the Justice Party manifesto. This will provide us some kind of an understanding regarding the social and political compulsions of the formation of a political party and its programme. In this context, the manifesto provided that though Brahmins are numerically less in number, but monopolized high government appointments as well as political power. It also identified the reasons of the supremacy of the Brahmins in the cultural, social, political and economic matters.

The Justice Party manifesto observed that, to achieve success in political power and government appointments, the individuals and the communities should 'act in concert' and establish 'efficient separate organizations' as 'modern weapon of publicity for attention and recognition'.[50] At the same time it pointed out the need for a 'progressive political development' based on 'trust in the people' and of 'timely and liberal concessions'. It advocated the need for the 'broadening and deepening' of the constitutional reforms so as to include 'every class, caste and community and their numerical strength', so as to provide them 'fiscal freedom and legislative autonomy in matters affecting their domestic and economic position'. It also suggested to pursue a 'more vigorous education policy' as well as 'association for the advancement of the education of the non-Brahmins classes'. It further suggested the need 'to ensure a continued educational, political, and economic development on a broad and enduring basis'.

The National Unionist Party

The Unionist Party in Punjab emerged out of a loose grouping of the rural members formed in the first Legislative Council. The Party adopted a 'secular and economy based front' in the elections to the Second Punjab Legislative Council (1923). The following are some important points of manifesto:[51] to attain dominion status within the British Commonwealth of Nations; to provide equal opportunities of advance to all and to direct in an increasing measure by constitutional means; to provide beneficent activities of the government to backward classes and areas; to secure a fair distribution of the burden of provincial taxes between agricultural and other classes; to secure a just and fair representation in the public services of the province to all classes and communities; to check the exploitation of economically backward classes by economically dominant classes; to promote indigenous industries and to encourage the use of Swadeshi articles; to banish illiteracy from the province; to encourage a policy of decentralization; to encourage the growth of local self-governing institutions; to diminish litigation; to secure economy in the administration; to suppress corruption and bribery; to promote temperance; to preserve intact the Punjab Land Alienation Act as a measure of protection to backward classes'.[52]

Elections

The elections under the Government of India Act 1919 were conducted for the Central Assembly and the Provincial Councils in 1920, 1923, 1926 and 1929–1930. However, except for the results of the second election held in November 1923, for the Central Assembly and the Provincial Councils (Table 2.7), as well as the Provincial Legislative Council elections of Assam (Table 2.8), no party-wise details both for the Central Assembly and the Provincial Councils are available.

Political parties and provincial councils

Since the emphasis of the study is on election-related issues, it is proposed to provide an analysis on political parties in terms of structure and organization, campaigning, publicity, electoral appeal and party manifestos.

Madras

In the context of the First General Election in Madras, it was reported that the political parties have been formed not on 'political principles' but on the basis of communal considerations or the 'personal influence of individuals'. It was also reported that 'There is no lack of general political 'planks in election manifesto'.[53]

In Madras, the first elections in November 1920 gave the Justice Party a decisive victory over the Brahmins. It was observed that voting was high in some urban constituencies. The significance of the election was analysed in the official review of the Government of India in the following words: 'For the first time in the history of India, the lower castes of Madras have asserted themselves against the intellectual

Table 2.7 Results of the second Provincial Election 1923.

	Central Assembly	*Madras*[a] *Council*	*Bombay Council*	*Bengal. Council*	*U.P. Council*	*Punjab Council*	*Bihar and Orissa Council*	*C.P. Council*	*Assam Council*	*Total*
Swarajists	42	-	32	36	31	9	13	40	13	216
Moderates	27	–	23	18	–	38	25	–	19	150
Independents	7	–	20	13	7	11	–	10	–	68
Non-Brahmins	–	61	6	–	–	–	–	–	–	67
Loyalists	6	–	–	–	–	–	19	–	–	25
Liberals	2	–	–	–	4	–	–	4	–	10
S.G.P. Committee	2	–	–	–	–	10	–	–	–	12
Brahmins	–	13	–	–	–	-	–	–	–	13
Muhammadans	–	13	–	–	8	–	–	–	–	21
Indian Christians	–	5	–	–	–	–	–	–	–	5
Europeans	–	5	5	18 (including Anglo-Indian)	4	–	–	–	6	39
Anglo-Indians	–	1	–	–	–	–	–	–	–	
Non-Swarajists	–	–	–	26	–	–	-	–	–	26
Landholders	–	–	-	–	43	–	–	–	–	43
Progressives	–	–	–	–	4	–	–	–	–	4
Khilafatists	–	–	–	-	–	3	–	–	–	4
Zamindars	–	–	–	–	–	–	15	–	1	15
No Party[b]	19	–	–	–	-	–	–	–	–	19
Not Known	–	–	–	-	–	–	1	–	–	1
Total	105	98	86	111	101	71	73	54	–	738

[a] There were seven Swarajists among the Brahmins and the non-Brahmins in Madras, while in Bengal there were thirteen Muhammadans among the Swarajists.

[b] The number of seats held by No Party was probably nineteen, not fifteen as recorded, for the total elected seats in the Assembly were 105, not 101.

Source: Home (Fol.) K.W. to File No. 82 of 1925 (Conf. Part I. App. A), p. 37 quoted in B.B Misra, *The Indian Political Parties: An Historical Analysis of Political Behaviour up to 1947*, Delhi: Oxford University Press, 1976, p. 221.

Table 2.8 Elections to the Assam Legislatures 1920–1937.

	1920	*1923*	*1926*	*1929*	*1937*
Total no. of candidates	81	89	88	n.a.	277
Returned unopposed	18	10	12	19	20
Contested seats	21	29	27	20	88
No. of regd. Voters	2,02,400	2,24,063	2,50,751	2,88,832	8,15,341
Votes polled	33,352	83,320	88,707		5,22,273
Percentage of votes polled for contested seats	25%	42%	43.5%		71.3%
Votes polled as percentage of the province's electorate	16.4%	37.2%	35.3%		64.0%

Source: ALCP (1924), Vol. 4, p. 3; ALCP (1927), Vol. 7, pp. 10–13; Return showing the Results of Election in India 1923 (Presented to Parliament, London, 1924), pp. 1–18 and 78–83; India in 1920: A report prepared for presentation to Parliament (Calcutta, 1921), appendix 3, p. 48; East India (Constitutional Reforms – Elections), Return Showing the Results of Elections in India 1925 and 1926 (PP. cmd 2923, London, 1927): East India (Constitutional Reforms) Indian Franchise Committee, Vol. I, Report of the Indian Franchise Committee, 1932 (London, 1932), p. 76. For the 1937 election, East India Constitutional Reforms: Elections – Return Showing the Results of Elections in India 1937 (New Delhi, 1937), p. 5, quoted in Amalendu Guha, *Planter-Raj to Swaraj: Freedom Struggle and Electoral Politics in Assam 1826–1947*, New Delhi: Indian Council of Historical Research, 155–156.

oligarchy of the upper, and have seized political power in their own hands'.[54]

Some of the important features of the Justice Party during the first Elections were complete unity in the party over political aims and methods. The party established its branches in almost all district headquarters in Madras Presidency. These branches were used as the main instruments for the support of the Justice Party. There were regular exchanges of visits between the branches and party headquarters. In the 1920 elections, it was reported that 'participation in the election seemed weak . . . but it was nonetheless an impressive demonstration of the growing political consciousness in the presidency'.[55] In the first election the party did 'some effective campaigning'.

However, in the 1923 election, due to the lack of electioneering as well as 'ineffectiveness of its local organizations', the Justice Party did not fare well. Besides, the Party was 'badly organized' and 'its newspapers were no longer effective as propaganda media'. It was observed that in comparison to 'Swaraj Party tactics and appeal' in the Justice Party 'there was simply not enough drive, imagination, creative leadership or organizational skill'.[56]

In the elections conducted in 1926, the Swarajists defeated the Justice Party and gained a majority in the Third Legislative Council.

In the elections of 1930, the Justice Party won the elections hands down. In the 1934 elections the Justice Party was completely defeated by the Congress. The Congress lifted its ban on Council Entry and won every seat that it contested. The Fourth Council worked until the end of 1936.

Punjab

In Punjab, the elections of 1920, both for the Central and the Provincial Councils, were 'low key affairs' with about 50 percent of the voters turning up. The first Punjab Legislative Council was almost totally an assembly which did not belong to any specific political party.[57]

The first election of Punjab legislative Council took place on December 5, 1920. In view of the appeal of the Indian National Congress for the boycott of the election the voter turnout was low. No organized party contested the election and as a result most of the representatives who were elected did not belong to any specific political party. By and large voting was exercised on the basis of the personality rather than the programme of the candidate.

The second Punjab Legislative Council elections (1923) were fought on the basis of the manifesto. Mainly it was contested by the 'Rural Blocks'. It was later renamed as the Punjab National Unionist Party. It is important to emphasize that this election was contested on the basis of 'new political ideology and new political programme'.[58]

The third elections of 1926 in Punjab for the reformed councils were significant due to the emergence of 'organized sectarian politics among the Hindus and Muslims'.[59] However the Unionist Party received a majority. The third Punjab Legislative Elections were held in November 1926. This election the politics was dominated 'by individual personalities with subjective aims and vested interests'.[60]

Elections for the Fourth Council were held in 1930, there was lack of interest in the election which is evident from the fact that, out of seventy-one seats in Councils, thirty-eight were returned unopposed.[61]

Bengal

During the first election of Bengal Legislative Council, there existed no definite political party and, as a result, there was no majority party to form a ministry. As a consequence, there was a lack of 'any real constructive programme'. In the second election in 1923, the Swaraj Party became the largest party. However they refused to accept the office. As a consequence, the second council did not achieve much by way of legislation. The party was guided by only by one policy, i.e. to obstruct the government in everything in order to destroy dyarchy. In the third Bengal Council, the Swarajists again emerged as the strongest party but with reduced numbers. The Fourth Council was convened in July 1929 and formed a ministry sometime in December 1929. It has been said about the Swaraj Party in Bengal that 'Its policy had little or no social and economic content and no mass appeal'.[62]

Bombay

In Bombay, in the 1920 elections for the Reformed Council, the percentage of voting was low. The total percentage of electors was 2.8 percent of the whole population. In the first elections, it has been reported that there were no organized parties. Besides, it was reported that 'The electorate has yet to learn the importance of returning representatives with a real sense of political responsibility for the welfare of the various peoples of the Presidency'.[63] As a matter of fact, it has been observed that the 1920 elections showed the 'listless attitude of the voter',[64] partly because of the low percentage of voting due to the boycott of the elections by the Congress Party.

In 1923 elections, the voting was higher because the electors which had boycotted the first election voted in support of the Swaraj Party. A number of reasons were attributed to the success of the Swaraj Party: 'a recognized leader, a definite programme, a sound organization, and party discipline'.[65]

It is also important to point out that, due to the difference of opinion within the Swaraj party in 1925, a large majority of the members of the Swaraj Party in the Legislative Council formed a Responsive Cooperation Party and the policy of obstruction was not pursed.[66] This spilt was complete by the time of the 1926 election. The behaviour of the various political parties in 1926 election has been analysed in the following words: the political disagreements within Congress and between Congress and its breakaways provides a glimpse of how the diversities of the province – linguistic, communal and economic – mirrored the differences between its political leaders at various levels. Each group took full advantage of these differences; for, after all, the object was success, however that may be achieved.[67]

United Provinces

The Report of the Government of United Provinces on the working of the reforms in the context of the elections of 1920 and the 1923 observed that the electors 'are pre-occupied with the difficulties of physical existence, responsive to the claims of their caste, community, passionately attached to their holdings, resentful of interference and oppression, but indifferent to any larger issue save religion; and religion in India is a disruptive force'.[68] Besides, the Report pointed out that the electors did not recognize that 'the legislature is their representative'. Except the Swarajist, the Report also observed the absence of well-organized parties. It was also commented on that, due to the 'divisions of race, religion, and interest [the] formation of stable combinations is difficult to achieve'. The Report concluded that 'neither the principle of responsibility to the electorate nor the principle of party cohesion has been established in any strength'.[69]

Bihar and Orissa

The election to the new council of Bihar and Orissa took place during November–December 1920. Nearly 41 percent of the total electorates voted in forty-six constituencies. The Report of Government of Bihar and Orissa observed that public meetings were unknown; few election addresses; no explanation of the political position, etc. The Report further observed on the second election of 1923 by stating that the 'three years of the reforms has educated the electorate to the meaning of an election and the business of a legislature'.[70] It was also observed that the first signs of the formation of a party system emerged only when the Swarajist candidates contested for elections. In 1926 election, the Swarajist captured the larger number of seats and provided consistent resistance to the government.

Central Provinces

The Report of the Central Provinces Government of the working of the first legislative council observed: 'The connection between the members and constituents members was very weak'; 'absence of any party organization, and lack of funds'. It was also pointed that, during the second election of 1923, the Swarajists party made no attempt to explain their policy of obstruction to the voters. Besides, the voters have not 'learned the value of their vote and also made no effort to control their representatives'. It was also pointed out that the electorates were handicapped not only due to illiteracy but were also devoid of any 'political sense'.

The working of dyarchy

From January 1921, the Government of India and the Provincial Governments started working under the Act of 1919. As mentioned earlier, the elections were completed in December 1920. However, within the span of three years, a number of limitations and obstacles were noticed both in the working of the Central and Provincial Governments.

The Government of India appointed a Reforms Enquiry Committee in 1924, under the Chairmanship of Sir Alexander Muddiman, 'to enquire into the difficulties arising from, or defects inherent in' with regard to the Central Government and the Provincial Governments. The Muddiman Committee, based on written and oral evidence of the Provincial Governments as well as former provincial ministers, analysed the reasons and defects in its working. It is interesting to point out in the context of this committee that two reports were submitted: the Majority Report[71] and the Minority Report.[72] However, in the context of defects of dyarchy, both the Reports contain nearly identical observations. Similarly the Simon Commission also analysed the limitations of the working of dyarchy both at the Centre and in the provinces. It was also analysed by some well-known scholars of Indian Constitutional history. Regarding the defects of dyarchy, there is lot of commonality in their observations in the government reports and related scholarly publications.[73]

In the working of the dyarchy, it was noticed that the division of functions between the Centre and the provinces and the division of provincial subjects between the Reserved and Transferred subjects were done in an arbitrary manner, i.e. without following any principles. In this context, many examples have been cited: education, agriculture, industries, etc. As a consequence, the Ministers were not in control over all the essential branches of any subject.

The purpose of the 1919 Act was to make a constitutional Governor. In this set up, it was stipulated that the ministers would be responsible to the legislative councils. However, the rules made under the transaction of business were framed, first, to 'concentrate power . . . in the hands of governor, and second, to encourage the practice of overruling the ministers. The governor, by dealing individually with the ministers, assumed greater power of control over the Transferred Department. As a result, the ministers had never possessed any real authority in any department'. The ministers never worked as a team and the dismissal and resignation of the minister did not affect his colleagues.

Another defect in the working of dyarchy was the ministers were not having adequate power over the permanent services. All matters relating to the services, appointment, postings and promotion were placed in the sole charge of the governor. In these matters, the ministers were left absolutely powerless. All this made the services practically independent of the ministers and made it difficult for ministers to obtain strict obedience. As a consequence, the implementation of the policy laid done by the ministers was largely left to the services over which the minister had no control.

The system of financial administration also adversely affected the working of the Reformed Constitution. Under the Devolution Rules, finance was made a reserved subject under the control of executive councilor. Its main function was to scrutinize and examine and advise on all schemes of new expenditures since all the Transferred subjects like education, sanitation, industries and agriculture were by their nature nation-building activities involving new expenditures. As a result the transferred subjects or departments were practically placed under the finance department and the finance members. It was reported to the Muddiman Committee by the former ministers that the finance department discouraged all new proposals and as such the ministers could not carry out schemes or new initiatives proposed by them. It was also reported that, in the both in the system of framing the budget (i.e. in the matter of imposition of taxes or shaping the expenditure), the ministers had no role to play.

Reforms committees on electorates

It is important to emphasize that the following Committees – Report of the Reforms Enquiry Committee 1924, Report of the Indian Statutory Commission 1930 and Report of the Indian Franchise Committee 1932 – had gone into the working of these Reforms. These Committees on the basis of written and oral evidence analysed their findings. A substantive part of the analysis included the following: the basis of representation, communal representation, obstacles to the growth of political parties, importance of party manifesto, percentage of population enfranchised, percentage of votes polled, election campaign, enfranchisement of women, etc.

Electorates

All the committees looking into the constitutional reforms in India addressed the problem of representation. The Muddiman Committee did not recommend any increase in the number of seats in the various legislatures. However the Committee recommended for the special representation for factory labourers, the removal of bar against women as members of the Indian legislators or the provincial councils, the representation of depressed classes in the Provincial Councils should be increased and that bribery, intimidation and the like should be made a penal offence.[74]

As mentioned earlier, some of the members of the Muddiman Committee[75] decided to write a separate Report about the electorates. This Report favoured the general broadening of the franchise. The Report observed:

> We have not been able to find the exact number of illiterates among the present electorates. But notwithstanding the fact that education in the three R's among the masses has been neglected in the past, we think that the average Indian voter, both rural and urban, is possessed of sufficient intelligence to understand issues directly affecting his local interests and capable of exercising a proper choice of his representatives. We think that the repeated use of the franchise will in itself be an education of potent value and the process of education must go hand in hand with the exercise of political power. We are, therefore, of the opinion that the franchise in every province should be carefully examined, and wherever it admits of lowering, it should be lowered, so as to secure the enfranchisement of a substantially large number of people.[76]

On the subject of communal representation, the Report was of the opinion that 'abolition of communal electorates is at present out of question, but we are entirely opposed to the extension of the principle any further'.[77]

The Indian Statutory Commission observed that the adoption of property qualification gave a 'monopoly in the vote to certain classes of the population'. This deprived a large section of a population from the franchise including all the women and the poor.[78]

The Indian Statutory Commission Report also pointed the need and importance of the elections of the political programme between parties aspiring to gain power. The Report observed 'The personal appeal, whether based on a zeal for service or on any other ambition, can be no substitute in the minds of the general population for the party contest and the political programme'.

The Indian Franchise Committee in May 1932 provided data regarding the interest evinced by the electorate in the elections of 1920, 1923 1926 (Table 2.9), 1929–1930 and 1934. The Report of the Committee pointed out that though it is true that a large majority of villagers in India have very little idea about the elections, and vote largely on personal grounds, however 'the interest now taken in politics and in elections is far more widespread than is always realized outside India'.[79]

The figures for 1929–1930 are given in Table 2.10. As in 1920, these figures were affected by the fact that the INC called upon its followers to abstain from the polls.

The Report of the Reform Enquiry Committee identified the following obstacles to the growth of political parties: limited franchise, subordinate character of legislatures in India, peculiar nature of dyarchy and its restricted ministries and, above all, the 'dominating aim of all

Table 2.9 Elections of 1920, 1923 and 1926.

Province	*Percentage of population enfranchised (1926)*	*Percentage of votes polled in the elections of*		
		1920	*1923*	*1926*
Madras	3.2	24.9	36.3 (11.4)	48.6 (19.2)
Bombay	3.9	16.2	38.4 (15.3)	39.0 (19.3)
Bengal	2.5	33.4	39.0	39.2 (13.0)
United Provinces	3.5	33.0	42.2 (2.8)	50.2 (10.0)
Punjab	3.4	32.0	49.3	52.4 (6.8)
Bihar and Orissa	1.1	41.0	52.0	61.0
Central Provinces	1.3	22.5	57.7	61.9
Assam	3.7	16.4	37.5	35.0 (not known)
The eight Provinces excluding Burma	2.8	29.0	39.9	42.6

Note: The figures in brackets give the percentage of women who voted to female electors, and it is clear that the enfranchisement of women has slightly retarded the general rate of improvement. The figures generally show a connection between a small electorate and a high proportion of voters.

The percentage for Madras, Punjab, Bihar and Orissa and Assam relate to contested elections only. For other Provinces the percentage of voters on the roll in all constituencies who polled their votes is shown. In all cases the figures cover special as well as general constituencies.

Source: *Report of the Indian Statutory Commission*, Volume I – Survey Calcutta: Government of India, Central Publication Branch, 1930, p. 197.

Table 2.10 Elections of 1929–1930.

Province	*Percentage of population enfranchised 1929–30*	*Percentage of votes polled in the elections of 1929–1930*
Madras	3.2	43.1 (18.1)
Bombay	3.9	11.4 (6.5)
Bengal	2.5	26.1 –
United Provinces	3.5	23.7 (3.9)
Punjab	3.1	38.5 (5.6)
Bihar and Orissa	1.1	33.2 (5.4)
Central Provinces	1.3	33.3 (8.8)
Assam	3.7	28.3 (6.5)

Note: The figures in parentheses give the percentage of women who voted for female electors.

Source: Indian Franchise Committee, *Report of the Indian Franchise Committee*, Second Edition, Calcutta: Government of India, Central Publication Branch, 1932 (1932), p. 30.

the groups is the same, namely, the attainment of responsible government'.[80] Besides, the Simon Commission Report observed that 'The various groupings, with kaleidoscopic changes of nomenclature, composition and leadership, have not often been on anything but communal lines, and their communal character has tended to become more rather than less pronounced'.[81]

Election campaign

Regarding the nature of election campaign the Report observed that public meetings were unknown and canvassing was limited to 'visiting the leading residents of the constituency'.[82] It was also mentioned that 'Election posters were used and hand bills circulated as the commonest means of appeal'. However, on the general elections of 1930,[83] it was observed that there was improvement in public meetings and method of canvassing. This Report also pointed out that, due to the growth of 'peasant consciousness', there was a decline of the influence of Zamindars.

Enfranchisement of women

The Indian Councils Act 1909 did not provide voting right to women. The Report on Indian Constitutional Reforms 1918 did not make any observation on the political rights of women in India. However, it suggested a 'broad' franchise with a substantial elected majority. It also recommended a special committee to 'measure the number of persons who can in the different parts of the country be reasonably entrusted with the duties of citizenship'.[84]

As a consequence, the Act 1919 provided that the qualification of electors for the different legislatures which were then being set up should be determined by 'rules made under the Act'. The Franchise Committee empowered the provincial councils by resolution to remove the sex barrier themselves, 'this should become an operative decision; and a corresponding faculty was conferred upon both Houses of the Indian Legislature'.[85] Madras was the first state to provide franchise to women in April 1921 and later on Bombay, Bengal, United Provinces, Punjab, Assam and Governors' Provinces gave this right to women, and this was done in every province by 1924.

The following table (Table 2.11) provides province-wise the numerical strength of electors (male and female) and their proportion to the population.

The number of women as electors was a lot less as the franchise was based on a property qualification. The women were enfranchised 'on the same terms as men' and in India women do not own property in their own right; as a result it remained more of a 'gesture'. The number of women who possessed in their own right the franchise qualification was, however, very small. For example, about 116,000 female voters in the Madras Presidency, 39,000 in Bombay, 37,000 in Bengal, 51,000 in the United Provinces, and 21,000 in the Punjab, i.e. the proportion of female electors to adult female population for that period varied from 1 to 0.2 percent.

The Report of the Reforms Enquiry Committee, 1924, observed that the question regarding women's franchise 'went deep into the social system and susceptibilities of India'.[86] It however noted with satisfaction that several of the provincial councils and the Legislative Assembly passed the necessary resolutions to remove the disqualifications for being an elector.

The committee on the issue of eligibility of women as members of the legislative bodies recommended that 'The bar against women being elected or nominated as members of either chamber of the Indian Legislature or of the provincial councils should be removable by the passing of resolutions after due notice in the chambers and the councils'.[87] By and large most of the legislative councils carried out this recommendation by 1926. The Indian Statutory Commission in its Report mentioned that 'In seven provinces out of nine the women became members of the legislatures as well as of the Legislative Assembly'.[88] It also provided that in several of the provincial councils, women were nominated as members and 'one of these has been unanimously elected by the Madras Legislature as its Deputy-President'. The Report further

Table 2.11 Male and female electors in the Provinces.

Province	*Population of the electoral areas in 1921 (Figures to nearest thousand)*	*Electors, male and female (Women electors in square brackets)*	*Proportion of electors to population*	*Proportion of male electors to adult male population*	*Proportion of female electors to adult female population*
			%	%	%
Madras	42,319,000	1,365,000 [116,000]	3.2	11.6	1.0
Bombay	19,292,000	759,000 [39,000]	3.9	13.4	.8
Bengal	46,241,000	1,173,000 [38,000]	2.5	9.7	.3
United Provinces	45,376,000	1,589,000 [51,000]	3.5	12.4	.4
Punjab	20,675,000	697,000 [21,000]	3.4	11.9	.5
Bihar and Orissa	33,820,000	373,000 [None]	1.1	4.6	–
Assam	6,735,000	250,000 [about 3,000]	3.7	14.2	.2
Central Provinces (including Berar).	12,780,000	169,000 [None]	1.3	5.2	–
Governors' Provinces excluding Burma	227,238,000	6,375,000 [268,000 in 6 provinces]	2.8	10.4	0.6 (for 6 provinces)
	11,073,000	1,926,000 [124,000]	17.4	60.3	4.6

Source: Report of the Indian Statutory Commission, Volume 1: Survey Calcutta: Government of India, Central Publication Branch 1930, p. 191.

pointed out 'The women members, . . . have done useful work as legislators: one of them (. . .) was responsible for the passage in Madras of the important measure known as the Devadasi Bill'.[89] S. Muthulakshmi Reddi was very active in the Women's Indian Association. She was nominated to the Madras Legislative Council and also served as its Deputy President. She was also a 'successful medical practitioner and a tireless social reformer for women's causes'.[90]

The development of the parliamentary experience

The growth and development of parliamentary experience in the context of Morley-Minto Councils (1909–1919) have already been delineated in the previous section. It is proposed to provide an overview of the growth of parliamentary experience from 1921 to 1937 under the Montague-Chelmsford Reforms.

The constitutional reforms of 1919 showed 'the attitude that the Indian mind had for representative institutions . . . a true appreciation of parliamentary responsibility and democratic institutions'.[91] The Simon Commission also had the identical view that

> Political ideas are so rapidly assimilated by Indian progressives and sense of novelty so quickly wears off that it is really necessary to pause and appreciate the extent of transformation. Less than ten years ago, there was not a province in Indian in which parliamentary institutions existed.[92]

In the context of the parliamentary experience, it is necessary to recount the contribution of Vithalbhai J. Patel, the first Indian to assume the office of the President (Speaker) of the Legislative Assembly (1925–1930). He displayed a high degree of independence and impartial behaviour in the conduct of the legislative business. President Patel had set up healthy conventions and helped in the growth of robust parliamentary procedures and practice. The Simon Commission observed:

> He claims, and employs, powers of interference which would be quite contrary to the stricter limits of the Speakership – reprimanding a government member of the Council of State for not attending and speaking at a debate in the Lower House, advising the Government not to proceed with impor tant business when the Swarajists walked out, explaining his view of the proper operation of the so-called Fiscal Convention, and so forth.[93]

At the Centre, a large volume of legislation was passed relating to fiscal, industrial, commercial, labour, currency and banking, etc. It had been reported that, upto 1928, about 199 government legislative proposals were passed by the Indian Assembly. Besides, in the conduct of legislative business for constitutional reforms – i.e. the Indianization of the Army, the Services and the Railways, etc. – the Indian members of the Legislative Assembly 'could exert pressure on the British'. Similarly, the legislative debates 'give an interesting insight into the efforts of Indian nationalist in opposing those measures which were motivated by imperial interests'.[94] Some such issues were the Steel Protection Bill, the Currency Bill, the Ottawa Trade Agreement and the Indo-British Pact.

Similarly, considerable amount of legislative work was undertaken by the provincial councils in almost all the activities entrusted in the provincial sphere.[95] The reorganization of municipalities and district boards were the first questions addressed by the ministers on assuming the office under the reformed constitution. A number of provinces enacted legislative measures in the field of local self-government. In Punjab, by 1923, three important enactments were passed: the Small Towns Act, the Village Franchise Amendments Act and the Town Improvements Act. In Bengal, in 1923, two important legislative measures were passed known as the Calcutta Municipal Bill[96] and the Bengal Municipal Bill 1923. In United Provinces, the District Board Bill was passed in 1922. In Bihar and Orissa, in 1923, three enactments regarding local bodies were passed: the Bihar and Orissa Municipal Bill, the Bihar and Orissa Local Self-Government (Amendment) Bill and the Bihar and Orissa Village (Administration) Act. In Bombay, in 1922, an enactment consolidated and amended the law relating to the local Boards. Similarly, in the Central Provinces in 1922, the Central Provinces Municipalities Act was passed. The Madras Village Panchayat Act was passed to enable a Panchayat to exercise the function of a Panchayat Court in 1923.

Another important legislation which was undertaken by a large number of provinces relates to urban and rural tenants. In this context, the Madras City Tenant Protection Bill of 1921, the Calcutta Rent Act of 1923 and the Oudh Rent Act of the United Provinces are significant.

Education was another important area where both legislative measures and progressive initiatives were undertaken at all levels by all the provinces. A number of new initiatives were taken in Bombay providing for the following: universal compulsory primary education; increased facilities for secondary, higher technical and professional education and special facilities for the depressed classes. In the United Provinces, initiatives were taken for expanding primary education and secondary education, for establishing a separate Board of High School and Intermediate Education and for reconstituting Allahabad University. In Madras, a number of initiatives were taken in enlarging and reorganizing the educational facility like these: a scheme of mass education, the reform of the secondary education and vocational-based education and the Madras University Reorganization Bill. In 1925, a bill was introduced to constitute a University for the Telugu-speaking districts of the Madras Presidency. It is also important to emphasize that other provincial governments also attempted to reform their universities on the lines suggested by the Calcutta University Commission. The Punjab and Dhaka University underwent extensive modifications and two new universities were established: Delhi (1922) and Nagpur (1923).

It is also important to mention that in some provinces some very progressive initiatives in the field of social legislation were undertaken. In this context, the Hindu Religious Endowment Act of Madras 1922, was the first attempt to legislate directly the matters related to Hindu religion. Besides in Bengal, a very important statute was enacted known as the Bengal Children's Act of 1922 with very progressive provisions.

Similarly, in the United Provinces, and in Bombay and in several other provinces, there were reforms introduced to reduce the consumption of alcohol and other intoxicants. This was done by initiating a policy to regulate both the quality and quantity of alcohol. In Bengal the Excise Amendment Act of 1922 was passed and in several provinces Licencing Boards were established.

Industrialization was another important sphere in which many new initiatives were undertaken. In 1921, a Department of Industries and Labour was created in the Central Government. In the Act of 1919, the development of industries became a provincial subject. In Madras, a bill was passed to regulate State-Aid to Industries.

Appadorai has provided some interesting statistical information which indicates the democratic experience between 1920 and 1937 on a large plane: four general elections (1920, 1923, 1926, 1929–1930) were conducted, voting percentage in each election increased and experience as Ministers of 93 public men and that of 121 as members of Governors' Executive Councils increased. Besides, during this period between 1,000 and 2,000 persons gained experience as legislators at the Centre and the Provincial levels.[97]

The Simon Commission, while discussing the proceedings in the legislatures, observed that 'the conduct of business . . . has been carried on with keenness, there has been much good debating, and the Government has been exposed to considerable challenge and comment from its opponents among the elected members'.[98]

Before the Constitutional Reforms of 1919, the legislative councils at the Centre and in the provinces were merely consultative bodies. They could not undertake without the previous sanction of the Governor-General or the Governor of a province any matter affecting the finance of India or a province. The legislatures before 1919 had no financial powers. It was only after the Government of India Act of 1919 that there was greater delegation of powers in financial matters to legislatures in India. The legislative procedure in the matter of the budget, i.e. presentation, general discussion and voting on the demands for grants, provided them opportunities for debate and discussion and larger implications of the budget proposals. It also provided opportunities to the members to move their cut motions, suggest reduction and criticize or support the demand. As a matter of fact, on the one hand, the power of voting on the budget and on the taxation proposal helped in bringing issues for redressal, and, on the other, helped the constitutional advancement of the country.

Under the provisions of the Act of 1919, the Public Accounts Committee was constituted both at the Centre and in the provinces in 1921. As a result, the procedures and processes involved in the conduct of Public Accounts Committee brought the civil servants and the legislators in close proximity. This provided the legislators an opportunity to look at the functioning of the government from close quarters on the matters related to expenditure. Similarly, the Standing Finance Committee also provided an opportunity to the members to scrutinize all proposals for new votable expenditure.[99] This has been a very significant mode of influencing the administration. Besides, the establishment of special subject committees also played a significant role. These committees were provided for in the Indian Legislature and Provincial Legislative Councils. These Committee were purely advisory in nature and the following subject matters were laid down in these committees: questions of departmental policy, schemes involving large expenditure, annual reports, etc. As such, the system of Committees became an important feature of the Reformed Constitution.

The resolutions discussed in all Councils dealt with important questions of public policy. While the Provincial Governments have justly refused to consider the resolutions to be mandatory, they have all along tried to give effect to them as recommendations emanating from popular representatives on which action should be taken, if possible.

The right of interpellation has been another potent instrument in the hands of the Council. By this method, the Council kept a strict watch on the administration. This right has gained in value as a check on the administration.

IV

Constitutional reforms 1927 to 1935

The Government of India Act, 1919, recommended the appointment of a Commission after ten years 'to review the constitutional position both as regards the Government of India and the provinces'. The Indian Statutory Commission was appointed in 1927, under the Chairmanship of Sir John Allsebrook Simon, for the purpose of inquiring into the working of the system of government. The Commission was appointed before the stipulated period because of the agitation carried on in India. The Commission consisted of following members: Harry Lawson Webster, Donald Sterling Palmer, Cecil George Cadogan, Stephen Walsh, George Richard Lane Fox and Clement Richard Attlee. The Commission was boycotted by all political parties of India as there was no Indian representation.

The subject of elections to legislative bodies through joint or separate electorates was in discussion among Hindu and Mussalman leaders in Delhi since March 1927. The absence of representation in the Simon Commission led to the appointment by All-Parties Conference of a committee with Motlial Nehru as Chairman to consider and determine a constitution for India. The Nehru Report, 1928, also contained some recommendations[100] on the problem of separate electorates. This Report also observed that 'separate electorates are bad for the growth of a national spirit' and recommended the following: joint mixed electorates throughout India, no reservation of seats except for Muslims in provinces where they are in a minority and the same provision for the non-Muslim population in the North-West Frontier Province. The Muslims or non-Muslims allowed to contest additional seats. Besides, no reservation of seats for any community in Bengal and the Punjab. The reservation of seats was to be a period of ten years. The Report also recommended the establishment of Sind as a separate province.

On the subject of elections, another important feature was Mohammad Ali Jinnah's Fourteen Points regarding the future constitution of India in March 1929.[101] It demanded the federal form of the future constitution and a uniform measure of autonomy to all provinces. In the context of elections for legislative bodies, it demanded the following: (1) adequate and effective representation of minorities in every Province, (2) one-third representation to Mussalman in the Central Legislature, (3) representation of communal groups by separate electorates, (4) no territorial redistribution should affect the Moslem majority in the Punjab, Bengal and N.W.F. Province and € Sind should be separated from the Bombay Presidency.

The Simon Commission recommendations

The Report of the Simon Commission was published in May 1930. The Report looked into 'as to whether and to what extent it is desirable to establish the principle of responsible government, or to extend, modify or restrict the degree of responsible government now existing'.[102] Some of the significant changes suggested at the Provincial level were these: termination of dyarchy, provincial Cabinet with joint responsibility for action and policy, wide franchise, enlarged financial resources, etc. The modifications suggested at the Centre were these: reconstitution of Legislative Assembly, continuation of the Council of State, continuation of existing legislative and financial powers of the two Houses and the Governor-General to select and appoint the Executive Councillors.[103] Besides, the Report observed that communal representation was an 'obstacle in the way of the growth of a sense of common citizenship'. In the context of communal representation, the Report praised the Nehru Report for its 'very ingenious and persuasive analysis which that Report contained of the distribution of religious opinion in Bengal and the Punjab'.[104]

Due to the condemnation of the Report, the British Government called a Round Table Conference in 1930–1931 to consider the future constitution of India. After the failure of the First and Second Round Table Conference on communal matters, the Prime Minister Ramsay MacDonald agreed to arbitrate on this matter. Some of the significant provisions made in this context relate to the Communal Award of 1932: elections to the seats allotted to the Muslim, European and Sikh constituencies were to be by voters (voting for separate communal electorates); revision of electoral arrangements; depressed classes to vote in general constituencies; reservation of seats to the depressed classes; women were given special representation on communal lines and allotments of seats to commerce and industry, mining and plantation, landholders (Table 2.12).

Table 2.12 Distribution of seats in the proposed Provincial Legislatures under the Communal Award, 1932.

Province	*General*	*Muslim*	*Sikh*	*Depressed classes*	*Backward Areas*	*Landholders*	*Christians*	*Commerce*	*Labour*	*Others**
Assam	44	34	–	4	9	–	1	11	4	1
Bengal	80	119	–	(not fixed)	–	5	2	19	8	17
Bihar and Orissa	99	42	–	7	8	5	2	4	4	4
Bombay[1]	97	63	–	10	1	3	3	8	8	7
Bombay[2]	109	30	–	10	1	2	3	7	7	6
C.P.	77	14	–	10	1	3	–	2	2	3
Madras	134	29	–	18	1	6	9	6	6	6
N.W.F.P.	9	36	3	–	–	2	–	–	–	–
Punjab	43	86	32	–	–	5	2	1	3	3
Sindh	19	34	–	–	–	2	–	2	1	2
U.P.	132	66	–	12	–	6	2	3	3	4

* Anglo-Indians, Europeans, University seats
[1] Bombay including Sindh
[2] Bombay excluding Sindh
Source: Communal Decision 1931–2 (Cmnd. 4147 of 1931–2) p. 7, quoted in B.R. Tomlinson *The Indian National Congress and the Raj, 1929–1942: The Penultimate Phase*, London: The Macmillan Press Ltd, 1976, p. 19.

Table 2.13 Communal Award as modified by Poona Pact.

	General total	*Reserved for depressed classes*	*Backward Areas*	*Muslims*	*Sikhs*	*Commerce*	*Christians*	*Landholders*	*Labour*	*Others*[*]
Bengal	78	30	–	117	–	19	2	5	8	21
U.P.	140	20	–	64	–	3	2	6	3	10
Madras	146	30	1	28	–	6	8	6	6	14
Bombay	114	15	1	29	–	7	3	2	7	12
Punjab	42	8	–	84	31	1	2	5	3	7
Bihar	86	15	7	39	–	4	1	4	3	8
C.P.	84	20	1	14	–	2	–	3	2	6
Assam	47	7	9	34	–	11	1	–	4	2
Sindh	48	–	–	33	–	2	–	2	1	4
Orissa	44	6	5	4	–	1	1	2	1	2
N.W.F.P.	9	–	–	36	3	–	–	2	–	–

[*] Anglo-Indian, European, University and Women's seats

Source: N. Gangulee, *The Making of Federal India* (London, 1936) p. 309 quoted in B.R. Tomlinson *The Indian National Congress and the Raj, 1929–1942: The Penultimate Phase*, London: The Macmillan Press LD, 1976. p. 20.

Mahatma Gandhi was totally opposed to the grant of separate electorate for the depressed classes. In a letter written in March 1932, he expressed his anguish and conveyed his decision to the Secretary of State for India to 'fast unto death'.[105] However, in a conference convened by Pandit Madan Mohan Malaviya, along with Dr. B.R. Ambedkar and other leaders, a scheme was formulated in Poona 'which met with the acceptance of all parties'.[106] The Poona Agreement was accepted by the British Government. Some of the significant provisions were the following: (1) reservations of seats for the depressed classes out of general electorates; (2) election by joint electorates, for this purpose all members of the depressed classes will form an electoral college which will elect a panel of four candidates belonging to the depressed classes by the method of single vote; (3) representation of the depressed classes in the Central Legislature on the principle of joint electorates and the same procedure were to be followed as in the case of the provinces; (4) 18 percent of the seats allotted to the general electorate were to be reserved for the depressed classes and (5) the system of primary election to the Central and Provincial Legislatures as provided above was to be abolished after ten years (Table 2.13).[107]

V

The Government of India Act, 1935

India was made federation and provinces were granted autonomy by the Act of 1935. The Act also provided that all the provinces were to join the Indian federation automatically, however, it was made voluntary in the case of the Indian states. The Act created eleven governor provinces and some areas as Chief Commissioner Provinces. The Act also provided the distribution of powers between Centre and the Provinces as per three lists, i.e. the Federal, the Provincial and the Concurrent.

The Federal Legislature consisted of the Federal Assembly and the Council of State. The period of Federal Assembly was five years while the Council of State was to be a permanent body of which one-third were to retired after three years. The Council of State was to consist of 156 representatives of British India and not more than 104 representatives of the Indian states (see Table 2.14). Of the 156 seats to be filled by representatives of British India, 150 seats were to be allocated to Governors' Provinces, Chief Commissioners' Provinces

Table 2.14 The Council of State: representatives of British India.

Province or Community	*Total seats*	*General seats*	*Seats for scheduled castes*	*Sikh seats*	*Muhammadan seats*	*Women's seats*
Madras	20	14	1	–	4	1
Bombay	16	10	1	–	4	1
Bengal	20	8	1	–	10	1
United Provinces	20	11	1	–	7	1
Punjab	16	3	–	4	8	1
Bihar	16	10	1	–	4	1
Central Provinces And Berar	8	6	1	–	1	–
Assam	5	3	–	–	2	–
North-West Frontier Province	5	1	–	–	4	–
Orissa	5	4	–	–	1	–
Sind	5	2	–	–	3	–
British Baluchistan	1	–	–	–	1	–
Delhi	1	1	–	–	–	–
Ajmer-Merwara	1	1	–	–	–	–
Coorg	1	1	–	–	–	–
Anglo-Indians	1	–	–	–	–	–
Europeans	7	–	–	–	–	–
Indian Christians	2	–	–	–	–	–
Totals	150	75	6	4.	49	6

Source: N. Rajagopala Aiyangar; *The Government of India Act 1935: With a Commentary, Critical and Explanatory*, Madras: The Madras Law Journal Office, 1937, p. 345.

and Communities. Six seats were to be filled by persons chose by the Governor-General. The Federal Assembly (see Table 2.15) consisted of 250 representatives of British India and not more than 125 representatives of the Indian states.

Under the Act the representatives of British India of the Council of State were to be chosen by the communities. The Hindu, Sikh and the Muhammadan communities were to choose their representatives by voting in territorial constituencies. Indirect election was retained for the representatives of the Anglo-Indian, European and Indian Christians communities. Their representatives were to be chosen by the members

Table 2.15 The Federal Assembly: representatives of British India.

Province	*Total Seats*	*General Seats*		*Sikh Seats*	*Muham madan Seats*	*Anglo Indian Seats*	*Euro Pean Seats*	*Indian Christian Seats*	*Seatsfor Reresen tatives of Commerce and industry*	*Land Holders Seats*	*Seatsfor Reresen tatives of labour*	*Women's Seats*
		Total of general seats of general searts	*General seats reserved for Scheduled Castes*									
Madras	37	19	4	–	8	1	1	2	2	1	1	2
Bombay	30	13	2	–	6	1	1	1	3	1	2	2
Bengal	37	10	3	–	17	1	1	1	3	1	2	1
Untied Provinces	37	19	3	–	12	1	1	1	–	1	1	1
Punjab	30	6	1	6	14	–	1	1	–	1	–	1
Bihar	30	16	2	–	9	–	1	1	–	1	1	1
Central Provinces and Berar	15	9	2	–	3	–	–	–	–	1	1	1
Assam	10	4	1	–	3	–	1	1	–	–	1	–
North-West Frontier Province	5	1	–	–	4	–	–	–	–	–	–	–
Oriisa	5	4	1	–	1	–	–	–	–	–	–	–
Simd	5	1	–	–	3	–	1	–	–	–	–	–
British Baluchistan	1	–	–	–	1	–	–	–	–	–	–	–
Delhi	2	1	–	–	1	–	–	–	–	–	–	–
Ajmer-Merwara	1	1	–	–	–	–	–	–	–	–	–	–
Coorg	1	1	–	–	–	–	–	–	–	–	–	–
Non-Provincial Seats	4	–	–	–	–	–	–	–	3	–	1	–
Totals	250	105	19	6	82	4	8	8	11	7	10	9

Source: N. Rajagopala Aiyangar; *The Government of India Act 1935: With a Commentary, Critical and Explanatory*, Madras: The Madras Law Journal Office, 1937, p. 347.

Table 2.16 Provincial Legislative Assemblies.

Province		*General seats*												*Seats for women*				
	Total seats	*Total of general seats*	*General seats reserved for Scheduled Castes*	*Seats for representatives of backward Areas and Tribes*	*Sikh seats*	*Muhammadan seats*	*Anglo-Indian seats*	*European seats*	*Indian Christian seats*	*Seats for representatives of commerce, Industry, mining and planting*	*Landholders seats*	*University seats*	*Seats for representatives of labour*	*General*	*Sikh*	*Muhammadan*	*Anglo-Indian*	*Indian Christian*
Madras	215	146	30	1	–	28	2	3	8	6	6	1	6	6	–	1	–	1
Bombay	175	114	15	1	–	29	2	3	3	7	2	1	7	5	–	1	–	–
Bengal	250	78	30	–	–	117	3	112	2	19	5	2	8	2	–	2	1	–
United Provinces	228	140	20	–	–	64	1	1	2	3	6	1	3	4	–	2	–	–
Punjab	175	42	8	–	31	84	1	2	2	1	5	1	3	1	1	21	–	–
Bihar	152	86	15	7	–	39	1	1	1	4	4	1	3	3	–	–	–	–
Central Provinces And Berar	112	84	20	1	–	14	1	1	–	2	3	1	2	3	–	–	–	–
Assam	108	47	7	9	–	34	–	–	1	11	–	–	4	1	–	–	–	–
North- Western Frontier Province	50	9	–	–	3	36	–	1	–	–	2	–	–	–	–	–	–	–
Orissa	60	44	6	5	–	4	–		1	1	2	–	1	2	––		–	–
Sind	60	18	–	–	–	33	–	–	–	2	2	–	1	1	––	1	–	–

Source: N. Rajagopala Aiyangar; With a Foreword by Alladi Krishnaswami Aiyar, *The Government of India Act 1935: With a Commentary, Critical and Explanatory*, Madras: The Madras Law Journal Office, 1937, p. 366.

Table 2.17 Provincial Legislative Councils.

Province	*Total of seats*	*General seats*	*Muhammadan seats*	*European seats*	*Indian Christian seats*	*Seats to be filled by Legislative Assembly*	*Seats to be filled by Governor*
Madras	Not less than 54	35	7	1	3	–	Not less than 8
	Not less than 56						Not more than 10
Bombay	Not lessthan 29	20	5	1	–	–	Not less than 3
	Not more than 30						Not more than 4
Bengal	Not less than 63	10	17	3	–	27	Not less than 6
	Not more than 65						Not more than 8
United	Not less than 58	34	17	1	–	–	Not less than 6
Provinces	Not more than 60		4	1	–	12	Not more than 8
	Not less than 29	9	6	2	–	–	Not less than 3
Bihar	Not more than 30						Not more than 4
Assam	Not less than 21	10	6	2	–	–	Not more than 3
	Not more than 22						Not more than 4

Source: N. Rajagopala Aiyangar; *The Government of India Act 1935: With a Commentary, Critical and Explanatory*, Madras: The Madras Law Journal Office, 1937, p. 367.

of the Electoral Colleges. The representatives of the states in the Council of the States were to be appointed by the Rulers of the states concerned on the basis of 'relative rank and importance of the State'.

The Federal Assembly

The majority of the seats were to be distributed on a communal basis. The Hindu, Muhammadan and Sikh seats were filled by the representatives of those communities in the Provincial Assemblies voting separately for a prescribed number of communal seats. Within the Hindu group, special arrangements were made for the Depressed Classes. The seats for Europeans, Anglo-Indians, Indian Christians, Representatives of commerce and industry, Landholders and Representatives of labour were to be filled by the representatives of these groups in the Provincial Assemblies, voting in ad hoc electoral colleges. Allocation of seats was on the principle of population.

The Act provided Dyarchy at the Centre under which certain subjects like Defence, External Affairs, Ecclesiastical Affairs and the administration of tribal areas were to be administered by the Governor-General with the assistance of three Executive Councillors. However, in respect of other federal subjects, the Governor-General was to be aided and advised by a Council of Ministers.

In the Government of India Act, 1935, in every province there was a Provincial Legislature. However, in the Provinces of Madras, Bombay, Bengal, the United Provinces, Bihar and Assam, bicameral principle was introduced for the first time. The chambers were to be known as the Legislative Council and Legislative Assembly. Representations in the Legislative Assembly were based on the allocation of seats to various communities and to specific interests. There were separate electorates for the Muhammadan, Sikh, Indian Christians, European communities and Anglo-Indians. The distribution was based on the communal Award of 1932 as modified by the Poona Pact (as explained in the previous section of the chapter)

Composition of Federal and Provincial Legislatures

The tables here provide the distribution of seats both province- and community-wise for (1) The Council of State, (2) the Federal Assembly, (3) Provincial Legislative Assemblies and (4) Provincial Legislatives Councils (Tables 2.16 and 2.17).

The Act of 1919 provided for an electorate of approximately 7,048,372 men and women or about 2.75 percent of the population of the British India. This franchise was based on property qualification. As mentioned earlier the Indian Statutory Commission expressed the view that the existing franchise was too narrow and recommended that about 10 percent of the population should be enfranchised. A committee known as the Indian Franchise Committee (1932) was appointed 'with a view to an increase of the electorate to a figure not less than the 10 per cent of the population suggested by the Statutory Commission nor more than the 25 per cent suggested at the First Session of the Round Table Conference'.[108] It was agreed that property qualification would be the basis of this franchise. To secure an adequate representation of women and the enfranchisement of approximately 10 percent of the Depressed Classes, certain educational qualification and related special qualification were added. Seats were also reserved for special interests like labour, landlords, commerce and retired persons with army background. Table 2.18 provides a comparative picture pertaining to the province-wise number of electorate

It is evident from the table that there was an increase of percentage of electorate from 2.75 in 1919 to 13.2 in 1935. Similarly, the average per seat in 1919 was 9,421 electors, which became 24,406 electors in 1935. The total number of electors in 1935 became 35,982,000 from 7048372 in 1919.

Table 2.18 A comparative figure pertaining to Province-wise number of electorate, 1919 and 1935.

	Total	*1919 electorate % of population*	*Average per seat*	*Total*	*1935 electorate % of population*	*Average per seat*
Madras	1,470,900	3.1	15,000	7,224,000	15.5	33,693
Bombay	888,801	4.1	10,335	3,726,000	17.1	18,630
Bengal	1,331,803	2.6	11,682	8,000,000	16.0	32,000
U.P.	1,646,290	3.4	16,463	7,500,000	15.5	32,895
Punjab	745,000	3.1	10,493	2,800,000	11.9	16,000
Bihar & Orissa	418, 324	1.1	5,504	3,500,000	9.3	20,000
C.P.	199,500	1.3	3,627	1,950,000	12.5	17,411
Assam	228,832	3.3	7,406	1,040,000	12.1	9,630
N.W.F.P.	119,922	-	4,283	242,000	9.9	48,400
Total	7,049,372	2.75	9,421	35,982,000	13.3	25,406

Source: Note on Franchise Committee Proposals, G.o.I. Reforms Office no. 102/32 R & KW N.A.I. quoted in B.R. Tomlinson, *The Indian National Congress 1929–1942: The Penultimate Phase* London: The Macmillan Press Ltd, 1976, p. 173.

Electoral system

Provisions regarding franchise were detailed in the Sixth Schedule in the Government of India Act, 1935.[109] Part I of the Schedule consisted of the general provisions and part II contained general requirement as to residence which varied from province to province.

Each province was divided into territorial constituencies for the purpose of elections to Legislative Assemblies – to fill the general seats, the Sikh seats, the Muhammadan seats, the Anglo-Indian seats, the European seats and the Indian Christian seats. The total number of seats available were distributed between the constituencies by the assignment of one or more of those seats to each constituency.

The territorial constituencies were the basis for elections to Legislative Councils. In the case of each such class of constituency the total number of seats available were distributed between the constituencies by the assignment of one or more of those seats to each constituency.

For every territorial constituency there was also a provision for an electoral roll. Every person included in the electoral roll was entitled to vote in that constituency. A person is included in the electoral roll only if he has attained the age of twenty-one years, and is either a British subject or the Ruler or a subject of a Federated State; no person is included in the electoral roll for a Sikh constituency, a Muhammadan constituency, an Anglo-Indian constituency, a European constituency or an Indian Christian constituency unless he is a Sikh, a Muhammadan, an Anglo-Indian, a European or an Indian Christian, as the case may be.

Regarding franchise, there was variation in each province regarding a requirement as to residence. In all constituencies the electoral rolls were prepared by authorities appointed by the Governor. In all constituencies and at all elections the Returning Officer was a person in the service of the Crown in India.

With respect to the enfranchisement of women, the franchise was extended to all women who had the following: (1) property qualification, (2) the pensioned widow or mother of a person who was in military service and (3) was literate.

Rules were made with respect to the matters mentioned later–(1) the delimitation of territorial constituencies for the purpose of elections under this Act; (2) the qualifications entitling persons to vote in territorial or other constituencies at such elections, and the preparation of electoral rolls; (3) the qualifications for being elected at such elections as a member of a legislative body (and the filling of causal vacancies in any such body); (4) the conduct of elections under this

Act and the methods of voting; (5) the expenses of candidates at such elections; (6) corrupt practices and other offences at or in connection with such elections and (7) the decision of doubts and disputes arising out of, or in connection with, such elections.[110]

The elections under the Government of India Act 1935

As mentioned previously, the Act provided for the establishment of responsible government in the eleven provinces of British India. It also provided for a federation of India consisting of the provinces and of states. The provincial part of the Act came into force on April 1, 1937. The federal part of the Act was to become 'operative only when and if a sufficient number of states (1) to occupy 52 of the 104 seats allotted to the states in the upper house of the federal legislature and (2) to make up half the total population of all the states, had acceded to the federation'.[111] However,

> By the time war was declared in 1939, the necessary number of princes had still not acceded to the federation and in October 1939, therefore, the federal provisions of the Act were suspended indefinitely. The Council of State and the Legislative Assembly continued to operate, therefore, until they were replaced by the Constituent Assembly (Legislative) as the central legislature for independent India in August 1947.[112]

The Elections under the Act were conducted during January and February 1937.

The Act of 1935 was criticized by all political parties in India. The INC, in one of the resolutions adopted in its Lucknow Session April 1936, observed that the Act

> is designed to facilitate and perpetuate the domination and exploitation of the people of India and is imposed on the country to the accompaniment of widespread repression and the suppression of civil liberties, the Congress reiterates its rejection of the new constitution in the entirety.[113]

The Congress Party also resolved to contest the election to the new Provincial Legislatures. It was also mentioned that the election should be contested on the basis of a 'detailed political and economic programme' and 'with our demand for a Constituent Assembly in the fore-front'. It was also expressed by Jawaharlal Nehru that the main objective for contesting election was 'to carry the message of the Congress to the millions of voters' so as to apprise them with the programme and policy of the Congress. This appeal was not restricted to the voters alone but also to those disfranchised, as most of them 'suffer from exploitation and are at the bottom of the social ladder'. He was also of the view that 'in order to win over the hesitating and compromising groups and individuals there should be . . . no toning down our programme and policy'.[114]

Election manifestos

It is proposed to provide some significant features of the election manifestos of the political parties which contested the 1937 elections and formed ministries either alone or in coalition with other parties. The manifestos of following parties are being analysed: Congress, Muslim League, Communist Party, National Unionist Party, Krishak Praja Party, etc. However, in this context, it is first proposed to provide a note on the debate on the ideology of the Congress Party from 1928 to 1937. This debate significantly impacted the Congress Party's election manifesto of 1937.

Debate on the ideology of the Congress Party

In the context of the Congress Party, there is a long history of debate and discussion on the social and economic ideology of the party. It is important to provide an account of this history, as it not only impacted the manifesto of the Congress Party but also impacted the Indian Constitution on the one hand and the manifestos of all other major parties – both national and regional. It is significant to point out that this manifesto emerged out of the debate on Indian problems between the right-wing and left-wing leaders in the Congress.

The debate and discussion on the ideology of the Congress Party between 1928 and 1937 constitute an important chapter in the modern Indian history. In this section, it is proposed to provide a chronological account of this debate.

National objective – need for

The policy of the Congress during the 1920s broadly consisted in carrying political work for the achievement of swaraj as well as the Gandhi Constructive Programme. This programme included the following: popularizing the *Khaddar* and promoting inter-communal unity and prohibition. On this approach, Dr. Bhagvan Das voiced concern regarding the absence of 'clearer definition of our national objective'. He observed 'the Indian people should make clear to themselves what they ought to understand by swaraj or self-government, to visualize as clearly as possible our goal, and the roads thereto, and not run blindly after unexplained and ill-understood words'.[115]

Jawaharlal Nehru endorsed this idea of Dr. Bhagvan Das, and questioned 'what kind of Swaraj we are aiming at'.[116] He further elaborated this view by pointing out that 'No one thought in terms of independence, of real freedom, of a transfer of power to a democratic India, of the solution of any of the vital and urgent economic problems facing the Indian people'.[117] He was of the view that the policy of the Congress should be to strengthen the masses and 'enable them to hold power when imperialism fades away from India'.[118]

Jawaharlal Nehru was deeply concerned with the problems of the masses – poverty, exploitation, etc. He was of the opinion that there is a need to bring economic and social programmes to bridge this gap. In his many addresses and statements in 1928, he made his orientation clear towards 'socialist outlook' on all vital problems.[119] On economic issues, Nehru's approach differed radically from that of Mahatma Gandhi.[120] On this Nehru observed 'You have criticized strongly the many obvious defects of industrialism and hardly paid any attention to its merits'.[121] On this aspect, Gandhi observed 'The differences between you and me appear to me to be so vast and so radical that there seems to be no meeting ground between us'.[122]

Economic objective

It was entirely due to the initiative of Jawaharlal Nehru that the Congress Working Committee, in its meeting at Bombay during May 1929, adopted for the first time the resolution on the economic reconstruction of Indian society as an integral part of its aim and object. The AICC in its meeting passed the following resolution:

> In the opinion of this Committee, the great poverty and misery of the Indian people are due, not only to foreign exploitation in India but also to the economic structure of society, which the alien rulers support so that their exploitation may continue. In order therefore to remove this poverty and misery and to ameliorate the condition of the Indian masses, it is essential, to make revolutionary changes in the present

economic and social structure of society and to remove the gross inequalities.[123]

Fundamental rights and economic programme

Another important development in the ideology of the Congress was the adoption of the Fundamental Rights and Duties and Economic Programme by the AICC at Karachi during April 1931.[124] Nehru took the initiative for this resolution shortly after Mahatma Gandhi's famous eleven-point programme which he termed as the 'substance of independence' Mahatma Gandhi had listed eleven points in his programme in January 31, 1930 as the substance of independence. These points by and large catalogued the sum and substance of the demands of both the classes and the masses: reduction of land revenue by 50 percent, abolition of the salt tax, total prohibition, a protective tariff on foreign cloth, enactment of a coastal reservation bill in favour of Indian shipping, revaluation of the rupee, reduction of Military expenditure by at least 50 percent, reduction of the salaries of the highest great services by half, release of all political prisoners nor condemned for murder or attempted murder and abolition or control of the Criminal Investigation Department Sitaramayya.[125]

The resolution on Fundamental Rights and Economic Policy originated as a result of discussion between Gandhi and Nehru during February-March 1931 in Delhi. In this context, Nehru observed

> I had referred to this matter, and he had welcomed the idea of having a resolution on economic matters. He asked me to bring the matter up at Karachi, and to draft a resolution and show it to him there. I did so at Karachi, and he made various changes and suggestions. He wanted both of us to agree on the wording, before we asked the Working Committee to consider it.[126]

The Resolution was amended at Bombay in August 1931.

The Resolution stated that 'In order to end the exploitation of the masses, political freedom must include real economic freedom of the starving millions. The Congress, therefore, declares that any constitution which may be agreed to on its behalf should provide, or enable the Swaraj Government to provide, for the following':

1 Under the category of Fundamental Rights and Duties some of the important provisions are as follows: the right of free expression

and association; freedom of conscience and religion; protection of language and culture; equality before the law; right of personal liberty and property subject to law; adult franchise; free and compulsory primary education; religious neutrality on the part of the state; right to keep and bear arms in accordance with regulations made in that behalf; protection of women and children; reform of the land tenure system; death duties; reduction of civil and military expenditure and fixing of a maximum salary; protection of indigenous cloth; prohibition; relief of agricultural indebtedness, freedom for every citizen to move throughout India, to acquire property and to follow any trade or calling and to be treated equally with regard to legal prosecution or protection in all parts of India, etc.

2 The Resolution also provided under the category of 'Labour' certain economic provisions to be fulfilled by the state: the organization of economic life must conform to the principle of justice; safeguard the interests of industrial workers and secure for them a living wage, provide limited hours of labour, healthy conditions of work, protection against old age, sickness and unemployment; labour to be freed from serfdom; protection of women workers; school-going children prohibited for employment in mines and factories; peasants and workers have the right to form unions

3 The Resolution also carried provisions regarding 'Economic and Social Programme'. These are the following: reduction of land revenue and rent; imposition of progressive income tax on agricultural incomes and death duties; reduction of military expenditure; reduction in expenditure and salaries of civil departments; no duty on salt; protection of indigenous cloth and other industries against foreign competition; total prohibition currency and exchange shall be regulated in the national interest; the state shall own or control key industries, services, mineral resources, railways, waterways, shipping and other means of public transport; relief of agricultural indebtedness and control of usury and military training of citizens.[127]

Nehru on the resolution on Fundamental Rights observed that he would 'personally like to go much further'. He also added that in the interests of the masses the 'vested interests in India will have to give up their special position and many of their privileges'. As such for him, 'revising vested interests in favour of the masses'[128] was the central question. Mahatma Gandhi agreed with Nehru on the question of vested interests, 'I am also in whole-hearted agreement with you when you say that without a material revision of vested interests the condition of the masses can never be improved'.[129] Mahatma Gandhi after the passing of this resolution observed that 'we make it clear to the world and to our own people what we propose to do as soon as we come into power'.[130] Nehru on the other hand observed that the Congress

> took a step, a very short step, in a socialist direction by advocating nationalization of key industries and services, and various other measures to lessen the burden on the poor and increase it on the rich. This was not socialism at all, and a capitalist state could easily accept almost everything contained in that resolution.[131]

'Whither India'

Another important initiative by Nehru professing his 'socialistic outlook' relates to the publication of 'Whither India', 1933, a series of three articles. These articles provide a theoretical overview of the need to devise a system, looking into the Indian national objective. The whole thrust of 'Whither India' was to economically improve the condition of the masses. For this purpose, he reiterated and referred about the vested interests.[132] He was critical of the Indian national movement as it works 'chiefly in the interests of the vested interests'.[133] For removing the basic inequalities of the capitalist system, he advocated the need for a 'more scientific system'.[134] He was also critical of the fact that to bring this fundamental change, we often think in terms of 'paper constitutions'. However, he was against 'this lawyer's mentality which ignores life and the vital economic issues and can only proceed on the basis of *status quo* and precedents'.[135] He concluded by highlighting that this requires fundamental changes of 'regime politically, economically and socially'.[136] In the context of bringing out the fundamental changes, he was of the view 'that coercion or pressure is necessary' however he preferred the 'non-violent method'.[137]

Congress Socialist Party

Another important event in the history of the socialistic ideas in India relates to the formation of a new party called the Congress Socialist Party within the Congress in May 1934. It has been pointed out that 'Whither India', 'provided food for thought among some younger leftist Congressmen . . . to form the Congress Socialist Party, a faction within the Congress, with Nehru as the acknowledged spiritual godfather'.[138]

It is important to provide the object, programme and plan of action of the Congress Socialist Party, as it will help in the proper appreciation of the difference with the right-wing of the Congress leadership. The first conference of the Congress Socialist Party, in May 1934, adopted the following objectives:

> Transfer of all power to the producing masses; the development of the economic life of the country to be planned and controlled by the state; the socialization of the key and principal industries, e.g. steel, cotton, jute, railways, shipping, mines, banks and public utilities; the organization of co-operatives for the production, distribution and credit in the unsocialized section of the economic life; state monopoly of foreign trade; the elimination of the princes and landlords and all other classes of exploiters; the redistribution of land to peasants; the encouragement and promotion of co-operative farming with a view to ultimate collectivization of all agriculture in the country; the liquidation of debts owed by the peasants and workers; the state to provide work to every able-bodied adult and social insurance against unemployment, old age, sickness, accident and maternity; 'to every one according to his needs' 'to be the ultimate basis of distribution of economic goods'; adult franchise on a functional basis; and abolition of discrimination on the basis of distinctions of religion, caste, community and sex.[139]

Besides, the Party also drew an action plan to work within the Indian National Congress with a view to develop it into a real anti-imperialist organization:

- Organization of peasant and labour unions, and entry into such unions where they exist, for the purpose of participating into the day-to-day struggle of peasants and workers and intensifying the class struggle of masses and of creating a powerful mass movement for the achievement of Independence and Socialism.
- Organization of, and participation in, youth leagues, women's organizations, volunteer organizations, etc. for the purpose of getting their support to the programme of the Party.
- Active opposition to all imperialist wars and the utilization of such and other crises for the intensification of national struggle.

- Refusal to enter at any stage into negotiations on the constitutional issue with the British Government.
- Convening after the capture of power of a Constituent Assembly elected by local committees of deputies of workers, peasants and other exploited classes for the purpose of formulating a constitution of the Indian state.[140]

Mahatma Gandhion Congress Socialist Party (CSP)

Gandhi was the first to react about Congress Socialist Party's objects, activities and plan for action. He observed that the Socialist Party's both objective and plan of action is based 'on coercion'. He further pointed out that the party 'ignore Indian conditions' and their 'assumptions of antagonism between the classes and the masses' and 'between the labourers and the capitalists' is facile. Besides, he described nationalization of instruments of production, distribution and exchange as 'too sweeping to be admissible'.[141] In his discussion with the students, he pleaded that we should not be 'obsessed with catchwords and seductive slogans imported from the West' and suggested to study our 'Eastern institutions in that spirit of scientific inquiry'.[142] On this issue Mahatma Gandhi, while answering to the Zamindars, further elaborated his stand – 'I am working for the co-operation and co-ordination of capital and labour and of landlords and tenants'[143]– and further observed that 'Socialism and communism of the West are based on certain conceptions which are fundamentally different from ours'.[144]

Mahatma Gandhi, took a more firm view, on the Patna resolution of the Socialist's Conference which requested him that 'he should use his influence with the Congress executive to adopt a Socialist Programme'. Mahatma told the Socialists 'that they should either be prepared to abide by the Congress decision without attempting to create unnecessary splits in Congress ranks or take over charge of the Congress machinery including its executive. He and other members of the executive were prepared to hand over control and make room for them if they so desired'.[145]

Further, Mahatma Gandhi, in a letter to Narendra Deva, finally summed up his position regarding the Congress Socialist Party

> But your enunciation of the socialist object frightens me. The implications of all the three principles are too vast for my comprehension. They make an intoxicating programme. I fear all intoxicants. . . . I do not contemplate the elimination of the princes and the landlords nor do I contemplate redistribution

> of land to peasants. . . . I plead for a drastic revision of the whole constitution. . . . I suggest your presenting the country with practical socialism in keeping with Indian conditions instead of scientific socialism as your programme has been called. I am glad that the programme you have given me is but draft though prepared by an influential committee appointed for the purpose. It would be wise, if when you settle your programme finally, you will associate with you men who have socialist leanings and have experience of actual conditions.[146]

After Mahatma Gandhi reaction to the Socialists Party, the Congress Working Committee in June 1934 at Wardha passed a resolution clearly defining the Congress attitude towards socialism, confiscation of property, etc. This Resolution pointed out that the policy of the Congress was clearly defined in its Resolution on Fundamental Rights and Economic Programme, 'which lays down certain principles, neither contemplates confiscation of private property without just cause or compensation nor advocacy of class war'.[147] The Working Committee was further of the opinion that 'confiscation and class war are contrary to the Congress creed of non-violence'. However, the Congress, 'in order to prevent the exploitation of the landless poor, also believed in wiser and juster use of private property and a healthier relationship between capital and labour'.

Congress Working Committee on CSP

The Congress Working Committee further responded to the Congress Socialist Party's objective and plan of action by revising and expanding the Gandhi Constructive Programme: production of khaddar; removal of untouchability; promotion of inter-communal unity; promotion of total abstinence from intoxicating drinks and drugs and advocacy of prohibition; promotion of education on national lines; promotion and development of useful small industries; organization and reconstruction of village alike in its economic, educational, social and hygienic aspects; spread of useful knowledge among the adult population in the villages; organization of industrial labour, etc.[148]

The Congress Working Committee in July 1934 further articulated and refined 'Congress Goal and the Means of its Attainment' by re-emphasizing the goal of complete independence by 'strictly non-violent and truthful' methods.[149] The Resolution defined complete independence as full national control, over the army, and other defence forces, external affairs, fiscal and commercial matters and financial and economic policy. In order to serve the masses, it also emphasized the need to carrying out the comprehensive internal and constructive programme.[150]

The debate on the resolution of the Working Committee on June 1934 was further followed by an exchange of letters between Jawaharlal Nehru and Mahatma Gandhi. Nehru in his letter made sharp attack on the resolution by commenting that it was

> avoiding real issues, toning down, . . . even the political objective of the Congress . . . time is overdue for the Congress to think clearly on social and economic issues . . . showed such an astounding ignorance of the elements of socialism . . . and overmastering desire of the committee was somehow to assure various vested interests even at the risk of talking nonsense.[151]

Mahatma Gandhi in a letter to Jawaharlal Nehru took full responsibility for the Working Committee resolutions as well as 'the whole conception surrounding them'. Mahatma Gandhi further explained his thinking on the resolutions by the concept of 'means and end'. Mahatma Gandhi stated 'the difference of our emphasis on the method or the means which to me are just as important as the goal'.[152] About the Socialist Party, Mahatma Gandhi observed 'a body to be in a hurry'. Further writing on a conciliatory note he observed that 'You are hard on the members of the Working Committee. They are our colleagues such as they are after all we are free institution'.

Immediately after the exchange of correspondence between Mahatma Gandhi and Jawaharlal Nehru as explained previously, Gandhi decided to retire from the active leadership of the Congress. In a letter to Vallabhbhai Patel, [153] and subsequently in a 'Statement to the Press', [154] Gandhi explained the reasons for his retirement from active politics that a very large body of Congress intelligentsia were tired of my method and views, and the programme based upon them, that I was a hindrance rather than a help to the natural growth of the Congress, that instead of remaining the most democratic and representative institution in the country, the Congress had degenerated into an organization dominated by my one personality and that in it there was no free play of reason. He further pointed out that 'there is a growing and vital difference of outlook between many Congressmen and myself'. On the formation of the Socialist Group within the Congress he observed that 'fundamental differences with them on the programme published in their authorized pamphlets'. He further viewed that 'as they may gain ascendancy in the Congress. . . .' I cannot remain in the Congress. In this context, he added 'For me to be in active opposition should be unthinkable'. In this letter, Gandhi further explained his differences with many Congressmen on the following issues: policy advocated in regard to the princely states; method and approach on untouchability, non-violence as a 'fundamental creed', 'means and end', etc.

Gandhi concluded this statement by emphasizing that 'the sum total of these differences which has sterilized the existing Congress Programme' and advocated the need to whole-heartedly adopt the Constructive Programme: 'Untouchability, Hindu-Muslim unity, total prohibition, hand-spinning with khadi and cent per cent swadeshi . . . the revival of village industries and general reorganization of seven lakhs of villages'. [155]

It is evident from the aforementioned that, since 1928, Jawaharlal Nehru's differences with Mahatma Gandhi on 'socialistic outlook' got more and more intense. With Mahatma Gandhi's resignation from the Congress Party and withdrawal from the active politics, the other Congress right-wing leaders like Vallabhbhai Patel, Jamnalal Bajaj and Rajendra Prasad started questioning within the Party, Nehru's 'socialistic outlook'. This is evident from Rajendra Prasad's Presidential Address, during Forty-eighth Session at Bombay in 1934. In this address, Prasad was critical of the ideology of the Congress Socialist Party as expressed in their party objective and plan of action.[156]

Widening of differences

The differences in the Congress between the right-wing and the left wing (socialistic outlook) further widened. It is evident from a letter written by Rajendra Prasad to Jawaharlal Nehru in December 1935. In this letter, Rajendra Prasad observed about 'a certain difference between your outlook and that of men like Vallabhbhai, Jamnalalji and myself and it is even of a fundamental character'. He suggested 'a radical change . . . in the programme and methods of our work'. He also observed that 'these differences may become more marked'.[157]

It is evident that the differences with the right-wing leadership and those holding 'socialistic outlook' within the Congress became more pronounced. All these differences came in full public view at the time of the declaration of the results of the Presidential election of the Party in January 1936. Jawaharlal Nehru was elected President of the Lucknow Session of the Congress Party.

During the Lucknow Session in a meeting of the Congress Working Committee, Nehru as President put forth the following proposals for the consideration of the party members: affiliation of trade union and peasant leagues with the Congress, political reform in the princely states, rejection of the 1935 Constitution and demand for a Constituent Assembly.

The Congress Working Committee adopted most of these proposals, however in the Subjects Committee some of these proposals were either rejected or modified.[158] In the context of the differences, Jawaharlal Nehru observed

> We must recognize that there are two sides, if not diametrically opposed, at least two definitely opposite sides of opinion that are honestly held. The best thing we can do is to try and convince each other as to the correctness of our viewpoints. Difference on this issue is a vital matter, and we must grasp the vital significance of the two opinions.[159]

Jawaharlal Nehru concluded his observation on these differences by observing that

> we ought to try and approach this question with a certain mentality – that mentality is that we cannot afford to split up, and break up the Congress. We may even differ now, to agree later and work together. Occasionally we may even act in different ways, but I will certainly do my utmost to try to function so as to help the growth of that mentality and common action in the Congress.[160]

Jawharlal Nehru Presidential address at the Forty ninth session of INC at Lucknow in April 1936 covered a large ground. He was more concerned on the question of poverty, exploitation as well as the association of the masses with the party: 'The Congress must be not only for the masses, as it claims to be, but of the masses; only then will it really be for the masses'.[161] He expressed that 'due to a certain narrowness of our Congress constitution we have failed to adapt ourselves, to a growing urgency of economic problems affecting the masses'.

Jawaharlal Nehru further expressed that the only way to solve the Indian problems of poverty, unemployment and degradation lies in socialism. This requires 'revolutionary changes' in our political and social structure as well as the elimination of vested interests in land and industry and feudal and autocratic system. This also means by and large the ending of private property and replacement of the present profit system by a co-operative system. He also advocated for the need of rapid industrialization of country and was of the view that 'khadi and village industries have a definite place in our economy'.

One important outcome in the Lucknow session was adoption of the Agrarian Programme. The programme recognized the 'appalling poverty, unemployment and indebtedness of the peasantry'. The following are some of the important provisions of the agrarian programme: reduction in rent and revenue; exemption from rent on uneconomic holdings; agricultural incomes should be assessed on progressive scale; irrigation rates be substantially lowered; forced labour should be abolished and made illegal; fixing of tenure with heritable rights; effort to introduce co-operative farming; rural debt should be removed and provision of cheap credit facilities; rights of the people in tanks, ponds, wells, forests and no encroachment on these rights and common pasture lands should be provided; provision for securing a living wage; peasant unions should be recognized.[162]

On Jawaharlal Nehru's Presidential Address at Lucknow, Mahatma Gandhi, in a letter to Agatha Harrison (April 1936), observed

> Jawaharlal's way is not my way. I accept his ideal about land, etc. But I do not accept practically any of his methods. I would strain every nerve to prevent a class war. So would he, I expect. . . . But though Jawaharlal is extreme in his presentation of his methods, he is sober in action. So far as I know him, he will not precipitate a conflict nor will he shirk it if it is forced on him.[163]

In the Congress Working Committee meeting doubts were expressed by one of his colleagues that how Jawaharlal Nehru 'will be able to withstand the combined opposition and influence of Gandhism. . . . And the Working Committee you have formed is bound to prove more reactionary than the one it has replaced'.[164]

The previous apprehension became clear by June 1936 in a letter addressed by Rajendra Prasad to Jawaharlal Nehru on the resignation of the following members from the Working Committee: Rajendra Prasad, C. Rajagopalachari, Jairamdas Doulatram, Jamnalal Bajaj, Vallabhbhai Patel, J.B. Kripalani, S.D. Dev.[165] The letter mentioned

> We feel that the preaching and emphasizing of socialism particularly at this stage by the President and other socialist members of the Working Committee while the Congress has not adopted it is prejudicial to the best interests of the country and to the success of the national struggle for freedom

> which we all hold to be the first and paramount concern of the country.[166]

The letter concluded by emphasizing that 'through your speeches and those of the other socialist colleagues . . . the Congress organization has been weakened'.[167]

Rajendra Prasad on July 1, 1936 sent another letter to Nehru regarding withdrawing their resignation. This letter was written after 'a long conversation with Mahatmaji and a prolonged consultation among ourselves'.[168] The letter of July 1 elaborated and clarified many of the points communicated in the resignation letter of June 29, 1936. The letter of July 1 pointed out that Jawaharlal Nehru in his election speeches was speaking not 'on the general Congress programme' but more 'as the mouthpiece of the minority of our colleagues on the Working Committee'.[169] It was also observed that

> There is a regular continuous campaign against us treating us as persons whose time is over, who represent and stand for ideas that are worn out and that have no present value, who are only obstructing the progress of the country and who deserve to be cast out of the position which they undeservedly hold.[170]

The letter mentioned that 'We also think that your handling of the situation in the country is doing damage to the constructive programme which we consider to be an essential and vital part of the Congress programme'.[171] Besides the letter also mentioned that 'we . . . strongly felt that the ideals and the policy for which we have stood all these sixteen or seventeen years and which we believe to be the only right ones for the country are being most assiduously undermined and that your own views and sympathies are with those who are engaged in that game'.[172]

Another significant development after the withdrawal of resignation of the right-wing leaders relate to Jawaharlal Nehru's Letter to Mahatma Gandhi 5 July 1936. Jawaharlal Nehru in this letter thanked Mahatma Gandhi for all the trouble. . . 'in smoothing over matters and in helping to avoid a crisis'. He further mentioned 'that a break of the kind suggested would have had serious consequences for all our work, including the elections'.[173]

Jawaharlal Nehru in this letter also mentioned that 'my present ideas . . . are not casual. They are part of me and though I might change them or vary them in future, so long as I hold them I must give expression to them'. However, he further observed that

> Because I attached importance to a larger unity I tried to express them in the mildest way possible and more as an invitation to thought than as fixed conclusions. I saw no conflict in this approach and in anything that the Congress was doing. So far as the elections were concerned I felt definitely that my approach was a definite asset to us as it enthused the masses. But my approach, mild and vague as it was, is considered dangerous and harmful by my colleagues. I was even told that my laying stress always on the poverty and unemployment in India was unwise, or at any rate the way I did it was wrong.[174]

Mahatma Gandhi in his reply to Jawaharlal Nehru on July 8, 1936, pointed out that on Nehru's resignation

> A.I.C.C. will be paralysed and powerless to deal with the crisis. It will be torn between two emotions. It would be most unfair to spring upon it a crisis, in the name of democracy, which it has never been called upon to face. You are exaggerating the implications of the letter. I must not argue. But I would urge you to consider the situation calmly and not succumb to it in a moment of depression so unworthy of you.[175]

In view of the Mahatma Gandhi's intervention, Jawaharlal Nehru agreed to withdraw his resignation, a spilt in the party was averted, partly due to the general election of 1937, and also in the larger context of the freedom movement. As the elections of 1937 were drawing to a close, the Congress Working Committee was entrusted with the task of drafting an election programme. This was largely done by Jawaharlal Nehru. It was discussed in the Working Committee; and several amendments were moved, however only two were accepted. This manifesto was adopted by the All India Congress Committee at Bombay on August 22, 1936.

Party manifestos

In this section, we propose to analyse the manifestos of the political parties contesting the election of 1937 under the Act of 1935. The election of 1937 has been historic due to a number of reasons. The

Congress contested the provincial elections for the first time. The Muslim League also entered the fray along with Communist Party, Unionist Party and Krishak Praja Party, etc. As a matter of fact almost all parties, which existed during that period contested the election. As has been the practice, all the parties came out with their manifestos.

Congress

The Congress manifesto dwelled at length on the question of poverty and emphasized the need for a 'radical remedy'. Besides, it also voiced concern needing special attention for the peasantry and industrial workers, artisans, traders and small merchants, etc. Another major aspect dealt by the manifesto relates to the rejection of the Constitution and its replacement by another Constitution based on political freedom for India and framed by the Constituent Assembly. However, it emphasized the need to contest the coming elections 'not to cooperate in any way with the Act but to combat and seek to end it'. To this end, the manifesto called the Congress representatives 'to resist' various regulations for oppression and work for the establishment of civil liberty.

With this background, the manifesto placed its general programme before the people. The first point relates to its commitment to the Congress resolution on Fundamental Rights of 1931. The manifesto emphasized 'the most important and urgent problem of the country is the appalling poverty, unemployment and indebtedness of the peasantry, fundamentally due to antiquated and repressive land tenure and revenue systems, and intensified in recent years by the great slump in prices of agricultural produce'.[176] The manifesto further expanded this programme by emphasizing the need for the following: reform of the system of land tenure, revenue and rent and an equitable adjustment of the burden on agriculture land; giving immediate relief to the smaller peasantry by a substantial reduction of agricultural rent and revenue and exempting uneconomic holdings from payment of rent and revenue.

On the question of indebtedness, it emphasized the need for 'the formulation of a scheme including the declaration of a moratorium, an enquiry into and scaling down of debts and the provision for cheap credit facilities by the State'. The manifesto further highlighted the need to extend this relief to the following: agricultural tenants, peasant proprietors, small landholders and petty traders.

In the context of the industrial workers, the manifesto emphasized securing them a decent standard of living, hours of work to be regulated; machinery for the settlement of disputes, relief during old age, sickness and unemployment and the right of workers to form unions and to strike for the protection of their interests.

In the context of women, the manifesto highlighted the need for the removal of legal or social disabilities in any sphere of public activity. It also emphasized the removal of untouchability and stressed the need for the social and economic upliftment of the Harijans and backward classes.

The manifesto emphasized the need for the encouragement of khadi and village industries, protection to the larger industries; protection to the rights of the workers and the producers of raw materials.

It discussed in detail the communal decision which formed part of 1935 Act and expressed the view that it encouraged 'fissiparous and disruptive tendencies' and undermined the unity of India. It advocated for a satisfactory solution based on 'the goodwill and co-operation of the principal communities concerned'.

The first manifesto of the Congress Party for the elections of 1937 mainly consisted of the Gandhi Constructive Programme of 1934 as well as the Fundamental Rights and Economic Programme of 1933. It was devoid of the entireradical plan of action of the Congress Socialist Party. The Congress manifesto of 1937 was a culmination of the debate which started in 1928 within the Congress. On the manifesto, Nehru observed 'that this curiously enough, was agreed to without much argument. A new atmosphere of co-operation surrounded us and the tension seemed to lessen'.[177]

Nehru attached lot of significance to the election manifesto. He viewed it as a document of great importance. In a circular communicated to the provincial Congress committees and parliamentary boards in December, he pointed out that

> We are fighting this election not on personal grounds but for certain principles and certain larger objectives. We miss the whole significance of this position of the Congress if we fail to lay stress on these vital issues. Individuals must not count for us in this election, it is the cause that counts.[178]

He further pointed that the candidates contesting election 'must base his entire campaign on this manifesto and should refer to it in any election statements that he might make'. He was also of the view that the copies of the manifesto should be distributed to the electorate and the general public widely and the candidate must make clear to all concerned 'what the congress stands for and what he or she, as a representative of the Congress, stands for'.

Jawaharlal Nehru in the following words explained not only the approach, significance, tone and tenor of the campaign but also the vision and the importance of the message contained in the manifesto:

> We went to our people and spoke to them of freedom and the ending of their exploitation; we went to that forgotten creature, the Indian peasant, and remembered that his poverty was the basic problem of India; we identified ourselves with him in his suffering and talked to him of how to get rid of it through political and social freedom. . . . We read out to him our election manifesto and explained its significance. He and his kind gathered in vast numbers to hear us and, listening to the Congress message, his sunken eyes glistened and his shrunken starved body rose up in enthusiasm and the wine of hope filled his veins.[179]

Muslim League

The Twenty-Fourth Session of the All-India Muslim League was held at Bombay April 11–12, 1936. There was no regular session of the League during 1934–1935. The League in a resolution emphatically protested against the Government of Indian Act, 1935. However, the League though not fully in favour of the 'Provincial Scheme' of the Constitution thought of utilizing it in the prevailing circumstances. It was also critical of the All India Federal Scheme calling it 'reactionary, retrograde, injurious, and fatal'.

The Muslim League in the Bombay Session also decided to contest the coming provincial elections. For this purpose, it also decided to formulate

> a well-defined policy and programme which facilitate the education of the electorate, and co-operation between groups with proximate aims and ideals and ensures the working of the constitution to the best advantage; and whereas to strengthen the solidarity of the Muslim community and to secure for the Muslims their proper and effective share in the provincial governments.[180]

In the Bombay Session a Central Election Board under the presidentship of M.A. Jinnah was appointed along with thirty-five members. The Board was empowered to constitute provincial election boards and 'devise ways and means for carrying out the aforesaid object'.

The Muslim League Election Manifesto was announced on June 11, 1936. The opening remarks in the manifesto dealt with the history of the formation of the Muslim League in 1906 and also provided the aims and objects of the party as adopted in December 1912. The manifesto also cited the Lucknow Pact of 1916 and observed that

> This pact will go down in the Indian History as a landmark in the political evolution of the country as a signal proof of identity of purpose and earnestness and co-operation between the two great sections of the people of India, in the task of attainment of responsible government.[181]

However, the manifesto expressed the view that as a minority 'their position in any future political constitutional structure should be protected and safeguarded'. The manifesto also expressed the view that 'the League is opposed to any movement that aims at expropriation of private property'.

Some of the significant aspects of the manifesto were the following: to protect the religious rights of the Musalmans and take steps for the amelioration of their general conditions; to secure the repeal of all repressive laws; to resist all measures detrimental to the interest of India with reference to 'fundamental liberties' and 'economic exploitation'; to allocate substantial funds for nation-building departments; to encourage development of industries and cottage industries; to regulate currency, exchange and prices in the interest of economic development of the country; to stand for the social, educational and economic uplift of the rural population; to sponsor measures for the relief of agricultural indebtedness; to make elementary education free and compulsory; to protect and promote Urdu language and script; to reduce the heavy burden of taxation; to create a healthy public opinion and general public consciousness throughout the country; 'to derive measures for the amelioration of the general conditions of Muslims'.[182]

National Unionist Party

The Unionist party contested all the elections conducted under the Act of 1919 for Punjab Legislative Assembly. The Unionist Party though predominantly Muslim in its composition, however, was not a communal organization. The election manifesto for the 1937 election expressed that 'communal conflict was not religious but economic and political in nature and . . . the three major communities should forget caste, class and creed, and form a party based on liberal and socialistic programmes'.[183]

Some of the significant issues which formed the election manifesto relate to: 'attainment of dominion status by "constitutional" means at an early practicable date; the securing of an honourable status for Indians living overseas; the establishment of "provincial autonomy in Punjab"; economic criteria as the basis for forming political parties; equal facility and opportunity for all, with special consideration for backward classes and rural areas'. It was also mentioned 'that the problems of the provinces were primarily economic and therefore required attention mainly in that direction with 90 percent of the population depending on agriculture or related occupations'.[184]

Krishak Praja Party

In Bengal, the Krishak Praja Party in its manifesto in November 1936 emphasized the following:

> abolition of zamindari without compensation; land rent should be reduced by fixing a maximum for each class of land; landlords right of pre-emption should be annulled; Debt Settlement Boards for indebtedness; compulsory and free primary education; resuscitation of dying rivers and *khals* through local manual labour; hospitals should be established at the rate of one in each thana of every district; full self-government in Bengal should be established; steps to reduce the cost of administration; steps to repeal all repressive laws and to release all political prisoners.[185]

National Agriculturalist Party (NAP)

The NAP of Agra and that of Oudh contested the 1937 elections for the Provincial Legislature of the United Provinces. P.D. Reeves, in a highly analytical article,[186] provides the political compulsions in which the party was formed; the electoral strategy; the funding of the party; the differences between the NAP of Agra and that of Oudh; the election manifesto of NAP of Agra and that of Oudh and the reasons for the failure of NAP in the elections of 1937.

There was marginal difference in the manifesto of Agra and that of Oudh National Agriculturalists' Parties. However, the manifesto of NAP Agra consisted of the following issues: to devise means for the peace prosperity and good government of the country; to adopt all constitutional means in order to obtain self-government in India; to create healthy public opinion; to protect and advance by all constitutional means the interests of the people generally and of the agricultural population particularly in these provinces; to help and advance the political, social, educational and economic uplift of the province; to create better and friendly relations between various classes and communities of the province; to encourage industries generally and cottage and agricultural industries particularly; to encourage the establishment of co-operative credit societies and land mortgage banks and to take steps to reduce the heavy burden of taxation; to help and improve medical and public health facilities generally and in the rural areas particularly; to regulate exchange policy in the interest of the country; to reduce expenditure and effect substantial economy in every branch of the government administration'.[187]

The manifesto of the NAP of Oudh consisted of the following: to adopt measures for the peace, prosperity and good government of the country; to oppose all subversive activities which tend to create class antagonism and cause political and social upheavals in the country; to create healthy and responsible public opinion and to inculcate the spirit of real service in the masses; to adopt all means necessary to promote the agricultural and economic advancement of the rural areas; to promote the cause of Swadeshi, and to assist in the development of Indian manufactures and industries especially cottage industries; to work for economy of administration and the reduction of the burden of taxation; to maintain relations between landlord and tenants; to adopt measures for the relief of agricultural indebtedness; to encourage the establishment of co-operative credit societies and land mortgage banks; to take effective steps for regulating the currency and exchange policy in the interest of the country'.[188]

Election related issues

To coordinate the election effort and maintain discipline within the party, the Congress Working Committee formed in March 1937, a parliamentary Sub-Committee consisting of the following members: Maulana Abdul Kalam Azad, Sardar Vallabhbhai Patel and Rajendra Prasad.[189] Sardar Patel was in charge of Bombay, Madras, Central Provinces and Sind; Maulana Azad was allotted Bengal, Uttar Pradesh, Punjab and the North-West Frontier Province; Rajendra Prasad was in charge of Bihar, Orissa and Assam. Similar committees were established also at the provincial level. Besides, district branches of the party were asked to form special committees to 'oversee the election effort' at the district level.

Tomlinson has given a detailed analysis of the processes regarding the selection of candidates; the election campaigns; the role of local, district, provincial and all-India leaders and their relationship and sources of finance.[190] Similarly D.A. Low in the context of the 'Congress and Mass Contacts' deliberated on the issues relating to ideology, interests and conflict over the basis of party representation.[191] Bimal Prasad has analysed the 1937 elections on the issue concerning 'electoral competition and communal strategy' between the Congress and the Muslim League.[192]

Tomlinson has also analysed in a very incisive manner the election campaign of the Congress Party. One important aspect highlighted by Tomlinson relate to the importance and 'the vital role given not to ideology but to the "intermediaries" or "brokers" – local magnates who can control and mobilize votes by dominance of local government, development agencies and informal systems of influence and linkage'.[193]

Election results

Tables 2.19 and 2.20 provide the results of 1937 elections to Legislative Assemblies and Legislative Councils. It is evident from Table 2.19 that the INC won absolute majority in the Legislative Assembly of five provinces: Bihar, Madras, U.P., Orissa and Central Provinces. It was the largest single party in four provinces: Bombay, Bengal, Assam and North-West Frontier Province. However, in Sind and Punjab, the Congress was comparatively a smaller party.

The Congress Ministries assumed office in July 1937 and remained till October–November 1939 in the following seven provinces: Bihar, Madras, U.P., Orissa, Central Provinces, North-West Frontier Province and Bombay. A coalition Ministry under a Congress Premier was established in Assam at the end of 1938.[194] In Bengal coalition of (Krishak Praja Party and Muslim League) in Punjab (Unionist Party and non-Congress Hindus) and in Sind (a succession of coalition ministries under different leaders) formed Ministries during April 1937 and remained in power at the end of 1942.[195]

The Congress ministries

The Congress Working Committee, in its meeting on March 1, 1937, adopted a resolution enunciating the Congress Policy in the Legislatures. Some of the significant points of the resolution were a policy of

Table 2.19 Final statement of results of elections to Legislative Assembly 1937.

Parties	*Assam*	*Bengal*	*Bihar*	*Bombay*	*C.P.*	*Madras*	*N.W.F.*	*Orissa*	*Punjab*	*Sind*	*U.P.*	*Total*
Total seats	108	250	152	175	112	215	50	60	175	60	228	1585
Congress	32	54	91	85	70	159	19	36	18	8	134	706
Muslim League	4	40	–	18	5	9	–	–	1	–	26	103
Oeioke's Party	–	–	–	–	–	1	–	–	–	–	–	1
Unionist Party	–	–	–	–	–	–	–	–	95	–	–	95
Justice Party	–	–	–	–	–	21	–	–	–	-	–	21
Non-Brahman	–	–	–	10	3	–	-	–	–	–	–	13
Independents	–	–	16	19	–	15	–	11	–	–	–	61
Muslim Progressive Party	–	–	–	–	–	1	–	–	–	–	–	1
Muslim Independents	30	42	–	12	8	–	2	–	5	9	24	132
Hindu Independents+	9	37	–	–	17	–	1	–	7	2	8	81
Hindu Sabha	–	2	–	–	1	–	–	–	–	11	29 (Zamindars)	43
Nationalist	–	3	–	1	3	–	7	4	–	–	–	18
Hindu Election Board	–	–	–	–	–	–	–	–	11	–	–	11
Sikh Independents	–	–	–	–	–	–	–	–	3	–	–	3
Khalsa Election Board	–	–	–	–	–	–	–	–	14	–	–	14
Akalis	–	–	–	–	–	–	–	–	10	–	–	10
Europeans, Anglo-Indians	–	32	–	8	2	9	–	–	–	–	6	57
Liberal and Indian Christian	–	–	–	–	–	–	–	–	–	–	1	1
Praja Party	–	35	–	–	–	–	–	–	–	–	–	35
Tipperah Krishak Party	–	5	–	–	–	–	–	–	–	–	–	5
Ahrar	–	–	3	–	–	–	–	–	2	–	–	5
United Party	–	–	6	–	–	–	–	5	–	18	–	29
Ambedhkar's Party (scheduled Caste)	6	–	4	13	1	–	–	4	4	–	–	32
No Party	27	–	32	–	–	–	21	–	–	4	–	84
Communist Party	–	–	–	1	–	–	–	–	–	–	–	1
Labour (Independent)	–	–	–	4	2	–	–	–	1	1	–	8
Democratic Swaraj Party	–	–	–	2	–	–	–	–	–	–	–	2
Sind Muslim Party	–	–	–	–	–	–	–	–	–	4	–	4
Socialist	–	–	–	–	–	–	–	–	1	–	–	1
Others	–	–	–	2	–	–	–	–	3	3	–	8

Source: App. II to Notes in Home (Pol.) File 111/37-Poll (I) of 1937 (Final Statement of Results of Elections to Provincial Legislatures, March 11, 1937) quoted in B.B Misra, *The Indian Political Parties: An Historical Analysis of Political Behaviour up to 1947*, Delhi: Oxford University Press, 1976, pp. 312–313.

non-cooperation with the government; the policy to resist the introduction of the Federal part of the Act; the demand for a Constituent Assembly; the carrying out of the Election Manifesto and the Congress agrarian resolution, etc.[196]

Before we analyse the working of the Congress ministries under the Act of 1935, it is proposed to provide a brief overview of Gandhi's advice to the Legislators and the Ministers on the working of the government. For this purpose, Gandhi encouraged the revival of the parliamentary wing of the Congress. He was of the view that work within the legislatures was the 'best outlet for the energies of some Congressmen'. He also believed that the new constitution provided an opportunity, however limited, 'to replace the rule of the sword by the rule of the majority'.[197] In this context, he suggested that 'If the Congress worked the new constitution, to achieve its goal of independence, it would avoid a bloody revolution and a mass civil disobedience movement'.[198]

After the formation of the Congress ministries, Gandhi advised them to set an example of simplicity and urged them to cultivate 'industry, ability, integrity, impartiality and an infinite capacity for mastering details'.[199] Gandhi not only questioned the personal attitude of the Ministers 'Will the Ministers require the Western style and expenditure on the Western scale?' But he also suggested that

> Congressmen have for the past seventeen years disciplined themselves in rigorous simplicity. The nation will expect the Ministers to introduce that simplicity in the administration of their provinces. They will not be ashamed of it, they will be proud of it. We are the poorest nation on earth, many millions living in semi-starvation. Its representatives dare not live in a style and manner out of all correspondence with their electors.[200]

In the legislative programme of the Congress Ministries, Gandhi particularly was keen on the strict enforcement of prohibition and education. Regarding education he placed his ideas before educational conference which met at Wardha in October 1937. A detailed scheme of elementary education was prepared by a committee headed by Dr. Zakir Hussain.

Congress manifesto and its implementation

It is proposed to provide an overview of the implementation of election manifestos by different political parties which formed Ministries in the eleven provinces under the Act of 1935. On the working of the Act, a number of scholarly publications are available which have examined how far the different political parties as governments, enforced their electoral programmes.[201] The Congress remained in power for about twenty-eight months and for the other political parties the period in power was approximately five years.

The All India Congress Committee adopted a resolution in Calcutta during October 1937 regarding 'Implementing of the Congress Programme by Congress Ministries'. This matter was taken up again in the Congress Working Committee at Wardha, February–March 1937. A resolution was adopted to the fact that 'the work of the Congress members of the Provincial Legislatures shall be governed by the following policy': to combat the 1935 Act, all activities directed to achieve complete independence, to resist the introduction and working of the Federal part of the Act demand for a Constituent Assembly. Besides, the Congress members should carry out the programme as enunciated in the Election Manifesto and the Congress agrarian resolution with particular reference to a substantial reduction in rent and revenue; assessment of income tax on a progressive scale on agricultural incomes; fixity of tenure; relief from the burden of rural debt; repeal of all repressive laws; release of political prisoners, restoration of lands and property confiscated by the government during Civil Disobedience Movements; eight-hour days of work for industrial workers and a living wage; prohibition; unemployment relief; reduction of high salaries, allowances and cost of administration of government.[202]

The first task of the Congress Ministry was to pass a resolution in their legislatures against the Government of India Act, 1935, and replace it with a constitution for a free India framed by a Constituent Assembly. Similarly, all Congress Legislatures adopted a resolution and condemned the scheme of federation. Besides, all the seven Congress ministries took measures for the removal of civil liberty as well as release of political prisoners. The political prisoners were released without any difficulty except in U.P. and Bihar, due to the refusal of Governors for the release of the political prisoners.

On the land question, R. Coupland has mentioned that, by and large, Congress policy was conservative, as no other attempt was made to 'upset the existing land-revenue system'. However, the agrarian policy of the Congress dealt vigorously 'with tenancy-rights and rents'.[203]

In the context of agrarian problems and rural indebtedness a number of legislations, were passed to mitigate the distress of the peasants. These tenancy reforms were carried out in all Congress-led ministries. A number of Moneylenders and Debtors' Relief Acts were passed in Bihar, Bombay and the Central Provinces, Madras, North-West Frontier

Table 2.20 Final Statement of Results of Elections to Legislative Council 1937.*

Parties	*Assam*	*Bengal*	*Bihar*	*Bombay*	*Madras*	*U.P.*
Total seats	18	57	26	26	46	52
Congress	–	9	8	14	26	8
Muslim League	–	11	–	2	3	–
Moderates	10	–	–	1	–	3
Independent Hindus	–	12	–	3	–	16
Independent Muslims	6	13	3	3	–	14
Independents	–	1	–	–	11	–
Justice Party	–	–	–	–	5	–
Democratic Swaraj	–	–	–	2	–	–
Europeans	2	6	1	1	1	1
Hindu Sabha	–	1	–	–	–	–
Nationalists	–	1	–	–	–	–
Praja Party	–	3	–	–	–	–
Muslim United Party	–	–	3	–	–	–
No Party	–	–	11	–	–	–
National Agriculturist (Zamindars)	–	–	–	–	–	10

*The following provinces did not have Councils: Central Provinces, North-West Frontier Province, Orissa, Punjab, Sind

Source: App. II to Notes in Home (Pol.) File 111/37-Poll (I) of 1937 (Final Statement of Results of Elections to Provincial Legislatures, March 11, 1937) quoted in B.B Misra, *The Indian Political Parties: An Historical Analysis of Political Behaviour up to 1947*, Delhi: Oxford University Press, 1976, p. 311.

Province and Orissa. In most of the Congress-led provinces, some rural construction programmes were started for the welfare of the masses on a modest scale. Similarly, a lot of encouragement was also given to the spread of khadi and the development of the village industries.

Prohibition was enforced in a substantial manner in almost all the Congress-led provinces. In the field of education the Congress ministries in different provinces introduced the scheme of basic education. Emphasis was also given in the field of adult education and to the spread of the depressed class education, female education and the reorganization of university education.[204]

However, it was noticed that in many areas the implementation of manifesto was not up to the mark. On this aspect, Nehru showed his unhappiness. In a letter to Mahatma Gandhi in April 1938, he stated:

> I feel strongly that the Congress Ministries are working inefficiently and not doing much that they could do. They are

> adapting themselves far too much to the old order and trying to justify it. But all this, bad as it is might be tolerated. What is far worse is that we are losing the high position that we have built up, with so much labour, in the hearts of the people. We are sinking to the level of ordinary politicians who have no principles to stand by and whose work is governed by a day-to-day opportunism.

This observation was elaborated by Rani Dhavan Shankardass in the specific context of Bombay (now Maharashtra).[205]

Rani Dhavan Shankardass's study brings out factors particularly responsible for the non-fulfilment of the election manifesto, 'many of their more radical schemes had to be modified and adapted to local conditions'. As a consequence,

> Once in office, the Congress entered the practical world of political action; and even when ideological goals were declared, promises had to be trimmed into possibilities. Proclamation of ideologies was not abandoned overnight, but the more realistic politicians in Congress increasingly played politics, according to the rules that most people in politics accepted as more realistic and practical. That meant that too great an emphasis on ideology was considered incongruous in an environment where the facts would belie the professed declarations.[206]

Non-Congress ministries and the enforcement of manifestos

In case of the non-Congress Government in Bengal, a number of progressive legislations were enacted relating to tenancy reform, relief of rural indebtedness, fund for relief and insurance against famine, assistance to the poor and unemployed in rural areas, etc.[207] Similarly, in Punjab, under the Unionist Party the government carried out the following: measures to restrict the sale or mortgage of agricultural land; relief for providing the liquidation on easy terms of all mortgages; legal measure to prevent malpractices in the markets; the Registration of Moneylenders Act; the Relief of Indebtedness Act; tax on urban immovable property, and a general sales tax, etc.[208] Coupland has also observed that 'The record of Assam and Sind both in legislation and in firm administration has been poorer'.[209]

The Second World War

The Second World War broke out in September 1939. The Congress Working Committee, in its meeting in Wardha on September 14, 1939, discussed the war crisis and took a view that it could not 'associate themselves or offer any cooperation in a war which is conducted on imperialist lines and which is meant to consolidate imperialism in India and elsewhere'.[210] By November 15, 1939, except Assam, all Congress Ministries resigned against the Viceroy's statement of October 1939. In Assam, the Congress coalition ministry resigned, but an alternative ministry was appointed. The remaining provinces of Bengal, the Punjab and Sindh continued as before.[211]

The decision of the Congress to resign was 'widely regretted'.[212] Jawaharlal Nehru realized that this had been an 'error'.[213] V.P. Menon in his book *The Transfer of Power in India* noted that the resignation of the Congress was of direct benefit to the Muslim League. The following are some of the observations of Menon on this decision:

> [a)] Lord Linlithgow's attitude automatically changed. There was no longer any necessity to woo the Congress so far as the war effort was concerned, since the administration of the Congress provinces had been taken over by the Governors. . . . b) Lord Linlithgow began to lean more on the support of the Muslim League and to discountenance any move on the part of the Congress to return to office except on his own terms . . . c) For all practical purposes Jinnah was given a veto on further constitutional progress and, adroit politician that he was, he made the very most of the situation.[214]

Subsequently, the resignation of Congress Ministries facilitated the Muslim League 'to operate in a political vacuum' by strengthening its position in the Muslim majority provinces. In Bengal, in March 1943, a Muslim League Ministry was formed; in Sind, the pro-Congress Ministry was dismissed and a Ministry was formed with the League's support. In the North-West Frontier province the Muslim League formed a Ministry in May 1943 and in Assam, also, the Muslim League formed the ministry.[215]

Some important developments took place after October 1939. These are the August Offer (1940) and Cripps Proposal (1942) the Quit India Resolution (1942) and Shimla Conference (1945).

August Offer 1940

The Viceroy on behalf of the British Government made an offer on August 8, 1940 for the following: the expansion of the Executive Council of Governor General and the establishment of Advisory War Council; to safeguard the position of the minority's full weight to minority opinion; the framing of the new constitution should be primarily the responsibility of Indians themselves and should originate from 'Indian conceptions of the social, economic and political structure of the Indian life'; the setting up of a representative Indian body to formulate the new constitution and for all parties and communities in India to co-operate in India's war effort. The August Offer was rejected by the Congress while the Muslim League neither accepted nor rejected it.

Cripps Proposals 1942

Another important constitutional development relates to the Cripps Proposals of 1942. In this proposal, India would be free to devise her own constitution; there would be participation of the Indian states in the Indian constitution-making body; His Majesty's Government would accept and implement forthwith the constitution so framed and be subject to the right of any province of British India, i.e. not prepared to accept the new constitution to retain its present constitutional position. There would also be provision for the representation of the Indian states in the constitution-making body. 'The right of secession was recognized. The device of a bilateral treaty for implementing the new Constitution and discharging the British obligations was introduced. The Muslims were also assured that they could have Pakistan if they so pleased'.[216] These proposals were criticized by the Congress. However, the response of the Muslim League was a mixed one.

The Quit India Resolution August 1942

The A.I.C.C. in its meeting in Bombay during August 1942 passed a resolution that emphasized the necessity of ending the British rule in India and announced 'the starting of a mass struggle on non-violent lines'.[217] This led to the arrest of Mahatma Gandhi and other senior prominent Congress leaders. There was a mass protest all over the country. This situation continued up to May 6, 1944, when Mahatma Gandhi was released. However, the other leaders of the Congress Working Committee were released in June 1945.

Wavell Plan 1945

The Wavell Plan 1945 consisted of 'the formation of a new Executive Council more representative of organised political opinion' and 'again undertake the tasks of government in the provinces now administered under Section 93 of the Constitution Act, and that these Ministries will be coalitions'.[218] To discuss the Wavell Plan, a conference was called at Simla June 1945 which failed due to disagreement with Jinnah regarding the inclusion of non-League Muslims in the list of the Governor-General.

General Elections of 1945–1946

The end of the Second World War and the victory of Labour Party in the British national election of July 1945 gave some hope and urgency for sympathetic consideration of India's problem. On September 16, 1945, Lord Wavell, the Viceroy, made the announcement regarding the elections to the Central and Provincial Legislatures during the coming winter season. The purpose was to discuss with the representatives of the Legislative Assemblies in the provinces regarding the proposals contained in the 1942 Declaration. This would also help in knowing 'the will of the Indian electorate'. No commitment was given to undertake any revision of the existing franchise system. However, assurance was given 'to revise the electoral rolls efficiently'. Lord Wavell also announced that after the elections 'discussions would be held with the Indian leaders and with the representatives of the Indian states to determine the form which the constitution-making body should take. This procedure appeared to be the best way to give India the opportunity of deciding her destiny'.[219] It was decided to organize the general elections in the following manner: first, elections to the Central Assembly, second, elections to the Provincial Legislatures where ministries were functioning and, lastly, to the Provincial Legislatures were not functioning.

For the elections of 1945–1946, the total number of seats in the Provincial Assemblies were 1,585 (including four non-elective seats in Orissa). These seats were distributed in the following thirteen electoral divisions:

General	657
Scheduled Castes	151
Muslims	482
Sikhs	34
Backward Tribes	24
Anglo-Indians	11
Europeans	26

Indian Christians	20
Commerce, etc.	56
Landholders	37
University	8
Labour	38
Women	41

Source: Asoka Mehta, *The Political Mind of India: An Analysis of the Results of the General Elections*, Bombay: A Socialist Party Publication, 1952, p. 83.

The AICC held its first meeting during September 21–23, 1945 after a gap of three years of suppression by the British Government. It passed a resolution, regarding Lord Wavell's proposal of the general elections and characterized the announcement as 'vague, inadequate and unsatisfactory'.[220] The resolution pointed out that, first, the Central Assembly was governed by the Act of 1919 and, second, that it was elected on a franchise of less than 1 percent of the population; as a consequence, the Central Assembly was 'undemocratic'. It requested for revised electoral rolls; restoration of civil liberties so as to provide space for free and fair elections. The resolution also constituted an Assembly Elections Committee for organizing elections to the legislatures.[221] The resolution also decided to prepare a manifesto containing the policy and programme of the Congress.

Before we analyse the election manifesto of the Congress, it is important to provide a brief overview of Mahatma Gandhi-Jawaharlal Nehru correspondence on economic modernization, which happened just before the release of the Congress Party manifesto. This is important, because it was for the last time that they were exchanging their views on economic objectives which started since 1928. In this correspondence, both of them kept their basic premise intact. This correspondence is of historic significance and has contemporary relevance.

Mahatma Gandhi and Jawaharlal Nehru on social and economic objectives in 1945

Following a discussion on social and economic objectives in the Congress Working Committee, Mahatma Gandhi wrote to Jawaharlal Nehru on October 5, 1945 about 'the sharp difference of opinion' that appeared between them. Mahatma Gandhi felt that 'If such a difference really exist people should also know about it for the work of *Swaraj* will suffer if they are kept in the dark'. In this letter, Mahatma Gandhi pointed out that 'I fully stand by the kind of governance which I have described in *Hind Swaraj*. . . . My experience has confirmed the truth of what I wrote in 1909', 'to achieve real freedom, . . . we shall have to go and live in the villages. . . . We can have the vision of that truth and non-violence only in the simplicity of the villages'. Mahatma Gandhi advocated 'That simplicity resides in the spinning-wheel and what is implied by the spinning-wheel. It does not frighten me al all that the world seems to be going in the opposite direction. For the matter of fact, when the moth approaches its doom it whirls round faster and faster till it is burnt up. It is possible that India will not be able to escape this moth-like circling' Mahatma Gandhi observed that 'The sum and substance of what I want to say is that the individual person should have control over the things that are necessary for the sustenance of life. If he cannot have such control the individual cannot survive'.[222]

Nehru on October 9, 1945, in his reply, pointed out the need for 'sufficiency of food, clothing, housing, education, sanitation, etc., which should be the minimum requirement for the country and for everyone'. Besides, there is a need to develop 'modern means of transport as well as many other modern developments must continue and be developed'. There is also a need for heavy industry.

Nehru pointed out that 'The question of independence and protection from foreign aggression, both political and economic, had also to be considered in this context'. Besides, 'for India to be really independent unless she is a technically advanced country'. He also advocated the need for a strong background of scientific research and every department. Nehru attributed to 'tremendous acquisitive tendency' as the most important reason for conflicts and wars. In this context, he suggested, 'That basis must go and be transformed into one of co-operation, not of isolation which is impossible. If this is admitted and is found feasible then attempts should be made to realize it not in terms of an economy which is cut off from the rest of the world but rather one which co-operates. From the economic or political point of view an isolated India may well be a kind of vacuum which increases the acquisitive tendencies of others and thus creates conflicts'.

Nehru also pointed out that *Hind Swaraj* 'seemed to me completely unreal'. He further mentioned that though 'In your writings and speeches since then I have found much that seemed to me an advance on that old position and an appreciation of modern trends'. He further pointed that 'I was therefore surprised when you told us that the old picture still remains intact in your mind. As you know, the Congress has never considered that picture, much less adopted it. You yourself have never asked it to adopt it except for certain relatively minor aspects of it'. Nehru concluded his letter by stating that 'since *Hind Swaraj* was written. The world has completely changed since then, possibly in a wrong direction. In any event any consideration of these questions must keep present facts, forces and the human material we have today in view, otherwise it will be divorced from reality'.[223]

While replying Nehru's letter Mahatma Gandhi, on November 13, 1945, observed 'I want that people should know us as we know each other. If in the end we find that our paths are different, then so be it. Our hearts will still remain one, for they are one'. Mahatma Gandhi pointed out that he agrees with the basic question which both share that 'how to ensure man's mental, economic, political and moral development'. For this, Mahatma Gandhi pleaded for providing every 'individual equal right and opportunity'. Mahatma Gandhi elaborated his views further by stating that From this point of view there should be 'equality between villages and cities' and to bring this condition 'people should produce their own cloth and food and build their own houses. So also, they should produce their own water and electricity'. For this purpose Mahatma Gandhi pleaded that 'the unit should be an ideal village or a social group which will be self-sufficient, but the members of which will be interdependent'. Mahatma Gandhi further pleaded that 'This conception will bring about a change in human relationship all over the world'.[224]

The election manifestos and related issues

It is proposed to provide some of the salient aspects of the manifestos of Congress, the Muslim League and the Communist Party of India which contested the elections of 1945–1946.

Congress Party

A composite manifesto[225] both for the Central and the Provincial Elections was adopted by the Congress Working Committee in December 1945. It envisaged fundamental rights and civil liberties to all its citizens guaranteed in the constitution. The manifesto stood for the unity of all communities and religious groups as well as for tolerance and goodwill between them. It also provided for the freedom of each group and territorial area within the nation to develop its own life and culture. It suggested a linguistic and cultural basis for the creation of provinces. It opposed any form of social tyranny and injustice. It provided for a federal constitution with autonomy for its constituent units. It advocated a minimum list of common and essential federal subjects. It envisaged elections under universal adult franchise.

The manifesto also discussed the numerous economic problems faced by the country. It pointed out the need to remove the 'curse of poverty' and raise the standard of the masses. The manifesto suggested that 'Industry and agriculture, the social services and public utilities must be encouraged and modernized'. It emphasized the need to undertake all these activities with the primary object of benefiting the masses and 'raising their economic, cultural and spiritual level', removing unemployment and adding to the 'dignity of the Individual'. For this purpose, the manifesto suggested ways and means 'to plan and co-ordinate social advance in all its many fields', 'to prevent the concentration of wealth and power in the hands of individuals and groups' and 'to prevent vested interests inimical to society from growing, and to have social control of the mineral resources, means of transport and the principal methods of production and distribution in land, industry and in other departments of national activity, so that free India may develop into a co-operative commonwealth'.[226]

The manifesto also suggested the need to constitute the river commission to develop the power resources of the country. The development of land and industry would require 'the harnessing and proper utilization of the vast energy that is represented by the great rivers of India'.

The manifesto also laid emphasis on the education of the masses so as to 'fit them for the new forms of work and services'. The manifesto called for the need to provide public health services along with special attention to the needs of the rural areas. The manifesto also pointed out the need for social security for all.

It also discussed the need to develop scientific research and its utilization in industrial, agricultural, national defence and cultural advance.

With regard to industrial labour the manifesto observed the need for the following: minimum wage, proper housing, reasonable work hours, good work conditions, suitable machinery for the settlement of disputes and the right to form unions. The manifesto emphasized industrial co-operatives for the development of small-scale industry on a democratic basis.

In international affairs, the manifesto advocated for the 'establishment of a world federation of free nations'. It also suggested the need to develop friendly relations with all nations and particularly with neighbours – 'the Far East, South East Asia and Western Asia'– for reasons of 'security and future trends of trade'. The manifesto also advocated the need for the 'elimination of imperialism'.

Muslim League

In order to appreciate the political developments from the perspective of the Muslim League, it is desirable to reflect on its status as a political organization before the elections of 1945–1946.

As described in an earlier section, after Jinnah became the President of Muslim League in early 1936, the League showed signs of revival and life. Jinnah appointed a Central Parliamentary Board to direct the elections. A manifesto was released for contesting the Central and Provincial Elections of 1937. The Congress formed ministries in all the provinces except in Bengal, Punjab and Sindh. When the Congress decided to 'accept office', there was a proposal that it should form coalition ministries with the Muslim League in the provinces where the League had representation. It is interesting to point out that, in the Provincial Legislatures of Bihar, Orissa and the Central Provinces, the League had no representation at all. This offer did not materialize, as the Congress decided to form 'homogenous ministries' of its own. This was the beginning of a serious rift between the Congress and the League and was a factor 'which induced neutral Muslim opinion to turn to the support of Jinnah'.[227]

It is also interesting to point out that Jinnah in his Presidential Address at Lucknow on October 15, 1937 observed

> The present leadership of the Congress, especially during the last ten years, has been responsible for alienating the Musalmans of India more and more by pursuing a policy which is exclusively Hindu, and since they have formed the Governments in six provinces where they are in a majority they have by their words, deeds and programme shown more and more that Musalmans cannot expect any justice or fair-play at their hands. Wherever they are in a majority and wherever it suited them, they refused to co-operate with the Muslim League Parties and demanded unconditional surrender and signing of their pledges.[228]

The other factors which widened the distance between the Congress and the League was the Congress programme of 'Muslim mass contact' after the elections of 1937. The Muslim League also passed a resolution criticizing the Congress attitude in 'foisting Bande Mataram'; making Hindi a compulsory language, the tricolour flag, the *Vidya Mandir* scheme of education. These issues helped Jinnah to consolidate his position and that of the Muslim League amongst the Muslim masses.

Some other factors responsible for the consolidation of the Muslim League as the single strongest political organization relate to the support of Jinnah and Muslim League to the British war effort and the bringing of all Muslim political parties under the umbrella of the Muslim League. Jinnah in his Presidential Address at the Lahore Session of All India-Muslim League in March 1940 demanded a separate homeland for Muslims. In this address he asserted that the

> Mussulmans are a nation according to any definition of a nation, and they must have their homelands, their territory and their state. . . . We wish our people to develop to the fullest our spiritual, cultural, economic, social and political life in a way that we think best and in consonance with our own ideals and according to the genius of our people.[229]

A resolution passed at the Lahore Session of the Muslim League on March 23, 1940 stated:

> Resolved that it is the considered view of this Session of the All-India Muslim League that no constitutional plan would be workable in this country or acceptable to the Muslims unless it is designed on the following basic principles, viz. that geographically contiguous units are demarcated into regions which should be so constituted, with such territorial readjustments as may be necessary, that the areas in which the Muslims are numerically in a majority as in the North-Western and Eastern zones of India should be grouped to constitute 'Independent States' in which the constituent units shall be autonomous and sovereign.[230]

The Lahore resolution saw 'a steady consolidation of the Muslim League's power and of Jinnah's personal position'. The two factors which further enhanced their position relate to the resignation of the Congress ministries in October 1939 and the Congress 'Quit India' resolution (August 1942), i.e. 'the demand for the withdrawal of British power from India'. These factors strengthened the Muslim League and enabled them 'to operate in a political vacuum. It gradually strengthened its support in the Muslim majority provinces, which it had to win to give reality to the Pakistan demand'.[231] It is also important to mention that, except in Punjab, 'after some very involved political infighting' in Bengal, a Muslim League ministry was formed in March 1943; in Sind a Ministry was formed with League support in September 1942; in North-West Frontier Province, League also formed a ministry in May 1943. This also happened in Assam where the League took over.[232] Another contributing factor was Wavell's proposal for which Jinnah made it clear 'that it would not agree to the inclusion of non-League Muslims'.

Along with the aforementioned developments, it is also important to emphasize that the League during the war years were able to bring within its fold many non-political Muslims like industrial and commercial entrepreneurs, students and professionals and clerical and salaried Muslim middle class. Besides, a Planning Committee of League was set up in its Karachi Session of 1943 'to devise plans for the economic development of the areas intended to form part of Pakistan'[233] and in 1944 an education committee was also appointed to make recommendations necessary 'for the preservation, fostering and promotion of Islamic traditions, culture and ideals'.

In the elections of 1945–1946, 'With a strong press, a well built political organization claiming the loyalty of almost every Muslim, with a more vigorous social and economic programme, the Muslim League had become a people's party. . . . The Muslim League fought the elections on the issue of Pakistan'.[234] In the context of elections of 1945–1946, Ayesha Jalal has analysed the League's electoral strategy, the issues involved in the election campaign, the role of the High Command, the problem of Muslim factionalism, the selection of candidates, etc., relating to Muslim majority provinces – the Punjab, Bengal, Sind and the North-West Frontier Province.[235] I.A. Talbot in an article devoted to the Punjab elections of 1946 attributed the success of Muslim League in these elections because of its 'religious appeals' and 'traditional channels of political mobilization'.[236]

The Muslim League contested the elections of 1945–1946 on the sole issue of Pakistan. In this context, it is interesting to point out the statement issued to the press on September 6, 1945 by the Working Committee of Bengal Provincial Muslim League titled 'Manifesto'. The 'Manifesto' declared the election of 1945 'as a plebiscite on Pakistan and a plebiscite on their claim to represent the whole of Muslim India'. For this purpose the manifesto pointed out the need to marshal and mobilize the resources; sinking the difference of opinion and emphasized the need for 'unity, and fraternity in the Muslim community'.[237]

Communist Party of India

The Communist Party of India contested the elections and issued its election manifesto in February 1946 with detailed strategy and tactics. The manifesto called for a 'united struggle of all freedom loving Indians against the British enslavers'.[238] The manifesto also included economic proposals with emphasis on state industrial planning and 'free and equal cooperation between the representatives of the state, Management and Labour'. The manifesto advocated the need to 1 develop cottage industry as well as large-scale industry to achieve 'maximum growth'. On the question of agrarian policy, it pleaded for the abolition of landlordism, but promised to protect the small landlord, the middle farmer and landless.[239] The manifesto also emphasized the need to take drastic steps for the control of the interests of profiteers and hoarders; the nationalization of all key industries, like chemicals, iron and steel, and of coal mines; and the control of all major industries and capital resources for the rapid development of the 'People's state'.[240] A very significant demand voiced by the Communist Party was that the 'illegal riches of the war profiteers "should" be confiscated and mobilized for people's needs after prompt investigation and summary trial through open and impartial tribunals'.[241]

Election results of 1945–1946

Table 2.21 shows the party-wise position of eleven Provincial Assemblies of the 1945–1946 elections.

It is evident from Table 2.21 that in the Provincial Legislatures the Congress obtained an absolute majority in all the Hindu-majority Provinces and in the Muslim majority Province of the North-West Frontier. The Congress formed ministries in all the eight provinces: Assam, Orissa, Bihar United Province, Bombay, Central Provinces, Madras and North-West Frontier. It is significant to point out that the Congress won a large number of seats without contest (UP, 79; Madras, 64; Bihar, 44; Orissa, 34). The Muslim League won 428 out of 492 in the Provincial Legislatures. The Muslim League formed ministries in Bengal and Sind but in the Punjab, a coalition of the Congress, the Unionists and the Akali Sikhs formed the ministry.

In these elections, the Congress and the Muslim League emerged as the two contenders for power in India and other parties were nearly eliminated. In the context of the representation of various political parties in the Legislative Assemblies in the election results of 1945–1946, Asoka Mehta provided a very fine analysis, which, in a way, covers

Table 2.21 Statement showing the party-wise composition of Provincial Assemblies during the elections of 1945–1946.

	Madras		
General: total members: 186		Muslim: total members: 29	
Congress	163	Muslim League	28
Nationalist Hindu	1	(Vacant)	1
Communists	2		
Europeans	7		
Anglo-Indians	2		
Indian Christians	3		
Landholders	3		
Commerce	2		
Independent (women)	1		
(Vacant)	2		
	Bombay		
General: total members: 144		Muslim: total members: 29	
Congress	128	Muslim League	29
Communists	2		
Radical Democrat	1		
Hindu Mahasabha	1		
Europeans	6		
Anglo-Indians	2		
Independents	4		
	United Provinces		
General: total members: 160		Muslim: total members: 68	
Congress	148	Muslim League	54
Europeans	3	Congress	4
Anglo-Indian	1	Ahrars	1
Indian Christian	1	Nationalist Muslims	7
Commerce	2	Independent Muslims	2
Landholders	5		

(Continued)

Table 2.21 (Continued)

		Bihar			
General: Total members: 112				Muslim: Total Members: 40	
Congress	97			Muslim League	34
Adibasis	3			Momins	5
Anglo-Indian	1			Congress	1
Indian Christian	1				
Europeans	3				
Commerce	2				
Landholders	4				
University	1				
		Central Provinces			
General: total members: 97				Muslim: total members: 15	
Congress	93			Muslim League	13
Scheduled Castes Federation	1			Congress	1
Hindu Mahasabha	1			Independent	1
European	1				
Anglo-Indian	1				
		Orissa			
General: total members: 56				Muslim: total members: 4	
Congress	47			Muslim League	4
Communist	1				
Landholders	2				
Backward Tribes (nominated)	4				
Independents	2				
		Punjab			
General: total members: 51		Muslim: total seats: 91		Sikh: total members: 33	
Congress	40	Muslim League	80	Akalis	23
Unionist	6	Unionists	6	Congress	10

Indian Christian	1	Ahrars	1
Independent Labour	1	(Vacant)	3
Independent	1		
Anglo-Indian	1		

North-West Frontier Province

General: total members: 9*		Muslim: total members: 38	
Congress	9	Congress	19
		Jamiat-ul-Ulema	2
		Muslim League	17

Sind

General: total members: 25		Muslim: total members: 35	
Congress	22	Muslim League	28
Europeans	3	Syed Group	4
		Nationalist Muslims	3

Bengal

General: total members: 127		Muslim: total members: 123	
Congress Hindu Mahasabha Communists Sch. Castes Federation Anglo-Indians Europeans Indian Christians Landholders Independents (Sch. Castes)	86131425214	Muslim League Krishak Praja Congress Independents	115314

Assam

General: total members: 74		Muslim: total members: 34	
Congress Europeans Tribal League Indian Christian Backward Tribes Labour	5891141	Muslim League Jamiat-ul-Ulema	313

*Excluding three Sikhs (Congress 2; Akalis 1)

Source: Very little information regarding the composite party-wise position of eleven Provincial Assemblies of the 1945–1946 elections is available. However, the Table of Representation as provided here was issued by the Press Information Bureau in June/July 1946. The Cabinet Mission's Statement of May 16, 1946 utilized 'the recently elected Provincial Legislative Assemblies as the election bodies' and the 'Party-wise composition of Provincial Assemblies at the time of elections to the Constituent Assembly', quoted in B. Shiva Rao, Chairman *The Framing of India's Constitution: Select Documents*, Vol. 1 New Delhi: The Indian Institute of Public Administration, 1966, pp. 288–291.

not only the growth and development of political parties since the Morley-Minto Reforms, but also the emergence within the Congress of various groups. Asoka Mehta's observations on the 1945–1946 elections are of great significance: 'Old parties that once administered provinces, like the Justice Party in Madras and the Non-Brahmin party in Bombay, have suffered a total eclipse. Parties that had broken away from the Congress in the past – the Liberals, the Responsivists, the Nationalists have experienced extinction. Among parties claiming nationwide organization and appeal, the Hindu Mahasabha has won barely three seats, the Scheduled Castes Federation just one'.[242] The Communist had captured eight seats and it was observed by Mehta 'If their was proportional representation, the Communists would have got 51 instead of 8 seats'.[243]

Cabinet Mission

The Cabinet Mission Plan of May 16, 1946 proposed that the Union of India responsible for defence, foreign affairs and communications and all the other subjects as well as residuary powers were to vest in the provinces. The provinces were free to form Groups with executive and legislatures and each group could determine the Provincial subjects to be taken in common. The Constitution was subject to revision ten years after its promulgation and every ten years thereafter. The Constitution of Union was to be formulated by a Constituent Assembly. The Cabinet Mission suggested for this purpose 'The only practicable course is to utilize the recently elected Provincial Legislative Assemblies as the electing bodies'.

The Cabinet Mission scheme was accepted partially by the Indian National Congress in June 1946, while the Muslim League accepted it in its entirety. The interim government under Jawaharlal Nehru took office on September 2, 1946, while the Muslim League refused to participate in it. The elections to the Constituent Assembly took place in July 1946 and the Constituent Assembly met for the first time on December 9, 1946 in New Delhi. The Muslim League refused to participate in its deliberations.

The Lord Mountbatten Plan of June 3, 1947 laid down the method by which power to be transferred. The Indian Independence Act, 1947, gave effect to the June 3 Plan of Lord Mountbatten. The Act provided the setting up of two independent Dominions India and Pakistan. The Act came into effect on August 15, 1947. Pending the framing of a new constitution, 'that the Government of each Dominion will be carried on as closely as possible in accordance with the provisions of the Act of 1935'. The legislative powers previously exercised by the Central Legislature were conferred temporarily on the Constituent Assembly in each Dominion. Thus, the Constituent Assemblies were given a dual role: the making of a constitution, for which purpose they have complete power to do anything, and the temporary function of acting as a Central Legislature for each Dominion in the exercise of the limited powers in the central field which were given to the Federal Legislature by the Act of 1935. To fit the new circumstances, there was extensive adaptation of the Act of 1935. This is to be done by Order made by the Governor-General under Clause 9 of the Bill. Clause 9 gives the Governor-General wide but temporary powers to make orders for effecting partition at the Centre and in the Provinces and for administering the common services and other Central functions pending their division between the two Dominions. It conferred similar powers for the purpose of partitioning in the Punjab, Bengal and Assam on the Governors of those Provinces.[244]

As mentioned in the previous section, the Provincial Assemblies elected in 1946 remained in office till 1951 when the New Constitution came into operation. In the context of the implementation of the election manifesto and the working of the provincial governments not much information is available. During the period 1946 to 1951, the Constitution was in the making; the Congress Working Committee was the only forum to discuss and make decisions on important policy issues and it 'emerged in these years as an important arena for informal discussions of all-India policy, discussions which served more or less officially as guidelines to the states'.[245] Even in these Working Committee meetings except the question of abolition of zamindari, not much effort was made concerning issues of development as mentioned in the election manifesto of 1946.[246] This aspect was discussed in detail by B.P. Sitaramayya in his Presidential Address at the Fifty-Fifth Session of Indian National Congress in December 1948. He talked about lack of 'congenial' conditions to implement the election manifesto which embodies certain principles and policies. In the context of industrialization, he mentioned 'The industrialization of the country is a problem of vast magnitude and is beset with unknown impediments. Capital goods are not available for love of money. Conditions change so swiftly that it is difficult to keep pace with their ever-recurring mutations'.[247] He further discussed that due to lack of capital it is difficult to undertake the abolition of zamindari, nationalization of key industries, etc. He voiced concern about the growing corruption which was to a large extent responsible for the inability of 'the Congress Governments . . . to give a glowing account of their achievements'.[248] He summed up his views on this problem by pointing out that 'These are all matters of high policy and administration and we trust ourselves to the trained talent of government for evolving proper solutions of problems of complicated nature'.[249]

The new Constitution of India came into force on January 26, 1950. The following chapter will look into constitutional provisions dealing with elections and related matters along with an overview of the general elections conducted from 1952 to 2014 for the Lok Sabha.

Notes

1 In India, the beginnings of constitutional representation commenced with Lord Ripon's Resolution on Local Self-Government, 1882. In the absence of any experience in conducting elections, Ripon suggested the need for introducing a variety of plans 'The simple vote, the cumulative vote, election by wards, election by the whole town or tract, suffrage of more or less extended qualification, election by castes or occupation- these and other methods might all be tried'. Ripon also laid down the conditions necessary for conducting the elections and in a way formalized the processes involved in introducing the elective system at the local level. A. Rangaswami Iyengar, *The Indian Constitution: An Introductory Study*, Second Edition-Revised and Enlarged, Madras: G.C. Loganadham Bros, 1913, Appendix, pp. civ–cxv. In the context of Local Self-Government Bill, Sir Sayyed Ahmad Khan on January 12, 1883 pointed out that in India where 'caste distinctions' and 'religious distinctions flourish' the introduction of the principle of election will not help. He favoured the power of Government of appointing one-third of the members of the local boards and district councils to ensure 'the success of local self- government, by securing and maintaining that due and just balance in the representation of the various sections of Indian population'. Abstract of the Proceedings of the Council of the Governor General of India, Assembled for the purpose of Making Laws and Regulations, 1883 with Index, Vol. XXII (Calcutta Office of the Superintendent of Government Printing, 1884), p. 20 quoted in A. Appadorai, *Documents on Political Thought in Modern India*, Vol. II, Bombay: Oxford University Press, 1976, pp. 255–256. For details concerning the elections conducted by various provinces for the local boards. See S. Gopal, *The Vice Royality of Lord Ripon, 1880–1884*, London: Oxford University Press, 1953, pp. 110–111. See also for an important sidelight, Samuel H. Beer, The Representation of Interests in British Government: Historical Background, *The American Political Science Review*, Vol. LI, No. 3 (September 1957), pp. 613–650; Harold A. Gould, *Grass Roots Politics in India: A Century of Political Evolution in Faizabad District*, New Delhi: Oxford * IBH Publishing Co. Pvt. Ltd, 1994, pp. 50–76 and Douglas E. Haynes, *Rhetoric and Ritual in Colonial India: The Shaping of a Public Culture in Surat City, 1852–1928*, New Delhi: Oxford University Press, 1992, pp. 145–174.

2 Lord Curzon, while introducing the Bill in the House of Commons on March 28, 1892, highlighted that the object of this Bill 'was to widen the

basis and expand the functions of the Government of India, to give further opportunities than at present existed to the non-official and native element in Indian society to take part in the work of government, and in that way to lend official recognition to that remarkable development both in political interest and capacity which had been visible among the higher classes of Indian society since the government was taken over by the Crown in 1858'. It is interesting in this context to quote observations of Gladstone, as leader of the opposition, on this Bill, 'In an Asiatic country like India, with its ancient civilization, with its institutions so peculiar, with such a diversity of races, religions and pursuits, with such an enormous extent of country, and such a multitude of human beings as probably, except in the case of China, were never before under a single Government, I can understand that there should be difficulties in carrying what we desire to see accomplished; but great as the difficulties are, the task is a noble task, and will require the utmost prudence and care in conducting it to a successful termination. But after the assurance we have had from persons of the highest capacity, and the greatest responsibility, I believe we are justified in looking forward, not merely to a nominal, but to a real living representation of the people of India'; quoted in Anil Chandra Banerjee, ed., *Indian Constitutional Documents, 1757–1939*, Vol. II, 1858–1917, Second Edition, Calcutta: A. Mukherjee, 1948, pp. 110 and 124.

3 Stanley A. Wolpert, *Morley and India: 1906–1910*, Berkeley, CA: University of California Press, 1967, pp. 132–133 and 144–149 and see also Stanley A. Wolpert, *Tilak and Gokhale: Revolution and Reform in the Making of Modern India*, California: University of California Press, 1962, pp. 184–189; B.R. Nanda, *Gokhale: The Indian Moderates and the British Raj*, New Delhi: Oxford University Press, 1977, pp. 320–353; Dietmar Rothermund, Constitutional Reforms Versus National Agitation in India, 1900–1950, *The Journal of Asian Studies*, Vol. XXI, No.4 (August 1962), pp. 505–522.

4 Wolpert, *Morley and India*, p. 148.

5 It consisted of Sir A.T. Arundel, chairman; Sir D. Ibbetson, E.N. Baker, Erle Richards, members; and H.H. Risley, as secretary of the Committee. Syed Razi Wasti, *Lord Minto and the Indian Nationalist Movement 1905 to 1910*, Oxford: Clarendon Press, 1964, p. 133.

6 Herbert Risley, *ICS, Secretary to the Government of India's Home Department, was earlier Director of the Ethnological Survey, Government of India, and the author' of, The People of India*, New Delhi: Oriental Books Reprint Corporation, Second Edition, 1969, p. 291. See also Ravinder Kumar, *Essays in the Social History of Modern India*, Bombay: Oxford University Press, 1983, pp. 47–67 and Dietmar Rothermund, Emancipation Or Re-Integration: The Politics of Gopal Krishna Gokhale and Herbert Risley in D.A. Low, ed., *Soundings in Modern South Asian History*, London: Weindenfeld & Nicolson, 1968, pp. 131–157.

7 Risley, *The People of India*, p. 286.

8 Ibid., p. 286.

9 Ibid., p. 293.

10 Indian Statutory Commission, *Report of the Indian Statutory Commission*, Vol. I–Survey Calcutta: Government of India Central Publication Branch, 1930, p. 184; M.N. Das, *India Under Morley and Minto: Politics*

Behind Revolution, Repression and Reforms, London: George Allen and Unwin Ltd, 1964, pp. 46–61 and pp. 228–249 and see also Countess Mary Minto, *India Minto and Morley, 1905–1910*, First Edition. London: The Macmillan Press Ltd, 1934, Reprinted 1935, pp. 45–48 and pp. 110–111.
11 Iyengar, *The Indian Constitution, Appendix*, pp. lxxxiv–lxxxv.
12 Ibid., pp. cxvi–cxix.
13 Secretary of State to GI (November 27, 1908), [Cd. 4426], Vol. LXXVI, pt. I, p. 52 quoted in J.H. Broomfield, *Elite Conflict in a Plural Society: Twentieth Century Bengal*, Berkeley, CA: University of California Press, 1968, p. 76.
14 The 1911 arrangements took careful account of Bengal's special needs, and Crewe, in his letter to Carmichael of January 15, 1912, emphasized the importance of encouraging the separate development of the province. The new Legislative Council regulations of 1912 provided another opportunity to make local adjustments, and it was one of Carmichael's basic tenets that Bengal was not to be treated like the rest of India. GB, Political, A 45–62 (March 1913), quoted in Broomfield, *Elite Conflict in a Plural Society*, 1968, p. 76. See also Mary Carmichael, *Lord Carmichael of Skirling: A Memoir Prepared by His Wife*, London: Hodder and Stoughton, 1929.
15 It is interesting, in this context, to point out that the definition of corrupt practices in the Regulations was taken from the Bombay District Municipalities Act. Quoted in Iyengar, *The Indian Constitution*, pp. cxix–cxxiii, and p. clviii.
16 Ibid., pp. cxxi–cxxviii.
17 Wolpert, *Morley and India*, p. 165.
18 J.H. Broomfield, The Vote and the Transfer of Power: A Study of the Bengal General Election, 1912–1913, *Journal of Asian Studies*, Vol. XXI, No. 2 (February 1962), pp. 163–181.
19 Broomfield, *Elite Conflict in a Plural Society*, p. 55. See also Sir Surendranath Banerjea, *A Nation in Making: Being the Reminiscences of Fifty Years of Public Life*, Calcutta: Oxford University Press, 1925, Reset and Reprinted 1963, p. 271.
20 Ibid., pp. 57–58.
21 Ibid.
22 Ibid., p. 60.
23 . Broomfield, The Vote and the Transfer of Power, p. 166.
24 Ibid., p. 169.
25 Ibid., p. 177.
26 Government of Bengal, Appointment Department proceedings. File I8L-3. $B_{427-33.}$ July 1914. (Subsequent references to proceedings of this department give only the file number and date.) Quoted in Broomfield, The Vote and the Transfer of Power, p. 164. Sir Surendranath Banerjea mentioned the following about Abdul Rasool: 'Mr. Rasool was a Bengalee Mohamedan and came from the district of Comilla in East Bengal. He was a graduate of Oxford University and was a member of the Calcutta High Court Bar. He was one of the very few Mohamedans who opposed the Partition of Bengal, after it had become an accomplished and a settled fact. He was always an unflinching advocate of the union between Hindus and Mohamedans for political purposes, and he regarded the Partition

as a national calamity, in the sense that it would alienate Hindus and Mohamedans, interfere with the solidarity of the Bengalee-speaking population, and weaken their political influence'. In Sir Surendranath Banerjea, *A Nation in Making: Being the Reminiscences of Fifty Years of Public Life*, Bombay: Oxford University Press, First Published 1925, Reset and Reprinted 1963, pp. 214–215.

27 Report of the 31st *Indian National Congress*, 1916, *All- India Congress Committee*, pp. 77–81 quoted in B.N. Pandey, ed., *The Indian Nationalist Movement, 1885–1947: Select Documents*, London: The Macmillan Press Ltd, 1979, pp. 20–22.

28 *Report on Indian Constitutional Reforms*, Calcutta: Superintendent Government Printing India, 1918, pp. 58–61 and Banerjea, *A Nation in Making*, pp. 60–61.

29 For the politics of Montague speech, see S.R. Mehrotra, The Politics Behind the Montague Declaration of 1917 in C.H. Philips, ed., *Politics and Society in India*, London: George Allen & Unwin Ltd, 1963, pp. 71–96. For setting up of the Franchise Committee and the Functions Committee, see *Report on Indian Constitutional Reforms*, pp. 146–147 and 153–155. The Franchise Committee consisted of the following: Lord Southborough (Chairman), Sir Frank Sly (Vice-Chairman), Sir Malcolm Hailey, Sir Malcom Hogg, Rt. Hon. Srinivas Shastri, Aftab Mohamed and S.N. Banerjea; see Banerjea, *A Nation in Making*, for insightful details into the inner working of the Franchise Committee, pp. 292–297. The Committee on the Division of Functions consisted of H. Feetham (Chairman), H.F.W. Gillman, Khan Bahadur Maulvi, Rahim Baksh, Dr. Tej Bahadur Sapru, Chimanlal Harilal Setalvad, H.L. Stephenson and J.P. Thompson. See R.R Sethi and Vidya Dhar Mahajan, *Constitutional History of India*, Third Edition, New Delhi: S. Chand & Co., 1956, p. 103.

30 *Report of the Indian Statutory Commission*, Vol.2, p. 88.

31 P.D. Reeves, B.D. Graham and J.M. Goodman, *A Handbook To Elections In Uttar Pradesh 1920–1951*, New Delhi: Manohar Book Service, 1975, pp. xiii–xxix.

32 *Report on Indian Constitutional Reforms*, p. 147 and see also *Report of the Indian Statutory Commission*, Vol.1, pp. 134–142 and pp. 190–202.

33 W.A.J. Archbold, *Outlines of Indian Constitutional History [British Period]*. London: Curzon Press, First published 1926 and New impression 1973, p. 187. See also *Report of the Statutory Commission*, Vol.2, p. 88.

34 Electoral Rules, Parts IV, VI, and VII; vide The Gazette of India (Extra) (July 30, 1923), quoted in Debendra Nath Banerjee, *The Indian Constitution and Its Actual Working*, Bombay: Orient Longmans Limited, Green & Co., 1926, pp. 107–114.

35 For details regarding the separation of the Liberals from the Congress, see C.Y. Chintamani, *Indian Politics since the Mutiny: Being an Account of the Development of Public Life and Political Institutions and of Prominent Political Personalities*, Waltair: Andhra University, 1937, pp. 99–111 and Banerjea, *A Nation in Making*, pp. 281–297.

36 Report of the Proceedings of the Second Session of the All-India Conference of the Moderate Party, pp. 115–116 quoted in Pandey, ed., *The Indian Nationalist Movement, 1885–1947*, pp. 89–90.

37 Indian Annual Register, 1921, pp. 206–207 quoted in. Pandey, ed., *The Indian Nationalist Movement, 1885–1947*, pp. 89–90.

38 As ministers and legislators, both at the Centre and Provinces from 1920 to 1937, the work carried by the Liberal Party have been 'considerable and creditable'. This work was undertaken in the area of education, local self-government, prohibition, industries, etc. Report on the Working of the Reformed Constitution (1923) and (1926), p. 143 and 87, respectively, quoted in B.D. Shukla, *A History of the Indian Liberal Party*, Allahabad: The Indian Press, 1960, pp. 217–242. See Banerjea, *A Nation in Making*, pp. 319–363; Reginald Craddock, *The Dilemma in India*, London: Constable & Co. Ltd, 1929, pp. 199–216 and R. Coupland, *The Constitutional Problem in India Part I: The Indian Problem, 1833–1935*. London: Oxford University Press, 1943, p. 20 and see also, *The Earl of Lyton, Governor of Bengal, 1922–27, Pundits and Elephants: Being the Experiences of Five Years as Governor of an Indian Province*, London: Peter Davies, 1942, pp. 40–65.

39 P. Sitaramayya, *The History of the Indian National Congress 1885–1935*, Vol. I, Bombay: Padma Publications Ltd, 1946 [1935] pp. 202–203.

40 The Congress Democratic Party did not contest the election as Tilak died on August1, 1920. On Tilak's approach to the Montague Chelmsford Reforms, the formation of the Congress Democratic Party and its manifesto, see D. V. Tahmankar, *Lokamanya Tilak: Father of Indian Unrest and Maker of Modern India*, London: John Murray, 1956, pp. 252–258 and 294–305.

41 In the context of Tilak's manifesto, the following two aspects are necessary to keep in mind: it is of significance to highlight that during, his stay in England (September 1918–October 1919), Tilak worked to enlighten the British people about Indian affairs. For this purpose, he established contacts with Labour leaders and their organizations to influence the public opinion on the matters of India. He issued and distributed many pamphlets to make the people aware about the problems of India. Two of the most significant pamphlets dealt with the question of the self-determination of India and Indian Constitutional Reforms. As a matter of fact, Tilak's manifesto by and large contained most of the conclusions drawn from these pamphlets. Besides, he gave many speeches as well as evidence before the Joint Parliamentary Committee (set up to consider the Government of India Bill). See G.P. Pradhan and A.K. Bhagwat, *Lokamanya Tilak: A Biography*, Bombay: Jaico Publishing House, 1958, pp. 320–330. See also Pattabhi Sitaramayya, *The History of the Indian National Congress*, Vol. I, Bombay: Padma Publications Ltd, 1947, pp. 194–196 and see also Theodore L. Shay, *The Legacy of the Lokamanya- The Political Philosophy of Bal Gangadhar Tilak*, Bombay: Oxford University Press, 1956, pp. 161–162.

42 While dealing with the evolution of manifesto in the electoral politics in the Introductory Chapter of this study, it was mentioned that the British Labour Party, since the 1920s, started using it as a document to bring orderly social change. Tilak's manifesto in this sense of the term can certainly be called the first document of this kind in the Indian context. Another important aspect relates to the sympathy of the British Labour Party with India's freedom. It is important to mention that the Labour

Party Manifesto, during general elections of 1918, mentioned for India the 'right of self-determination within the British Commonwealth of Free Nations'. F.W.S. Craig, compiled and edited, *British General Election Manifestos 1900–1974*, Revised Edition, London: The Macmillan Press Ltd, 1975, pp. 31–32. Besides, the following observation on Tilak by Ramsay MacDonald is of great significance 'Believe me when I say that Mr. Tilak (who is fortunately with us tonight) is the very embodiment of all the grievances and hardships under which the people of India are suffering and the very embodiment of the spirit of resistance which is manifest in India today. He has personally come here to request you to support and help the Indian people's struggle for political independence. I assure him on your behalf that the Independent Labour Party will give him and his people the support and help he is asking for. We Socialists do not believe in the narrow concept of nationalism. Our ideal is the brotherhood of man. We will work always for the establishment of democratic institutions based on justice and peoples' will, everywhere in the world' See Tahmankar, *Lokamanya Tilak*, p. 282.

43 For a detailed narration of the events after Ahmedabad conference to the Report of the Civil Disobedience Movement (December 1921–October 1922), see K.M. Panikkar and A. Pershad, eds., *The Voice of Freedom: Selected Speeches of Pandit Motilal Nehru*, Bombay: Asia Publishing House, 1961, pp. 505–513. The Civil Disobedience Inquiry Committee consisted of Hakim Ajmal Khan, Motilal Nehru, C. Rajagopalachari, Dr. M.A. Ansari, Vithalbhai Patel and Kasturiranga Aiyengar. See M.R. Jayakar, *The Story of My Life*, Vol.1, 1873–1922, Bombay: Asia Publishing House, 1958, pp. 504–614; and, for the formation of the Swaraj Party, see M.R. Jayakar, *The Story of My Life*, Vol.2, 1922–1925, Bombay: Asia Publishing House, 1959, pp. 71–181.

44 Panikkar, Pershad, eds., *The Voice of Freedom*, pp. 505–513, It is important to emphasize that M.R. Jayakar made an important contribution in the preparation of the manifesto of the Swaraj Party. This is evident from a letter which he wrote to C.R. Das on January 6, 1923 stressing that the 'destructive aspect of our agitation should not be given unnecessarily prominent place in our programme. . . . Let us put our programme on a stable, sane, constructive and permanent basis of amelioration, giving a subordinate place, if at all, to the possibilities of destruction, which after all may not arise. . . . Our strength, in such a contest, will mainly lie in our programme of work of permanent value to the country, in the soundness of which we believe and which affords sufficient flexibility to the worker and adequate hope of amelioration to the voter'. See M.R. Jayakar, *The Story of My Life*, Vol.2, 1922–1925, Bombay: Asia Publishing House, 1959, pp. 73–76.

45 A. Pershad and Promilla Suri Motilal Nehru, *A Short Political Biography*, New Delhi: S. Chand & Co., 1961, p. 42.

46 Gwyer and Appadorai, *Speeches and Documents on Indian Constitution 1921–47*, Vol. I, pp. 4–5.

47 *The Indian Annual Register*, Vol. II, 1926, pp. 37–39 quoted in Sir Maurice Gwyer and A. Appadorai, *Speeches and Documents on the Indian Constitution 1921–47*, Vol. I, Bombay: Oxford University Press, 1957, pp. 6–8.

48 Ibid., pp. 5–6.
49 Eugene Irschick, *Politics and Social Conflicts in South India*, Berkeley, CA: University of California Press, 1969, p. 70.
50 Ibid., pp. 358–367.
51 Raghuvendra Tanwar, *Politics of Sharing Power: The Punjab Unionist Party 1923–1947*, New Delhi: Manohar Book Service, 1999, pp. 46–47.
52 I.A. Talbot, Deserted Collaborators: The Political Background to the Rise and Fall of the Punjab Unionist Party, 1923–1947, *The Journal of Imperial and Commonwealth History*, Vol. XI, No. 1 (1982), p. 78. See also Tanwar, *Politics of Sharing Power*, pp. 46–47.
53 *Report of the Reforms Enquiry Committee*, p. 3.
54 Government of India, India in 1921–1922, Comp., L.F. R. Williams (Calcutta: Central Bureau of Information, Government of India, 1923), p. 221 quoted in Robert Hardgrave, *The Dravidian Movement*, Bombay: Popular Prakashan, 1965, p. 20.
55 Irschick, *Politics and Social Conflicts in South India*, p. 178.
56 Ibid., p. 264.
57 Tanwar, *Politics of Sharing Power*, pp. 42–43.
58 Ibid., pp. 46–48.
59 Satya M. Rai, *Legislative Politics and the Freedom Struggle in the Panjab 1897–1947*, New Delhi: Indian Council of Historical Research, 1984, p. 145.
60 Tanwar, *Politics of Sharing Power*, p. 65.
61 Sir Firoz Khan Noon, *From Memory*, Lahore: Ferozsons, 1966 p. 113, quoted in Tanwar, *The Politics of Sharing Power*, p. 71.
62 Misra, *The Indian Political Parties*, New Delhi: Oxford University Press, 1976, p. 242.
63 *Report of the Reforms Enquiry Committee*, 1924, p. 4.
64 *Times of India*(October 25, 1923), p. 10 quoted in Rani Dhavan Shankardass, *The First Congress Raj: Provincial Autonomy in Bombay*, New Delhi: Macmillan India Limited, 1982, p. 49.
65 Misra, *The Indian Political Parties*, p. 236.
66 Ibid., p. 237.
67 Shankardass, *The First Congress Raj*, p. 22. See also *Report of the Indian Statutory Commission*, Vol. I–Survey, pp. 258–261 and Pattabhi Sitaramayya, *The History of the Indian National Congress*, Vol. I, Bombay: Padma Publications Ltd, 1947, pp. 299–301.
68 *Report of the Reforms Enquiry Committee*, 1924, p. 7.
69 Ibid., p. 8.
70 Ibid., p. 12 See also Misra, *The Indian Political Parties*, pp. 247–249.
71 The Reforms Enquiry Committee, 1924, consisted of the following: Sir Alexander Muddiman (Chairman), Members: Dr. Mian Sir Muhammad Shafi, Sir Bijay Chand Mahtab, Sir Tej Bahadur Sapru, Air Arthur Froom, Sir Sivaswami Iyer, Sir Henry Moncrieff Smith, Mr. M.A. Jinnah, Dr. R.P. Paranjype. The Majority Report was signed by the following: A.P. Muddiman, M. D. Shafi, B.C. Mahtab of Burdwan, A.H. Froom and H. Moncrieff- Smith and H. Tonkinson see *Report of the Reforms Enquiry Committee*, 1924, pp. 25–42 and 46–52.
72 The Minority Report of the Reforms Enquiry Committee was signed by the following: Tej Bahadur Sapru, P.S. Sivaswamy Aiyer, M.A. Jinnah and

R.P. Paranjype). See *Report of the Reforms Enquiry Committee*, 1924, pp. 25–42 and pp. 46–52.

73 *Report of the Reforms Enquiry Committee*, 1924, pp. 25–42 and 46–52; *Report of the Indian Statutory Commission*, 1930, Vol. I, pp. 203–219; A. Appadorai, *Dyarchy in Practice*, London: Longmans, 1937, pp. 204–257; Kerala Putra, *The Working of Dyarchy in India*, Bombay: D.B. Taraporevala Sons & Co., 1928, pp. 44–60; P.N. Masaldan, *Evolution of Provincial Autonomy in India*, Bombay: Hind Kitabs Ltd, 1953, pp. 74–101. Arthur Berriedale Keith, *A Constitutional History of India1600–1935*, Allahabad: Central Book Depot, First Published, 1936, Reprint 1961, pp. 247–273; R. Coupland, *The Constitutional Problem in India*, pp. 54–79.

74 Ibid., p. 108.

75 See note 52.

76 Ibid., p. 176.

77 Ibid., p. 189.

78 *Report of the Indian Statutory Commission*, p. 191.

79 Ibid., p. 197. See also Gwyer and Appadorai *Speeches and Documents on the Indian Constitution 1921–47*, p. 142.

80 *Report of the Reforms Enquiry Committee*, p. 151.

81 *Report of the Statutory Commission*, p. 209.

82 Sifton, *Report on the General Elections* of 1923 (Bihar and Orissa), p. 11, para.53 quoted in Misra, *The Indian Political Parties*, p. 247. See also, Coupland, *The Constitutional Problem in India*, pp. 66–79.

83 H.F. Horsfield, *Report on the General Elections* of 1930 (Bihar and Orissa), p. 4, para. 14. Also Views of the Local Governments on the Working of the Reforms (1927), p. 428, para. 25(c), quoted in Misra, *The Indian Political Parties*, p. 247.

84 *Report on Indian Constitutional Reforms*, p. 146.

85 *Report of the Indian Statutory Commission*, p. 49.

86 *Report on Indian Constitutional Reforms*, p. 57.

87 *Report of the Reforms Enquiry Committee*, p. 107.

88 *Report of the Indian Statutory Commission*, p. 49.

89 Ibid., p. 49.

90 Quoted from S. Muthulakshmi Reddi, Papers: Speeches and Writings, Vol. II, part 2 in Katherine Mayo, Mother India, edited and with an Introduction by Mrinalini Sinha, Ann Arbor: The University of Michigan Press, 2000, p. 276.

91 Kerala Putra, *The Working of Dyarchy in India*, Bombay: D. B. Taraporevala Sons & Co., 1928, pp. 115–116.

92 *Report of the Indian Statutory Commission*, p. 132.

93 *Report of the Indian Statutory Commission*, p. 226 and for details regard ing the role of V.J. Patel as President of the Legislative Assembly; see Subhash C. Kashyap, *Parliamentary Procedure: The Law, Privileges, Practice and Precedents*, Vol. I, New Delhi: Universal Law Publishing Co. Pvt. Ltd, pp. 41 50. See G.S. Dhillon, The Contribution of Shri Vithalbhai Patel to the Office of the Speaker in R.K. Nayak, *Executive Editor, Vithalbhai Patel: Patriot and President*, New Delhi: National Forum of Lawyers and Legal Aid, 1976, pp. 278–289.

94 Manoranjan Jha, *Role of Central Legislature in the Freedom Struggle*, New Delhi: National Book Trust, 1972, p. 309.

95 A large part of the following monographs deal with the debate and discussion on legislation carried out in the provincial councils before independence: Satya M. Rai Legislative, *Politics and the Freedom Struggle in the Punjab 1897–1947*, New Delhi: Indian Council of Historical Research, 1984; Amalendu Guha, *Planter Raj to Swaraj Freedom Struggle and Electoral Politics in Assam, 1826–1947*, New Delhi: Indian Council of Historical Research, 1977; S. Krishnaswamy, *The Role of Madras Legislature in the Freedom Struggle 1861–1947*, New Delhi: Indian Council of Historical Research, 1989; K.M. Patra, *Orissa State Legislature and Freedom Struggle 1912–47*, New Delhi: Indian Council of Historical Research, 1979; Amit Kumar Gupta, *North- West Frontier Province legislature and Freedom Struggle 1932–47*, New Delhi: Indian Council of Historical Research, 1976; see also Shukla, *History of the Indian Liberal Party*; Banerjea, *A Nation in Making*, Christopher John Baker, *The Politics of South India 1920–1937*, New Delhi: Vikas Publishing House Pvt. Ltd, 1976.

96 Banerjea, *A Nation in Making*, pp. 333–340.

97 Appadorai, *Dyarchy in Practice*, p. 72.

98 Report of the Indian Statutory Commission, p. 219. The Central Legislative Assemblies (1921–1947) produced some very distinguished parliamentarians: Motilal Nehru, Madan Mohan Malaviya, S. Satyamurthi, Mohammad Ali Jinnah, Lala Lajpat Rai, T. Rangachariar, Dr. H.S. Gour, G.V. Mavalankar, Vithalbhai Patel, Sir A. Rahim, Bhulabhai Desai, Govind Ballabh Pant, M.S. Aney, Liaquat Ali Khan, B.C. Pal, N.M. Joshi, Dewan Chaman Lal, Jamnadas Mehta, Sir Sivaswamy Aiyar, Rafi Ahmad Kidwai, K.C. Neogy, Shanmukham Chetty, M.R. Jayakar, N.C. Nelkar, Fazrul Haq. See Subhash C. Kashyap, History of the Parliament of India, Vol. I, C. P. R. Shipra, New Delhi, 1994, Chapter6, quoted in Kashyap, *Parliamentary Procedure*, pp. 25–26.

99 Ibid., p. 38.

100 *The Nehru Report: An Anti- Separatist Manifesto*, New Delhi: Michiko & Panjathan, 1928, Reprinted 1975, pp. 202–203 and see also Reginald Craddock, *The Dilemma in India*, London: Constable & Co. Ltd, 1929, pp. 229–236.

101 Pandey, *The Indian Nationalist Movement, 1885–1947*, pp. 82–83.

102 *Report of the Indian Statutory Commission*, Vol.2, Recommendations, p. 311.

103 Ibid., pp. 311–313.

104 Ibid., p. 56.

105 Sitaramayya, *The History of the Indian Congress*, p. 532 and see also H.H. Dodwell, *The Cambridge History of India*, Vol. VI, The Indian Empire, Cambridge: Cambridge University Press, 1932.

106 Ibid., p. 534.

107 Ibid., p. 553.

108 J.P. Eddy and F.H. Lawton, *India's New Constitution: A Survey of the Government of India Act 1935*, London: The Macmillan Press Ltd, 1935, p. 81. See also Indian Franchise Committee, *Report of the Indian Franchise Committee*, Vol. I, Second Edition, Calcutta: Government of India, Central Publication Branch, 1932, pp. 7–35.

109 N. Rajagopala Aiyangar, *The Government of India Act*, 1935: with a commentary, critical and explanatory, Madras: The Madras Law Journal Office, 1937, pp. 368–407.
110 Ibid., p. 300.
111 S.R. Mehrotra, The Congress and the Partition of India in C.H. Philips and Mary Doreen Wainwright, eds., *The Partition of India: Policies and Perspectives 1935–1947*, London: George Allen and Unwin Ltd, 1970, pp. 188–221.
112 Reeves, Graham and Goodman, *A Handbook to Elections in Uttar Pradesh 1920–1951*, p. xx.
113 A.M. Zaidi, *INC: The Glorious Tradition*, Vol.3, 1928–1938. Texts of the resolutions passed by the INC, the AICC and the CWC, New Delhi: Indian Institute of Applied Political Research, 1987, p. 323.
114 Zaidi, *Congress Presidential Addresses*, p. 440.
115 Dr. Bhagvan Das (January 1869–September 1958), Freedom Fighter, Congress leader, Philosopher and Member of Central Legislative Assembly, Awarded Bharat Ratna in 1955. Bhagavan Das, *The Philosophy of Non-Cooperation and of Spiritual- Political Swaraj*, Madras: Tagore & Co., 1922, p. vi.
116 Jawaharlal Nehru, *Eighteen Months in India 1936–1937: Being Further Essays and Writings*, Allahabad: Kitabistan, 1938, p. 38.
117 Jawaharlal Nehru, *An Autobiography, Jawaharlal Nehru Memorial Fund*, Oxford University Press, First Published 1936, Fifteenth Impression 2002, pp. 293–294.
118 Nehru, *Eighteen Months in India 1936–1937*, p. 38.
119 'Political Addresses and Statements'. Some of the important addresses during 1928 are the following: Presidential Address at the Kerala Provincial Conference, May27, 1928, pp. 234–240; The Landholders and Socialism (July19, 1928), pp. 246–248. On the Zamindari Question (August26, 1928), p. 249 and Presidential Address at the U.P. Provincial Conference (October27, 1928), pp. 255–262 in S. Gopal, ed., *Selected Works of Jawaharlal Nehru*, Vol.3, New Delhi: Michiko Memorial Fund, Orient Longman Limited, 1972, pp. 217–268.
120 Ibid., p. 14 and p. 18 (fn2).
121 This was the second letter of Jawaharlal Nehru to Mahatma Gandhi dated 11–01–1928, 'The first letter is not available' in Gopal, ed., *Selected Works of Jawaharlal Nehru*, Vol.3, pp. 14–15.
122 The text of this letter dated (January 17, 1928) is in D.G. Tendulkar, *Mahatma. Life of Mohandas Karamchand Gandhi*, Vol.8, Bombay: Vithalbhai K. Jhaveri, 1947–1948, p. 351.
123 A.M. Zaidi, *A Trust with Destiny: A Study of Economic Policy Resolutions on INC Passed During the Last 100 Years*, New Delhi: Publication Department, Indian Institute of Applied Political Research, 1985, p. 54.
124 The Motilal Nehru Committee Report in 1928 for the first time recommended the following fundamental rights: right of free expression, freedom of conscience, equality before the law, no state religion, freedom of association, equal rights for men and women, living wage for every worker, right to free elementary education. *The Nehru Report: An Anti-Separatist Manifesto, The Committee appointed by the All Parties*

Conference 1928, New Delhi: Michiko & Panjathan, Reprinted 1975, pp. 100–124. This committee consisted of the following: Motilal Nehru (Chairman), Members: Tej Bahadur Supru, S. Ali Iman, Madan Mohan Malaviya, Annie Besant, M.A. Ansari, M.R. Jayakar, Abul Kalam Azad, Mangal Singh, M.S. Aney, Subhas Chandra Bose, Vijiaraghavachaiar and Abdul Kadir Kasuri.

125 In Sitaramayya, *The History of the Indian National Congress*, Vol. 1 (1855–1935), p. 366.

126 Nehru, *An Autobiography*, p. 268.

127 Jawaharlal Nehru, *The Unity of India: Collected Writings, 1937–1940*, London: Drummond, 1942, pp. 406–408.

128 The text of the Gandhi-Nehru correspondence in September 1933 is in The Collected Works of Mahatma Gandhi, Vol. LV (April 23–September 15, 1933), *The Publications Division: Ministry of Information and Broadcasting, Government of India*, 1973, Appendix XIV, p. 457.

129 The text of the Gandhi-Nehru correspondence letter (September 13, 1933) is in D.G. Tendulkar, *Mahatma: Life of Mohandas Karamch and Gandhi*, Vol.3, 1930–1934, Bombay: Vithalbhai K. Javeri and G. Tendulkar, 1952, p. 375.

130 Ibid., p. 113.

131 Nehru, *An Autobiography*, p. 266.

132 Jawaharlal Nehru, *India and the World: Essays*, London: George Allen & Unwin Ltd, 1936, p. 40.

133 Ibid., p. 41.

134 Ibid., p. 53.

135 Ibid., p. 58.

136 Ibid., p. 62. See also Michael Brecher, *Nehru: A Political Biography*, London: Oxford University Press, 1959, pp. 195–196.

137 'Some Criticisms Considered' relating to 'Whither India', in Jawaharlal Nehru, *Recent Essays and Writings: On the Future of India, Communalism and Other Subjects*, Allahabad: Kitabistan, Second Impression, 1934, pp. 34–35.

138 Brecher, *Nehru: A Political Biography*, p. 196. See also Dietmar Rothermund, Nehru and Early Indian Socialism in S.N. Mukherjee, ed., *South Asian Affairs, Number Two: The Movement for National Freedom in India, St. Antony's Papers – Number 18*, London: Oxford University Press, 1966, pp. 106–107. This article is important as it is based on Dietmar Rothermund's interview with Nehru in 1962 and discussions with E.M.S. Namboodiripad, Jayaprakash Narayan, Achut Patwardhan, M.R. Masani, Y.B. Chavan, and many others. Besides, it also elaborates on Swami Vivekandanda's influence on Nehru.

139 Some of the prominent national leaders who joined the party under the Presidentship of Sampurnananda were Jayaprakash Narayan, M.R. Masani, Mohanlal Gautam, N.G. Gore, E.M.S. Namboodripad, Narendra Dev, Kamaladevi Chattopadhyaya, Rammanohar Lohia and S.M. Joshi. Indian Annual Register, 1934, Vol. II, pp. 295–296 quoted in B.N. Pandey, ed., *A Centenary History of the Indian National Congress*, Vol.3 (1935–1947) *Jointly Published by All India Congress Committee*, New Delhi: Vikas Publishing House Pvt Ltd, 1985, pp. 226–227.

140 Pandey, ed., A Centenary History of the Indian National Congress, Vol. 3 (1935–1947), pp. 228–229.
141 Observations on M.R. Masani's, *Socialistic Programme*, May 29, 1934 is in *The Collected Works of Mahatma Gandhi*, Vol. LVIII (May 18–September 15, 1934), New Delhi: The Publications Division, Ministry of Information & Broadcasting, Government of India, 1974, pp. 36–37.
142 Discussion with Students (July 21, 1934), *The Collected Works of Mahatma Gandhi*, Vol. LVIII (May 18–September 15, 1934), p. 219.
143 Answers to Zamindars (July 25, 1934) is in ibid., p. 247.
144 Ibid., p. 248.
145 Discussion with Socialists Deputation (July 27, 1934) is in *The Collected Works of Mahatma Gandhi*, Vol. LVIII (May 18–September 15, 1934), p. 254.
146 The text of this letter dated (August 2, 1934) is in *The Collected Works of Mahatma Gandhi*, Vol. LVIII (May 18–September 15, 1934), pp. 274–276.
147 Congress Working Committee Wardha (June 12 and 13, 1934) in A.M. Zaidi, *INC: The Glorious Tradition*, Vol.3, Texts of the resolutions passed by the INC, the AICC and the CWC, Vol.3, 1928–1938, New Delhi: Indian Institute of Applied Political Research, 1987, p. 263.
148 Ibid., pp. 258–259.
149 Ibid., pp. 267–268.
150 Ibid.
151 *The Collected Works of Mahatma Gandhi*, Vol. LVIII (May 18–September 15, 1934), p. 462.
152 The text of this letter dated (August 17, 1934) is in *The Collected Works of Mahatma Gandhi*, Vol. LVIII (May 18–September 15, 1934), p. 318 and VII.
153 The text of this letter, dated (September 5, 1934) is in *The Collected Works of Mahatma Gandhi*, Vol. LVIII (May 18–September 15, 1934), pp. 403–406.
154 The text of this letter (September17, 1934) is in *The Collected Works of Mahatma Gandhi*, Vol. LIX (September 16–December 15, 1934), pp. 3–12.
155 The text of this speech dated May 19, 1934 in *The Collected Works of Mahatma Gandhi*, Vol. LVIII (May 18–September 15, 1934), p. 11.
156 Zaidi, *Congress Presidential Addresses*, p. 418.
157 The text of this letter dated (December 19, 1935) is in Jawaharlal Nehru, *A Bunch of Old Letters*, Bombay: Asia Publishing House, 1958, p. 136.
158 A.M. Zaidi, *INC: The Glorious Tradition*, Vol.3, p. 272. The Working Committee consisted of the following members: Sardar Vallabhbhai Patel, Dr. M.A. Ansari, Maulana Abul Kalam Azad, Mrs. Sarojini Naidu, Seth Jamnalal Bajaj, Syt. C. Rajagopalachariar, Khan Abdul Ghaffar Khan, Sardar Sardul Singh Caveeshar, Dr. Pattabhi Sitaramayya, Syt. Gangadharrao Deshpande, Syt. Jairamdas Doulatram, Pandit Jawaharlal Nehru, Dr. Syed Mahmud, Syt. J.B. Kripalani.
159 S. Gopal, ed., *Selected Works of Jawaharlal Nehru*, Vol.7, *A Project of the Jawaharlal Nehru Memorial Fund*, New Delhi: Orient Longman Limited, 1975, p. 168.

160 On Acceptance of Office – Speech at the subjects committee meeting, Lucknow (April 11, 1936), From *The Hindustan Times*(April 11, 1936) in Gopal, ed., *Selected Works of Jawaharlal Nehru*, Vol. 7, p. 169 and see also Nehru, *The Unity of India 1936–39*, p. 98.
161 The Presidential Address – Lucknow (April 12, 1936). *The Bombay Chronicle* (April 13, 1936) in Gopal, ed., *Selected Works of Jawaharlal Nehru*, Vol.7, pp. 170–195.
162 Nehru, *The Unity of India*, pp. 408–409.
163 Nehru, *A Bunch of Old Letters*, pp. 175–176.
164 From Rafi Ahmad Kidwai (April 20, 1936), found in *A Bunch of Letters*, pp. 174–175. The President selected the following fourteen members for the Working Committee on April 16, 1936: J.B. Kriplani (General Secretary), Jamnalai Bajaj (Treasurer), Maulana Abul Kalam Azad, Rajendra Prasad, Vallabhbhai J, Patel, Khan Abdul Ghaffar Khan, C. Rajagopalachari Subhash Chandra Bose, Narendra Dev, Jairamdas Daulatram, S.D. Deo, Jaya Prakash Narayan, Bhulabhai Desai and Achyut Patwardhan. In Zaidi, Vol.3, p. 345.
165 From Rajendra Prasad and Others (June 29, 1936) in Nehru, *A Bunch of Old Letters*, p. 185.
166 Ibid., p. 182.
167 Ibid, p. 185.
168 Ibid.
169 From Rajendra Prasad to Nehru (July 1, 1936), in Nehru, *A Bunch of Old Letters*, pp. 185–186.
170 Ibid., p. 186.
171 Ibid.
172 Ibid., pp. 186–187.
173 Nehru to Mahatma Gandhi (July 5, 1936) is in Nehru, *A Bunch of Old Letters*, pp. 188–189.
174 Ibid., p. 190.
175 From Mahatma Gandhi to Nehru (July 8, 1936) is in Nehru, *A Bunch of Old Letters*, p. 192.
176 Nehru, *The Unity of India*, p. 406.
177 Ibid., p. 102. See also Narendra Deva, *Favourite of Fortune in Nehru Abhinandan Granth, Presented to Nehru on his Sixtieth Birthday*, New Delhi: Nehru Abhinandan Granth Committee, 1949, p. 109.
178 Gopal, ed., *Selected works of Jawaharlal Nehru*, Vol. 7, p. 556.
179 Ibid., Vol. 8, 1976, p. 64.
180 K.K. Aziz (edited with notes) *Muslims Under Congress Rule 1937–1939: A Documentary Record*, Vol.1, New Delhi: Renaissance Publishing House, 1978, Reprint in India 1986, p. 39 and see also Z. H. Zaidi, Aspects of the Development of Muslim League Policy, 1937–47 in Philips, *The Partition of India*, pp. 245–275.
181 Ibid., p. 41.
182 Ibid., pp. 40–45.
183 Tanwar, *Politics of Sharing Power*, pp. 88–105.
184 The election manifesto was prepared mainly by Sir Chhotu Ram, ibid., p. 93.
185 Shile Sen, *Muslim Politics in Bengal 1937–1947*, New Delhi: Impex India, 1976, pp. 79–80.

186 P.D. Reeves, Landlords and Party Politics in the United Provinces, 1937–7 in Low, ed., *Soundings in Modern South Asian History*, London: Weidenfeld & Nicolson, 1968, pp. 292–293.
187 Proceedings of the meeting of the Board of the NAP, U.P., held on August 5, 1934, p. 3. U.P.Z. Assn. Printed in Landholders' *Journal*, Vol. II, No.12, Calcutta (July 1934), p. 852 quoted in P.D. Reeves, Landlords and Party Politics in the United Provinces, 1937–7 in Low, ed., *Soundings in Modern South Asian History*, pp. 292–293. See also Peter Reeves, Adjusting to Congress Dominance: The UP Landlords, 1937–1947 quoted in Richard Sisson and Stanley Wolpert, *Congress and Indian Nationalism: The Pre-Independence Phase*, New Delhi: Oxford University Press, 1988, pp. 159–181.
188 P.D. Reeves, Landlords and Party Politics in the United Provinces, 1937–7 in Low, ed., *Soundings in Modern South Asian History*, London: Weidenfeld & Nicolson, pp. 292–293.
189 Ibid., p. 396.
190 B.R. Tomlinson, *The Indian National Congress and the Raj, 1929–1942: The Penultimate Phase*, London: The Macmillan Press Ltd, 1976, pp. 52–91.
191 For derails see D.A, Low, Congress and 'Mass Contacts', 1936–1937: Ideology, Interests, and Conflicts over the basis of Party Representation in Sisson, Richard and Wolpert, Stanley, *Congress and Indian Nationalism*, pp. 134–158.
192 Bimal Prasad, Congress versus the Muslim League, 1935–1937. See also Mushirul Hasan, The Muslim Mass Contacts Campaign: Analysis of a Strategy of Political Mobilization, in Sisson and Wolpert, *Congress and Indian Nationalism*, pp. 305–329 and pp. 198–222.
193 Tomlinson, *The Indian National Congress and the Raj, 1929–1942*, p. 75.
194 Coupland, *The Constitutional Problem in India*, Part II, p. 308.
195 Ibid., p. 16 and p. 308.
196 Zaidi., *INC The Glorious Tradition 1929–1938*, Vol. 3, pp. 392–393.
197 B.R. Nanda, *Mahatma Gandhi: A Biography*, London: George Allen & Unwin Ltd, 1958, p. 388.
198 Ibid.
199 Ibid., p. 390.
200 M.K. Gandhi, *Gandhiji Expects*, pp. 42–43. See also Collected Works of Mahatma Gandhi, Vol. LXV (March 15–July 31, 1937), The Publications Division: Ministry of Information and Broadcasting Government of India, 1976, p. 407.
201 Coupland, *The Constitutional Problem in India*, Part II, pp. 1–157. See also Sitaramayya, *The History of the Indian National Congress*, Vol. II (1935–1947), 1947; Rani Dhavan Shankardass, *The First Congress Raj: Provincial Autonomy in Bombay*, New Delhi: Macmillan India Limited, 1982, pp. 257–267; Vinita Damodaran, *Broken Promises: Popular Protest, Indian Nationalism and the Congress Party in Bihar, 1935 1946*, New Delhi: Oxford University Press, 1992, pp. 370–375 and also Tomlinson, *The Indian National Congress and the Raj, 1929–1942*, pp. 113–136.
202 Zaidi, *INC: The Glorious Tradition*, Vol.3, 1928–1938, pp. 391–394.
203 Coupland, *The Constitutional Problem in India*, Part II, p. 138 and see also Kishori Mohan Patra, The First Congress Ministries: Problems and

Prospects (1937–1939) in B.N. Pandey, *General Editor A Centenary History of the Indian National Congress (1885–1985)*, New Delhi: Jointly Published by All India Congress Committee and Vikas Publishing House Pvt. Ltd, 1985, Vol.3, p. 157.

204 Ibid., pp. 147–217.

205 Nehru, *A Bunch of Old Letters*, pp. 276–277.

206 Shankardass, *The First Congress Raj: Provincial Autonomy in Bombay*, p. 262. See also Vinita Damodaran, *Broken Promises, Popular Protest, Indian Nationalism and the Congress Party in Bihar, 1935–41946*, New Delhi: Oxford University Press, 1992, pp. 370–372.

207 Coupland, *The Constitutional Problem in India*, Part II, pp. 37–40.

208 Ibid., pp. 53–55.

209 Ibid., p. 308.

210 Zaidi, *INC: The Glorious Tradition*, Vol. 4, 1939–1950, 1988, p. 66.

211 V.P. Menon, *The Transfer of Power in India*, Bombay: Sangam Books Ltd, 1957, pp. 66–67.

212 Ibid., p. 68.

213 Misra, *The Indian Political Parties*, p. 361.

214 Menon, *The Transfer of Power in India*, pp. 69–70 and see also Misra, *The Indian Political Parties*, pp. 353–362.

215 P. Hardy, *The Muslims of British India*, Cambridge: Cambridge University Press, 1972, p. 234.

216 Dodwell, ed., *The Cambridge History of India*, Vol. VI, The Indian Empire, 1858–1918, p. 668.

217 Zaidi, *INC: The Glorious Tradition*, Vol.4, 1939–1950, pp. 164–165.

218 Menon, *The Transfer of Power in India*, Appendix-II, pp. 459–461.

219 Ibid., p. 219.

220 Zaidi, *INC: The Glorious Tradition*, pp. 200–201.

221 The Committee consisted of the following members: Maulana Abul Kalam Azad, Sardar Vallabhbhai Patel, Dr. Rajendra Prasad, Pandit Govind Vallabh Pant. Asaf Ali, Dr. Pattabhi Sitaramayya and Shanker Rao Deo. In A.M. Zaidi, *INC: The Glorious Tradition: Texts of the Resolutions Passed by the INC, the AICC and the CWC*, Vol.4, 1939–1950, New Delhi: Indian Institute of Applied Political Research, 1988, p. 202.

222 *Collected Works of Mahatma Gandhi*, Vol. LXXXI, New Delhi: The Publications Division, *Ministry of Information and Broadcasting, Government of India*, pp. 319–320. See also Pyare Lal, *Mahatma Gandhi: The Last Phase*, Vol. II, Ahmedabad: Navajivan Publishing House, 1958, pp. 24–26. In the context of this letter, Mahatma Gandhi mentioned the following: 'I have long been intending to write to you but can do so only today. I have also been wondering whether I should write in English or Hindustani. In the end I have decided to write in Hindustani'.

223 Gopal, ed., *Selected Works of Jawaharlal Nehru*, Vol. 14, New Delhi: Jawaharlal Nehru Memorial Fund, Orient Longmans Limited, 1981, p. 554.

224 Collected Works of Mahatma Gandhi, Vol. LXXXII, p. 72.

225 Sitaramayya, *The History of the Indian National Congress*, Vol. II (1935–1947) Appendices, pp. i–v.

226 Ibid., p. iii.

227 Menon, *The Transfer of Power in India*, p. 56.

228 Aziz, ed., *Muslim Under Congress Rule 1937–1939*, Vol. I, p. 146.
229 Gwyer and Appadorai, *Speeches and Documents on the Indian Constitution*, Vol. II (1921–47) pp. 442–443.
230 Ibid., p. 443.
231 Hardy, *The Muslims of British India*, pp. 233–234.
232 Ibid., p. 234.
233 Z.H. Zaidi, Aspects of the Development of Muslim League Policy, 1937–47 in Philips and Wainwright, eds., *The Partition of India*, p. 267.
234 Ibid., p. 272.
235 Ayesha Jalal, *The Sole Spokesman: Jinnah, the Muslim League and the Demand for Pakistan*, Cambridge: Cambridge University Press, 1985, p. 126–173.
236 I.A. Talbot, The 1946 Punjab Elections, *Modern Asian Studies*, Vol. 14, No. 1 (1980), p. 89.
237 Sen, *Muslim Politics in Bengal 1937–1947*, pp. 276–279.
238 P.C. Joshi, *For the Final Bid for Power! Freedom Programme of Indian Communists*, Bombay: People's Publishing House, n.d. [1945?], pp. 101–122 quoted in Gene D. Overstreet and Marshall Windmiller, *Communism in India*, Berkeley, CA: University of California Press, 1959, p. 229.
239 *Communist Party of India, Election Manifesto of the Communist Party of India*, Bombay: People's Publishing House, 1946, pp. 6–7 quoted in Sobhanlal Datta Gupta, *Justice and the Political Order in India: An Inquiry into the Institutions and Ideologies: 1950–1972*, Calcutta: KP Bagchi & Company, 1979, pp. 199–200 and see also Overstreet and Windmiller, *Communism in India*, pp. 229–237 and see also P.N. Chopra, *India's Struggle for Freedom: Role of Associated Movements*, Vol.1, New Delhi: Agam Prakashan, 1985, p. 630.
240 Ibid., pp. 7–8 in Gupta, *Justice and the Political Order in India*, pp. 199–200.
241 Ibid., p. 8 in Gupta, *Justice and the Political Order in India*, pp. 199–200.
242 Mehta, ibid., p. 86.
243 Ibid., p. 89 and Menon, *The Transfer of Power in India*, pp. 229–232. See Indian Annual Register (1946), Vol. I, pp. 229–231.
244 B. Shiva Rao, *The Framing of India's Constitution: Select Documents*, Vol. 1, New Delhi: Indian Institute of Public Administration, 1966, p. 536.
245 Stanley A. Kochanek, *The Congress Party of India: The Dynamics of One-Party Democracy*, Princeton, NJ: Princeton University Press, 1968, p. 188.
246 Zaidi, *INC: The Glorious Tradition*, Vol.4, 1939–1950, pp. 313–314.
247 Zaidi (ed), *Congress Presidential Addresses*, Vol.5 (1940–1985), pp. 87–88.
248 Ibid., p. 89.
249 Ibid., p. 88.

3

ELECTORAL SYSTEM, POLITICAL PARTIES AND LOK SABHA ELECTIONS

Chapter 2 provided an overview of the emergence of the electoral system, political parties and party manifestos before independence. The Indian National Congress since 1885, in its annual sessions, made a demand for the representation of the people in the Legislative Councils. In the context of franchise, it is interesting to point out that, in October/November 1916, nineteen non-official elected members of the Imperial Legislative Council[1] submitted a memorandum to the Viceroy outlining a scheme of self-government for India. This memorandum suggested that all the Legislative Councils in India 'should have a substantial majority of elected representatives'. It was suggested that it should be 'broadened and extended directly to the people' and proper representation should be provided to Muhammadans or Hindus in consonance to their numerical strength.

The Motilal Nehru Committee 1928 is the first document which provides the nationalistic perspective on the problem of franchise. By this time, as recommended in the Morley-Minto and Montague-Chelmsford Reforms, elections for the legislative councils both of the Centre and the provinces were conducted (1909–1910, 1912–1913, 1916, 1920, 1923, 1926, 1929–1930). In the context of electorates, two important facets of these reforms relate to restricted franchise and separate electorates. The Nehru Committee members were aware of the problems of disharmony and communal divide arising from the prevailing system of representation. As a result, the Committee took note of these aspects and suggested adult suffrage despite the 'illiteracy of the masses and their lack of political experience'. It was of the view that 'Political experience can only be acquired by an active participation in political institutions and does not entirely depend on literacy. There should be equal opportunities available to all to acquire this experience'.[2] Regarding separate electorates, the Committee observed that these are not only 'bad for the growth of national spirit' but 'Extreme communalists flourish' under this system and suggested joint or mixed electorates. Some of the specific recommendations of the Committee in this regard are as follows:

1 Joint mixed electorates for the House of Representative and the Provincial Legislature.
2 No reservation of seats for the House of Representatives except for Muslims in provinces where they are in a minority and non-Muslims in the N.W.F. Province.
3 In the provinces:
   a No reservation of seats for any community in the Punjab and Bengal
   b No reservation of seats for Muslims minorities on population basis in provinces other than the Punjab and Bengal with the right to contest additional seats.
   c Similar reservation of seats for non-Muslims in the N.W.F. Province with the right to contest other seats.
4 Reservation of seats for a fixed period of ten years.[3]

Regarding the method of election and representation, a large number of members favoured the system of proportional representation.[4]

In the context of the franchise, it is also necessary to put in perspective the views of national leaders like Mahatma Gandhi and Jawaharlal Nehru. Mahatma Gandhi favoured the franchise of all adults, males and females, above the age of twenty-one, or even eighteen.[5] He was against the idea that 'a man who has got wealth should have the vote'.[6] More than anyone else, Jawaharlal Nehru was critical of the communalization of electorates in India. He was of the view that it 'weakened the groups that were already weak or backward', 'encouraged separatist tendencies', 'prevented the growth of national unity', and helped in the emergence of 'new vested interests of the most reactionary kind', and diverted attention from the 'real economic problems'. He further observed that 'the injury they have caused to every department of Indian life has been prodigious. Out of them have grown all manner of separatist tendencies and finally the demand for a splitting up of India'.[7] Nehru believed that elections were an 'essential and inseparable part of the democratic process'. He favoured the adult franchise and its adoption in India.

Constituent assembly debates on the electoral system

The discussion on election and the importance of manifesto was articulated by K.T. Shah in *A Note On Fundamental Rights* on December 23, 1946,

> The consent of the people or of the citizens is expressed by means of free elections of the representatives. This is achieved usually by secret ballot, so that, notwithstanding the presence of party machines, party discipline, and party propaganda, the individual citizen can express, through his vote for a representative, the general trend of public opinion on given issues which the Ministry formed on the results of these elections will have to deal with.[8]

In the Constituent Assembly, the Fundamental Rights Sub-Committee and the Minorities Sub-Committee in its interim report April 23, 1947 agreed that the following should be included in the Constitution:

- Every citizen not below 21 years of age shall have the right to vote.
- The law shall provide for free and secret voting and for periodical elections to the legislature.
- The superintendence, direction and control of all elections to the legislature, whether of the Union or of a unit, . . . shall be vested in an election commission for the Union or the unit, as the case may be, appointed, in all cases, in accordance with the law of the Union.[9]

The provisions of Draft Constitution pertaining to Elections were debated in the Constituent Assembly, clause by clause on June 15 and 16, 1949. It is proposed to highlight significant amendments suggested by the members on each provision.

Election Commission

It is of interest to note that the idea of Election Commission was accepted as far back as January 1947. In the Draft Constitution, there was provision for a separate Election Commission for each province under the guidance of the Governor and the local government. However, a large number of members agreed with the suggestion of Dr. B.R. Ambedkar that 'in the interests of purity and freedom of elections to the legislative bodies, it was of the utmost importance that they should be freed from any kind of interference from the executive of the day'.[10] Ambedkar, while presenting the motion, stressed the importance of centralized election machinery not working under the Provincial Government, but working under the superintendence and control of the Central Election Commission. He was of the view that 'to prevent injustice being done by Provincial Governments to people other than those who belong to the province racially, linguistically and culturally, it is felt desirable to depart from the original proposal of having a separate Election Commission for each province'.[11] He emphasized the need for a Central Election Commission with power to 'issue directives to returning officers, polling officers and others engaged in the preparation and revision of electoral rolls so that no injustice may be done to any citizen in India, who under this Constitution is entitled to be brought on the electoral rolls'.[12]

Ambedkar was also of the view that the conditions of service and tenure of office, etc., of the Election Commissioners should be determined by Parliament or by law. Shibban Lal Saksena suggested an amendment that the appointments of Chief Election Commissioner and other Election Commissioners shall be by the President 'subject to confirmation by a two-thirds majority both Houses of Parliament sitting and voting in a joint session'.[13]

K.M. Munshi while discussing the Central Election Commission and the need for its independence both from the Central Government as well as from the Provincial Governments observed:

> if there is going to be democracy, the sovereign people of India must be in a position to elect their own representatives in a manner which is above suspicion, above partiality. Corrupt practices do not necessarily apply to the candidates. There may be corrupt practices by a Government of the day. Therefore, it is necessary that we should not consider this question from the point of view of any theoretical provincial autonomy, a point which is being trotted out again and again in this House.[14]

He was also of the view that the function of the government is to hold the elections. However, in the context of the huge electorates require a 'large army of section officers, of clerks, of persons to control the booths etc.' These can only be provided 'by the Central Government, by the Provincial Government or by the local authorities'. He was not in favour of assigning the work of election to an entirely independent organ of the government. He was also of the view that the electoral matters 'should be placed beyond the reach of temporary passions in the provinces'[15]

Hirday Nath Kunzru was of the view that electoral machinery should not only be free from provincial political influences but also from Central political influences. He felt that 'If the electoral machinery is defective or is not efficient or is worked by people whose integrity cannot be depended upon, democracy will be poisoned at the source'.[16]

These were some up the important points of discussion in the Constituent Assembly with regard to the setting of independent Election Commission (Article 324). It was finally decided to have an Election Commission to superintend, direct and control all elections to Parliament and to the State Legislatures and to the offices of President and Vice-President.

The joint electorates

In the context of representation through communal electorates, it was held by many members of the Constituent Assembly that it created a permanent communal majority in the government and legislatures. Apart from this, continuance of separate electorates led to the evolution of political parties on religious lines. Besides, it was also an obstacle in the growth of political parties divided on broad issues of policy and differences in economic interests or political ideals. Regarding the need to provide adequate representation of different communities and interests, it was felt that there is no need for any specific provision in the context of special representation for any interests. It was suggested that the system of proportional representation provides enough protection.[17]

The Advisory Committee on the subject of minority rights submitted its Report to the Constituent Assembly on August 8, 1947.[18] The Report dealt primarily with the issue of 'political safeguards of minorities'. Other important issues taken by this Committee relate to the representation in legislatures, joint verses separate electorates and weightage. The Report pointed out that the system of separate electorates 'sharpened communal differences to a dangerous extent and has proved one of the main stumbling blocks to the development of a healthy national life'.[19] The Report recommended that all elections to the Central and Provincial Legislatures should be held on the basis of joint electorates. On the question of weightage, the Report recommended that the communities should be represented according to the proportion of their population.

The Sub-Committee on Fundamental Rights, February–April 1947 provided to the Schedule Castes the right to the representation in the legislature equal to the ratio of their population to the total population. It also recommended that the system of election introduced by the Poona Pact shall be abolished. The Sub-Committee was of the opinion that 'Separation in religion is not the only test of a minority. . . . Social discrimination constitutes the real test for determining whether a social group is or is not a minority'.[20] The Committee further elaborated this point by stating 'the nature of the electorates is determined not by reference to religion but by reference to social considerations'.[21] It recommended that seats for the different recognized minorities shall be reserved in the various legislatures on the basis of their population initially for a period of ten years.

These recommendations of the Advisory Committee were accepted by the Constituent Assembly and embodied in the draft Constitution. However, a number of spokesmen for the various minorities came forward with the proposal that the question of reservation of seats be re-examined. On May 11, 1949, the Advisory Committee passed the resolution of H.C. Mookherjee: 'That the system of reservation for minorities other than Scheduled Castes in Legislatures be abolished'.[22]

Electoral rolls

Another important issue in the Constituent Assembly relates to the preparation of electoral rolls. It was felt that for the composition of the future Central and Provincial Legislatures, there is needed not only necessary electoral machinery but also the preparation of electoral rolls, and qualifications for voters, within a certain time frame. A motion was moved by Dr. B.R. Ambedkar for this purpose. It was a mentioned that if a person is not a citizen of India and if he is of unsound mind, he shall not be included in electoral roll of any constituency. It was also resolved that a person shall be qualified to be included in the electoral roll if he has resided in the constituency not less than 180 days.

Some of the members of the Constituent Assembly were critical of the aforementioned motion primarily on the question that in the absence of passing of an article in the Constituent Assembly on citizenship, it may raise difficulties in the preparation of electoral rolls. In this context, the Prime Minister, Pandit Jawaharlal Nehru, was of the view, that 'Whatever the future decision of the Assembly in regard to the citizenship clause might be, it will only affect the preparation of those rolls slightly'.[23] However, Algu Rai Shastri was of the view that it is a difficult to prepare electoral rolls 'unless a decision about the delimitation of constituencies has been taken'. He was of the opinion that 'citizenship and delimitation of constituencies are the keystones of any scheme of electoral rolls'.[24]

In this context, however, Dr. B.R. Ambedkar proposed an amendment:

> There shall be one general electoral roll for every territorial constituency for election to either House of Parliament or to the House or either House of the Legislature of a State and no person shall be ineligible for inclusion in, or claim to be excluded from, any such roll on grounds only of religion, race, caste, sex or any of them.[25]

The object of this was nearly to give effect to the decision of the House of no separate electorate at all.

These were more some of the important points of debate regarding Article 325 which provides that there shall be one general electoral roll for every territorial constituency for election to either House of Parliament, or to the House or either House of a State Legislature.

Adult suffrage

As mentioned in the previous section, the Fundamental Rights Sub-Committee in its interim report recommended that every citizen not below twenty-one years of age shall have the right to vote. It was also pointed out by Shibban Lal Saksena that the 'right of adult franchise should not only be guaranteed by the Constitution but its proper exercise should also be guaranteed in practice . . . so that the elected people will represent the true will of the people of the country'.[26]

Alladi Krishnaswami Ayyar observed, about adopting the principle of adult suffrage, that

> If democracy is to be broad based and the system of government that is to function is to have the ultimate sanction of the people as a whole, in a country where the large mass of the people are illiterate and the people owning property are so few, the introduction of any property or educational qualifications for the exercise of the franchise would be a negation of the principles of democracy. . . . It cannot after all be assumed that a person with a poor elementary education and with a knowledge of the three Rs. is in a better position to exercise

> the franchise than a labourer, a cultivator or a tenant who may be expected to know what his interests are and to choose his representatives. Possibly a large-scale universal suffrage may also have the effect of rooting out corruption what may turn out incidental to democratic election.[27]

He further pointed out that the provision of adult suffrage 'is so important and significant that even if there had not been any other provision in it, it would have yet retained fully a democratic character'

Article 326 provides for adult suffrage as the basis for elections to the House of the People and the Legislative Assembly of every state. Every person who is a citizen of India and who is not less than twenty-one years of age, and who is not otherwise disqualified under the law on the grounds of non-residence, unsoundness of mind, crime or corrupt or illegal practice, shall be entitled to be registered as a voter at any such election. Granville Austin in the context of adult suffrage was of the opinion that 'Adult suffrage gave a voice, indeed power, to millions who had previously to depend on the whim of others for even a vague representation of their interests'.[28]

A number of members at various stages of the discussion on the Draft Constitution were of the view that a large section of the people has been particularly unprepared for the voting rights. It is important to emphasize in the context of universal adult franchise that during the third reading of the draft constitution in the Constituent Assembly, some members had serious reservations regarding voting rights to all citizens. The main argument against this provision was based on the illiteracy of the people and the need for educating them. It was pointed by N.V. Gadgil that 'Unless the electorate is sufficiently educated in a general way, capable of weighing not the details of a big problem, but its broad outlines, unless they have some capacity to distinguish between men and men the democracy that we are contemplating will not be successful.'[29]

Dr. P.S. Deshmukh observed that adult franchise is one factor which 'will make a tremendous difference to the nature of representation in the various legislative bodies'. And this is possible 'if the present Constitution is worked in the right spirit, if the adult franchise makes a difference and we get the right people from the common and average men as their representatives, then alone will it be possible for the people to receive that benefit which they are aspiring for'.[30] On the other hand, M. Thirumala Rao observed 'Without proper education, without the proper development of patriotism in this country, I am afraid this is a dangerous weapon'.[31]

Frank Anthony was of the view that it would have been desirable not to extend the franchise 'at one bound to universal suffrage'. 'Democracy has always carried the postulate, the implication that at least the exercise of the franchise would be made, if not on an essentially rationalistic basis, would be made at least on a common-sense basis'. In this matter of franchise, he was of the opinion that 'we will have proceeded progressively not necessarily gradually but progressively'. He also was of the view that

> with an electorate . . . predominantly illiterate, with an electorate which will be predominantly unaware of exercising the franchise on a basis of being able to analyse political issues in a rational way, that this electorate will not be stampeded by empty slogans by meretricious shibboleths into chasing political chimeras which will not only lead to chaos but to the very destruction of the democracy which we have chosen to give them.[32]

Power of Parliament to make provision with respect to elections to legislatures

There was general agreement on the motion proposed by Dr. B.R. Ambedkar regarding the power of Parliament to make provision with respect to elections to legislatures. However, an amendment was proposed by Thakur Das Bhargava which stated that the responsibility for making laws in regard to elections would be left to the Central Legislature alone. He observed that 'If we want uniformity in the conduct of elections we should see that Parliament alone has this power'.[33] On this issue, it was suggested by M. Ananthasayanam Ayyangar that 'There may be certain matters where for the sake of uniformity. Parliament may make law and the state legislature may make the rest of the laws'.[34]

B.R. Ambedkar with regard to the power of Parliament to make provisions with respect to elections to legislatures, finally substituted the following:

> Subject to the provisions of this Constitution, Parliament may from time to time by law make provisions with respect to all matters relating to, or in connection with, elections to either House of Parliament or to the House or either House of the Legislature of a State including the preparation of electoral

rolls and all other matters necessary for securing the due constitution of such House or Houses.

Power of the legislature of a state to make provision with respect to elections

It was observed by H.V. Kamath that there is a need to define and demarcate the powers relating to elections to be bestowed in Parliament and in the State Legislature. He pleaded to provide some powers to the State Legislature 'so as to promote greater harmony'. 'The Parliament should not be given entire authority to make, laws with respect to all matters relating to elections'.[35] Dr. B.R. Ambedkar, while clarifying the distinction between the power of Parliament and that of State Legislature in matters of election, pointed out that 'There are other matters which Parliament may think are of such local character and liable to variations from province to province that it would be better for Parliament to leave them to the Local Legislature'.[36]

Article 328 confers powers on State Legislatures to make laws relating to elections to the House, either the House of the Legislature of the State, including the preparation of electoral rolls and all other matters necessary for securing the due constitution of such House or Houses.

Bar to interference by courts in electoral matters

Dr. B.R. Ambedkar while moving the motion on this aspect provided the following:[37]

(a) The validity of any law relating to the delimitation of constituencies or the allotment of seats to such constituencies, made or purporting to be made under article 290 or article 291 of this Constitution shall not be called in question in any court.
(b) No election to either House of Parliament or to the House or either House of the Legislature of a State shall be called in question except by an election petition presented to such authority and in such manner as may be provided for by or under any law made by the appropriate legislature.
(c) Provision may be made by or under any law made by the appropriate legislature for the finality of proceedings relating to or in connection with any such election at any stage of such election.

However, an amendment was moved to omit clause (c), which was adopted. Article 329 bars interference by courts in electoral matters regarding any law relating to the delimitation of constituencies or the allotment of seats to such constituencies. It also provides that no election may be called in question except through an election petition, presented to such authority and in such manner as may be provided by a law.

Legal framework of electoral process

According to the Article 327, Parliament has legislative power to make laws regarding all matters relating to election. In this context, Parliament has enacted the Representation of the People Act, 1950, with regards to the allocation of seats and delimitation of Constituencies for the purpose of election, the qualifications of voters at such elections, the electoral machinery at the state level and the district level preparation of electoral rolls for parliamentary and Assembly Constituencies and Constitution of electoral college. Besides, the Parliament has also enacted the Representation of the People Act in 1951, to provide for the conduct of elections to the Houses of Parliament and to the House or Houses of the Legislature of each state, the qualifications and disqualifications for membership of those Houses, disqualification on the grounds of corrupt practices, disqualifications for voting, notification of general elections, administrative machinery for the conduct of elections, registration of political parties, general procedure at elections, the poll, election expenses, disputes regarding elections, election petitions, corrupt practices and electoral offences, counting of votes, publication of election results, powers of Election Commission in connection with inquiries is to disqualification of members, etc. These Rules were framed by the Central Government in consultation with the Election Commission. It is important to mention that in this context that 'In 1956, both these sets of Rules were replaced by two new sets of Rules bearing the same nomenclatures'.[38] In 1960, the rules relating to the preparation of electoral rolls were replaced by the Registration of Electors Rules 1960. Besides, in 1961, the Conduct of Elections Rules were also framed. These rules deal with nomination paper, symbols for elections, postal ballot, voting by electronic machines, counting of votes, election expenses, etc. These sets of rules provide the legal framework of election as a process in India.

It has been rightly pointed out that 'The introduction of adult suffrage in the Constitution was an act of great faith on the part of Constituent Assembly'. As mentioned earlier, in 1935, about 35 million voters were franchised which represented approximately 20 percent of the adult population of British India. However, the introduction of adult franchise meant a five-fold increase, i.e. about 176 million voters during the first general election held in 1952.[39]

Political parties after independence

In Chapter 2, an attempt was made to analyse the emergence of political parties after the Constitutional reforms of 1909, 1919 and 1935. These reforms recommended the system of representation based on classes and interests and not on the principle of territorial representation. Except the Indian National Congress, which was founded in 1885 (with the objective initially of bringing reform in the representative character of the government and later on independence for the country), these reforms caused the growth of political parties based on communal and sectional interest. As a consequence, the Muslim League, the Justice Party, the Krishak Party, the Foreword Bloc, the National Agriculturist Party, and the Unionist Party, the Akali Dal, the Nationalist Party, etc., came into existence. Besides, the Hindu Mahasabha was founded in 1910 by Hindus who felt that the Congress was not sufficiently representative of Hindu interests. In the beginning, it considered itself the Hindu wing of the Congress and did not function as a separate political organization. The Communist Party was founded in 1924. It was closely related to the Congress Party for many years for political purposes. It was declared an illegal party in 1934, and went underground. The Party was organized in 1942 as a legal body. The Congress Socialist was another group that was organized in 1934, and it worked within the fold of the Congress for many years. The main objective of the party was to give a Socialist orientation to the nationalist movement. It got separated from the Indian National Congress in March 1948.

One important problem with which the national leadership dealt after independence related to the organizational aspects of various political groups which were functioning within the Indian National Congress. Myron Weiner has a very interesting analysis of the emergence of political parties after independence and the reasons for the break away of a number of political groups for the Congress mainstream. 'So long as Congress was a movement which united all those who subscribed to the goal of independence, the leadership tolerated a wide variety of ideological and policy differences. . . . Once it became clear that Congress would now contest elections against many of these groups, it was evident that Congress could no longer tolerate a situation in which there were organized parties within itself'. In 1948 an amendment to the Congress constitution was passed which forbade any party member to belong to 'any other political party, communal or other, which has a separate membership, constitution and programme'. With the passage of this amendment, 'the Congress Socialist party members withdrew from Congress'.[40]

It is evident from the previous that during the pre-independence period, political parties in India played a very significant role both in the freedom movement as well as contesting elections for the Provincial and Central Legislatures. The Constitution of India does not define a political party. However, it was only by the Constitution (Fifty-second Amendment) Act, 1985, 'that their existence and functioning in the political field came to be recognized for the first time by the Constitution'.[41] However, the Representation of the People Act 1951, under Section 29A, provides that any association or body of individual citizens of India 'calling itself a political party' may apply for its registration as a political party to the Election Commission. During the first general election in 1952, it was a realized that, due to the poor illiteracy rate, it is essential to evolve a system so that a large majority of illiterate voters could exercise their franchise meaningfully. For this purpose, the Election Commission decided in favour of the symbol system.[42]

In the context of party recognition rules, during the period between 1952 and 1967, the Election Commission recognized the political parties 'Without the application of any objective set of standards and criteria. . . . The *ad hoc* character of party recognition resulted in a number of anomalies'.[43]

The Election Commission in 1968 promulgated The Election Symbols (Reservation and Allotment) Order 1968 for the specification, reservation, choice and allotment of symbols for recognition of political parties and in relation there to. This Order classified political parties in two categories: the recognized political party and the unrecognized political party. This Order introduced and made obligatory that associations and bodies must be registered with the Election Commission as a political party. The Order classified political parties in India in three categories: registered parties, recognized state parties and recognized national parties. At the 4 percent threshold requirement, a state party was granted recognition in either the state or the national elections in a state; however, where a party met this threshold in at least four states national party status was conferred. Political parties that failed to meet these criteria could still be recognized at the state level upon demonstrating their active involvement in political life for five continuous years. Political Parties which failed to get these criteria, but actively involved in political life for five years, are recognized at the state level.

In the context of political parties, it is important to mention the Constitution (Fifty-Second Amendment) Act, 1985. The purpose of the amendment is 'outlawing defection'. The problem of defections became a matter of 'national concern' and it was felt that if not checked it would 'undermine the very foundations of our democracy and the principles which sustain it'. According to this Act, if a member of any house (Parliament or Legislative Assembly) votes or abstains from voting contrary to any direction of such issued by the political party to which he belongs, he shall be disqualified from being a member of that House. The Act does not recognize disqualification on the grounds of defection in the case of a faction of a legislature party consisting of not less than one-third of the members of such legislature's party spilt from the original political party. The Act also specifies that disqualifications on the grounds of defection does not apply in case of merger if not less two-thirds of the members of the legislatures party have agreed to such merger. The Act also specifies that no courts shall have any jurisdiction over any matter connected with the disqualification of a member. In this matter the Speaker of the House has the responsibility to make its decision and only technical issues can be taken to court.

The Election Symbols Order 1968 was revised in December 2000 and May 2005.[44] According to this Order, the political parties are either recognized political parties or unrecognized political parties. However, a recognized political party shall either be a National Party or a State Party.

State Party

A party may be recognized as a State Party if any of the following conditions is fulfilled:

- The candidates set up by the party have secured not less than 6 percent of the total valid votes polled in the state, and the party has returned at least two members to the Legislative Assembly of that state.
- The candidates set up by the party have secured not less than 6 percent of the total valid votes polled in the state; and, the party has returned at least one member to the House of the People from that state. The party has won at least 3 percent of the total number of seats Legislative Assembly, or at least three seats in the Assembly, whichever is more.
- At the last general election to the House of the People from the state, the party has returned at least one member to the House of the People for every twenty-five members.

National Party

A party may be recognized as a National Party if any of the following conditions is fulfilled:

- The candidates set up by the party in any four or more states, have secured not less than 6 percent of the total valid votes polled in each of those states at that general election and has returned at least four members to the House of the People.
- The party has won at least 2 percent of the total number of seats in the House of the People at the last general election to the House of the People, any fraction exceeding half being counted as one; and the said candidates have been elected to that House from not less than three states.
- The party is recognized as State Party in at least four states.

The Table 3.1 gives the number of recognized national and state parties.

Table 3.1 Number of recognized national and state parties: 1952–2014.

Election	*National parties*	*State parties*	*Total*
Year			
1952	14	60	74
1957	4	12	16
1962*	–	16	16
1967*	–	21	21
1971	8	17	25
1977	5	18	23
1980	6	19	25
1984	7	19	26
1989	8	20	28
1991	9	27	36
1996	8	30	38
1998	7	30	37
1999	7	40	47
2004	7	45	52
2009	6	55	61
2014	6	39	45

* As parties were given recognition only on a state-by-state basis, there were no national parties in 1962 and 1967.

Source: David Bulter, Ashok Lahiri and Prannoy Roy *India Decides: Elections 1952–1995*, New Delhi: Books & Things, Third edition, 1995, p. 24. See also Douglas V. Verney How has the Proliferation of Parties Affected the Indian Federation? A Comparative Approach in Zoya Hasan, E. Sridharan and R. Sudarashan (eds) *India's Living Constitution: Ideas, Practices, Controversies* New Delhi: Permanent Black, 2002, p. 142.

At present there are six national recognized parties: The Indian National Congress, The Bharatiya Janata Party, The Communist Party of India (CPI), The Communist Party of India (Marxist), The Bahujan Samaj Party and the Nationalist Congress Party. The total number of State Parties is thirty-nine.

Preparation for conducting First General Elections 1951–1952

The Constitution came into force on January 26, 1950. However, the elections could be held only after a lapse of two years. The reasons given by the Election Commission for conducting elections after two years were as follows:

- The electoral law was to be enacted by Parliament.
- The Scheduled Castes and the Scheduled Tribes had to be specified. The population strength of these could not, therefore, be determined. As the extent of reservation of seats in the legislatures for the Scheduled Castes and Scheduled Tribes depends strictly on the exact proportion that their numbers bear to the total population in any State or in the country as a whole, no decision could be taken at that stage regarding the number of seats reserved for them in the various legislatures.
- The work of delimiting the constituencies could not be taken up in the absence of the determination of the population of the states and different areas in each state. The Census Commissioner was asked to prepare the estimates of the population.
- The preparation of electoral rolls was also a time-consuming task.
- The state of preparedness for elections varied considerably in the different states.[45]

Because most voters were illiterate, arrangements were made to enable people to vote intelligently through the use of symbols for the parties, and the multiple ballot-box technique facilitated in dropping the ballot paper.

In order to conduct general elections to the legislatures under the new Constitution in the year 1950, the Vice-President of the Constituent Assembly moved a motion regarding 'Preparation of Electoral Rolls'[46] on January 8, 1949. The members of the Constituent Assembly were critical on this motion as there was no provision in the Rules of the Assembly by which such a motion can be brought by the Chair and, second, usually the motions from the Chair were not subject to debate. It is interesting to point out that in absence of the discussion on the provisions regarding the electoral system, most of the members raised objections regarding some of the technical difficulties concerning clauses relating to the following: 'citizenship of India, unsound mind and stand by a competent court, proof of residence and in the case of refugees a declaration of his intention to reside permanently in that constituency', etc.

It is interesting to point out that Jawaharlal Nehru in his capacity as a member of the Constituent Assembly moved the Resolution which was identical to the one which was put forth by the Vice-President of the Assembly. It was pointed out that the Resolution had come from the 'Steering Committee.' And the government 'as such has not moved this Resolution and Government as such is not functioning in this Assembly'.[47] He further pointed out that

> 'the Government is concerned, the Government some time back took steps to ask the Provincial Governments to get electoral rolls prepared. As a matter of fact, even if this Resolution was not passed, the Government of course can proceed with the preparation of those rolls, but there will be this difficulty, that in the event of the Constituent Assembly at a later stage perhaps varying the qualifications or something, then all the electoral rolls that have been prepared or might be prepared might become useless'.[48]

A large number of members also pointed out that the preparation of electoral rolls is not possible until the appointment of Delimitation Commission because, unless the constituencies are delimited, 'we will not know the area for which the electoral rolls will have to be prepared'. K. Santhanam in this context pointed out that 'this Resolution is in the nature of provisional directions to the government of India on behalf of the Constituent Assembly to prepare the spade work. The final directions will have to be given by the President or such authority as will come into existence after August 15th next, if fortunately we are able to put the Constitution into force by that date'.[49] After much debate, the Resolution, as amended, was adopted. The Resolution is as follows:

> resolved that instructions be issued forthwith to the authorities concerned for the preparation of electoral rolls and for

taking all necessary steps so that elections to the legislatures under the new Constitution may be held as early as possible in the year 1950.

Resolved further that the State electoral rolls be prepared on the basis of the provisions of the new Constitution agreed to by this Assembly and in accordance with the principles thereinafter mentioned, namely the following:

- That no person shall be included in the electoral roll of any area if he is of unsound mind and stands so declared by a competent court.
- That 1st January 1949 shall be the date with reference to which the age of the electors is to be determined.
- That a person shall not be qualified to be included in the electoral roll for any area unless he has resided in that area for a period of not less than 180 days in the year ending on the 31st March 1948. For the purposes of this paragraph, a person shall be deemed to be resident in any area if he ordinarily resides in that area or has a permanent place of residence therein.
- That notwithstanding anything in paragraph above, a person who has migrated into a Province or Acceding State on account of disturbances or fear of disturbances in his former place of residence shall be entitled to be included in the electoral roll of an area if he files or makes a declaration of his intention to reside permanently in that area.[50]

Jawaharlal Nehru on elections

Jawaharlal Nehru was closely associated with the elections of 1936–1937 and 1945–1946. His interventions in the Constituent Assembly regarding some issues relating to the election process have also been commented upon. However, his views on many aspects of the electoral system are not only important but has a good deal of contemporary significance in laying 'the firm foundations of the democratic structure' of India.

In a speech broadcast from the All-India Radio on November 22, 1951, he spelled out his views on a number of issues relating to the electoral process. He was in favour of maintaining 'a high level of propriety and decorous behaviour' during election campaigns. He was of the view that the propaganda of a party should deal with the policies and programmes and 'should not and degenerate into personal criticism'. He was keen for the people to realize 'the deep significance of this great adventure of the Indian people'. Here is given an except from this speech:

> Hundreds of millions of people in India will determine the future of this country. They will put their voting papers in tens of thousands of ballot boxes indicating their choice and will or should do so peacefully. Out of these voting papers will emerge the Members of the Parliament of India and of the State Assemblies and we shall accept the result of this election without question.
>
> That is the essence of democracy. All of us naturally want the cause we represent to triumph and we strive for that end. In a democracy, we have to know how to win and also how to lose with grace. Those who win should not allow this to go to their heads, those who lose should not feel dejected.
>
> The manner of winning or losing is even more important than the result. It is better to lose in the right way than to win in the wrong way. Indeed, if success comes through misconceived effort or wrong means, then the value of that success itself is lost . . .
>
> I lay stress upon this because it is important and because there is a tendency, during election time, to disregard all standards of behaviour. I earnestly hope that every candidate along with his supporters will remember that to some extent he has the honour of India in his keeping and conduct himself accordingly.[51]

Elections in India 1952–2014: an overview

It is proposed to analyse in this section some significant aspects of the Indian Elections to the Lok Sabha since 1952. The size of the electorate has gone from173,212,343 in the 1952 elections to 814,591,184 in 2014. It has been estimated that this number is more than the electorates of both the European Union and the United States of America. This has been made possible due to the introduction of universal adult suffrage. It has brought every person, as a voter, into the mainstream of political life. Jawaharlal Nehru paid tribute to the political maturity of the Indian masses by pointing out that 'even though largely illiterate, they showed a broad understanding of issues. . . . Indeed, oddly enough the so-called illiterate voter has done probably better than

Table 3.2 Party-seats, seats shares and vote shares of the Lok Sabha elections, 1952–2009.*

	1952	*1957*	*1962*	*1967*	*1971*	*1977*	*1980*	*1984*	*1989*	*1991*	*1996*	*1998*	*1999*	*2004*	*2009*
Total seats	489	494	494	520	518	542	542	542	543	543	543	543	543	543	543
Indian National Congress (INC), (INCI) in 1980	364(479) 45.0%	371(490) 47.8%	361(488) 44.7%	283(516) 40.8%	352(441) 43.7%	154(492) 34.5%	353(492) 42.7%	415(517) 48.1%	197(510) 39.5%	232(492) 36.5%	140(529) 28.8%	141(474) 25.9%	114(453) 28.3%	145(416) 26.64%	206(440)
Bharatiya Janata Party (BJP), (BLD) in 1977, (BJS) till 1971	3(94) 3.1%	4(130) 5.9%	14(196) 6.4%	35(251) 9.4%	22(160) 7.4%	295(405) 41.3%		2(229) 7.4%	86(226) 11.5%	120(468) 20.1%	161(471) 20.3%	179(384) 25.5%	(182339) 23.8%	138(364) 22.16%	116(433)
Janata Dal (United) (JDU) in 1999, (JD) 1989–1998, (SWA) till 1971			18(173) 7.9%	44(178) 8.7%	8(5[illegible]) 3.1%				142(243) 17.7%	59(307) 11.8%	46(196) 8.1%	6(190) 3.2%	21(60) 3.1%	6(33) 1.85%	19
Communist Party of India (CPI)	16(49) 3.3%	27(110) 8.9%	29(137) 9.9%	23(106) 5.0%	23(87) 4.7%	7(91) 2.8%	11(48) 2.6%	6(66) 2.7%	12(50) 2.6%	14(42) 2.5%	12(43) 2.0%	9(58) 1.8%	4(54) 1.5%	10(34) 1.40%	4(56)
Communist Party of India Marxist (CPIM)				19(62) 4.4%	25(85) 5.1%	22(53) 4.3%	36(63) 6.1%	22(64) 5.7%	33(64) 6.5%	35(60) 6.2%	32(75) 6.1%	32(71) 5.2%	33(72) 5.4%	43(69) 5.73%	16(82)
Lok Dal (LKD), (JPS) in 1980, INCO till 1977					16(238) 10.4%	3(19) 1.7%	41(294) 9.4%	3(174) 5.6%	0(117) 0.2%	0(78) 0.1%					
Samajwadi Party (SP), in 1991, (JP) till 1989							31(432) 19.0%	10(219) 6.7%	0(156) 1.0%	5(345) 3.4%	17(111) 3.3%	20(164) 5.0%	26(151) 3.8%	36(102) 3.88%	22
Telugu Desam (TDP)								30(34) 4.1%	2(33) 3.3%	13(35) 3.0%	16 2.99%	12 2.78%	29(34)	5(33) 3.06%	6
Praja Socialist Party (PSP), (KMPP) in 1952	9(145) 5.8%	19(189) 10.4%	12(168) 6.8%	13(109) 3.1%	2(63) 1.0%										
Samyukta Socialist Party (SSP), (SOC) till 1962	12(254) 10.6%		6(107) 2.7%	23(122) 4.9%	3(93) 2.4%										
Bhaujan Samaj Party (BSP)											11(117) 3.6%	5(249) 4.7%	14(225) 4.2%	19(436) 5.43%	21(500)

(*Continued*)

Table 3.2 (Continued)

	1952	*1957*	*1962*	*1967*	*1971*	*1977*	*1980*	*1984*	*1989*	*1991*	*1996*	*1998*	*1999*	*2004*	*2009*
Nationalist Congress Party (NCP)													8(130)	9(33) 1.79%	9(68)
Rashtriya Janata Dal (RJD)											16	17	7(60)	21(28)	4(44)
Others	47(320) 16.5%	31(119) 7.6%	34(236) 10.5%	45(161) 10.0%	53(427) 13.8%	52(155) 9.9%	35(262) 8.5%	44(273) 10.0%	44(1035) 12.2%	41(126) 12.1%	115 21.5%	141 26.3%	143 27.1%	20(1260) 5.65%	111
Independents (IND)	38(533) 15.9%	42(481) 19.4%	20(480) 11.1%	35(864) 13.7%	14(1134) 8.4%	9(1224) 5.5%	9(2826) 6.4%	5(3878) 8.1%	12(3712) 5.2%	1(5536) 3.9%	9 6.3%	6 2.4%	6 2.8%	4(2384) 4.16	9(3831)

Source: David Butler, Ashok Lahiri and Pranoy Roy, *India Decides: Elections 1952–1995*, New Delhi: Books and Things, 1995; Election Commission of India, *Statistical Report on General Elections*, vol. I (ver. I) National and State Abstracts and Parliament of India, *Who's Who* for 1996(11th), 1998(12th), 1999(13th), 2004(14th) Lok Sabha and 2009(15th) Lok Sabha. Complied from Government of India, *India 2010: A Reference Manual*, Publication Division, Ministry of Information and Broadcasting, New Delhi, pp. 1271–1286.

BLD – Bharatiya Lok Dal

BJS – Bharatiya Jana Sangh

SWA – Swantantra Party

INCU – Indian National Congress (Urs)

JPS – Janata Party Secular

JD(U) – Janata Dal (United)

INCO – Indian National Congress (Organized)

JP – Janata Party

KMPP – Kisan Mozdoor Praja Party

SOC – Socialist Party

SJP – Samajwadi Janata Party (Now SP- Samajwadi Party)

NCP – Nationalist Congress Party

RJD – Rashtriya Janata Dal

Notes: [a] Elections were not held in thirteen constituencies: twelve in Assam and one in Meghalaya.
[b] Elections were not held in Assam (fourteen seats).
[c] Elections were not held in Jammu&Kashmir (six seats) and Punjab (thirteen seats); three counter manded seats results excluded.
[d] Figures in parenthesis are seats contested, upper percentage is seat share, lower percentage is vote share

many of the literates'.[52] The Report of the Election Commission commended the adoption of universal suffrage as 'an act of faith – faith in the common man of India and in his practical common sense. This decision launched a great and fateful experiment unique in the world in its stupendousness and complexities'.[53] Despite a high percentage of electorates being illiterate, Brecher observed 'The deeply rooted belief in the West that democratic processes are suitable only to highly literate societies was seriously questioned by the Indian elections in 1951–1952'.[54] Table 3.2 refers to each election result from 1952 to 2009.

The First General Elections (October 25, 1951–February 21, 1952) were conducted on a very vast scale. This vastness can be understood from the fact that there were over 90,000 polling stations and 224,000 polling booths, and the number of ballot papers use exceeded 620,000,000, and over 1,800 candidates contested for the 489 seats of the Lok Sabha while another 15,000 candidates contested for the 3,283 seats in the State Assemblies.[55] Michael Brecher, while praising the success of the First General Elections in India, observed that

> On the purely technical level the election of 1951–2 was a striking success: at only seven of the 133,000 polling stations was the voting adjourned because of violence; in 193 other cases a re-vote was necessary; all told, 1,250 offences were recorded, but more than 800 fell into the category of impersonation. The achievement was especially impressive in view of the high rate of illiteracy, the unfamiliarity of many candidates, officials and voters with the electoral procedure, and the relative haste with which the administrative preparations were completed; less than two years had elapsed between the inauguration of the Constitution and the actual polling.[56]

With the introduction of the constitutional framework in 1950, due to regional, religious, ethnic, linguistic, social and cultural diversity of India, around seventy-four political parties took part in the elections. Out of these, only fourteen claim to function on all-India basis while sixty were state parties. One important development in India since independence has been the growth of state parties.

The Congress won 364 seats. It secured 45 percent of the total votes cast, capturing 74.4 percent of the Lok Sabha seats. While in the category of other parties, which essentially included state-based parties, it won forty-seven seats capturing 9.6 percent of the seats share and 16.5 percent of the votes. Besides, the independent candidates, also significantly won thirty-eight seats capturing 7.6 percent of seats and 16 percent of vote share.

In the context of Second General Elections, it is important to point out that a major initiative was taken by the Communist Party of India on electoral alliance. The Central Committee of the Communist Party of India, on July 11, 1956, issued a document highlighting the need to all socialists, democrats and progressive people 'to unite into a common front against the Congress Government and contest the Congress candidates at all levels', on the 'basis of a mutually agreed minimum programme'.[57] In this context, the Manifesto of the Party further emphasized that 'The emergence of a democratic opposition will strengthen the fight for the rights and liberties of the people. It will strengthen the forces of socialism and democracy in our political and economic life'.[58] During the Second General Elections of 1957, although at the national level alliances were not achieved; however, in several states, arrangements were made among groups of parties to present a united opposition to the ruling party. The most significant of these alliances were those in Maharashtra, Gujarat, West Bengal, Kerala, Rajasthan, Uttar Pradesh, Assam and Madhya Pradesh.

During the Second General Elections (February 24, 1957–June 9, 1957),[59] the entire period of the poll was reduced to just over fifteen days. The Election Commission observed that during the First General Elections the task was enormously difficult due to illiteracy of high percentage of population and by the lack of experience in elections of 'princely' India. One important aspect of the Second General Elections was the changes in the political map of the country, due to the State Reorganization Act, 1956, which resulted in massive readjustments in the administrative system and revision of the constituencies.

During the 1957 Second General Elections, the Congress Party won 371 seats, i.e. about 75 percent of seats with 47.8 percent of the total votes polled for the Lok Sabha elections. The CPI with twenty-seven seats became the largest party after the Congress. However, in opposition to the Congress Party, the regional parties won more seats in the State Assemblies and the Lok Sabha than any national party. This made Selig Harrison observe that 'Indian political life since Independence has witnessed the steady growth of regionally based forces and the corresponding erosion of the system of national party competition which was implicitly envisaged by the drafters of the Indian Constitution'.[60] Harrison also characterized the independent candidates as 'ubiquitous' and 'ready to bargain with the highest bidder'. He further provided his most prophetic observation 'the regionalization of Indian politics has carried with it an additional, potentially ominous, development in the mushrooming rise of militant parochial parties which are in no mood for bargaining and which have as their *raison d'etre*, in fact, the elimination of the national party presence in their territory'.[61]

The Third General Elections of 1962 (February 16–June 6)[62] was completed within a period of one and half weeks. For the first time the country was divided into single member constituencies, some of them being reserved for Scheduled Castes and Scheduled Tribes. The Congress Party secured 361 seats, i.e. 73 percent of the seats with 44.7 percent of the valid votes cast at the polls. The ballot marking system was introduced for the first time in India. Prior to this, the voters had to put their ballots in boxes marked for individual contesters. Upto 1962, the CPI was one opposition party which was steadily securing more seats in each election: 1952(16), 1957(27) and 1962(29).

The Fourth General Elections of 1967 (February 15–February 28)[63] brought large changes in the political structure of the country. The Indian National Congress had lost its right to rule in eight States: Uttar Pradesh, Bihar, West Bengal, Orissa, Madras, Kerala, Punjab, Rajasthan and the Union Territory of Delhi. Besides, its majority in the Lok Sabha was drastically reduced. The Congress Party won only 283 seats, a loss of seventy-eightseats in comparison to the 1962 General Elections.

The election results also saw the emergence of different regional parties and national parties coming to power in different States (as no single party commanded a majority, coalition governments were formed). For example: in Kerala and West Bengal, the governments were formed by a group of left parties; in Madras, the DMK; in Orissa, the Swatantra Party and Jana Congress formed an alliance; in Bihar, Uttar Pradesh, Punjab and Rajasthan, a mixed group of parties including Swantantra, Jana Sangh, Praja Socialist Party (PSP), Samyukta Socialist Party (SSP), Congress and the Communist. This has been attributed due to the major defections from the Congress Party 'over the allocation of party tickets' in some states,[64] besides, 'the Indian voter was reaching maturity and could no longer be taken for granted by any political party, however well-established and well-entrenched it might be'.[65]

The Fifth General Elections were held in 1971 (March 1–March 13)[66] about fourteen months before the expiration of its normal period. The Congress Party suffered a spilt in November 1969[67] and, as a consequence, the clear majority of the party in power had eroded. To seek a fresh mandate from the people, elections were announced. This election is also important because, for the first time, it was decided to delink Parliamentary and State Assembly Elections. The elections of 1971 saw the emergence of two major electoral forces opposed to one another. A Four-Party Alliance consisting of Jana Sangh, Congress (O), Swatantra and Samyukta Socialist Party was formed on an All-India basis. In this alliance, the constituencies were distributed between the four partners. Besides, the Congress made 'limited local adjustments' with the CPI in Uttar Pradesh, Bihar and Andhra Pradesh and DMK in Tamil Nadu.[68] In these elections the electoral performance of the regional parties was very noticeable. In terms of popular vote, these parties were the first or second largest party in eight of the eighteen states.[69] The Congress Party came back with a two-thirds majority in the Lok Sabha with 352 seats and 43.7 percent votes

In the context of these elections, the manifesto of the Congress Party, highlighted that due to the 'mass upsurge and awakening', 'Only a genuine radical programme of economic and social development could meet the challenge of this new situation'. The manifesto emphasized that 'the policies and programme to which it stands pledged are in accordance with the principles laid down in the Constitution of India'. The Congress manifesto in order to strengthen this argument, quoted the Directive Principles of State Policy, particularly articles 37, 38, 39(b) and (c). The manifesto further emphasized that 'Public policy has to respond to the requirements of the vast majority of our people. We must call for a mass approach to the basic problems of the people'. In this context, Myron Weiner observed

> By nationalizing banks, disinheriting the princes, proposing ceilings on rural land holdings and urban property and publicly challenging big business, she (Indira Gandhi) sought to move the electorate toward issues and way from the politics of patronage. By splitting the party – one might say in retrospect, by expelling from the party those who did not believe in her kind of politics – she repudiated those who operated under these old assumptions.[70]

The Sixth General Elections (March 16, 1977–March 20, 1977)[71] represented certain basic shifts in the party system in India. The declaration of the emergency in June 1975, the postponement of the elections scheduled for March 1976 and the discussion on revising the constitution mark the beginning of a new phase of Indian politics. Myron Weiner has very aptly observed that 'The Indian parliamentary elections of March 1977 brought to an end thirty years of Congress Party rule, eleven years of government under the prime ministership of

Indira Gandhi, and twenty-one months of an emergency that had set the nation on an authoritarian course. If, instead of elections, a violent upheaval had marked this turning point, we might be writing about India's democratic revolution'.[72]

In the context of the 1977 General Elections, the formation of the Janata Party 'was dictated by the instinct of survival of the opposition parties'.[73] The Janata Party manifesto pointed out that 'It is not a mere alliance of parties but a new national party to which the Congress (O), the Bharatiya Lok Dal, the Jana Sangh, the Socialist Party, Independent Congressmen and many others stand firmly committed. This manifesto is a solemn reaffirmation of that common resolve'.[74] Besides, it was the first attempt of forming a coalition government at the national level. The nomenclature used in the manifesto to spell out their intentions and programmes like 'Political Charter', 'Economic Charter' and 'Social Charter' were not only different from the previous manifestos but also were sharply focused and pin-pointed.

This election resulted in the total rejection of the ruling Congress Party. The Janata Party got 295 seats and Congress got only 154 seats. The Congress Party was totally wiped out in Bihar, Haryana, Himachal Pradesh, Nagaland, Punjab, Uttar Pradesh and Delhi, while in Madhya Pradesh and Rajasthan the Congress Party got one seat each. On the other hand the Janata Party in Kerala and Tamil Nadu was totally wiped out, but in Karnataka and Andhra Pradesh, the Party got two seats and one seat respectively. In the western India (Maharashtra and Gujarat) the Janata Party marginally got more seats than the Congress, i.e. the Janata Party got thirty-five seats while Congress got thirty seats.[75]

The Janata Party experiment came to an end when some of the constituent parties like Bharatiya Lok Dal, Socialist Party and Congress for Democracy walked out, during the parliamentary session in July 1979. The Prime Minister Moraji Desai resigned, sensing the defeat. Charan Singh was elected leader of a coalition consisting of breakaway Janata, the Congress (Swaran group) and other minor parties along with the support of Congress (I) from outside. Subsequently, the Congress withdrew the support and the Charan Singh Ministry resigned, without facing the Parliament. The Sixth Lok Sabha was dissolved on August 22, 1979.

The elections to the Seventh Lok Sabha 1980 (January 3–January 6)[76] was the second mid-term poll. The First mid-term poll was the fifth general election in 1971. It is interesting to point that the Janata Dal (Secular) won forty-one seats with 9.4 percent of the votes polled. One interesting aspect of the 1980 elections pertain to electoral alliances.

Though there was no All-India-based electoral alliances. However, some kind of programmatic alliances were made amongst the left parties limited to West Bengal, Kerala and Tripura. Another interesting pattern was between the Congress (I) and DMK on the one hand and Janata alliance with AIADMK based only in Tamil Nadu. Similarly, the Congress (I) had the support of the National Conference in Jammu and Kashmir and with All-India Muslim League in Tamil Nadu and Kerala. In these alliances there was a state-wide sharing of seats and a common campaigning and understanding of staying together after elections. The performance of the Congress Party was spectacular as it won 353 seats and its polling percentage was only 42.7. The Janata Party won only thirty-one seats though it polled 19 percent of votes.

In the Eighth Lok Sabha Elections 1984 (December 24–December 28),[77] the Congress Party won 415 seats out of 542 total seats. In terms of percentage the Congress got 76.6 percent of the seats and 48.1 of the votes. The number of seats and the number of votes has been the highest received by the Congress Party so far. From this point of view it has been an historic general election for the Congress Party. It won all the seats in Haryana, Himachal Pradesh, Madhya Pradesh, Manipur, Meghalaya, Nagaland, Rajasthan, Arunachal Pradesh, Chandigarh, Delhi, Goa, Lakshwadeep, Mizoram, Pondicherry. Besides in Gujarat out of twenty-six total seats, the Congress won twenty-four, and in Orissa out of twenty-one seats, the Congress won twenty seats.[78] About this outcome, mainly two reasons were normally spoken, first related to 'sympathy vote' and the other regarding a 'Hindu backlash'. However, it has been said that both these reasons were misleading. The real reasons have been, first, there was no unity among the Opposition parties and, second, the overwhelming majority of the electorates 'could not possibly rely on any other party to provide the government that could defend the country from external and internal threats'.[79] Such massive mandate to the Congress has been attributed to 'a vote for keeping India together, a vote for its defence and integrity'.[80] In this election, the Congress (I) had an electoral adjustment with AIADMK. In most of the constituencies, there were multicornerd contest due to the presence of a large number of independent candidates.

The CPI (M) was the only opposition party which could come back with twenty-two seats from Bengal and Tripura. The regional Party Telugu Desam did remarkably well by winning thirty seats and after Congress it was the largest party in the Lok Sabha. While the BJP fielded 229 candidates in fourteen states, it won only two seats, their lowest representation so far.

Era of coalition governments – 1989–2014

The Table 3.3 depicts the constituent parties which formed the coalition governments between 1989 and 2014, along with the period these governments functioned. It also shows the pre-electoral and post-electoral alliances amongst the constituent parties.

The Ninth General Elections of 1989 (November 22–November 26)[81] did not give any clear verdict to any particular party. Though the Congress emerged as the largest single party with 197 seats, it decided not to stake its claim to form a government. On August 6, 1989, six national parties namely the Janata Dal, CPI, CPI(M), TDP, DMK and Congress (S) formed a National Front with the Andhra Pradesh Chief Minister N.T. Rama Rao as its Chairman and V.P. Singh as Convenor. The emergence of the National Front, towards the end of the year led to the fall of the Congress (I) government at the Centre. The following parties constituted the National Front at the time of its inception – Janata party, Lok Dal, Congress(S), TDP, DMK, AGP, JM. The constitution of the National Front in its article XI specifically pointed out that the Lok Sabha would be fought based on agreed national common minimum programme. It further emphasized that 'The constituent parties may also have supplementary manifestos keeping in view the special conditions prevailing in their States, but not inconsistent with the manifesto of the National Front'.[82] It further pointed out that 'The AGP, DMK and TDP parties in Assam, Tamil Nadu and Andhra Pradesh shall take initiative and will have a decisive role in seat adjustments with other political parties in their respective States'.[83] The National Front though secured lesser seats than the Congress, formed the government with support of the BJP and Left Front. As mentioned earlier, the left front gave conditional support from outside to the National Front Government.

The CPI in its Central Executive Committee meetings during November–December 1989, decided to support the National Front Government at the Centre from outside. This support was based on

> secular and democratic policies, provided the government does not include representatives of communal parties like the BJP and the Muslim League and shall not water down its programme, particularly of safeguarding the rights of the minorities and weaker sections of the people, upholds democratic setup of the country and the policy of nonalignment.

Table 3.3 Coalition and minority governments in India: 1989–2014.

Year	*Prime Minister*	*Coalition constituents*
December 4, 1989–November 10, 1990	V.P. Singh National Front Minority Coalition Government	JD, Cong(S), TDP, LD, DMK, AGP, JM Outside support of the BJP and the Left Front
November 10, 1990–June 21, 1991	Chandrasekhar Minority Government Coalition	Outside support of the Congress
June 21, 1991–July 28, 1993–December 31, 1993–May 16, 1996	P.V. Narashima Rao Congress Minority Government	It lost minority status after the JMM and JD (Ajit) helped defeat the no-confidence motion and these groups were admitted into the Congress Party. As a consequence, the Congress attained a majority on its own.
June 1, 1996–April 21, 1997	H.D. Deve Gowda United Front Minority Coalition Government	JD, SP, TDP (Naidu), RJD, DMK, AGP, ASDC, CPI(M), CPI, RSP, AIFB, TMC, Cong (Tiwari). With Congress support
April 21, 1997–November 28, 1997	I.K. Gujral United Front Minority Coalition Government	JD, SP, TDP (Naidu), RJD, DMK, AGP, ASDC, CPI (M), CPI, RSP, AIFB, TMC, Cong (Tiwari). With Congress support
March 19, 1998–April 17, 1999	A.B. Vajpayee Minority Government led by BJP	Pre-electoral: BJP, TC, SHS, JNP, HVP, SAD, AIADMK, PMK, MDMK, LKS, BJD, TRC, SMT, Post-electoral-Independent (Maneka Gandhi), Independent (Satnam S. Kainth), Independent (Buta Singh), TDP, JKNC, HLD(R), AC, MSCP, SDF, Anglo-Indians, BSMC, Citizen Common Front, RJP (Anand Mohan)
October 13, 1999–May 13, 2004	A.B.Vajpayee National Democratic Alliance – BJP's Minority Government	Pre-electoral – BJP, JD (U), BJD, DMK, SHS, TC, INLD, SAD-B, MDMK, PMK, HVC, MDMK, ABLTC, MSCP, SDF, Independent (Maneka Gandhi), Janatantrik BSP, AC, DBSM, Post-electoral: TRC, JKNC, RLD. Outside support from TDP

May 19, 2004–May 2009	Manmohan Singh Congress-led United Progressive Alliance-I	Pre-electoral: Cong, TRS, IND(Cong), RJD, LJNP, NCP, JMM, PDP, MUL, KCM, JDS, RPI, RPI(A), PRBP, DMK, MDMK, PMK, PDS, AC Supported by the Left Parties
May 22, 2009–May 2014	Manmohan Singh Congress-led United Progressive Alliance-II	Pre-electoral: Congress, TC, DMK, NCP, NC, JMM, MUL, AIMIM, KCM VCK, Bodoland People's Front

Source: Data regarding constituent parties from 1989 to 1990 from A.M. Zaidi, ed. *The Annual Register of Indian Political Parties: Proceedings and Fundamental Texts 1989*: Part Two, Publication Department, Indian Institute of Applied Political Research, New Delhi, 1992, pp. 413–417. Data regarding constituent parties from 1990 to 1991, 1991 to 1993, 1996 to 1997, April 1997 to November 1997, see Subhendu Ranjan Raj *Coalition Politics in India: Dimensions of Federal Power Sharing*, New Delhi: Manak Publications Pvt. Ltd., 2009, p. 110. Data regarding constituent parties from 1998 to 1999, 1999 to 2004, 2004 to 2009, and 2009 from E. Sridharan, The Party System in Niraja Gopal Jayal, Pratap Bhanu Mehta, eds *The Oxford Companion to Politics in India*, New Delhi, Oxford University Press, 2010, pp. 125–127; See also for 1998 pre-electoral coalition *constituents National Agenda for Governance: BJP and Alliance Partners*

It was further pointed out that 'the National Front Government should seek national consensus on certain pressing national issues like Punjab, Babri Masjid, Ram Janmabhoomi, Centre-state relations, etc., and solve them'.[84]

The Third Front in Indian politics provided an ideological alternative to the major political parties represented by the Congress and the Bharatiya Janata Party. The National Front consisted of JD, TDP, DMK and Congress (S), the outside support was given by the BJP and the Left Front. The general elections of 1989 are also significant as the Congress was voted out or power for the second time since 1952 elections; and in 1989, for the first time, India came to be governed by the National Front Government (minority government) and the outside support was provided by the BJP and the Left Front.

The National Front manifesto incorporated the two most significant changes in the political system of the country relating first to the mobilization of the Other Backward Class (OBCs) and other lower castes and providing them an identity and, second, for the first time Ram Janmabhoomi/Babri Masjid issue became a part of all national political parties. The National Front manifesto made a pointed reference to this issue by stressing that 'The National Front feels that the Babri Masjid should not be demolished. At the same time, the Hindu sentiments to have a temple dedicated to Lord Rama should be respected'. The BJP support to the minority government of the National Front from outside in a way helped in bringing this issue in the mainstream of the political system. It is in this context it is important to highlight the Mandal issue and the Mandir issues were part of the manifesto of the National Front.

The V.P. Singh government was brought down by the withdrawal of BJP's support on the Rath Yatra and Ayodhya issue. 'Janata Dal (Samajwadi) came into being as a result of the split in the Janata Dal in November 1990'. Due to the 'long simmering discontent' with the Janata Dal, Prime Minister V.P. Singh expelled Chandra Shekhar and twenty-four other members of Lok Sabha and five members of Rajya Sabha from Janata Dal Parliamentary Party for 'Anti-Party' activities on November 5, 1991. The same day, sixty-eight members belonging to the breakaway Janata Dal group of Lok Sabha MPs unanimously elected Chandra Shekhar as their leader. 'This event led to the formation of Janata Dal (Samajwadi) on the same fateful day i.e. November 5, 1991'.[85] The left opposed the Janata Dal (Samajwadi) Government, headed by Chandra Shekhar and his group of defectors, numbered less than sixty in all and were totally dependent for survival on the Congress (I). In order to avoid being defeated on the floor of the house by the opposition, Chandra Shekhar resigned. As a consequence, the Lok Sabha was dissolved and fresh elections were ordered.

The main reason attributed for the collapse of the National Front Government was the fact that

> there was no common ideology, outlook or programme between the National Front and its outside supporters. Nor was there any ideological or programmatic compatibility between the outside supporters themselves. Indeed, there was little in common even among the various factions of the Janata Dal and even less among the diverse parties constituting the National Front. The unnatural coming together of all these incompatible factions and parties was inherently flawed.[86]

India's Tenth Lok Sabha Elections were conducted during 1991 (May 20–June 15, 1991).[87] This election like the previous election failed to produce a parliamentary majority. The Congress Party failed to get the majority but won the largest number of seats (232, which about thirty-five seats more than the 1989 elections). There was also an increase in BJP strength (86 in 1989 to 120 in 1991). P.V. Narasimha Rao headed India's third minority government within two years. He was given four weeks to provide a proof of vote of confidence in the Lok Sabha. The purpose was to prove that the Congress (I) could command the parliamentary support necessary to govern as a minority government. The vote of confidence came on July 15, 1991, as no party was prepared to face new elections. Congress (I) and its alliances cast 241 votes in favour of the motion; the BJP with 120 members voted against; and 112 of the National Front and the Left Front members of Lok Sabha abstained. The opposition parties were willing to support the government on an 'issue to issue basis'.

The 1991 election manifesto of Indian National Congress (I) not only outlined its agenda for action but also promised a definite time frame for its implementation. It identified a large number of socio, political, economic issues for implementation, with different stipulated time frames.

Another important feature of the tenth elections relate to a common manifesto of all the constituent parties of the National Front, Janata Dal, Congress(S), DMK, Asom Gana Parishad (AGP) and Telgu Desam Party. The 1991 manifesto of the National Front regarding its governance during the eleven months tenure observed

> Perhaps this is the first time that a ruling party took its Manifesto seriously and tried to implement schemes and policies

> for the benefit of the poor and the deprived, as well as to correct the structural distortions which the democratic polity had suffered under the Congress rule.[88]

In the Eleventh General Elections 1996 (April 27 to May 7),[89] none of the political formations – the Congress, the BJP, National Front or the Left Front – gained a clear majority. The Congress along with its allies won only 140 seats. The BJP turned out as the single largest party in Lok Sabha and along with its electoral allies; it had 161 seats. The BJP as the single largest party having 161 seats formed the government under A.B. Vajpayee. However, he had to resign after thirteen days when it became clear that a no confidence vote would be passed against the government.

In these elections, on the other hand, some parties – TMC (20) and DMK (17) in Tamil Nadu; the SMP (17) and the BSP (11) in Uttar Pradesh, TDP (16) in Andhra Pradesh; and SHS (15) in Maharashtra – did extremely well considering the number of seats from these states. Both the Congress and the BJP tried to form alliances with regional and state parties, but a number of regional and state level parties did not align with any of the major political formations.

The United Front (UF) was formed after the 1996 Lok Sabha Elections. After the BJP and the Congress, in terms of seats, it was in the number three position. As such, no single party or no single pre-election combination of parties secured an absolute majority. The United Front Government, which came to govern India in 1996, was constituted primarily by parties which are based in and limited to a particular state: TDP (Andhra Pradesh), DMK (Tamil Nadu), TMC (Tamil Nadu) and AGP (Assam).

The United Front set before its own government an agenda in the form of 'A Common Approach to Major Policy Matters and a Minimum Programme'. This programme was founded on the 'pillars of unity, secularism, stability, development and distributive justice'. The United Front remained in power for eighteen months. The Congress voluntarily extended outside support to the United Front. After the withdrawal of the Congress support, the mid-term polls were announced. As a coalition partner, the CPI were opposed to the idea of joining the United Front Government.

The General Election of 1998 (February 16 to February 28),[90] the Bharatiya Janata Party had pre-pole arrangement with twelve parties.[91] In this election, the BJP, with 179 seats, emerged as the largest party in terms of number of seats in the Lok Sabha. The Congress Party got 141 seats. As such, during 1998 elections neither of the parties came close to a majority in the Lok Sabha. The BJP along with its electoral allies after the elections consolidated its position by including some minor parties to take its post-electoral coalitional tally to 283. This included some post-electoral alliance partners.[92] It is evident that the BJP was the only national level party in this coalition. Almost all the other parties were state-level regional parties, functioning in one state or the other.

One high point of the BJP-led minority government was 'National Agenda for Governance' which shows the spirit of change and accommodation by BJP with other parties. The coalition government of BJP and its alliance partners presented to the country a 'National Agenda for Governance'. This was 'a joint commitment, and an assurance' that these parties gave to the country. The Agenda was adopted unanimously by both Houses of Parliament. This Agenda 'spelled out its concerns as well as an outline of solving the problems facing the country'. Broadly the following issues were dealt in the Agenda: governance, economy, unemployment, food security and price stability, empowerment of women, constitutional and legal reforms, national security, social justice, international relations, etc. The Agenda also mentioned to develop 'national consensus on all major issues confronting the nation by involving the opposition parties and all sections of society in dialogue'. The Agenda further mentioned for a 'consensual mode of governance'.

Another interesting development regarding the 1998 General Elections relate to the manifesto of the left parties. The Left parties – Communist Party of India (Marxist) Communist Party of India, Revoluntary Socialist Party, and All Indian Forward Bloc – for the first time presented a common manifesto before the people 'their alternative policies and the way to make India a vibrant democratic and just society'. The manifesto emphasized that the Left Parties will work for a strong secular-democratic system, a just socio-economic order for all oppressed sections, economic growth with equity, corruption-free governance and accountability.

The 1998 general elections, the Indian National Congress included a 'Preamble' which provided the importance of a manifesto in the context of elections in a democratic system. Some of the important points made in the Preamble are the following: (1) 'A manifesto provides an opportunity periodically for any political party to articulate its loftiest hopes and noblest aspirations', (2) 'A manifesto is a movement to offer to our people a freshness of vision, a boldness of intent and a clarity of purpose' and (3) 'a manifesto is a solemn pledge that a political party takes to fulfill promises and renew its commitments'.

The Vajpayee Government lost in the Lok Sabha by just one vote on April 17, 1999. The following factors have been attributed towards the collapse of the Vajpayee Government: lack of effective coordination, lack of consultation on major policy issues, coalition partners unable to influence policies and7 the BJP tendency to 'push forward its own reserve agenda provoked sharp protest, notably its policy towards religious minorities and the resultant attacks on Christian missionaries'.[93]

In the General Elections of 1999 (September 5 to October 3),[94] the BJP had electoral arrangements with twenty-three parties.[95] The National Democratic Alliance (NDA) was formed under the leadership of Atal Bihari Vajpayee. The NDA, in its manifesto, sought a mandate 'to complete the unfinished agenda'. One significant aspect of this alliance was that BJP could spread its influence with the help of Telugu Desam, DMK, BJD, JDU and Trinamool Congress in the southern, north-eastern, and eastern states of the country. The BJP in its allies formed a Coalition Government with 282 seats.

The alliance prepared a joint manifesto under the title *The National Agenda for Governance – the Basis of Our Joint Commitment for Stable Government*. The manifesto of NDA expressed 'the signatory political parties came together as an act of national commitment and founded the National Democratic Alliance (NDA), under the leadership of Atal Bihari Vajpee, to set the Indian polity on a new course for the future'. The preamble of the manifesto also cited the reason for creating the NDA 'to lift the spirit of the nation at large, to draw its people together and, most importantly, to rebuild the bonds of common purpose that are the very roots of our democratic polity'. The manifesto very forcefully pointed out that the NDA was formed as 'our young democracy cannot bear the fits and tremors of frequent elections which will undermine the peoples' in the democratic process'. The manifesto of this alliance was based

> with a consensus on a common cause and a common set of principles we have sunk over differences to weld ourselves into a solid phalanx of a single dominant political formation and thereby we fulfill the resolve of the Indian people to give themselves a stable, strong and progressive Government.

It is significant to emphasize that both in the 1998 and 1999 General Elections in which the BJP-led alliances formed the governments, on the issue of secularism, all alliance parties projected a view which was more encompassing and comprehensive than a view normally undertaken by the BJP. On the issue of secularism, the NDA, committed itself for a 'civilized, humane and just social order'. On the one hand, it promised non-discrimination on account of caste, religion, colour, race, etc. It also promised to 'uphold and practice the concept of secularism consistent with the Indian tradition of equal respect with all faiths'. It also stressed the need to take effective steps for the economic, social and educational development of the minorities.

In 2004 elections (April 20 and May 10)[96] the Congress-led alliance consisted of nineteen parties. The Congress-led alliance got 222 seats (the Congress won 145 seats and the alliance partners got 77 seats). The NDA consisting of the (BJP and its allied partners) got 189 seats. Out of these, the BJP won 138 seats, only seven seats less than the Congress. However, the UPA were supported from outside by the Left Parties (sixty-one seats) and the SP (thirty-six seats) and the BSP (nineteen seats).

The 2004 election manifesto of the Congress under the title 'change and continuity' described how it responded to new challenges during the 1950s, 1960s, 1970s and 1980s. The manifesto also reiterated that within 100 days of receiving the mandate, the party will release a detailed action plan on the promises and commitments made in the manifesto. The Congress-led United Progressive Alliance (UPA)-I was constituted only after the election results were announced. The UPA comprised of Indian National Congress, and its pre-poll partners[97] supported by like-minded parties.

The manifesto of Indian National Congress for the 2004 general elections provided the foundation of a Common Minimum Programme of the UPA. The UPA Government formulated six basic principles for governance: protect and promote social harmony; ensure 7–8 percent growth of economy per year; enhance the welfare and well-being of farmers, farm labour and workers; empowering women; equality of opportunity for Scheduled Castes, Scheduled Tribes, OBCs and religious minorities and unleash the creative energies of entrepreneurs, businessmen, scientists, engineers and all other professionals. The UPA made also a solemn pledge 'to provide a corruption free, transparent, accountable, responsible and responsive government'. The most significant highlight of this programme was formulating an inventory of the critical issues in each sector and identifying the implementing Ministry/Department as well as putting the action needed on each issue.

In the 2009 elections (April 16 to May 13),[98] the UPA coalition consisting of the Congress along with its pre-electoral partners won 263 seats. Out of this the Congress won 206 seats (sixty-one seats more than the 2004 elections tally) and its electoral partners won fifty-seven seats. In this election, the Congress did not go for a national alliance and for a common programme. However, there were post-electoral negotiations relating to cabinet formation consisting of the Congress, TC, DMK, NCP, NC and MUL. On the other hand the NDA got 159 seats. Out of these the BJP won 116 seats and its allied partners got forty-three seats. The NDA got thirty seats less in comparison to the 2004 general elections. There was a reduction in the number of electoral partners in the case of BJP, which got reduced from twenty-four in 1999 to thirteen in 2004 and nine in 2009. One significant aspect of 2009 elections relate to the fact that there was no national level alliance made by both the Congress and the BJP.

The Congress manifesto of 2009 with regard to its alliance partners pointed out that 'Over the past five years, the Indian National Congress has managed a coalition government at the Centre, accommodating the views of its partners but without compromising on any of the essential principles of nation-building'.

Lok Sabha general election 2014

One of the significant aspects of the 16th Lok Sabha election[99] has been the coming back to power of a single party majority (Table 3.4) in the Lok Sabha after a gap of 30 years. The BJP with its 282 seats and the alliance NDA got 336 seats. On the other hand, the INC had to suffer the most humiliating defeat, securing only forty-four seats and the combination it headed the UPA getting fifty-nine seats. The INC party at forty-four seats is lower than the number of seats required to be recognized as the official opposition party in the Lok Sabha. Another important aspect regarding the BJP relates to the fact that its candidates won seats in almost all states. The BJP won all seats in Gujarat, Rajasthan, Delhi, Uttarakhand, Himachal Pradesh and Goa and won most of the seats in Uttar Pradesh, Chattisgarh, Jharkhand and Bihar. Besides, the regional political parties like SP, BSP, RJD, JDU lost heavily in this election. However, there are some regional parties came up with spectacular performances like AIADMK, BJD and TMC.

It has also been observed that the people's verdict represents a 'paradigm shift'. The rise of the BJP as a pan-India party has simultaneously resulted in the Congress losing that stature. The resentment against the Congress and the United Progressive Alliance (UPA) Government led to the decimation of the country's oldest party, which recorded its lowest-ever tally.

Table 3.4 Lok Sabha general election 2014.

Party	*Seats*	*Vote percentage*
Bharatiya Janata Party	282	31.0%
Communist Party	1	0.8%
Communist Party of India (Marxist)	9	3.2%
Indian National Congress	44	19.3%
Nationalist Congress Party	6	
Aam Aadmi Party	4	2.0%
All India Anna Dravida Munnetra Kazhagam	37	3.3%
All India N.R. Congress	1	
All India Trinamool Congress	34	3.8%
All India United Democratic Front	3	0.4%
Biju Janata Dal	20	1.7%
Indian National Lok Dal	2	0.5%
Indian Union Muslim League	2	0.1%
Jammu & Kashmir Peoples Democratic Party	3	
Janata Dal (Secular)	2	0.7%
Janata Dal (United)	2	1.1%
Jharkhand Mukti Morcha	2	0.3%
Kerala Congress (M)	1	
Lok Jan Shakti Party	6	0.4%
Naga Peoples Front	1	0.2%
National Peoples Party	1	
Pattali Makkal Katchi	1	0.3%
Rashtriya Janata Dal	4	1.3%
Revolutionary Socialist Party	1	0.3%
Samajwadi Party	5	0.2%
Shiromani Akali Dal	4	0.7%
Shiv Sena	18	
Sikkim Democratic Front	1	
Telangana Rahtra Samithi	11	1.2%
Telgu Desam	16	2.5%
All India Majlis-E-Ittehadul Muslimeen	1	
Apna Dal	2	0.1%
Rashtriya Lok Samta Party	3	
Swabhimani Paksha	1	3.4%
Yuvajana Sramika Rythu Congress Party	9	2.5%
Independent	3	
Total	543	

Note: The vote percentage shares of the following parties are not available: Jammu & Kashmir Peoples Democratic Party; Nationalist Congress Party; Kerala Congress (M); National Peoples Party; Shiv Sena; All India Majlis E Ittehadul Muslimeen; Rashtriya Lok Samta Party; Independent.

Source: Election Commission of India, http://eciresults.nic.in/

Notes

1 Memorandum on Post-War Reforms (By nineteen members of the Imperial Legislative Council) 1916 in B. Shiva Rao, *The Framing of India's Constitution: Select Documents*, Vol. I, New Delhi: Indian Institute of Public Administration, 1966, pp. 19–24. The signatories to the memorandum were the following: Manindra Chandra Nandy of Kasimbazar, Dinshaw E. Wacha, Bhupendranath Basu, Bishan Dutt, Shukul, Madan Mohan Malaviya, K.V. Rangaswamiengar, Mazharul Haque, V.S. Srinivasa Sastri, Tej Bahadur Sapru, Ibrahim Rahimtoola, B. Narasimheswara Sarma, Mir Asad Ali, Kamini Kumar Chanda, Krishna Sahay, R.N. Bhanja Deo of Kanika, M.B. Dadabhoy, Sita Nath Roy, Mohamed Ali Mohamed, M.A. Jinnah.
2 *The Nehru Report: An Anti-Separatist Manifesto*, The Committee Appointed by The All Parties' Conference 1928, New Delhi: Michiko & Panjathan, Reprinted 1975, p. 94.
3 Ibid., p. 123.
4 Ibid., pp. 35–36.
5 Harijan (January 14, 1939), p. 421 quoted in H.M. Vyas (compiled), *Gandhiji Expects: Why the Father of the Nation expected of People's Representatives*, Ahmedabad: Navajivan Publishing House, 1965, pp. 37–38.
6 Harijan (March 2, 1947), p. 45 quoted in Vyas (compiled), *Gandhiji Expects*, pp. 37–38.
7 Jawaharlal Nehru, *The Discovery of India*, New Delhi: Jawaharlal Nehru Memorial Fund, Oxford University Press, 1946; Seventeenth Impression, 1997, p. 355.
8 Rao, *The Framing of India's Constitution*, Vol. II, 1967, p. 44.
9 Ibid., pp. 295–296.
10 *Constitutional Assembly Debates: Official Report*, Vol. VIII, New Delhi: Lok Sabha Secretariat, Reprinted 1989, p. 905.
11 Ibid., p. 906.
12 Ibid.
13 Ibid., p. 908.
14 Ibid., p. 926.
15 Ibid., pp. 924–925.
16 Ibid., p. 923.
17 Rao, *The Framing of India's Constitution*, Vol. II, pp. 352, 353, 377–78, 531–532, 627.
18 *Constituent Assembly Debates*, Vol. V, pp. 197–280.
19 Ibid., p. 243.
20 Rao, *The Framing of India's Constitution*, p. 109.
21 Ibid., pp. 109–110. In the context of minorities and Scheduled Castes and Scheduled Tribes representation and electoral reservation in India, the following are some important publications: Rochana Bajpai, *Constituent Assembly Debates and Minority Rights, Economic and Political Weekly*(May 27, 2000), pp. 1837–1845; Alistair Mcmlllan, *Standing at the Margins Representation and Electoral Reservation in India*, New Delhi: Oxford University Press, 2005, p. 340.
22 Rao, *The Framing of India's Constitution*, Vol. IV, p. 601.

23 *Constituent Assembly Debates*, Vol. VII, p. 1363.
24 Ibid., p. 1366.
25 Ibid., Vol. VIII, p. 930.
26 Ibid., pp. 907.
27 Ibid., Vol. XI, p. 835.
28 Granville Austin, *The Indian Constitution: Cornerstone of a Nation*, New Delhi: Oxford University Press, First Published 1966 Eighth Impression, 2004, p. 47. See also David Gilmanton, Election Law and the 'People' in Colonial and Postcolonial India in Dipesh Chakravarty, Rochna Majumdar and Andrew Sartori, *From the Colonial to the Postcolonial: India and Pakistan in Transition*, New Delhi: Oxford University Press, 2007, p. 56 and A.H. Somjee, *Political Capacity in Developing Societies*, London: The Macmillan Press Ltd, 1982, p. 32.
29 *Constituent Assembly Debates: Official Report*, Vol. XI, New Delhi: Lok Sabha Secretariat, 1989, p. 660.
30 Ibid., p. 777.
31 Ibid., p. 818.
32 Ibid., p. 939.
33 Ibid., Vol. VIII, pp. 932–933.
34 Ibid., p. 933.
35 Ibid., pp. 934–935.
36 Ibid., p. 935.
37 Ibid., p. 936.
38 V. S. Rama Devi and S. K. Mendiratta, *How India Votes: Election Laws, Practice and Procedure*, First Edition, New Delhi: Butterworths, 2000, p. 22.
39 B. Shiva Rao, *The Framing of India's Constitution: A Study*, Vol. V, New Delhi: The Indian Institute of Public Administration, 1968, p. 835 and see also W.H. Morris Jones, *The Indian Elections in The Economic Weekly*(June 28, 1952), pp. 655–656.
40 Myron Weiner, *Party Building in a New Nation: The Indian National Congress*, Chicago: The University of Chicago Press, 1967, p. 40. It is interesting in this context to point out that that the possession of political power brought new responsibilities to the Congress. Besides, as explained in part two, since 1885, the party passed many resolutions which gave prominence to the political, social and economic issues of the country with special emphasis on poverty. However, the Congress Party after independence started thinking of framing a party constitution with a different object and programme in the context of a free India. The draft of the revised constitution was shown to Mahatma Gandhi who revised the draft and pointed out that 'the Congress in its present shape and form, i.e., as a propaganda vehicle and parliamentary machine, has outlived its use. India has still to attain social, moral and economic independence in terms of its seven hundred thousand villages. . . . It must be kept out of unhealthy competition with political parties and communal bodies. For these and other similar reasons, the A.I.C.C. resolves to disband the existing Congress organization and flower into a Lok Sevak Singh'. Mahatma Gandhi's views were so radical that the Congress did not accept them. In February 1948, the Congress approved the following amendment in its

Constitution – the object of the Congress from 'complete independence' by all legitimate and peaceful means, was changed to bring 'well-being and advancement of the people of India and the establishment in India by peaceful and legitimate means of a Co-operative Commonwealth based on equality of opportunity and of political, economic and social rights and aiming at world peace and fellowship'. Another amendment was passed which disallowed, any party member 'of any political party, communal or other, which has a separate membership, constitution and programme'. See also M.V. Ramana Rao, *Development of the Congress Constitution*, New Delhi: All India Congress Committee, 1958, p. 72.

41 V. S. Rama Devi and S. K. Mendiratta, *How India Votes: Election Laws, Practice and Procedure*, First Edition, New Delhi: Butterworths, 2000, p. 479.

42 Ibid., pp. 480–483.

43 Csaba Nikolenyi, Recognition Rules, Party Labels and the Number of Parties in India: A Research Note, in *Party Politics*, Vol. 14, No.2 (2008), p. 215. See also Pradeep Chibber, Ken Kollman, *The Formation of National Party Systems: Federalism and Party Competition in Canada, Great Britain, India, And the United States Princeton*, Princeton, NJ: Princeton University Press, 2004.

44 V. S. Rama Devi and S. K. Mendiratta, *How India Votes: Election Laws, Practice and Procedure*, New Delhi: Butterworths, 2007, pp. 580–588.

45 Election Commission, Report on the First General Elections in India 1951–52, Vol. I, New Delhi: Government of India Press, 1955, pp. 22–23.

46 *Constituent Assembly Debates*, Vol. VII, pp. 1355–1391.

47 Ibid., p. 1362.

48 Ibid.

49 Ibid., p. 1380.

50 Ibid., p. 1387. See the correspondence amongst the President of India, the Prime Minister, the Law Minister, Government of India, the Election Commission and various State Governments on holding the General Elections under the new Constitution and the problems associated regarding preparation of electoral rolls. For representation of the People Bill and provisions relating to delimitation of constituencies, see Valmiki Choudhary, ed., *Dr. Rajendra Prasad: Correspondence and Select Documents*, Vol.12 (January–June 1950) *Presidency Period*, Ahmedabad: Allied Publishers Limited, 1989, pp. 270–278.

51 Jawaharlal Nehru's, *Speeches 1949–1953, Second Impression*, New Delhi: The Publications Division, Ministry of Information and Broadcasting, Government of India, 1957, pp. 22–23.

52 Congress Bulletin, No. 1 (January–February 1952), pp. 11–16 quoted in Michael Brecher, *Nehru: A Political Biography*, London: Oxford University Press, 1959, p. 447.

53 Election Commission, *Report on the First General Elections in India 1951–52*, Vol. I, New Delhi: Government of India Press, 1955, p. 10.

54 Brecher, *Nehru: A Political Biography*, p. 444.

55 For details, see Asoka Mehta, *The Political Mind of India: An Analysis of the Results of the General Elections*, Bombay: A Socialist Party Publication, 1952, pp. 5–12; Ramachandra Guha, Democracy's Biggest Gamble:

India's First Free Elections in 1952, *WorldPolicy Journal*, Spring 2002, pp. 95–103; Irene Tinker and Mil Walker, The First General Elections in India and Indonesia, *Far Eastern Survey*, Vol. XXV, No.7 (July 1956), pp. 97–110.

56 Brecher, *Nehru: A Political Biography*, p. 438.

57 New Age (July 15, 1956). See also text of a letter written by Jaya Prakash Narayan regarding electoral adjustments in Janata (September23, 1956) and the text of Asoka Mehta's Statement as a rejoinder to JayaPrakash Narayan's Letter in *Bombay Chronicle* (September21, 1956).

58 *Election Manifesto of the Communist Party of India*, New Delhi: Communist Party Publication, 1957, p. 43.

59 For details, see *Report on the Second General Elections in India*, 1957, Vol. I (General), New Delhi: Election Commission, 1958, p. 1; 'Congress Election Manifesto' (Editorial) *The Economic Weekly*, Vol. IX, No. 2 (January 12, 1957), pp. 33–34; The Parliament(Editorial) *The Economic Weekly*, Vol. IV (May 17, 1952), pp. 463–464; S.L. Poplai, ed., *National Politics and 1957 Elections in India*, New Delhi: Metropolitan Book Co. Private Ltd, 1957.

60 Selig S. Harrison, Hindu Society and the State: The Indian Union in K.H. Silvert, ed., *Expectant Peoples: Nationalism and Development*, New York: Random House, 1963, p. 286.

61 Ibid.

62 For details see Election Commission, *Report on the Third General Elections in India*, 1962, Vol. I (General), New Delhi: Election Commission, pp. 3–13; Rajni Kothari, The Congress 'System' in India in Rajni Kothari, etal., *Party System and Election Studies, Centre for the Study of Developing Societies Occasional Papers: Number 1*, Bombay: Allied Publishers, 1967, pp. 1–18 and Wayne A Wilcox, Towards a Theory of Indian Politics: A Comment, *The Economic Weekly* (December 15, 1962), pp. 1911–1912 and Surindar Suri, Towards a Theory of Indian Politics: Some Implications of the Results of the General Election, *The Economic Weekly* (December 1, 1962), pp. 1847–1852 and see also for the development of the party system after independence as well as dominance of the Congress Party and a detailed analysis of the results of 1962 elections – Gopal Krishan, One Party Dominance – Development and Trends, *Perspectives*, supplement to the *Indian Journal of Public Administration*, Vol. XII, No. 1 (January–March 1966), pp. 1–65.

63 For details, see M. Pattabhiram, ed., *General Election in India 1967: An Exhaustive Study of Main Political Trends*, Bombay: Allied Publishers, 1967; Sulekh C. Gupta, Fourth General Elections: Its Dimension and Dialectics, *Mainstream* (March 11, 1967), pp. 30–31; Norman D. Palmer, India's Fourth General Elections, *Asian Survey*, Vol. VII, No. 5 (May 1967), pp. 275–291 and S.P. Varma and Iqbal Narain, eds., *Fourth General Election in India, Volume One Political Surveys*, Bombay: Orient Longmans Limited, 1968, pp. 1–37; *Seminar* No. 89 Your Vote.

64 Rajni Kothari, Continuity and Change in India's Party System, *Asian Survey*, Vol. X, No. 11, 1970, p. 947.

65 Election Commission, *Report on the Mid-term General Elections in India 1968–69*, New Delhi: Government of India Press, p. 7.

66 Election Commission, *Report on the Fifth General Elections in India 1971–71. Narrative and Reflective Part*, New Delhi: Government of India Press, pp. i–iii and pp. 235–245.

67 For a detailed account of the origin of this spilt, see A. Moin Zaidi, *The Great Upheaval 1969–1972: The Case of the Indian National Congress in Ferment Based on Documents Emanating From Official Sources*, New Delhi: Orientalia, 1972, pp. 35–176.

68 W.H. Morris-Jones, India Elects for Change and Stability, *Asian Survey*, Vol. XI, No. 8 (July 1971), pp. 719–741.

69 Myron Weiner, The 1971 Elections and the Indian Party System, *Asian Survey*, Vol. XI, No. 12 (December 1971), pp. 1153–1166.

70 Weiner, *The 1971 Elections and the Indian Party System*, p. 1156.

71 For details see Madhu Limaye, *Janata Party Experiment: An Insider's Account of Opposition Politics: 1975–1977*, Vol.1, New Delhi: B.R. Publishing Corporation, 1994; S. Devadas Pillai, ed., *The Incredible Elections: 1977: A blow-by-Blow Document as reported in the Indian Express*, Bombay: Popular Prakashan, 1977; Stanley A. Kochanek, Mrs. Gandhi's Pyramid: The New Congress in Henry C. Hart, ed., *Indira Gandhi's India : A political System Reappraised,* Boulder, CO: Westview Press, 1976, pp. 93–124; Ram Joshi and Kirtidev Desai, Towards a More Competitive Party System in India, *Asian Survey*, Vol. xviii, No. 1 (November 1978), pp. 1091–1117; Oliver Mendelsohn, The Collapse of the Indian National Congress, *Pacific Affairs*, Vol.51, No.1, Spring (1978), pp. 41–66; Myron Weiner, The 1977 Parliamentary Elections in India, *Asian Survey*, Vol. XVII, No. 7 (July 1977), pp. 619–626; Norman D. Palmer, The Two Elections: A Comparative Analysis, *Asian Survey*, Vol. XVII, No.7 (July 1977), pp. 648–666; Harry W. Blair, Mrs. Gandhi's Emergency, The Indian Elections of 1977, Pluralism and Marxism: Problems with Paradigms Modern, *Asian Studies*, Vol. 14, No. 2 (1980), pp. 237–271; D.A. Low, *Eclipse of Empire*, Cambridge: Cambridge University Press, 1991, pp. 148–163. Jyotirindra Das Gupta, India 1979: The Prize Chair and the People's Share – Electoral Diversion and Economic Reversal, *Asian Survey*, Vol. XX, No. 2 (February 1980); Kuldip Nayar, *The Judgement,* New Delhi: VikasPublishing House Pvt. Ltd, 1977; Norman D. Palmer, India in 1976: The Politics of Depoliticization, *Asian Survey*, Vol. XVII, No.2 (February 1977), pp. 160–180.

72 Myron Weiner, *India at the Polls: The Parliamentary Elections of 1977*, Washington, DC: American Enterprise Institute for Public Policy Research, 1978, p. 1.

73 C.P. Bhambhri, *The Janata Party: A Profile*, New Delhi: National Publishing House, 1980, p. 16.

74 Ibid., p. 149.

75 David Butler, *Ashok Lahiri and Prannoy Roy, India Decides: Elections 1952–1995*, Third Edition, New Delhi: Books and Things, 1995, pp. 88–89.

76 For details, see S.K. Chaturvedi, *The Seventh Lok Sabha Election: An Analysis of Peoples' Verdict*, Kanpur: Grantham, 1981, pp. 33–114; Javeed Alam, The Vote for 'Political Stability' and the Implication: An Analysis of 1980 Election Results, *Political Science Review*, Vol. 21, No. 4 (October–December 1982), pp. 289–318; Y.C. Bhatnagar and Moin

Shakir, The Seventh Lok Sabha Elections, *Indian Journal of Political Science*, Vol. 41 (1980), pp. 69–78 and N.D. Arora, Analysis of 7th Lok Sabha Elections in the State of Punjab, Haryana and J & K, *The Indian Political Science Review*, Election Issue (July 1980), p. 198; Henry C. Hart, The Indian Constitution: Political Development and Decay, *Asian Survey*, Vol. XX, No. 4 (April 1980), pp. 428–451.

77 For details, see V. Bhaskara Rao, ed., *General Elections in India: Some Issues of Eighth Lok Sabha Elections*, New Delhi: Uppal Publishing House, 1987, pp. 29–35; J.R. Siwach, Eighth Lok Sabha Elections, *The Indian Journal of Political Studies*, Vol.9 (December 1985), pp. 25–44; Walter Hauser and Wendy Singer, The Democratic Rite: Celebration and Participation in the Indian Elections, *Asian Survey*, Vol. XXVI, No.9 (September 1986), pp. 941–958; Party Manifestos, Paper Promises (Special), *India Today*(December 31, 1984), pp. 46–49; Iqbal Narain, India in 1985: Triumph of Democracy, *Asian Survey*, Vol. XXVI, No.2 (February 1986), pp. 253–269; Harold A. Gould, A Sociological Perspective on the Eighth General Election in India, *Asian Survey*, Vol. XXVI, No. 6 (June 1986), pp. 630–652; David Butler, The Winter's Election, *Representation*, Vol. 25, No. 98 (March 1985), pp. 1–2.

78 Butler, Lahiri and Roy, *India Decides: Elections 1952–1995*, Third Edition, New Delhi: Books and Things, 1995, pp. 96–97.

79 Mandate and After (Editor's Notebook), *Mainstream*, Vol. XXIII, No. 19 (January 5, 1985), p. 2.

80 Ibid.

81 For details see Harold A. Gould and Sumit Ganguly, eds., *India Votes: Alliance Politics and Minority Governments in the Ninth and Tenth General Elections*, Boulder, CO: Westview Press, 1993, pp. 1–220; Mahendra Prasad Singh, ed., *Lok Sabha Elections 1989: Indian Politics in 1990's*, New Delhi: Kalinga Publications, 1992, pp. 37–49; Mahendra Prasad Singh, Ideological Spectrum in Mahendra Prasad Singh and Rekha Saxena, eds., *India's Political Agenda: Perspectives on the Party System*, New Delhi: Kalinga Publications, 1996, pp. 1–34; Dipankar Sinha V.P. Singh, Chandra Shekhar, And 'Nowhere Politics' In India, *Asian Survey*, Vol. XXXI, No.7 (July 1991), pp. 598–612; *The 'People's Verdict'*, *Seminar* No. 368 (April 1990), pp. 12–17; Dennis Austin and Anirudha Gupta, India's Ninth General Election, *The Round Table*, No. 314, 1990, pp. 137–146; Walter K. Anderson, Election 1989 in India: The Dawn of Coalition Politics?, *Asian Survey*, Vol. XXX, No. 6 (June 1990), pp. 527–540; Atul Kohli, From Majority to Minority Rule: Making Sense of the 'New' Indian Politics in Marshall M. Bouton and Philip Oldenburg, eds., *India Briefing*, 1990, Boulder, CO: Westview Press, 1990.

82 A.M. Zaidi, ed., *The Annual Register of Indian Political Parties: Proceedings and Fundamental Texts 1989: Part Two*, New Delhi: Publication Department, Indian Institute of Applied Political Research, 1992, pp. 416–417.

83 Ibid., p. 417.

84 Ibid., pp. 199–200.

85 Zaidi, ed., *The Annual Register of Indian Political Parties 1991: Part One*, 1993, p. 454.

86 Election Manifesto, *General Election 1991 Indian National Congress (I)*, New Delhi: All Indian Congress Committee, p. 2.

87 For details see Gould and Ganguly, eds., *India Votes*, pp. 221–315; Robert L. Hardgrave, After the Dynasty: Politics in India, *Current History*(March 1992), pp. 106–112; for analyses of the election see *India Today*(July 15, 1991), pp. 10–44; Walter K. Andersen, India's 1991 Elections: The Uncertain Verdict, *Asian Survey*, Vol. 31, No. 10 (October 1991); Mitu Sengupta, How the State Changed Its Mind: Power, Politics and the Origins of India's Market Reforms, *Economic & Political Weekly* (Special Article) (May 24, 2008), pp. 35–42; A.G. Noorani, Ayodhya again: The BJP's unconstitutional project, *Frontline*(July 6–19, 1991), pp. 103–104.

88 Manifesto of National Front, *Lok Sabha Elections 1991*, p. 444 quoted in Zaidi, ed., *The Annual Register of Indian Political Parties,* New Delhi: Applied PoliticaL Research, *1991: Part Two.*

89 For details, see Pramod K Kantha, General Elections, 1996: BJP Politics: Looking beyond the Impasse, *Economic and Political Weekly* (November 29, 1997), pp. 3090–3100; Walter Andersen, India in 1995: Year of the Long Campaign, *Asian Survey*, Vol. XXXVI, No.2 (February 1996), pp. 165–178; Aditya Nigam, India After the 1996 Elections: Nation, Locality and Representation, *Asian Survey*, Vol. XXXVI, No. 12 (December 1996), pp. 1159–1169; Sudha Pai, Transformation of the Indian Party System: The 1996 Lok Sabha Elections, *Asian Survey*, Vol. XXXVI, No.12 (December 1996), pp. 1170–1183; BM, UF Government Emerging in True Colours, *Economic and Political Weekly* (June 22, 1996), pp. 1568–1569; Paul Wallace, General Elections, 1996: Regional Parties Dominant in Punjab and Haryana, *Economic and Political Weekly* (November 15, 1997), pp. 2963–2969; Sudipta Kaviraj, The General Elections in India, *Government and Opposition*, Vol. 32 (1997), pp. 3–24; E. Sridharan, *Coalition Politics, Seminar* No. 437 (January 1996), pp. 53–57; Prannoy Roy and Dorab Sopariwala, Political Alliances: Fatal Attraction, *India Today* (April 15, 1996), pp. 36–41.

90 For details, see Paul Wallace, Introduction: India's 1998 Election – Hindutva, the Tail Wags the Elephant, and Pokhran in Ramashray Roy and Paul Wallace, eds., *Indian Politics and 1998 Election: Regionalism, Hindutva and State Politics*, New Delhi: Sage Publications, 1999, pp. 15–35; Sudha Pai, *State Politics New Dimension: Party System, Liberalisation and Politics of Identity*. New Delhi: Shipra Publications, 2000, pp. 37–57.

91 Bharatiya Janata Party, All-India Anna Dravida Munnetra Kazhagam, Samata Party, Biju Janata Dal, Shiromant Akali Dal, Trinamool Congress, Shiv Sena, Marumalarchi Dravida Munnetra Kazhagam, Pattali Makkal Katchi, Lok Shakti, Haryana Vikas Party, Tamizhaga Rajiv Congress, Janata Party. See Coalition constituents National Agenda for Governance: BJP and Alliance Partners, p. 1.

92 Namely the Indian National Lok Dal, Arunchal Congress, Sikkim Democratic Front, Manipur State Congress, Citizens Common Front, Bodoland State Movement. Committee, Telgu Desam, National Conference, Anglo-Indians, Unattached. See Balveer Arora, Negotiating Differences: Federal Coalitions and National Cohesion in Francine R. Frankel, et al., eds.,

Transforming India: Social and Political Dynamics of Democracy, New Delhi: Oxford University Press, 2000, p. 194.

93 Balveer Arora, Negotiating Differences: Federal Coalitions and National Cohesion in Francine R. Frankel, et al., eds., *Transforming India: Social and Political Dynamics of Democracy*, New Delhi: Oxford University Press, 2000, p. 199.

94 For details, see *Cruel Choices, Seminar* No. 480 (August 1999), pp. 12–29; Aditya Nigam and Yogendra Yadav, Electoral Politics in Indian States, 1989–99, *Economic and Political Weekly* (August 21–28, 1999), pp. 2391–2399; Rob Jenkins, Appearance and Reality in Indian Politics: Making Sense of the 1999 General Election, *Government and Opposition*, Vol. 35, No.1 (2000), pp. 49–66; Nagindas Sanghavi and Usha Thakkar, Regionalisation of Indian Politics, *Economic and Political Weekly* (February 12, 2000), pp. 514–518; Yogendra Yadav and Suhas Palshikar, From Hegemony to Convergence Party System and Electoral Politics in the Indian States, 1952–2002, *Journal of Indian School of Political Economy*, Vol. 15, No. 1 and 2 (January–June, 2000), pp. 6–44.

95 Pre-electoral – Bharatiya Janata Party, Janta Dal (United), Biju Janata Dal, Dravida Munnetra Kazhagam, Shiva Sena, Trinamool Congress, Indian National Lok Dal, Shiromani Akali Dal, Marmaraichi Dravida Munnetra Kazhagam, Pattali Makkal Katchi, Himachal Vikas Congress, MGR Anna Dravida Munnetra Kazhagam, Akhil Bharatiya Lok Tantrik Congress, Manipur State Congress Party, Sikkim Democratic Front, Independent (Maneka Gandhi), Janatantrik Bahujan Samaj Party, Arunachal Congress, Democratic Bahujan Samaj Morcha, -: TRC, JKNC, RLD. Outside support from Telugu Desam Party see Bidyut Chakrabarty, *Forging Power: Coalition Politics in India*, New Delhi: Oxford University Press, 2006, p. 199.

96 For details, see Dunu Roy, From Promises to Performance: Political Manifestos and Budget 2004–05, *Economic and Political Weekly*(August 7, 2004), pp. 3583–3585; R Sthanumoorthy and Leena Mary Eapen, Economic Issues in Elections: Recent Trends, *Economic and Political Weekly* (March 6, 2004), pp. 1019–1021; Christophe Jaffrelot, The BJP and the 2004 general election: Dimensions, Causes and Implications of an Unexpected Defeat in Katharine Adeney and Lawrence Saez, *Coalition Politics and Hindu Nationalism*, New York: Routledge, 2005, pp. 237–253; *A Mandate for Change, Seminar* No. 539 (July 2004), pp. 12–43.

97 Indian National Congress, Rashtriya Janata Dal (RJD), Dravida Munnetra Kazhagam (DMK), Nationalist Congress Party (NCP), Pattali Makkal Katchi (PMK), Telengana Rashtra Samilti, Jharkhand Mukti Morcha (JMM), Marumalarchi Davida Munnetra Kazhagam (MDMK), Lok Janashakti Party (LJP), People's Democratic Party (PDP), Republican Party of India(A) (RPI (A), Muslim League, Kerala State Committee (MUL), Independents (IND), Janata Dal (Secular) JD(S), Republican Party of India (RPI), People's Republican Party (PRBP), Arunachal Congress (AC) See Bidyut Chakrabarty, *Forging Power: Coalition Politics in India*, New Delhi: Oxford University Press, 2006, p. 226.

98 For details, see Ramashray Roy, Regional Base and National Dream: Alliance Formation, 2009 National Elections in Paul Wallace and Ramashray Roy, eds., *India's 2009 Elections: Coalition Politics, Party Competition,*

and Congress Continuity, London: Sage Publications, 2011, pp. 21–41; Ajay K. Mehra, ed., *Emerging Trends in Indian Politics: The 15th General Election*, London: Routledge, 2010; Verdict 2009: Myths and Hypotheses, *Economic and Political Weekly* (May 23, 2009), pp. 5–6; National Election Study 2009, *Economic and Political Weekly* (September 26–October 2, 2009), pp. 33–82.

99 National Election Study 2014, *Economic and Political Weekly*, Vol. 49, No. 39 (September 27, 2014), pp. 39–98.

4

A COMPARATIVE ANALYSIS OF PARTY MANIFESTOS OF NATIONAL POLITICAL PARTIES

Before we analyse the party manifestos of national political parties from 1952 to 2014, it is necessary to provide a brief outline of the initiatives taken regarding the social and economic reconstruction of the country between 1946 and 1951. These initiatives provide a background of the efforts made for social and economic modernization before the beginning of competitive electoral politics. These initiatives came from three different entities: the Constitution of India, the Government of India and the national political parties.

The first important initiative relates to the Directive Principles of State Policy of the Indian Constitution. In the Constituent Assembly, a Committee under the Chairmanship of J.B. Kriplani submitted the Report on Fundamental Rights in April 1947. Along with a list of Fundamental Rights which are enforceable by appropriate legal process also contained certain provisions 'which are in the nature of fundamental principles of the social policy that is to regulate the governments concerned'. The Committee observed that while drawing up these principles it has kept 'in view the complexity of Indian conditions and the peculiarities of the Indian situation'.

Directive principles of state policy

It is proposed to provide an outline of these principles. Under Article 39 the state is called upon to direct its policy towards securing, amongst other objectives, these: (1) that all citizens have the right to an adequate means of livelihood; (2) that the ownership and control of the material resources of the community are so distributed as best to subserve the common good; (3) that the operation of economic system does not result in the concentration of wealth and means of production to the common detriment; (4) that there is equal pay for equal work for both men and women; (5) that childhood and youth, men and women are protected against exploitation and moral and material abandonment. Article 40 instructs the state, in conformity with the importance of village *panchayats* or councils in ancient India, to organize such local authorities and provide them with the powers enabling them to function effectively as units of self-government

The Principles (vide Articles 41, 42 and 43) direct the state, within the limits of its economic capacity and development, to secure the right to work, the right to education and the right to public assistance for the unemployed, aged, sick and disabled; to secure proper conditions of work and maternity relief and to secure by suitable laws or economic organization for all workers a living wage and full enjoyment of leisure. These principles also stress the need to promote cottage industries on an individual or co-operative basis in rural areas. Article 44 pleads – 'the State shall endeavour to secure for the citizens a uniform civil code throughout the territory of India'. Article 45 calls upon the state to provide, within a period of ten years, free compulsory education for all children upto the age of fourteen years.

Article 46 calls upon the state to concentrate upon promoting the educational and economic interests of the weaker sections of the people, in particular the tribes, lower castes, and outcastes, protecting them from social injustice and all forms of exploitation. Article 47 dedicates the state to raising the level of nutrition and the standard of living as a primary duty, with an attempt to prohibit the consumption, except for medicinal purposes, 'of intoxicating drinks' and injurious drugs; while Article 48 calls for the preservation and improvement of cattle breeds and the prohibition of their slaughter. Article 49 deals with protection of monuments and places and objects of national importance; Article 50 involves the separation of the judiciary from the executive; Article 51 promotes international peace and security.

The Constituent Assembly discussed these provisions as part of the Draft Constitution during November 1948. A number of members were critical of the fact that 'welfare and well-being' of the people of India has not been made justiceable. Dr. P.S. Deshmukh epitomized the views of many others by observing 'This Report . . . represents that part of the Constitution which the masses of India are looking forward to for the fulfilment of the promises made to them by their leaders'.[1] He even went to the extent of expressing that 'the Committee viewed the whole question from an utterly wrong stand-point: Our Constitution framers appear as if they merely studied the existing Constitutions and chose what they thought would probably serve as a sop to the socialists and communists'.[2] He observed 'We expected, . . . that the Indian society would in the future be regulated on definite principles. . . . Instead of having all these several items, let the framers of our Constitution give us a definite programme that they are determined to give effect to'.[3]

In summing up the debate on the Directive Principles of State Policy, Dr. B.R. Ambedkar justified the inclusion of these principles by stating that the Constitution provides only a machinery for the government of the country. In a democracy, the people of the country will decide 'who should be in power'. However, Ambedkar cautioned that 'whoever captures power will not be free to do what he likes with it'. But in the exercise of power,

> he will have to respect these instruments of instructions which are called Directive Principles. He cannot ignore them. He may not have to answer for their breach in a Court of Law. But he will certainly have to answer for them before the electorate at election time. What great value these directive principles possess will be realized better when the forces of right contrive to capture power.[4]

The Planning Commission

The second initiative regarding nation-building and economic modernization relates to the setting up of the Planning Commission by a resolution of the Government of India in March 1950.[5] This resolution defined the scope of its work by stating the following: the state shall strive to promote the welfare of the people by securing and protecting as effectively as it may a social order in which justice (social, economic and political) shall inform all the institutions of the national life, and shall direct its policy towards securing, among other things, (1) that the citizens, men and women equally, have the right to an adequate means of livelihood; (2) that the ownership and control of the material resources of the community are so distributed as best to subserve the common good; and (3) that the operation of the economic system does not result in the concentration of wealth and means of production to the common detriment.

From January 2015, the Planning Commission has been replaced by a new institution called NITIAayog (National Institution for Transforming India). The objectives of the NITIAayog are the following: to evolve a shared vision of national development, to foster co-operative federalism, to develop mechanisms to formulate creditable plans, to pay special attention to the poor and downtrodden, to design long-term policy and to plan frameworks, etc.

Approach of national political parties

The third initiative in the context of social and economic reconstruction of the country came from the national political parties: INC, SP, BJS, CPI and SCF. These parties started preparing reports, draft statements and papers mostly to debate and discuss so as to evolve a strategy for national development. This strategy was needed primarily to formulate the party programme (manifesto) for the coming general elections of 1951–1952.

Congress Party

In this context, the INC, with a resolution of the AICC onNovember 17, 1947, observed the following 'Political independence having been achieved, the Congress must address itself to the next great task, namely, the establishment of real democracy in the country and a society based on social justice and equality'.[6] For this purpose, an Economic Programme Committee was appointed under the chairmanship of Jawaharlal Nehru for the drawing up the Economic Programme of the Congress.[7] The Committee, in its report in January 1948, made detailed recommendations with regard to agriculture, village and cottage industry; industry, industrial relations and co-operation.

The following are the some of the recommendations made by the sub-committee on agriculture: between the tiller and the state, all intermediaries and middlemen should be replaced by co-operatives functioning as non-profit making agencies; there should be equitable exchange relations between agricultural and non-agricultural products; the maximum size of holdings should be fixed, and the surplus land to be acquired should be placed with the village co-operatives; there should be a priority for the development of river-valley projects for the production and distribution of cheap electricity for rural industries and agricultural purposes; assuring protected water supply to the rural areas; there should be 'Statutory village Panchayats' for self-governing purposes with well-defined powers and adequate financial resources, and 'with supervisory jurisdiction over all other institutions in the locality'; and progressive taxation of agricultural income, etc.

The sub-committee on Village and Cottage Industries stressed the need of the following: 'full employment of human, animal and natural resources'; 'encourage research for the purpose of developing these industries efficiently and for better utiliziation of available natural resources'; 'the small scale and cottage industries should be promoted on non-profit lines through industrial co-operative societies'; and 'no state-aid should be given to an individual except through his co-operative society'.

The sub-committee on industry suggested the following: 'industries producing articles of food, clothing and other consumer goods should constitute the decentralized sector . . . be developed and run on a cooperative basis'; spheres of large-scale, small-scale and cottage industries should be demarcated 'to avoid economic insecurity and destructive competition'; regional self-sufficiency; public ownership for undertakings in defence; key and public utility industries should be started; public ownership for undertakings which are in the nature of monopolies; in respect of existing undertakings the process of transfer from private to public ownership should commence after a period of five years; the system of managing agency should be abolished; regulations and controls for private industry for fulfilling the objectives of national policy; state-directed investment; setting-up of Finance Corporations for financing industries and Banking and Insurance sectors should be nationalized.

The sub-committee on Industrial Relations recommended the following: increasing the association of labour with management in industry and through profit sharing; establishing a Works Committees to settle differences; establishing Regional Labour Boards to determine wages and conditions of labour; creating machinery of conciliation, arbitration and adjudication for all disputes between employers and workmen.

The sub-committee on co-operation recommended the following: the need to promote 'cooperative-distribution' as an important component of an economic plan for the country; to establish 'a multipurpose cooperative society with branches for agricultural producers, consumers and small industries should be set up to develop an integrated economy for the village'; to promote and encourage the cooperative consumers' societies to control a large and growing volume of the retail trade; 'the State should grant special facilities for transport, storage, etc., . . . available to co-operative societies'; to control the wages and the prices of agricultural products and manufactured articles and that 'the distribution of consumer goods should be controlled by the encouragement of cooperative effort'.[8]

The Report of the Economic Programme Committee concluded by suggesting the following: to review the present tax structure and amend it 'to fit into the economic policy'; that the structure of the country's foreign trade should be fully analysed; to 'build up its economic structure on a sound basis so as to make it possible for the nation to provide its primary needs and thus buttress its independent position' and that 'the place of foreign capital should be carefully examined so as to ensure that the economic controls remain with the nationals of the country'.[9] The AICC gave its general approval to the Report of the Economic Programme Committee in February 1948.

Communist Party of India

The CPI Politbureau in April 1951 adopted a 'Draft Programme' and a tentative 'Statement of Policy', as a part of the strategy of social and economic reconstruction.[10] These documents formed the basis for discussion. In October 1951, the party approved the 'Draft Programme'.

> This programme pointed out the new stage of the revolution in India was not socialist and that the urgent task was the completion of the anti-imperialist and anti-feudal revolution. The programme stated that in order to achieve this task, it is necessary to build a united front of the working class, *Kisans*, petty bourgeoisie and the national bourgeoisie interested in freedom and national advance. It is only by fulfilling this task that the working class can lay the basis for socialist transformation.[11]

The party also issued a policy statement which

> underlined the need for India evolving its own path of revolution, taking into consideration the concrete features of our country and its specific conditions. The policy statement also emphasized the need, in the new situation, to combine extra-parliamentary mass struggles and mass movements with the struggle inside Parliament and the State Assemblies.[12]

The 'Draft Programme' and 'Statement of Policy' was adopted by the Party with minor amendments in October 1951.

The Socialist Party

As back as in October 1947, a discussion paper 'Programme' was issued containing some of the most 'vital problems of reconstruction'. Regarding its economic policy the Paper covered the following aspects: industry, planning, socialisation, controlled industry, new industry; labour, banking and trade, taxation, black markets, agriculture, subsidiary rural and small industries; it also provided the following general philosophy of the party:

> To make a start towards socialism, the present economy must be brought under social control and subordinated to an overall plan of development; certain sectors of it must be socialized immediately; investments must be rigidly controlled and directed by the State; taxation must toned down vast income disparities such property relationships as zamindari must be abolished forthwith and a living wage, a decent shelter, must be guaranteed to the worker.[13]

The paper further highlighted the 'need of raising production, i.e. utilizing present equipment and manpower to the best advantage, to further industrial and agricultural development'. The Paper also emphasized the need to address immediately on problems of shortage of food, cloth and housing. The Paper in general suggested that 'The social state must evoke in the Indian citizen a new consciousness of social cohesiveness. The individual must respond to new incentives and assume larger responsibilities'.

The Jana Sangh

The Jana Sangh came into existence on October 21, 1951. Its object, as approved by a conference of original members of the party, stated that

> The object of the Bharatiya Jana Sangh is the rebuilding of Bharat on the basis of Bharatiya *Sanskriti* and *Maryada* as a political, social and economic democracy granting equality of opportunity and liberty to individuals so as to make her a prosperous, powerful and united nation, progressive, modern and enlightened, able to withstand the aggressive designs of others and to pull her weight in the council of nations for the establishment of world peace.[14]

The party's economic programme consisted of the following: paying attention to the supply of food and cloth at a reasonable price; securing reductions in the prices of other essential commodities; adopting a programme which will inspire all sections of the people to work for a common national purpose; creating long-term schemes like river-valley projects and reclamation of land for increasing the production of agricultural commodities and raising the yield per acre through small-scale irrigation schemes and the more plentiful supply of seeds, manure and implements. Also, they advocated for the following: uncultivated land will be requisitioned wherever necessary and co-operative farming will be encouraged; a rational procurement polity; that economic salvation lies in increasing production and in adopting a fair and more equitable system of distribution; a planned decentralization of industries; the development of small and medium-size industries aiming at regional self-sufficiency; the improvement of relations between capital and labour; a planned reorientation of the education system in all its stages; and attention to the improvement of the social, economic and educational advancement of the backward sections of the population. The party stands for democratic government and the democratic way of life, the corner-stones of which are free public opinion and the rule of law, fighting corruption, black-marketing and profiteering and to create a healthy public opinion in favour of raising the standard of honesty and efficiency of the administration.

All India scheduled castes federation

Besides the approach of the aforementioned political parties on national reconstruction, it is proposed to provide the draft manifesto of the All India Scheduled Castes Federation, as spelled out by Dr. B.R. Ambedkar in October 1951. Its approach to solve social and economic problems is radically different from the approach made by other national political parties. This difference emanates from the fact that Dr. Ambedkar was of the view that

> old time Constitutional Lawyers believed that the scope and function of Constitutional Law was to prescribe the shape and form of the political structure of society. They never realized that it was equally essential to prescribe the shape and form of the economic structure of society, if Democracy is to live up to its principle of one man, one value. Time has come to take a bold step and define both the economic structure as well as political structure of society by the Law of the Constitution. All countries like India which are late-comers in the field of Constitution-making should not copy the faults of other countries. They should profit by the experience of their predecessors.[15]

Keeping with this objective, Dr. Ambedkar prepared the party manifesto,[16] providing its principles, its policies and its programmes along with its terms of co-operation with other political parties. Before we outline the approach of the party on economic development, it is important to understand the basic philosophy of the party on this aspect:

> The policy of the Party is not tied to any particular dogma or ideology such as Communism or Socialism, Gandhism, or any other ism. The Party will be ready to adopt any plan of social and economic betterment of the people irrespective of its origin and provided it is consistent with its principles.

In order to increase production, the draft manifesto pointed out 'The pattern of industrial enterprise will be a matter regulated by the needs of the time and circumstances'. The manifesto further spelled out that 'no other consideration except that of greater production and still greater production can be the primary and paramount condition'.[17]

Besides the rapid industrialization of the country, the manifesto equally emphasized the need for the 're-construction of Indian Agriculture'. For this purpose the manifesto emphasized the need for the mechanization of agriculture and introduction of co-operative farms and collective farms. In the planning of agriculture development, the state was assigned a very important role. The manifesto further emphasized the need to bring cultivable waste land under cultivation. It also highlighted the need for the proper maintenance of forests belts.[18] 'Without forest belts proper degree of rainfall will not be assured and agriculture in India will continue to be the gamble in rain as it has always been in the past'. The draft manifesto further emphasized the need to supplement effort in agriculture by development in cottage industries. The manifesto also highlighted the need for further development of river valley projects, which will help in irrigation, production of electricity and minimizing floods.

The draft manifesto called for the alleviation of poverty and suggested the need for 'more production both in agriculture and industry'. However, in the context of poverty, the manifesto emphatically stressed the need of 'controlling the excessive growth of population'. For reducing population, the manifesto suggested an 'intensive propaganda in favour of birth control; opening of birth control clinics all over the country and it went to the extent of advocating more drastic methods of controlling it'.[19]

The manifesto also spelled out the ways to raise the finances for the development of the country and suggested the following: a reduction of expenditure over the army, the re-levy of salt taxes, the abolition of prohibition and saving of excise revenue and the nationalization of insurance.

The manifesto also addressed the creation of the linguistic states; in order to restore purity in Administration, the manifesto also suggested that there should be 'stern action against ministers or officers who are corrupt'. The manifesto highlighted the need to raise 'the standard of administration'. The manifesto also discussed the problem of the control and black-marketeers along with the problem of inflation

Swatantra Party (SWP)

The SWP came into existence in 1959 and contested the elections from 1962 only. The party in its meeting in Bombay in August 1959 adopted a twenty-one-point Statement of Principles. This statement constitutes the core of party's economic thinking and fundamental philosophy.

Some of the important principles are:

> Equality for all people without distinction of religion, caste, occupation or political affiliation; individual initiative enterprise, and energy i.e. maximum freedom for the individual and minimum interference by the state; adheres to the principle of Trusteeship admired by Gandhiji; to foster and maintain spiritual values and preserve what is good in our culture and tradition; strict adherence to the Fundamental Rights and Guarantees specified in the Constitution; priority must be assigned to the basic needs of the people- food, water, housing and clothing; every citizen has a fundamental right to educate his children and the state should afford facilities for such education without discrimination; increasing food production . . . to the self-employed peasant- proprietor . . . opposed to collectivisation and bureaucratic management of the rural economy; restriction of state enterprise to heavy industries . . . opposed to the state entering the field of trade and distribution; preservation of the freedom of the small and self-employed artisans, craftsmen, and traders; opposed to a programme of development based on crippling taxation, abnormal deficit financing and foreign loans; opposed to all policies that lead to excessive inflation; the cost of Public Administration should be reduced considerably; stands for

> the rule of law and independence judiciary, and for the full play of the powers of judicial review given, to the Courts of the Constitution.[20]

Importance of party manifestos

Jawaharlal Nehru was of the view that for the people of the country the elections are meant 'to give expression to their views, or their approval of policies and programmes put before the country'.[21] He underscored the utility and purpose of the general elections,

> one to gain further contacts with people, and secondly to explain things to them. I want the general elections to be a kind of a vast university for the masses of the people to discuss political and economic subjects and domestic and international problems.[22]

Nehru clarified the importance of party programmes or manifestos in the general elections:

> the whole object of democratic elections is to ascertain the views of the electorate on major problems and to enable the electorate to select their representatives. Political Parties place their programmes before the public and carry on intensive propaganda to convince the electorate of the virtues of each individual programme as well as of the demerits of other programmes. These conflicting approaches are supposed to educate and enlighten the electorate and enable it to choose rightly.[23]

The manifestos are prepared after considerable intra-party discussions with party leadership. Highest consideration is given by the top leadership of the party in the preparation of the manifesto. For example, in the context of the Congress Party, during the first general election of 1952, the manifesto of the Congress Party was prepared by Jawaharlal Nehru.[24] It was presented at the AICC Session at Bangalore on July 13, 1951 and adopted on July 14. The manifesto was again moved and adopted at the A.I.C.C. meeting at New Delhi on October 16, 1951. In the debate at the AICC meeting on the draft election manifesto, a number of members participated. A number of questions were asked on issues related to planning, land reforms, foreign policy, prohibition, linguistic provinces, military training, ban on cow slaughter, co-operative farming, corruption and bribery, etc.

The final document which emerged took into consideration all these points. Nehru during the course of debate pointed out that the 'actual manifesto will, of course, contain what you approve of with little minor changes, minor additions, etc. Anyhow, it is for this House to agree to this basic provision which this draft contains'.[25] Debate, discussion and approval in the party conclave is an essential part of drawing up the manifestos. The significance of the manifestos in the party's programme is obvious. The manifesto reflects the faith and ideologies of a political party.

A comparative perspective

This study deals with the ideologies (political programmes) of national political parties as reflected in their manifestos. An effort has been made to analyse from a comparative perspective the party manifestos since 1952, in terms of their expressed views in the context of the complex issues. Each manifesto also provides an extensive note on the areas of concern where the government policies and programmes have not made any significant contribution.

In the context of party manifestos of the last sixteen general elections, the following parties have been studied: the Indian National Congress (1952–2014), the Bharatiya Jana Sangh (1952–1984)/Bharatiya Janata Party (1984–2014), the Communist Party of India (1952–2014), the Communist Party of India (Marxist) (1967–2014), the Socialist Party (1952–1962), Swantantra Party (1962–1971), the Praja Socialist Party (1967–1971), the Samyukta Socialist Party (1967–1971), the Janata Party (1977–1984), the National Front (1989–1991) and the United Front/Janata Dal (1996–1998).

Another noticeable aspect of political parties' manifestos relate to the size of their text: Between 1952 and 1967, the size varied from four to twenty-four pages; from 1971 to 1984, eight to forty-two pages; from 1989 to 1999, five to seventy-nine pages, from 2004 to 2009, twenty to forty-eight pages. The increase in the size of the manifestos since 1971 is largely attributed due to their coverage of a large number of issues while also providing a detailed analysis and corrective action on each problem or issue. The BJP manifesto of 1996 was printed in nearly eighty pages. However, this holds true, by and large, of other political parties except the CPI and CPI(M). The British political parties' manifestos, on the contrary, have been very brief, running four to five pages, The British party manifestos do not provide much details and treat their approach to a problem in a generalized manner.[26]

It is our objective to investigate the manifestos of national political parties so as to facilitate comparisons on key issues. The analysis of the election manifesto of different national political parties from 1952 to 2014 is based on the approach of these parties on various social, political, economic and international issues including defence. The resolution of these issues is necessary for nation-building and economic modernization. In this background, the party manifestos have a very important role in articulating their views as well as spelling out their approach to the problems and issues facing the country.

It is from this perspective that it is proposed to analyse the party manifestos of national political parties from 1952 to 2014. To provide a certain degree of uniformity on the issues compared, a framework of this comparison has been developed which covers all the issues contained in these manifestos. The comparison has been made broadly on the following issues: political – character of the state, Ram Janmabhoomi, electoral reforms, civil liberties, human rights, Panchayati Raj, Constitution, Centre-state relations, corruption, internal security, the insurgency and terrorism of Jammu and Kashmir, North-East, judicial reforms, reorganization of the states, law and order and police reforms and terrorism. Economic – objective of economic organization, agricultural policy (tenancy reform, agricultural labour, agriculture production and irrigation) and industrial policy (small-scale industries and industrial relations). Financial – taxation and banking and insurance financial management, including debt management, capital markets, fiscal management, resource mobilization and economy. Human and social development – education, health, family planning, public distribution system for women and youth), Scheduled Castes and Scheduled Tribes, minorities, media and mass communication, sports, cinema and culture. Infrastructure – science and technology, environment, energy, transport, e-governance information technology and urban development. Foreign policy and defence – United Nations Organization, India-Soviet relations, India-China relations, regional issues, nuclear capability, new concerns and defence.

To bring this comparison in tandem with the current thinking, the issues are put under the aforementioned subject headings. In analysing the manifestos, the main basis has been not to provide election-wise cataloguing of the party manifestos. On the contrary, effort has been made to highlight the basic similarities or uniformities and identification of significant points of difference in the approach to the core issues in each problem.[27]

Comparative analysis of party manifestos

It is proposed to analyse, from the first general election 1952 to the sixteenth general election conducted in 2014, the manifestos of national political parties on important issues relating to political, economic, social, infrastructure, foreign affairs and defence subjects.

Political issues

Character of the state

During the general elections of 1952, 1957, 1962 and 1967, the political parties like INC, CPI, SP and PSP in their manifestos expressed their commitment to uphold the constitutional provisions relating to secularism – characterizing it as the basic character of the Indian state. To inculcate the spirit of secularism, the CPI in one of its manifesto mentioned incorporation of 'democratic and secular cultural policies, incorporating the humanist and tolerant teachings of the social reformers'. The CPI (M) voiced the need by the state to promote 'secular value . . . in all spheres'. The JD expressed to take caution against any 'weakening of secularism' and to 'promote religious tolerance and intellectual dissent'. While the BJS expressed 'revival of Bharatiya culture and revitalization of true Bharatiya nationalism', and pointed out the need to 'give a positive, patriotic and moral content to education' 'foster the feeling of Indianness in all sections of society'.

In the context of maintaining the basic character of the Indian polity, the INC and CPI advocated the need to strengthen a national consensus against political, cultural and social organization which seek to undermine it. The CPI(M) emphasized the need for

> enacting a comprehensive law against communal violence; ensuring speedy justice and adequate compensation to the victims of communal violence . . .; purging all school textbooks of content reflecting communal bias and prejudices; reining in organizations and institutions involved in spreading communal hate and attacking minorities through appropriate legal measures; enforcing the Protection of Places of Worship Act to prevent raising of disputes on religious places.

The BJP, in its manifesto of 1984, gave a new ideological orientation to this issue by expressing that it is committed to the 'positive concept of secularism'. This concept has been defined by stating that 'in Indian tradition, since times immemorial, the state has always been a civil institution, which makes no distinction between one citizen and another on grounds of his religion. The very idea of a theocratic state is alien to Indian political history; when India became independent in 1947, we very naturally declared ourselves a secular state'. However, the manifesto further explained that 'Secularism should not be allowed to become a euphemism for appeasement, alternately of this community, or that, a sordid political device to garner bloc-votes'.

Ram Janmabhoomi

Regarding the Ram Janmabhoomi, the INC, CPI and CPI (M) broadly hold identical views on this issue, i.e. separation of religion from politics, resolution either through a negotiated settlement or by due processes of law, strict implementation of the status quo of religious places as of August 15, 1947 and prohibition on the use of religious issues for electoral purposes by political parties. The CPI also advocated for the need to form an anti-riot or a peace-keeping force with a mixed composition for the purpose of using them in the event of religious related disputes.

The BJP in its manifestos of 1991, 1996, 1998 on the other hand emphasized the need for the construction of 'Shri Ram Mandir Janma Sansthan in Ayodhya'. In its election manifesto for the 16th Lok Sabha 2014, the BJP reiterated and expanded its stand on the Ram Mandir by stating that 'it will explore all possibilities within the framework of the Constitution to facilitate the construction of the Ram Temple in Ayodhya'. The BJP manifesto also suggested to provide resources 'for the maintenance and restoration of all national heritage sites'. It also pleaded to create a National Mission for 'beautifying and improving the infrastructure and amenities at pilgrimage centres of all faiths'.

Electoral reforms

Since the first general election, a large number of electoral reforms have been suggested by the political parties. These suggestions deal with issues like the right to recall, lowering the age of voting, defection, the funding of elections, prohibiting criminal persons to contest elections and the institutional aspect of the electoral system.

On the issue of right to recall, the CPI, the SP, the PSP and JP expressed the view to enact legislation providing the right to recall, so that the electorate has complete control over its elected representatives and a fresh election should take place. The INC, the CPI, the CPI(M), and the BJP in its manifestos advocated the need for lowering the age for voting right from twenty-one to eighteen. The PSP and Janata Party advocated the need to stop the menace of defection by pointing out that a defector must cease to be a legislator if he crosses the floor.

The Janata Party and BJP favoured state funding of elections, as in the case of Germany, Japan and most other democratic countries and public audit of party funds. Besides the CPI(M) and the BJP were in favour of prohibiting corporate funding to political parties. On the other hand, the INC on this issue expressed the view to introduce transparency in financing of political activities and expanding state funding for elections.

The BJP and CPI(M) all were in favour of taking effective steps to prohibit persons with a criminal background from contesting elections. However, the INC expanded this issue further by stating the need for 'strengthening the legal and judicial framework for disqualifying persons convicted of crimes against women and weaker sections and disqualifying those who subvert the integrity of the electoral process'.

Regarding reforms in the election processes, the BJP and NDA pledged for maintaining a 'National Register of Citizens' for introducing the compulsory voting for all citizens, for introducing identity cards for voters, for giving the right of Postal Ballot to Indian citizens living abroad for ensuring the right of franchise of the Armed Forces through proxy or any other method;

In the context of bringing changes in the institutional aspect of the electoral system, the BJP also expressed that the members of the Election Commission should be appointed by the President of India on the advice of a committee consisting of the Prime Minister, the Leader of the Opposition and Chief Justice of the Supreme Court. The Election Commissioners must be legally debarred from enjoying any office after retirement. The Representation of the People's Act needs to be amended to specify the jurisdiction of election observers; a constitutional amendment needs specify Election Commission's jurisdiction vis-à-vis law and order in order to avoid conflict with the elected State Governments. The BJP have been voicing in their manifestos the need to evolve a method of holding Lok Sabha and Assembly elections simultaneously as well as revising expenditure limit realistically.

To ensure free, fair and fearless elections, since 1989, the CPI, CPI (M), BJP, INC, pleaded for a comprehensive Electoral Reforms Bill on the basis of agreements arrived at the All-Party meetings on the subject.

Some of the significant aspects of the issues expressed in the manifestos of 2014 election relate to the suggestion of BJP regarding revising expenditure limits realistically; while the INC suggested introducing transparency in the financing of political activities and in expanding state funding for elections and CPI was against corporate funding to political parties. The INC suggested to enact the Women's Reservation Bill to ensure one-third reservation for women in Parliament and state legislatures.

Civil liberties

In the context of the emergency of 1974, the CPI, CPI(M), BJP and JP expressed the following: to lift the emergency; to restore the fundamental freedoms that were suspended by Presidential Order and to repeal Maintenance of Internal Security Act (MISA). The CPI (M) expressed further the 'total dismantling of the authoritarian framework introduced in the Constitution during the Emergency; deletion of the existing provision in the Constitution for prevention detention; President's power to declare Emergency to operate only in case of an outbreak of war'. The CPI(M) and the JP advocated for the need to enact laws to ensure that no political or social organization is banned without independent judicial enquiry. The CPI(M) and the BJS expressed the view to formulate a code of conduct for agitations and movements and ensure that they are conducted in a democratic way.

Human rights

The INC was the first national party to suggest a Human Rights Commission 'to investigate and adjudicate complaints of violations of human rights' (1991). Besides, the UF and JD, in the context of human rights, suggested the need to recommend and amend the Indian Penal Code, the Criminal Procedure Code and other penal laws to make their provision consistent with the sanctity of human rights. The JD and BJP hold similar views regarding providing all assistance to the National Human Rights Commission so that it continues to act independently. On this issue, the INC remains 'committed to the resolute defence of human rights in India consistent with our Constitution and with the international law and covenants'.

The JD suggested the need to review 'special laws enacted to handle the extraordinary situations in several insurgency prone areas'. The BJP pledged 'to inculcate among security forces a greater appreciation of the need to safeguard innocent citizens from being harassed in insurgency-affected areas'. The JD and the BJP also advocated the need for human rights education in school and college curriculum.

Panchayati Raj

Since the beginning, the SP was for progressive decentralization. It came out with the suggestion to 'democratize the constitution and the administration in the directions both of decentralization and people's control'; to create the four-pillar state which divides sovereignty at all levels of the village, district, province and the centre; to transfer police powers to district and village control and to have the village council acquire a quarter share in all revenues and expenditures of the Republic. These councils will also serve as sovereign agencies of legislation and planning on properly delineated subjects. Members of the village and district panchayat should also participate in the election of the President of the Republic.

The CPI expressed the need to provide greater power for the Panchayats and other local bodies as well as adequate resources for them. All local development works should be entrusted to Panchayats. Elections must be direct and by secret ballot without any bureaucratic interference, ending all bureaucratic control over local bodies and raising their status and dignity.

Along with CPI and SP, the BJS also favoured the need to decentralize political power. However, the BJS expressed the view that Local Bodies and Zila Parishads derive their power from the Constitution. The BJP in 1991 advocated the need to effective decentralization of power; constitutional status to local bodies from Village Panchayats to Metropolitan Corporation, involvement of Panchayats in development and to make 10 percent of the budget available to them.

The CPI (M), JP, BJP and CPI advocated suitable changes in the 73th and 74th Amendments in the Constitution so as to define the functions of Panchayati Raj Institutions (PRI's) with precision and to curb the discretionary power that the states enjoy in this respect. The INC and BJP also advocated the need to suitably strengthen the Gram Sabha. The CPI(M), JP and BJP also pleaded to make the PRI financially self-reliant so as to enable a full discussion on development projects, scrutinize the allocation and spending of funds and evaluate the performance of elected and government functionaries. The JP advocated the need for the 'decentralization through units of self-government upto the village level, making the periodic elections to panchayat mandatory and bringing panchayats and local bodies elections under the purview of the Election Commission, and the establishment of the State Finance Commission to 'ensure a fair share of State revenues for the Panchayati and local bodies '. In this context, the BJP advocated the need 'work for the effective financial and administrative empowerment of Panchayati Raj institutions and Urban Local Bodies in respect of funds, functions and functionaries'.

In the manifesto of BJP during the 2014 elections, the BJP suggested empowering Panchayati Raj Institutions with extensive devolution of functions, functionaries and funds as well as strengthening the institution of Gram Sabha. The INC proposed to set up a 'National Panchayati Raj Commission' with branches in each state to ensure probity and transparency in the functions of Panchayats. The manifesto also pleaded for the strengthening of Gram Sabhas.

Constitution

The Constitution of India and its various provisions formed an important part of manifestos in almost all the general elections conducted since 1952. The PSP suggested to 'use the forum of Parliament and State Legislatures for voicing in a democratic way, people's urges and aspirations, and for introducing progressive legislation'. Besides, different political parties during the course of last sixteen general elections expressed their concern on many issues. An attempt has been made below to identify these views party-wise.

The CPI, in this context, made references to the following: the Directive Principles of State Policy should be speedily implemented and made a part of fundamental rights of citizens which should be justiciable; the Upper House in the State Legislature should be abolished; the states should be vested with wide powers in the sphere of finance; the emergency powers of the President must be abolished; the power of the President and the Central Government to dismiss a State Government must be annulled; the Governors must be directly elected; proportional representation should be introduced in all elections; there should be Standing Committees in Parliament and in the State Legislatures with requisites statutory powers so that all parties and groups represented in the Legislature may be directly and actively associated with the initiation and formulation of policies by different ministries and government, along with the power to review the implementation of government policies and the work of the administration and a rejection of all proposals of a Presidential form of government

The SP held the view regarding 'the convening of a Constituent Assembly' on the basis of adult suffrage with a view to framing a new Constitution. They also advocated for the following: some provisions in the Constitution itself for the formation of representative bodies at grass-roots level; the redundant offices of the Governor and the Collector being abolished; the police and the general administration in the district or city should function under the panchayats concerned; the right to property should be deleted in the list of Fundamental Rights; food, clothes, shelter, education, employment and medical aid to every citizen should be included in the list of Fundamental Rights; basic changes in the Centre-State relations; in the financial setup, the state and the local panchayats should be able to mobilize resources in such a way that they deem fit; the Directive Principles of state policy should be made justiceable; Sections 107, 109, 117, 144, 151 etc. of the Criminal Procedure Code need to be removed; the abolition of capital punishment and all the heavy industries and all the foreign capital should be socialized. The SSP in the context of formulation of laws stressed the need for an 'understanding of the inter-relationship between legal enactment and popular force for laws to bring about big changes in society'.

The NDA suggested the following: to 'Appoint a Commission to review the Constitution of India of the entire post-independence period', and to make suitable recommendations devolution of more financial and administrative powers and functions to the states; to ensure harmonious Centre-State relations in the light of the recommendations of the Sarkaria Commission; to effect decentralization by activating and involving Panchayats and local bodies; to appoint a Backward Area Commission for each state of the Union to identify the least-developed areas and recommend comprehensive measures for their development; to appoint a Committee to study the feasibility of treating all nineteen languages included in Schedule 8 of the Constitution as official languages; to examine problems of border states; to take measures for ensuring a fixed a term (five years) for all elected bodies including legislatures and to examine replacing the present No Confidence Motion with the German system of 'Constructive vote of No-Confidence'.

The JP held the view that to 'prevent future misuse or undemocratic use of power by the President, the Prime Minister or the holder of any other high office, bring forward laws or changes in the Constitution' for this purpose; delegate more powers to the states and further down; extend and reinforce Panchayati Raj.

The NF suggested the need to establish an Inter-State Council under Article 263 of the Constitution and activate the National Development Council (NDC). Constitutional status should be awarded to the Planning Commission to ensure that it functions as an executive arm of the National Development Council. Also suggested were the following issues: constitutional accountability of the Governor should be ensured by bringing necessary amendments to the Constitution; they should devolve adequate financial and administrative powers to states; a genuine devolution of powers, functions and resources to Panchayati Raj Institutions should be promoted; the electronic media should be converted into autonomous corporations and the Constitution should be amended to ensure the citizen's right to information. Also, the NF desired to check by appropriate fiscal policies and through strict enforcement, like the Foreign Exchange Regulation Act and the Monopoly and Restricted Trade Practices Act, elitist consumption, luxurious living and five-star culture.

The CPI (M) viewed the problems which needed the following: 'basic changes in the Constitution to eliminate the grip of the big bourgeois-landlord classes over the State'; complete guarantee of freedom of the Press; right to work as a fundamental right in the Constitution; new constitutional provisions to expand the powers of the state and guarantee their autonomy; residuary powers to be with the states; Articles 356–360 dealing with President's rule in the states to be deleted; 'drastic reduction of the Concurrent List'. The CPI(M) manifesto of 2014 suggested the need to amend Article 3 of the Constitution to provide for the consent of the state legislature concerned before a state is to be bifurcated or reorganized by Parliament; amend the Constitution to make parliamentary approval mandatory for any international treaty; repeal the Armed Forces Special Powers Act and remove the death penal from the statutes.

Centre-state relations

Since 1952, various political parties are expressing their views to bring harmony in the relationship between the Centre and States. An attempt has been made hereto provide these views form 1952–2014.

The BJS suggested the need to appoint a high-power commission to enquire into and arbitrate on all disputes between one state and another as well as between a State and the Centre. Its decision will be binding. It also suggested to appoint an Inter-State Council under Article 263 of the Constitution to advise government in respect of all issues pertaining to Centre-State relations. The BJP also advocated the need to 'support and strengthen state Governments – and not destabilize and topple them'; to appoint State Governors in consultation with State Governments; to limit the number of ministers to 10 percent of legislature; to give the states a fairer share of Central revenues and increase the financial powers of the States. BJP: In the context of the Centre-State Relation the BJP 2014 manifesto pleaded to revive the 'National Development Council', the 'Inter-State Council' and the creation of Regional Council of State, with common problems and concerns and to involve the State Governments in the promotion of foreign trade and commerce etc.

The CPI and CPI (M) in the context of strengthening federalism advocated for the constitutional amendments for devolving more powers to the states in the economic, fiscal and administrative areas; for the decentralization of powers to the district bodies and panchayats; for ensuring local participation in the formulation of plans and projects; for replacing Article 356 with suitable provisions; for maximum autonomy for the state of Jammu and Kashmir to be provided for within the ambit of Article 370 and for reversing the process of central dictates on devolving finances to the states by imposing conditionalities to pursue the Central Government's economic policy directives.

The CPI (M) suggested to bring changes in the Constitution, specifically for the

> abolition of the post of Governors and of President's rule in States; revision of powers and functions between the States and Centre; most of the subjects in the Concurrent List of the 7th Schedule to the Constitution to be transferred to the State; 75 percent share of all the taxes centrally collected to go to the states; complete control by the State Governments over all its officials.

The CPI suggested the 'Restructuring of Centre-State relations' to expand the powers of the states and provide them adequate resources. This should be done in the true spirit of federalism, giving greater autonomy to states, allowing for the redistribution of legislative, administrative and fiscal powers between the Centre and the states; creating measures to prevent misuse of the powers of the President and the Governors (abrogation of Article 356 of the Constitution) and ensuring that the fate of a state government to be decided only 'on the floor of the house'. They also advocated for the inclusion of Tripura (if the tribals so desire) in the Sixth Schedule of the Constitution. The CPI further pleaded for the 'Activisation of Inter-State Council and empowering National Development Council with adequate powers on planning.'.

The JP advocated the need for the following: a constructive review of the Centre, State and concurrent lists of subjects; the establishment of an Inter-State Council; a review of the role of the Governors; an amendment of Article 356 to prevent its misuse; the financial viability of the states through constitutional legal and fiscal arrangements;

an appropriate reorganization of states; an inner democratic structure to submit audited accounts regularly; a review of the existing political and administrative divisions to evolve a new system where political constituencies are co-terminus with administrative divisions; the administrators being responsible to local and regional political institutions and not to distant masters; an amendment of the constitution to make local governments responsible for primary health, education, and public order apart from civic services like sanitation and water and the 'encouragement of local governments to raise resources with the assurance of matching grants'.

The NF pleaded to introduce a new system of governance founded on the principle of decentralization of power at all levels: the states to enjoy autonomy – political, legislative, economic, fiscal and administrative – within the federal framework; the Inter-State Council to undertake a comprehensive view of Union-State Relations; the Inter-State Council and the National Development Council to be effectively activated to ensure co-operation and coordination between the States and the Centre and the role, powers and functions of Governors and Articles 356 of the Constitution to be reviewed. The JD was of the view that the State ought to enjoy genuine autonomy-political, legislative, economic, fiscal and administrative within the federal framework; adequate financial resources and administrative powers will be devolved on the States to enable them to discharge their responsibilities to the people; the Inter-State Council to undertake a comprehensive review of Union-State relations; the Inter-State Council and the National Development Council (NDC) to be effectively activated to ensure co-operation and coordination between the States and the Centre and to make India a truly federal republic. The role of Governors and their powers and functions to be reviewed, so as to ensure, their constitutional accountability. Article 356, of the Constitution to be reviewed; appoint a Commission to go into demands for the creation of smaller states and make appropriate recommendations.

The CPI(M) manifesto suggested

> amending Articles 355 and 356 to prevent their misuse; Governors to be appointed by the President from a list of three eminent persons suggested by the Chief Minister of a State; devolving 50% of the total pool of collection of Central taxes to the States; raising state's share of market borrowing to 50%; conditionalities imposed upon the States like the passage of Fiscal Responsibility and Budget Management (FRBM) Act to be withdrawn; States to have a say in the composition

> and terms of reference of the Finance Commissions; transferring Centrally Sponsored Schemes under the State subject with funds to the States; constitutional amendment to make the decisions of the Inter-State Council binding on the Union Government; NDC to be granted Constitutional status; Planning Commission to act as an executive wing of the NDC; setting a target minimum level of Local Self-Government expenditure to GDP; funds devolved to the local bodies to be routed through the State Governments.

The CPI(M) manifesto of 2014 suggested the following: amending Articles 355 and 356 to prevent their misuse; devolving 50 percent of the total pool of collection of Central taxes to the states; transferring Centrally Sponsored Schemes under the state subject with funds to the states and creating a new Constitutional amendment to make the decisions of the Inter-State Council binding on the Union Government.

Corruption

The problem of corruption has been a major issue in the manifestos of all the national political parties since the third general election of 1967. The CPI, SWP and BJS advocated the need to check corruption by a setting up an independent, impartial commission at the Centre as well as the state levels for probing all cases of corruption, malpractices and improprieties. The SWP expressed the view that the authority should be on the lines of Ombudsman in Scandinavian countries. The PSP and the CPI particularly emphasized the need of an authority, independent of the Executive, for the redress of citizens' grievances against the administration and particularly regarding the misuse of power and arbitrary exercise of discretion by Ministers. The SSP not only pleaded for an independent commission to enquire into the misuse of state power by officials and non-officials but also emphasized that such enquiries would also cover businessman connected with them. It also emphasized that 'on misuse of state power being proved, the money will be confiscated'.

The BJS specifically mentioned the corruption at political levels and suggested a code of conduct for representatives of the people and a special law to be enacted to penalize corruption at that level. It suggested that all ministers and highly placed officials as well as all ex-ministers and other officials will be subject to such inquiries.

Since the 1984 general elections, the issue of corruption became more focused specifically in the context of an effective law, institutional mechanism and its ambit. The BJP, CPI, CPI(M), INC and JD have, since the 1980s, advocated the need for setting up of *Lokpal* with jurisdiction over public men holding high positions – all Legislators (MPs and MLAs), Ministers, Chief Ministers, Prime Minister and Class I Officers. Regarding the composition of *Lokpal*, the JD suggested a Multi-Member *Lokpal* appointed by the President of India, in consultation with Chief Justice of India, Speaker of Lok Sabha, Chairman of Rajya Sabha and leaders of Government and Opposition in two Houses of Parliament. Besides, it was also suggested that the Member of Parliament, Legislators and members of local bodies declare their assets and place them before Parliament and Assemblies. The JD also pointed out the need for scrutiny of such assets by an Independent Commission.

The CPI suggested setting up of Citizens' Committees at different levels with the right to initiate proceedings before *Lokpal* Institutions. The INC also suggested the 'involvement of the public in vigilance and control of corruption through public hearings, access to information and promotion of voluntary organizations'.

The INC suggested a review of the work of the enforcement agencies at the Centre and in the states with a view to accord adequate autonomy and insulate them from interference. It also suggested 'Strong measures against tax evasion, smuggling and other economic offence; strengthening existing procedures and mechanism for detecting and punishing corrupt practices, promote an ethic of austerity and simplicity'. However, the JD advocated that the Central Bureau of Investigation (CBI) to be freed from the control of the Department of Personnel and made autonomous and suggested for the investigation of white collar offences: a separate autonomous organization on the lines of CBI. In the context of corruption, the BJP suggested the need to ensure that investigative and intelligence agencies like Research Analysis Wing (RAW), Intelligence Bureau (IB) and CBI are not used to subserve the political designs of the ruling party. The CPI, CPI (M) and the INC also suggested that the CBI and other investigating agencies get functional autonomy to investigate cases leading upto prosecution. The CPI (M) specifically suggested 'that proceedings including trial of cases should be completed within a period of two years from the date of complaint' and suitable legislative changes to be brought to empower regulators and investigating agencies to thoroughly probe corporate crimes.

The INC in its manifesto of 2014 advocated for a better delivery of services and eliminating corruption and leakages by providing priority in the passage of the following Bills: the Right of Citizens for Time

Bound Delivery of Goods and Services and Redressal of their Grievances Bill, 2011; the Prevention of Bribery of Foreign Public Officials and Officials of Public International Organizations Bill 2011; the Prevention of Corruption (Amendment) Bill (which enlarges the definition of taking a bribe and covering commercial organizations) and the Public Procurement Bill, 2012 (which regulates public procurement by all Ministries and Departments of the Central Government and Central Public Sector Enterprises to promote competition and enhance efficiency in procurement processes).

On the other hand, the CPI(M), in its manifesto of 2014, pleaded for the following: amending and strengthening the Prevention of Corruption Act and the *Lokpal* Act to widen its purview and bring all contracts, agreements or MOUs of any kind between the government and the private sector within its purview; empowering regulators and investigating agencies to thoroughly probe corporate crimes; ensuring that private Financial sector institutions, the banking and insurance sector in particular, and all public-private partnership projects are brought under the purview of *Lokpal* Act, Whistleblowers Protection Act and other related anti-corruption legislations and instituting effective mechanisms for providing protection to RTI users and anti-corruption crusaders.

The BJP in its manifesto of 2014 suggested establishing a system which eliminates the scope for corruption; provides technology-enabled e-Governance; ensures system-based, policy-driven governance and provides a rationalization and simplification of the tax regime. On the issue of black money, the manifesto advocated to make an effort to ensure the minimization of the generation of black money and to initiate the process of tracking down and bringing back black money stashed in foreign banks.

Internal security

Regarding internal security, the BJP 2014 manifesto provides the following: revive the anti-terror mechanism to strengthen the role of National Investigation Agency (NIA); reform the National Security Council to make it the hub of all sector-related assessments; be accountable for real-time intelligence dissemination; completely revamp the intelligence-gathering system by modernizing the intelligence department; provide the state governments with all assistance to modernize their respective police forces and equip them with the latest technology; chalk up a national plan to address the challenges posed by the Maoists's insurgency and plan urgent steps for the safety of the migrant workers and communities from the North-East and other states.

The INC on the other hand advocated for the following: the need to equip police force with modern weapons and technology; the state resources to be mobilized to maintain law and order; the security forces posted in Left-Wing Extremism (LWE) affected areas to be strengthened; a development agenda to empower the people in LWE affected areas; the deployment of specialist battalions and the recruitment of additional personnel.

The CPI(M) pleaded for revamping the intelligence machinery and enhanced coordination between security and intelligence agencies; the National Investigating Agency to function without violating the federal structure and ensuring association of state governments for investigation within a particular state; the modernization of the Police forces; the amendment of the Unlawful Activities (Prevention) Act to remove draconian provisions like detention without bail for 180 days, and three-years imprisonment for withholding information etc.

Insurgency and terrorism – Jammu and Kashmir and North-East

The problems relating to insurgency and terrorism with respect to Jammu and Kashmir and North-East have been constantly finding a mention in the manifestos of national political parties since the early 1960s.

The BJS in the context of Jammu and Kashmir promised to make the whole of Jammu and Kashmir an integral part of India and suggested take steps to delete Article 370. It promised to do away with 'provision[s] that discriminate against citizen of India residing in the state or in the rest of the country'. The border with Pakistan should be effectively guarded by creating a security belt to stop infiltration of trained terrorists and the smuggling of arms and ammunition, narcotics and other contraband commodities. The manifesto emphasized that

> While recognizing that the Constitution provides for certain transient and temporary provisions for Jammu and Kashmir, . . . the immediate challenge before the Centre and the State is to involve all sections of society in eliminating terrorism, accelerating economic development and strengthening popular governance that can provide people-friendly administration.

It also advocated that the party is 'committed to ensuring early return of Kashmiri Pandits and other displaced people to their native places'. It also suggested balanced development of the three regions of the States i.e. Jammu, Kashmir and Ladakh. In this context, the manifesto pointed out that the BJP its committed to a three-point programme (1) 'Autonomous Regional Councils for Jammu and Ladakh with adequate financial and administrative powers', (2) protection of the original demographic identity of the three regions and (3) equitable distribution of funds from the Centre.

In the post-2000 election manifestos BJP further emphasized that Jammu and Kashmir was and shall remain an integral part of the Union of India. Its status is non-negotiable and, as successive elections have comprehensively demonstrated, the people of Jammu and Kashmir see themselves as part of the Indian national mainstream.

In dealing with issues relating to Jammu and Kashmir, the manifesto further observed that the BJP will be guided by the following principles: the territorial integrity of India is inviolable; the unanimous Parliamentary Resolution of 1994 reiterates this point and shall remain the cornerstone of future decisions and actions of our government; an agenda of equal development of its three regions – Jammu, Kashmir and Ladakh – should be promoted; the Pandits who had to leave their home and hearth in the Kashmir Valley, on account of separatist violence and terrorism, are fully deserving of all support and assistance, which will be provided to them in full measure and the long-pending problems and demands of refugees from Pakistan-occupied Kashmir will be addressed. In the context of the 2014 election, the BJP emphasized three specific aspects-committed to the abrogation of the Article 370; return of Kashmiri Pandits to the land of their ancestors 'with full dignity, security and assured livelihood'.

The INC, regarding Jammu and Kashmir, emphasized the need to take 'stern action against secessionist forces'; special attention to facilitating augmenting employment for the unemployed youth; advocated 'open to dialogue and discussion with any group within the framework of the Constitution'; and suggested to speed up 'the issue of regional autonomy will be given serious and critical consideration. It also expressed that the Congress stands committed to respecting Article 370 in letter and spirit'.

The CPI and the CPI(M) suggested maximum autonomy for Jammu and Kashmir by maintaining Article 370 of the Constitution as well as providing 'regional autonomy to Jammu and Ladakh regions within this state framework 'and advocated for strong steps to be taken to prevent excesses by security forces. CPI wants more frequent people to people contact between the divided parts of Kashmir and more confidence-building measures between India and Pakistan.

Regarding the problem of Jammu and Kashmir the UF suggested that it is committed to respecting Article 370 of the Constitution as well as the wishes of the people, the problems of Jammu and Kashmir will be resolved through giving the people of that state the maximum degree of autonomy.

North-East

The INC advocated the need to set up a High-Power Commission to examine and suggest solutions to the problems faced by the North-Eastern states. It suggested to contain the problem of insurgency and militancy through speedy all-round development of the region and mutual understanding and negotiations with the various groups. It also proposed an expanded role to North-East Council as well as larger funds and greater financial powers, and wider administrative and financial powers to Autonomous District Council. It also suggested to effectively check 'illegal infiltration into the region and special efforts to develop forestry, tourism, handicrafts, and other employment-oriented industries'.

Regarding the North-East, the BJP suggested the following: steps to be taken to stem the tide of illegal immigration from Bangladesh; insurgent groups will be dealt with firmly; the land and culture of indigenous ethnic groups will be protected; flood control in Assam and river water management will receive special attention; appropriate resources will be allocated for land development, agriculture, housing, nutrition, health, education, rural connectivity and irrigation; job-generating schemes will be initiated, especially in the service sector and special emphasis will be given to connectivity with and within North-Eastern States. In the context of the 2014 manifesto, the BJP advocated the following: enhancing the connectivity within the region and to the rest of the country; having a special emphasis on massive infrastructure development; addressing the issue of flood control in Assam; addressing the issue of infiltration and illegal immigrants in the North East region on a priority basis and taking measures for the safety of North-Eastern students studying across the country.

On the other hand, the CPI and CPI (M) advocated for the need for conducting negotiations with all those groups who are advocating separatism, while firmly defending the integrity of the Indian Union as well as the provision for the development of the North-Eastern region. However, the CPI criticized the Armed Forces Special Powers Act, and treat it as an attack on their identity and human rights that must be repealed.

While the CPI(M) in its manifesto of 2014 emphasized the following: for the North-East to be declared a priority region for development; for developing physical infrastructure and special employment schemes for the youth; for border fencing to be completed expeditiously; for protecting and expanding the administrative and financial powers under the Sixth Schedule and for the enactment of anti-racist laws and other measures to ensure greater security for people from the North-East in other parts of the country.

Regarding the problem of Assam and North-Eastern States, the UF suggested that government will take up special programmes for the economic development of Assam and the North-Eastern region.

The NF, regarding the North-Eastern region, suggested to fulfill 'the legitimate aspirations of the people' and provide more funds to the North-East Council for the development purposes. It also suggested giving sympathetic consideration to the demands for the application of the Sixth Schedule of the Constitution to put some restrictions in the North-Eastern States.

Judicial reforms

Since the First General Election (1951–1952), Judicial Reforms have always been an important component in the party manifestos. Some of the issues which have been advocated by all political parties are these: separation of Judiciary from Executive at all levels; justice being cheap and speedy; legal defence of the poor; mobile courts for small offences; increase in the number of judges; appointment of special judges to clear the arrears; steps to fill vacancies in the Supreme Court and the High Courts; existing legal aid facilities expanded and strengthened in weaker sections; fast-track courts extended to all layers of the judiciary; alternative dispute redressal mechanisms expanded through LokAdalats and Tribunals and by-law Nyaya Panchayats established in all states.

The SP, in its manifesto as early as Second General Election 1957, voiced the need 'to appoint a Law Commission to examine all existing laws so that they conform to the Constitution and to the notions of equality and democracy'.

The INC and the CPI suggested the need for a National Judicial Reforms Commission to formulate a detailed blueprint of a judicial system.

The CPI (M), in its 1971 manifesto, also advocated the need for a thorough reorganization of the judiciary due to the 'requirements of a rapidly changing democratic public opinion in the country and the reactionary viewpoint held by Supreme and other High Courts many of whose judgements have been admitted being "political" rather than judicial'. The manifesto suggested a through reorganization of the judiciary 'by replacing those who are demonstrably prejudiced in favour of vested interests by those who are committed to rapid change in socio-economic set-up in the country'.

The system of judicial appointment, their promotion and re-employment have been a subject of debate and discussion since the beginning. The SP advocated that the system must be revised so as to give the government little scope for patronage after their retirement. The CPI as early as 1971 General Election pointed out that

> Judges, including the Chief Justices of the Supreme Court and High Courts, shall be appointed from among the names of the panels approved by Parliament in the case of Supreme Court and by the concerned State Assemblies in the case of High Courts. The seniority shall not alone determine as to who should be appointed as the Chief Justice of the Supreme Court or a High Court. There shall be no legal restriction on the number of Judges of the Supreme Court. It will be open to Parliament to remove any judge from the Supreme Court by a resolution passed by a simple majority in the Lok Sabha alone.

Since the 1990s, all political parties (like CPI, CPI(M), BJP and INC) advocated for the need for setting up a National Judicial Commission and for making judicial appointments of Judges of Supreme Court and High Courts. The manifesto of CPI elaborated on its composition comprising of representative from judiciary, executive, legislature and bar. A BJP manifesto advocated the need to provide 'guidelines on objective criteria to determine merit'.

The CPI and CPI (M) in a recent manifesto also voiced the need that all Judges 'should be required by law to declare their assets'. The BJP also suggested that the National Judicial Commission will also draw 'a code of ethics for the judges'.

In the 2014 election manifestos, the BJP, INC and CPI(M) all emphasized the need to set up a National Judicial Commission for the appointment of judges in higher judiciary. While the CPI(M) also emphasized making this body for the 'transfer and dismissal of judges and to ensure judicial accountability'. On the other hand, INC emphasized providing 'a new method of appointing judges through a Judicial Commission'.

Reorganization of the states

Reorganization of the states on a linguistic basis was favoured in many Congress Resolutions before independence. During the First General Election 1952, the INC, SP and CPI emphasized the need for the formation of the states on a linguistic basis. However, the INC, and SP pointed out that, besides the linguistic reasons, there is need to look also into geographical contiguity, economic viability and administrative and financial factors. This view was also supported by the PSP.

In 1999, both the INC and NDA proposed the formation of Uttarakhand, Chattisgarh and Jharkhand as new states. The INC manifesto also advocated to set up 'Sub-regional Development Boards' in states having 'striking economic disparities' with meaningful autonomy for the implementation of development schemes. The BJP supported 'the creation of Telangana as a separate State of the Union of India'. It also pointed out the need to 'sympathetically examine and appropriately consider the long-pending demands of the 'Gorkhas, the Adivasis and other people of Darjeeling districts Dooars region'.

The BJP in a recent manifesto stated that it recognizes the special needs and unique problems of hill and desert states and advocated 'Development- based, State-specific model to meet aspirations of the people'. In 2014, the BJP reiterated again for 'greater decentralization through smaller states'.

Regarding the border disputes between states, the CPI voiced that 'this problem must be solved by faithfully adhering to the triple principle of linguistic and cultural homogeneity, geographical contiguity and taking village not tehsil or taluq or district as the unit'. In its manifesto of 2014, the CPI(M) expressed an amendment in Article 3 of the Constitution so to provide for the consent of the state legislature concerned before a state is bifurcated or reorganized by Parliament.

Law and order and police reform

The CPI in its manifesto during the first general election proposed the revision of British-framed police codes to bring them in line with democratic standards. 'The Police must be taught to be people-friendly. Deaths in police look-ups must stop. Police reforms must be accompanied by jail reforms'.

The INC and CPI voiced the need to do the following: implement the recommendations of the National Police Commission to free the police force from undue political interference and provide independence to function in an impartial and professional manner; to take steps to ensure that the police is seen to be functioning in a humane manner; to equip the police force with the latest equipment, tools and systems to make it more effective; to institute a special scheme for funding the modernization of the police force in all states; to undertake constant training of police personnel at all levels and sensitize them to the concerns of ordinary citizen; to induce more women into the police force; to raise a specialized force to deal with terrorism in its various dimensions within the country; to embark on a sensitive review of the entire network of intelligence establishments in the country; to upgrade the professional expertise of the intelligence organizations substantially; to coordinate among the various agencies that have to be institutionalized for timely analysis and to assess the intelligence information.

The BJP, INC and CPI suggested modernizing the police force into an efficient and impartial instrument of law and order. The CPI, besides modernization, also suggested 'detoxifying it of all communal virus and making it people friendly'. The BJP suggested to enact a Central Law and constitute a federal agency to deal with federal crimes

In the 2014 manifesto, both the BJP and INC emphasized the following: modernizing the police force, equipping them with the latest technology; strengthening investigations and making them swift, transparent, fair, clear and decisive. The INC emphasized the need to make the police administration more progressive and sensitive to the needs of people.

Terrorism

Terrorism since the 1990s found a place as one of the major issues in the agenda of political parties. In the context of terrorism, the INC pleaded to do the following: fight against terrorism and all other anti-national activities with special development efforts in states and regions which continue to be disturbed; strengthen the steps to protect our borders on land and sea in dealing with infiltration of foreigners, smuggling and narco-trafficking and eliminate the criminal nexus with influential segments and control of organized crimes.

The BJP in its 1996 manifesto emphasized the need to enact a suitable law to tackle terrorism; to timely assistance to state governments to maintain law and order; to hold district officers squarely accountable for mismanagement of public order, to improve the intelligence-gathering mechanism; to launch a nationwide derive to identify the influx of arms; to crack down on narcotics smuggling, to rationalize the number, structure, composition and role of para-military and special forces.

The CPI expressed the following: revamping the intelligence machinery and enhanced coordination between security and intelligence agencies; the Federal Investigating Agency functioning without violating the federal structure and ensuring association of state governments for investigation within a particular state; modernizing the Police Force; strengthening of the coastal security system and amending the Unlawful Activities (Prevention) Act to remove draconian provisions like detention without bail for 180 days, three years imprisonment for withholding information, etc.

Economic issues

Objective of economic organization

The manifestos of 1952 and 1957 dealt with the issue of objective of economic organization. In these manifestos, by and large, all national parties favoured a planned approach to the various aspects of national life. The INC called it a mixed economy based on controlled capitalism, for BJS, it was welfare capitalism and for the CPI and SP it was socialist society and, for PSP, a mixed economy with emphasis on decentralized industry and reduction in the disparities of income. On the other hand, the SWP in its manifesto of 1962 advocated for abolishing planning and the Planning Commission. It pleaded that the Cabinet is an appropriate organization for such planning, because the Cabinet is responsible to the Parliament, and through it to the people. However, the SWP subsequently suggested replacing the Planning Commission with a genuine expert advisory body in various sectors to help the government plan its business. Its manifesto observed that it is in favour of democratic planning, however, opposed to 'Soviet type coercive planning'.

Another important observation enumerated by the political parties in their manifestos during the election of 1952 and 1957 relates to the lessening disparities in incomes. In this context, the INC suggested 'A national minimum in the general standard of living should be aimed at, so that everyone has the necessaries of life and opportunity for education, for maintaining his health and for productive work'. The SP and PSP suggested to initiate measures to narrow down existing differences of incomes, aiming at a ratio of 1:10. The CPI was in favour of 'A national minimum wage to be fixed and workers should be assisted to secure fair wages'.

Agricultural policy

Tenancy reform

As far as the reform in the tenancy system is concerned, all the political parties were in favour of abolition of zamindari system. However, there were differences in the means to be adopted. The INC and BJS were in favour of giving compensation and distributing the land to the tillers. The BJS favoured the following: the 'Land shall belong to the tiller of the soil and there will be no intermediary between the *Kisan* and the state. Persons displaced by abolition of Zamindari and Jagirdari will be rehabilitated'; to 'redistribute land to provide holdings to the landless'; and 'The minimum and maximum holding shall be 5 and 30 acres of well irrigated land or its equivalent respectively'. On the other hand, the INC emphasized that 'On the land, all intermediaries must be progressively removed, so that land is owned by the cultivator himself'. While the SP emphasized that

> Private ownership of land about three times the size of the minimum holding that is a holding which a family of five can cultivate without employing hired labour or heavy mechanization, will be permitted. All lands in excess of these will be distributed among poor peasants and landless labourers.

On the other hand, the CPI emphasized that 'Ceilings should not exceed three times a family holding and all land in excess of the ceiling should be distributed among agricultural workers and peasants without payment'. The CPI regarding agrarian reforms subsequently pleaded that all land transfers must be re-examined and fictitious land transfers and all loopholes in the existing land legislation must be removed. The CPI (M) demanded for the 'taking over of the land of the big landlords and their distribution *gratis* among agricultural workers and peasants'. In subsequent manifestos, the CPI approached the problem of land reform by emphasizing the need of 'Radical ceiling legislations on the basis of drastic reduction of the present high ceilings and family as unit for ceiling and the scraping of exemptions'. The CPI further emphasized the need to 'stop all moves to reverse ceiling laws for corportising agriculture; and prohibit sale of agricultural land to foreign companies for agri business'.

However, the SWP approached the problem of land reforms with the suggestion to 'respect the property rights of the peasants in their holdings, big or small'. The party was of the view to bring land reforms without expropriation in any form. It also suggested repeal of the 17th Amendment of the Constitution, to expropriate land belonging to peasant proprietors on payment of grossly inadequate compensation.

For implementing the agrarian reform, the CPI favoured democratically elected agricultural labourers committees, whereas the PSP was in favour of using various Panchayats as the key agency for implementing land reform.

The manifestos of BJP and INC did not mention the problem of tenancy reforms in their manifesto of 2014. However, the CPI (M) highlighted the following tenancy issues: reverse the current thrust to dilute land-ceiling laws; prevent the encroachment and takeover of common lands; protect all government and public sector land from transfer to the private sector; takeover and distribute all surplus land to landless and poor peasant households.

Agricultural labour

Agricultural labour has been an issue in all the general elections. All the national political parties provided their approach on the issues of agricultural labour in their manifestos. In the beginning, the emphasis was on the redistribution of surplus land. However, since the second general election, along with the distribution of surplus land, payment of minimum wages was also included as an approach to solve the problems of agriculture labour. Emphasis was also given for providing alternative employment in schemes such as village road building, drainage, soil conservation, land reclamation, cottage and rural industries, etc. Besides, cancellations of debts and providing social benefits have also been suggested by almost all national political parties.

In the 2014 election, the following are some of the important issues focused on by different political parties.

1 The CPI(M) suggested the following: increasing minimum wages for agricultural workers to Rs 300 per day; ensuring equal wages for women agricultural workers; revamping the regulatory and implementing mechanism for effective and strict enforcement of the minimum wages act; enacting a separate and comprehensive legislation for agricultural workers to ensure minimum wages, the right to bargain collectively and measures of social security such as pensions, accident compensation etc. with central funding.
2 The INC suggested the following: health insurance and pension coverage; strict implementation of Contract Labour (Regulation and Abolition Act) of 1970 to end exploitation of workers; focus

on workers in hazardous industries; *Aadhaar* becoming a tool of social inclusion, all migrant labour being covered under *Aadhaar* in next one year; implementation of Unorganized Workers Social Security Act, 2008 in letter and spirit.

3 The BJP emphasized the following issues: issue identity cards to workers in the unorganized sector and make arrangements to provide quality healthcare and education services; extend access to modern financial services to labour; strengthen pension and health insurance safety nets for all kinds of labourers.

Agriculture production

It is proposed to provide the approach of the political parties regarding agriculture production in their manifestos during the elections conducted in the 1950s and early 1960s. For an increase in the agricultural production, the INC manifesto emphasized the need for 'cooperative farming' and providing top priority to river valley schemes. For this, it was suggested to make the whole or a greater part of the village a unit of co-operative management. In the case of the BJS, the emphasis was on the following: campaign to educate the cultivator; better storage facility, consolidation of holdings; popularization of better seeds; improved method of agriculture; use of mechanical appliances and provision of irrigation facilities to build small dams, sink wells, tube wells, and small irrigation projects etc. The CPI emphasized the need for irrigation works for increasing production of food and raw materials. The SP emphasized the need that 'the State will have to help the tiller in solving many of the difficulties that face him'. The party manifesto further included provisions for better manure, seeds, implements, better marketing facilities, cheaper finance and technical assistance implemented through co-operative banks, grain banks, warehouses, model forms and by the administrative reorganization of agricultural administration.

It is interesting to spell out the administrative measures suggested by the SP regarding agricultural administration. It suggested that 'The village panchayats will have pivotal place in the new setup. Above the panchayats there will be three layers of administrative bodies – Regional, State and Union'; (1) the panchayats will be elected on the basis of universal suffrage by a village or a group of villages. They will tabulate the resources of the village and assess their productive potential. They will prepare a crop plan for their village and send it to the higher organs of the Planning Commission; (2) over the village panchayats there would be Regional Land Commissions. They will coordinate the crop plans and agricultural resources in their region; (3) over the Regional Commission there will be a State Land Commission in each State. This will be in charge of planning, development and management of the rural economy; (4) 'the Union Land Commission will be in charge of such items as agricultural planning on all-India basis, movement of crops, multi-purpose development projects including river-training and flood control'.

From late 1960s to 1980s, all the political parties, for the purpose of increasing agricultural production, emphasized the need for the following: the application of scientific methods, a network of irrigation works, service co-operatives for marketing, a supply of improved tools, improved seeds, manures, fertilizers, pesticides and other inputs credit facilities and remunerative prices for food crops, the free movement of farm commodities etc.

Two important aspects which have been emphasized, since late 1990s, almost by all parties, relate to increased public investment in agriculture with focus on the backward and poor regions and amendment in the Land Acquisition Act. Besides, there has been an emphasis to adopt a National Land Use Policy to regulate and facilitate land management and to amend the SEZ Act and Rules.

The CPI(M), INC and BJP focused on the following issues in the 2014 elections. The CPI(M) emphasized the following: effect a substantial increase in public expenditure on the rural sector, increase public investment and expand public institutions for agricultural research and extension; re-impose trade restrictions to prevent both dumping and excessive exports that jeopardize national food security; provide cheap institutional credit to the agricultural sector at a maximum 4 percent rate of interest; expand public investment in power supply in rural areas and stop the privatization of electricity.

The INC emphasized the following: introduce the FDI in multibrand retail to create beneficial value chain; continue to promote PPPs for increasing investments in value chains; create a special emphasis on livestock development and animal husbandry; ensure access to and quality in agriculture education and continue to provide higher minimum support price to increase profitability of agriculture of farmers.

The BJP focused on the following: increase in public investment in agriculture and rural development; ensure minimum 50 percent over cost of production, cheaper agriculture inputs and credit; introduce latest technologies for farming and high-yielding seeds and link Mahatma Gandhi National Rural Employment Guarantee Act (MGNREGA) to agriculture.

Irrigation

All the national political parties emphasized the need for developing both large-scale river valley projects as well as small irrigation schemes for generating sufficient water resources and cheap hydro-electric power. However, since early 1990s, the emphasis has changed to building check dams; rain water harvesting; a rational water management approach for fulfilling the needs of the local population; expeditious solution to Inter-State water dispute and a new water policy.

Regarding pollution in the rivers the SP came out with a novel suggestion of the draining impure water from factories and sewage water from cities into rivers should be made illegal. For stopping the pollution of rivers, 'It should be taken through pipes to fallow tracks nearby, where fertilizer plants should be set up'.

In the 2014 election manifesto, the BJP focused on promoting low water-consuming irrigation techniques and the optimum utilization of water resources. On the other hand the CPI(M) emphasized the new National Water Policy to be formulated to treat water as a scarce public good in such a manner as to increase waster re-charge and water conservation while simultaneously enhancing water availability for domestic use, irrigation and industry through effective regulation and demand management. It also provides for the following: equitable provision of potable drinking water to all habitations to be accorded priority; no privatization of water resources; tackling depletion of ground water through more effective regulation, strengthening regulatory bodies and appropriate legislation.

Industrial policy

Regarding industrial development, during the first general election, the INC emphasized that 'basic industries should be owned or controlled by the State'. It also emphasized the need of the private sector, but the private sector must accept the 'objectives of the National Plan and fit into it'. It also stressed the need for the progressive extension of the public sector according to the 'results achieved the resources available and the capacity of the country at the moment'. In brief the INC favoured 'the mixed economy'. During the second general election, the party manifesto clarified that it is not intended to nationalize the existing private industries, 'except where such is considered necessary in terms of planning or where they occupy a strategic position in economy'. The party favoured the nationalization of State Bank as well as

Life Insurance, as it provides strategic control for planning and other purposes of the state

The CPI was in favour of nationalizing the foreign-owned industries in India. It also emphasized that the industries of India will be developed 'with the aid of nationalized capital and by enlisting the co-operation of the private industrialists who will be assured legitimate profit and protection of their interests'. For the industrial development of the country the CPI welcomed the assistance of private capitalist and foreign governments 'on terms that are in conformity with our national interests'. Subsequently the CPI favoured and extended the nationalization of banking, general insurance, coal mining, aluminium, manganese, copper, iron and gold. It also emphasized the development of the heavy and basic industries in the state sector, and the state should also have monopoly of foreign trade.

The BJS only advocated state ownership of those industries which were concerned or connected with defence needs of the country. The Party was of the view not to bring other large industries under state ownership, as generally this had 'not worked efficiently and economically' in India. The Party pointed out that 'unlimited state capitalism may also lead to totalitarianism'. The Party was of the view that instead talking about nationalization in vague terms, it will encourage expansion of private enterprise 'in the interests of consumers and producers alike'. Within this perspective of industrial policy, the BJS also emphasized to take effective steps to check on profiteering and concentration of economic power 'in the hands of the big few through cartels and combinations'.

Subsequently the BJS emphasized and extended its industrial policy by suggesting the nationalization of basic industries along with defence industries but providing full opportunity to all industries to develop freely subject to supervision and regulation. It also pleaded for the Indianization of foreign industries in the area of mining, tea-plantation, coffee, rubber etc. The BJS further also advocated taking 'steps to revive the spirit of Swadeshi for the development of industries and saving foreign exchange'. In the late 1960s, the BJS pleaded for a change in the investment pattern as the industrialization has been excessively capital intensive. For investment pattern, it favoured that 'Decentralization, Swadeshi and labour intensity should be the criteria for our industrial development'.

The SP was in favour of dividing the industry into three sectors – nationalized sector, the medium-scale private sector and the small-scale co-operative sector. It advocated for the nationalization of key industries like iron and steel, electric power, heavy chemicals, mines and plantation, textile, sugar and cement as well as credit institutions and insurances. The SP also emphasize a limited role to the private enterprise and initiative, however 'it will be well defined and free from erratic interference'. The party also suggested for nationalized industry to be run 'by public corporations, autonomous but subject to the overall control of the state in general matters of policy. The nationalized sector will subserve the need of the public and independent and co-operative producers'. The party also advocated encouragement to producer's co-operatives both in the private and small-scale sector. In such ventures, the state will provide special credit, marketing, technology, training of technical personnel, etc. It advocated for the municipalization of all public utility services like electricity, gas, water, etc.

The PSP in its first manifesto favoured the nationalization of key industries, foreign trade and those sectors of the economy 'where capital tends to accumulate and power concentrate'. The PSP advocated the need to 'nationalize and socialize all large-scale industries' and set up an independent autonomous corporation representing labour, consumers and the government to administer these industries. The nationalization will be worked out through autonomous corporations to enable 'democratic checks and participation'. Besides, the party advocated decentralization of industry, mainly with the help of local resources, in man, material and skill. It also emphasized the need and encouragement to the spirit of 'austerity and of swadeshi', for the goods manufactured by decentralized industries. Subsequently, the PSP also advocated to develop cooperatively the natural resources of the country such as fishing, forest and water resources. Besides, it also suggested an emphasis on regional development to mitigate the imbalance between different regions through utilizing the special resources, aptitudes and opportunities in different regions.

The SWP was the only party which had a different approach to the problem of industrial development. The party was opposed to nationalization. It defined the role of government in industry by stating that it 'should be that of a helper and regulator, but not a participant'. The party stood for the balanced development of capital goods, consumer goods and rural industries. The party was in favour of 'encouragement of private enterprise'. The party emphasized that it will 'rectify the confusion and corruption which had entered the economy on account of controls, permits, licenses and quotas'.

By the early 1960s, the INC, the SP and the CPI were having an identical approach to nationalization and providing dominant role to the public sector.

By the late 1970s, the JP came out with a fresh look at the pattern and perspective of industrialization. It emphasized the need to produce the wage goods necessary for mass consumption and to choose a pattern for industrialization that will provide full employment to the people. This will help in holding back inflation, assuring the minimum needs of the population and serve as a base for further development. It also favoured statutory spheres of production for big, small and cottage industries. This industrial policy was also broadly advocated by different national political parties till the 1980s.

Small-scale industries

The INC emphasized that the small-scale and cottage industries must be developed and protected 'with the aid of the state and coordinated with other forms of industry'. It was suggested that to make these industries effective and economic 'the best techniques should be employed'. It was also emphasized that the cottage industries should be organized in 'industrial co-operatives' wherever possible.

The BJS pointed out the development of small-scale and cottage industries on the model of Japan. It also suggested to make the country self-sufficient in consumer goods through the development of these industries. To achieve this goal, it proposed to take steps like the speedy development of hydro-electric energy and the establishment of rural polytechnics for training purposes, marketing facilities and encouragement to join in co-operative efforts for the establishment of such industries.

The PSP advocated for the decentralization of industry and envisaged 'the development of a new technology based on small machines operated by power, capable of distribution in small units'. The SP advocated 'devoted attention of the state to the small-scale industry'. It was expressed that the small-scale industries must occupy a place of pride in a country 'rich in manpower and short of capital'.

The manifesto of CPI in the 1977 election advocated the need to encourage the small and medium units through adequate credit and provision of raw material and marketing facilities. It further suggested the 'effective ban on the control, direct or indirect, of small-scale and cottage industries by monopoly houses'. It also advocated all necessary protection to the handloom industries.

The JP advocated to take appropriate measures 'to demarcate areas of differential technology and to provide for statutory reservations of spheres of production of high-small and cottage industries'. The manifesto of NF emphasized producing wage goods and services required for consumption by the mass of the people. For this purpose, the manifesto advocated 'Agro-processing industries, industries based on the craft of rural artisans, village industries of particular benefit to women and rural households will receive full support by way of credit, extension service, supply of inputs, marketing organization etc.' 'Manufacture of items of mass consumption, which can be produced by the cottage and small-scale industries, will be reserved'.

Industrial policy – post-liberalization phase, 1991–2014

Due to severe balance of payments crisis of 1991, all the major national political parties in their manifestos pronounced fundamental change in their approach to economic policy and related issues. The approach of political parties on the question of economic restructuring has been analysed here based on the content analysis of these manifestos from 1991 to 2014. This analysis compares the basic thrust of these parties on different aspects of the economic policy.

The BJP in its approach to economic liberalization pleaded that it would be its endeavour in every economic and industrial activity to 'foster Swadeshi spirit'. This was elaborated by stating that the national economic growth would be based on the principle that 'India shall be built by Indians'. The United Front elaborated its policy on liberalization by highlighting the need in its overall approach to adopt such growth-oriented policies that lead to greater self-reliance. It also stressed the need that the bulk of industries' requirements will come from within the country. The Janata Dal and the Janata Dal (S) were of the view to follow a balanced approach towards globalization and liberalization, keeping in view the objectives of India's autonomous development and the need to utilize the maximum potential employment opportunities. The approach of CPI and CPI (M) on this issue was to preserve economic independence and self-reliance. These parties also pleaded for reversal of IMF-World Bank – dictated economic policies.

One significant aspect of party manifestos consisted in bringing reform in the regulatory framework of economic development. The INC, BJP, Janata Dal, CPI(M) and CPI have been pleading for bringing simplification to the regulatory system, i.e. de-bureaucratize, cut down the plethora of controls and strengthen the regulatory bodies to prevent and minimize the scope for corruption.

On the issue of industrial development, the INC emphasized the need through special effort to revive the Indian manufacturing industry by 'a comprehensive entrepreneurship development programme with linkages to education institutions, banks and industrial promotion agencies'. While the BJP pleaded to achieve growth rate on a sustainable basis by mobilizing our own domestic resources and making Indian products and services competitive. The emphasis of National Front was to promote industrial development in such a way 'as to maximize employment' and produce wage goods and services required for consumption by the mass of our people. While the CPI and CPI(M) pleaded for a new policy to strengthen indigenous industry and domestic capacities as well as curbs on monopoly houses and transnational groups.

In these manifestos, there was also a mention of the development of Small and Medium Enterprises (SME). The INC pleaded to give SMEs access to finance, technology, marketing facilities and improved infrastructure. It also advocated the need to liberate them from multiplicity of laws and forms and freeing them from the clutches of inspectors. The manifesto of BJP also pleaded for the promotion of SMEs in retail sectors and also to bring reforms, to improve productivity and greater capital formation and impose countervailing restriction on foreign countries specially in service sector. While CPI and CPI(M) were also in favour of SMEs in labour-intensive sectors.

In almost all the manifestos of major national parties, one important constituent of the economic reforms and restructuring consisted of redefining the role of the public sector. The INC on this issue emphasized the need of a 'gradual withdrawal of the public sector' from areas where 'private and joint sector had developed capabilities'. It also emphasized the need to operate on the public sector on commercial lines to provide autonomy and accountability. The BJP's views, by and large, on the public sector, have been similar to that of INC, i.e. improving the efficiency and profitability of crucial public-sector units; pruning the public sector and 'confining to sensitive areas' relating to nations physical and economic security; professionally managing the public sector and least interference by the government and keeping the interests of the worker. On the other hand CPI and CPI(M) were against wholesale privatization of public sector. On the contrary, their views were to strengthen public sector in core and strategic areas, to promote its autonomy and efficiency and to halt the privatization of profit-making public enterprises.

Regarding the role of foreign capital, almost all national political parties – BJP, INC, CPI, CPI(M), and JD – were in agreement that it should be in harmony with and advance the national objectives. All national parties were also of the view that the main objectives of bringing foreign investments should be to obtain higher technology, increase exports and to expand production base but not at the cost of self-reliance. However, for the BJP, 'national development will be largely funded by capital generated within the country and foreign investment will play a small role'. While Janata Dal in principle agreed regarding 'competition from multinational corporations for promoting excellence, however, it was of the view that 'solid steps must be taken for creating a level-playing field before opening up of the economy'. The BJP and the Janata Dal also pleaded for foreign collaboration in infrastructure sector where there are technological gaps and deficiencies. While the BJP, Janata Dal, CPI and CPI(M) were against the foreign capital to be channelled in those areas for which clear-cut priorities are set. These priorities are to be determined by the need for developing new production capacities and acquiring new technology.

Due to their contemporary significance, an attempt has been made to provide an overview of economic policy of INC, BJP and the CPI(M) as specified in their respective manifestos of the 2014 elections. There is lot of similarity between the views of BJP and INC on economic policy. Both BJP and INC are in favour of providing an enabling environment for doing business in India.

Congress: create a stable and predictable business environment, sustain an investment climate which is welcoming and supportive of FDI, strengthen multilateral trade systems and investment flows for future prosperity, create national investment manufacturing zones as greenfield integrated industrial townships, create industrial corridors to catalyze economic growth.

BJP: create, conducive, enabling environment to make 'doing business' in India easy; focus on cutting red tape, simplifying procedures and removing bottlenecks; make decision-making on environment clearances transparent and time bound; develop world-class investment and industrial regions as global units of manufacturing; set up a task force to review and revive the Micro, Small and Medium Enterprises (MSME) sector; give high priority to the growth of manufacturing; increase public spending on research and development; facilitate setting up of software and hardware manufacturing units.

CPI(M): give priority to manufacturing sector growth through a long-term industrial policy that strategizes investment and creates incentives for employment generation; encourage small and medium enterprises in labour intensive sectors with adequate incentives, infrastructure support and sufficient credit from banks; protect domestic industry from indiscriminate lowering of import duties and takeover of existing Indian companies by foreign companies; prohibit FDI in Retail Trade; reverse FDI guidelines to prevent backdoor entry of

FDI and prevent FDI through acquisition route of domestic industries; channel foreign capital for building productive capacities and acquiring new technology; strengthen and expand the public sector in the core and strategic areas by injecting fresh capital and technology; promote autonomy and efficiency in the public sector; complete halt to disinvestment and privatization of profit-making and potentially viable PSUs.

Industrial relations

The INC during the First General Election emphasized the need for improving the implementation of those laws which were passed from 1947 to 1952: compulsory recognition of unions, conferring bargaining rights on unions, compulsory government adjudication of disputes, reduction of weekly working hours and introduction of compulsory welfare provisions for workers in large factories. It also emphasized the need for providing housing for workers and the need to improve the procedure relating to arbitration and adjudication of disputes. Subsequently, the manifesto of the INC advocated the need for continuing attention to the 'training and wellbeing of the workers' and suggested the need for progressively associating them in the management of the enterprises.

The BJS advocated the need for 'making labour sharer in profits of industries based on production'. It also advocated, during the transition period, that 'all strikes and lock-out would be discouraged'. All disputes to be settled by industrial tribunals which would be binding on industrialists and labour.

For SP, the workers will be consulted regarding the conduct of the industry. Sickness insurance, maternity benefits and old-age pension funds will be contributed to in all these matters the responsibility of social security is incumbent upon the state. The SP also advocated the need to organize the unions nationally, on an industry-wise basis, with branches in every region. Besides, legal safeguards will be provided to preserve fullest internal democracy.

The CPI advocated giving a living wage to the workers and to providing social security measures against every form of disability, sickness and unemployment. It recognized their trade unions and the rights of collective bargaining. It also advocated that 'profits will be controlled and joint production council set up'.

The CPI in the late 1960s advocated that all trade unions laws and rights 'will apply equally to the private and public sectors'. It also suggested the need to introduce legislation to ensure proper linking of dearness allowance with the cost of living index, rightful share of the workers in profits as bonus, unemployment insurance, improvement of social security schemes etc. It also advocated that the right to strike should be guaranteed and democratically exercised. In the subsequent manifestos, i.e. the 1970s and 1980s, the CPI advocated the need to fix a national minimum wage for the workers and also pleaded that the workers should assert to secure fair wages in all organized industries. It also advocated that a Pay Commission should be appointed to examine the pay scale, dearness allowance, security of service and also trade union rights of all government employees and workers. It also pleaded for social insurance and provision of unemployment benefits. It also advocated measures 'which help the workers to unite in one trade union in each industry on the basis of trade union democracy'.

The PSP advocated to the industrial workers the rights of association and collective bargaining with option to strike. It encouraged the development of a free and independent trade union movement on democratic lines. The participation of workers in management would be widely introduced. The worker earnings would be raised to a living wage.

The SP advocated for effective representation of industrial workers in the state co-operations through works council and production committees. It encouraged the development of a free and independent trade union movements on democratic lines, the appointment of a National Wage Commission to determine fair wages to various categories of workers and to bring an amendment in the employees' state insurance scheme so as to provide more benefits.

The SWP advocated the workers' right to organize themselves in order to improve their conditions of life and work. It suggested that 'Strong and responsible trade unions managed by the workers themselves . . . are an integral part of a democratic industrial, order'. The party was in favour for the workers' right to collective bargaining, including the right to withdraw their labour. It advocated for a closer association of the workers and management so that 'a spirit of partnership may be developed among all those engaged in production'. The Party opposed to the exploitation of the workers and their organization by any political party. It supported workers association with management and 'a fair deal based on an equitable sharing of the gains of productivity and resulting prosperity'.

The JP believed that 'economic policies should subserve the interests of workers and affirmed the rights of workers and trade unions'. It advocated to introduce through legislation the minimum wages to all categories of workers. It also advocated that 'A fair wage must be the minimum wage and workers must derived proportional benefits from increases in productivity'.

The JD opposed the demand for 'Exit policy, to facilitate industrial restructuring'. It advocated for the need to re-orient Indian industrial relations law in respect of the following issues: registration and recognition of trade unions, need for an independent machinery to oversee Trade Unions, revamping implementation machinery concerning Labour Laws and consolidation of various Labour Laws. Also it proposed social security of workers to be guaranteed and further expanded by undertaking sympathetic review of the exiting laws, payment of social security under a single-window scheme, setting up of Industrial Workers Rehabilitation Fund and enacting appropriate legislation to promote the interests of workers of the unorganized sector of the economy.

Financial issues

Taxation

During the 1950s and 1960s the purpose of the taxation policy was to use it as an instrument to bring, as pointed out in the 1952 manifesto of the INC, 'economic equality and social justice must proceed side by side with economic progress', a redirection of public expenditure and an examination of the tax structure for 'bringing about a reasonable relationship between the minimum and maximum incomes both in the public and private sector'. It also suggested the need to curb 'with a strong hand' 'Inequalities . . . accentuated . . . largely in consequence of illegitimate gains from black marketing, tax evasion, certain forms of speculation and other anti-social activities'. The views of the SP and the PSP were also concerned with to use the tax policy to correct the embedded inequalities of our society as well as need for graduated tax on wealth, capital gains stacks, excess profit tax, inheritance tax, gift tax etc.

Like the INC, the SP and the PSP also emphasized the need to revise the taxation policy to narrow down existing differences of income and to limit the minimum and maximum incomes to the ratio of 1:10 and to improve the economic and social status of person of small means through expenditure on social services. The CPI during this period also basically emphasized the need for a heavier taxation on corporate profits, a ceiling on personal and family incomes, a tax on personal wealth, effective measures against income tax evasion, effective measures to combat wastage in government undertakings and effective measures to unearth black money.

In the post-liberalization phase, the party manifestos by and large of the INC have been advocating the need to take steps in the following directions: having a firm commitment to eliminating the revenue deficit; supplying more resources for investments in social and physical infrastructure; undertaking major tax reforms to significantly expand the base of taxpayers; substantially increasing tax compliance; to making the tax administrative more citizen friendly; introducing a system of Value-Added Taxation (VAT) and giving full managerial autonomy to public sector banks. Banks will be encouraged in every way to expand lending, particularly to agriculture, agro-industry value-added agriculture, small-scale industry and infrastructure. Interest rates must be such so as to stimulate not just investments, but also to provide adequate returns to savers.

Similarly, the BJP during the 1990s also realized that taxation alone cannot be the base for revenue. For this purpose, it suggested the following: to structure fiscal reforms to augment savings to help in higher order investment; mitigate the rigours of indirect taxes; equally distribute the sharing of taxes among affluent sections of society; devise a suitably structured VAT; hike excise duties on items of mass consumption; give operational autonomy to Reserve bank of India; provide firm measures to prevent the generation of black money and rationalize and simplify the tax structure.

The CPI (M), in order to mobilize resources, proposed the following steps: effective tax speculative capital gains, black money, increase tax for the super-rich, introduce inheritance tax and review Double Taxation Avoidance Agreement.

Banking and insurance

The INC manifesto of 1967 advocated for the need to bring banking institutions under social control in order 'to serve the cause of economic growth and fulfil our social purposes more effectively'. The CPI also advocated for the need to bring 'the whole financial capital under the state control and planning and it suggested the nationalization of all banks. The investment and use of funds will be guided by the state'. However, the SWP in its 1971 was opposed to the idea of the nationalization of banks. It was of the opinion that it 'would retard development besides being fatal to monetary stability and security by placing the savings of lakhs of small depositors at the mercy of the Government seeking to lay its hand on all available resources'. In the context of bank nationalization, the BJS advocated to convert the nationalized banking industry into Autonomous Monetary Authority, headed by Reserve Bank of India with the objectives of 'price- regulation through currency control and full employment through credit polices'.

Almost all the national political parties during elections from 1991 to 2014 highlighted in their manifestos that the health of the financial system in general and the banking system in particular is the key to the performance of Indian economy. It was also felt by these parties that banks have to be given greater autonomy and the non-performing asset ratio of the banks must be reduced.

The INC advocated the need for mergers and consolidation in the banking industry to be encouraged. However, the CPI and CPI(M) were opposed to the following: trends of privatizing the banking sector; reforms to make banks accountable and restore social priorities; proper regulations of non-banking finance companies to safeguard interests of depositors; no privatization of pension funds; no diversion of pension and provident funds to stock market.

The CPI, CPI(M), and JD favoured Tarapurwala Committee recommendations: reimposing strict controls on the outflow and inflow of finance capital; prohibiting participatory notes used by the Foreign Institutional Investors (FIIs); discouraging speculative finance; halting any further dilution of government equity in public sector banks; strengthening the public sector in banking and insurance and ensuring strict adherence to priority sector lending norms; scrapping the Banking Regulation (Amendment) Bill and preventing the takeover of Indian banks by foreign banks.

In the context of the insurance sector, the INC favoured to open up the health insurance and pension businesses both in the public and private sector. It also favoured joint ventures in the insurance business with majority equity with Indian companies. While the United Front suggested that there is room for public sector companies and private sector companies to co-exist and compete in the financial sector, restructuring of the insurance industry. The Janata Dal suggested insulating the sensitive areas of financial services, like insurance and capital markets, etc., from the influence of international financial cartels. The Janata Dal was also against opening up of the country's insurance sector for foreign companies. On the other hand, the CPI and CPI(M) were against the privatization of the insurance sector and also suggested barring the foreign companies into the insurance sector.

Financial management

Debt management

In the context of debt management, the INC advocated for the need to pursue prudent debt management policies, avoid disbursement delays in externally assisted projects and efficiently utilize borrowed funds. The INC manifesto of 1999 also suggested the need to look into the 'feasibility of a Constitutional ceiling' on the growth of public debt. The United Front pleaded for severely restricted public borrowing (borrowed money was not be used for consumption expenditure); for growth in domestic debt to be slowed down and for a portion of the debt be retired in a phased manner. The CPI(M) pleaded for 'planned efforts to reduce external and internal debts within a time-bound period'. The BJP stressed the need to 'lighten the debt burden' so as to 'contribute to interest rate stabilization'.

Capital markets

The INC in its approach to the capital markets stressed the need, immediate steps to restore the health of the capital markets. Institutions like Unit Trust of India (UTI), Life Insurance Corporation (LIC) and General Insurance Corporation (GIC) should be equipped to become efficient market participants. The debt market will be developed; Foreign Institutional Investors (FIIs) will be encouraged. There will be a disinvestment of government shareholding in public sector companies and of financial institutions. It also stressed the need to revive the capital market and offer new investment opportunities to the people, as well as to regulate the capital market to efficiently protect the interest of small ordinary investors.

In the context of industrial policy, the BJP observed to ensure a healthy capital market with the twin objectives of increasing capital investment in the corporate sector of providing protection to the investing public.

Fiscal management

The INC and the BJP both stressed the need to bring a Fiscal Responsibility Act for maintaining a fiscal discipline in a transparent manner. The INC and the BJP pointed out the need to bring about a national consensus on the scope, nature, level and growth of public expenditures, including implicit and explicit subsidies; to bring about a fundamental reorientation in the structure of government expenditure at both the central and state levels and to bring about a firm commitment to eliminating the revenue deficit of the Central Government. The CPI and CPI(M) also highlighted the need to minimize wasteful expenditure and the growing misuse of public money by officialdom and public servants. The Janata Dal and BJP also stressed the need for curtailing the administrative expenditure and non-productive expenditure.

Resource mobilization

All national political parties – BJP, INC, CPI, CPI(M) and Janata Dal – on the issue of resource mobilization suggested the need to broaden the direct taxes base; raise the tax rates on the affluent sections and ensure strict compliance; deal firmly with tax evasion and unearth black money kept inside and outside the country and tap it for productive purposes.

Economy

It is proposed to provide an overview of the manifesto of INC, BJP, CPI(M), regarding the financial management of national development. In the manifestos of 2014 elections, some important issues are given here:

1 Congress: basic rights and welfare package for all working people; priority will be to bring India back to 8 percent inclusive growth path; zero aversion to foreign investment; to increase aggregate revenue bring 'Direct tax Code' and 'Goods and Services Tax' Bills; detailed 'Jobs Agenda' to ensure ten crore new jobs; incentivize domestic manufacturing and exports by providing minimum tariff protection and speed up the Industrial Corridor projects; provide rebate or waive off all taxes on Central and State exports and set up a National Investment Facilitation Authority. While formulating monetary policy it was suggested to strike a balance between price stability and growth. For infrastructure projects, it was suggested that the Public Private Partnership (PPP) model must be made more transparent and competitive and more widely used, that a minimum tariff protection be in place so that that there is an incentive to manufacture goods in India; that we must choose the subsidies that are absolutely necessary and give them only to the absolutely deserving.

2 BJP: will push for fiscal autonomy of states, additional tax benefits and higher interest rates for senior citizens; will review labour laws; will strategically develop industries such as electronics assembly, tourism, textiles, footwear, food-processing; will prohibit FDI in retail, FDI will be allowed in sectors wherever needed for job and asset creation, infrastructure and acquisition of niche technology and specialized expertise; will rationalize and simplify the tax regime, will strictly implement fiscal discipline; will undertake banking reforms; will bring all governments onboard for GST; will bring out a National Land Use Policy single window for project clearances and speedy environment clearances; will unbundle FCI operations into procurement, storage and distribution for greater efficiency and to tackle price rise; will undertake Banking reforms to enhance ease and access, as well as accountability; will encourage savings as an important driver of investment and growth; barring the multi-brand retail sector, FDI will be allowed in sectors wherever needed for job and asset creation, infrastructure and acquisition of niche technology and specialized expertise. BJP is committed to protecting the interest of small and medium retailers, SMEs and those employed by them. The FIPBs (Foreign Investment Promotion Board) functioning shall be made more efficient and investor-friendly.

3 The views of the CPI(M) are as follows: manufacturing sector growth to be given priority through a long-term industrial policy that strategizes investment for employment operation. GST to be implemented only after ensuring a higher rate for the states so as to at least partially correct the present fiscal imbalance. Also, to prohibit FDI in Retail Trade; reverse FDI guidelines to prevent backdoor entry of FDI and prevent FDI through acquisition route of domestic industries; regulate domestic corporate retailers through a licencing policy; launch a drive to unearth black money, especially those stashed in Swiss bank and other offshore tax havens; increase wealth tax for the super-rich and introduce inheritance tax; reviewing Double Taxation Avoidance Agreement; increase corporate profit tax; and implement the General Sales Tax (GST) only after ensuring a higher rate for the states.

Human and social development issues

It is proposed to provide a comparative analysis and an overview of the suggestions advocated by different national political parties since the First General Election relating to human and social development issues, like education, health and family planning, public distribution system, and sports, women, youth, Scheduled Castes and Scheduled Tribes, minorities, media and mass communication, sports, cinema, culture, etc.

Education

Since the First General Election 1952, almost all national political parties – INC, SP, PSP, CPI, and BJS – advocated free and compulsory education at primary and secondary stages and free education to the poor. However, the UF, the CPI and the CPI (M) also advocated the need to make elementary education a Fundamental Right and enforced through suitable statutory measures. The INC advocated to raise 'public spending in education to at least 6 percent of GDP and half of this amount being spent in primary and secondary schools'. It was suggested by the SP 'the first precondition of equality of opportunity is equality in education. All the primary schools should be equal in matters of expenditure, salary, buildings, books, etc.'

Regarding the budgetary allocation, the SP suggested the need to earmark 'Twenty percent of the States' revenues and ten percent of the Central revenues for education'. On the other hand, the CPI favoured the allocation of 10 percent of the Union Budget and 30 percent of States Budget for education. Subsequently, the CPI, the INC, BJP, UF, NF and JD advocated the need to raise 'public spending on education to at least 6 percent of GDP'.

The INC, BJP and CPI suggested time-bound programmes for the abolition of illiteracy and arrangement for adult education. While the SP suggested the formation of 'a literacy army of unemployed educated youth' to end illiteracy within ten years. The NF suggested to promote adult education for awareness of human rights and duties, environment, scientific tamper, fight against communal and casteist divisions, national unity, secularism and democracy. The INC suggested to use electronic media increasingly for the purpose of adult education programmes.

Regarding the medium of instructions, the BJS emphasized the need for the development of regional languages while the SP suggested that English medium should be ended forthwith.

The SWP pleaded for the establishment of central universities for maintaining 'common academic standards throughout the country' The SP, in the context of university education, suggested the need 'aiming at research and knowledge of subjects'. The SWP, INC and BJS voiced the need to provide of autonomy to universities and institutions of higher learning in science, technology, social sciences and management. The INC also suggested 'academic excellence and professional competence would be the sole criteria for all appointments to bodies like ICHR, ICSSR, UGC, NCERT, etc.'

While the INC in the context of rapid economic development emphasized 'the deepening of the expansion of scientific and technical education', as well as to integrate programmes of technical educational development with training facility in newer industries. The INC and BJP also advocated to reduce pressure for expansion of higher education by delinking degrees for recruitment to jobs. It also suggested to improve management structures 'for creating healthy and vigorous community'. It also advocated to modernize the courses at higher education levels 'to bring them in line with the emerging requirements for new skills in industry, commerce, agriculture and other spheres'. A similar approach was also suggested by the NF.

The SWP in its first manifesto of 1962 suggested the need to introduce in education 'a spiritual element' so as to provide an adequate background of 'human values for the citizen of the future'. For this purpose, the voluntary agencies will be encouraged 'to impart moral and religious education to the young, without forcing any such instruction on section belonging to other denominations'. These programmes would be voluntary in nature. The PSP emphasized the need of developing 'a sense of discipline and national service' in students through NCC training, voluntary work and training in democratic citizenship. The BJP and INC suggested to make some school texts 'common throughout the country for national integration; consciously promote feelings of patriotism and commitment to the nation'. The BJP stressed the need for 'increasing the moral and cultural content in syllabi and restoring the neglected focus on character-building'.

The CPI while commending the role of charitable and private societies in the field of education, however opposed 'privatization and commercialization of education'. However, the CPI subsequently suggested in the context of private educational institutions, some social control 'for regulation of admissions, fees and content of education'. For this purpose the party suggested a central legislation 'to empower the States to regulate self-financing institutions'. The INC suggested to establish 'a Education Development Finance Company to provide loans at affordable rates for higher education in science, engineering and medicine'.

The PSP stressed the need for greater emphasis to correspondence course and to utilize the services of All India Radio for this purpose. A similar approach was also suggested by INC by expanding distance education and establishing open universities. The SP, PSP and the BJS supported the view to provide instructions up to the highest class in the regional language.

In the manifesto of 2014 election, the BJP, INC and CPI(M) all were in favour of the universalization of secondary school education with a focus on rural tribal areas to reduce dropouts and improve the quality of education and infrastructure. Another important issue related to the opening up of higher education systems to investment from India and abroad while the INC was in favour of this proposition but the CPI(M) was against this approach. Another issue raised by BJP relate to restructuring of UGC and transforming it into a Higher Education Commission; while the INC was emphasizing the need to establish Rashrtiya Uchhatar Shiksha. The INC was in favour of an independent regulatory mechanism to ensure standardization and quality of education, while the CPI(M) was in favour of regulation of private higher educational institutions.

Health and family planning

Health

Since the First General Election, a National Health Scheme to provide free and subsidized medical care to the people has been an important component of political party manifestos of SP, PSP, CPI, INC and BJS. Later on, the CPI (M), BJP and NF also emphasized the same. The BJS, UF and BJP in this respect pointed out to need to establish one primary health centre for every village. In the context of the village health centre, the CPI and the BJP also emphasized making a provision for maternity and child welfare centres. The JD pointed out that to introduce in the National Health Scheme, a revolving fund contributed by the Central Government must be made to which the poor people can become members by making a nominal contribution. Their health expenditure will be covered under the scheme and they will be entitled to get treatment in any government hospital.

The CPI and CPI (M) have been emphasizing the need to increase the expenditure on public health to 5 percent of the GNP and 'radically improving' the health services in all districts and primary village health centres. The BJP stressed the need regarding public-private partnerships in the health sector on a widest possible scale. Similarly, it also emphasized private and foreign investment in tertiary and super specialty healthcare. The BJP also pointed out to make 'concerted efforts to make India as a centre or health tourism'. In the health set up of the country, the INC expressed the view to set up 'a network of superb-specialty hospitals, all over the country, with the assistance of all sectors'.

The INC approached the problems of the health-related issues by observing the need to formulate a co-operative approach to public health. i.e. governmental action along with some changes in the habits of the people. In this context, a number of political parties like INC, BJP, NDA, NF and CPI emphasized the need to provide safe drinking water and general sanitation. The SP and NF in particular emphasized that the 'health departments pay attention to the well-being of the people through preventive medicine and nutritious food rather than through fancy medicine'.

Due recognition, and promotion of Ayurveda, Homoeopathy, Unani, and Naturopathy and Yoga systems of indigenous medicines have been highlighted by BJS, BJP, INC and NF consistently from the First General Election. However, the BJS also advocated the need 'to develop Ayurveda as a national system of medicine by establishing a dispensary in every village and establishment of research laboratories in various parts of the country for research in, and manufacture of Ayurvedic medicines'.

The CPI, INC, NF, BJP and CPI(M) have been highlighting the supply of essential drugs to the people at affordable prices. The BJP and NF suggested the need to revise the drug policy in line with the recommendations of the Hathi Committee. The CPI in this context also suggested developing basic drugs in the public sector. Besides, the BJP also stressed the need 'to make the country self-sufficient in the manufacture of all medicines'.

The INC, the BJP, and the CPI emphasized the need to formulate a national programme for the containment and control of communicable diseases. The INC in this context suggested setting up 'epidemiological surveillance system' all over the country to facilitate early detection and prompt response for rapid containment and control of the disease. The JD and the BJP emphasized the need to attain 100 percent of universal immunization by vigorously attacking eradicable diseases

The INC suggested the need to review the existing pattern of medical education and also revise medical training programmes and promote research in frontier areas such as biotechnology and use of electronics in health programmes. The INC, also on this issue, pointed out setting up an Education Commission in Health Sciences on the lines of the University Grants Commission to provide requisite financial and technical support for professional and para-professional education in the health sciences.

The following are some of the important aspects on health-related issues by political parties in 2014 elections:

1 INC: bring in Right to Health, raise healthcare spending to 3 percent of the GDP; expand the Rashtriya Swasthya Bima Yojana – a cashless insurance scheme; create sixty lakh new jobs in the health sector by 2020; strengthen primary infrastructure and bring mobile health facilities to every district.
2 BJP: bring in 'National Health Assurance Mission' with a mandate for universal healthcare; initiate new National Healthcare Policy; encourage Indian System of Medicine (ISM), modern science and Ayurgenomics and set up an AIIMS-like institute in every state.
3 CPI(M): public expenditure on health to be raised to at least 5 percent of the GDP; regulate the private healthcare sector, reversing the trend of privatization of hospital sector through urgent and stringent measures; ensure uninterrupted supply of all medicines, free of cost, in all public health facilities and strictly control and regulate clinical trials.

Family planning

The population problem has been given due recognition by almost all the major national political parties. Almost all political parties suggested the need to take effective steps for family planning. In this context, it is significant to present the suggestion of INC: 'the standard of the people continue to be depressed and the problem of unemployment will become increasingly difficult, unless family planning and birth control are attended to adequately'.

The INC, BJP and CPI in particular suggested the need to encourage the voluntary adoption of the 'two child' norm. In this context, the CPI and the BJP suggested this norm without any gender bias. The BJP suggested to adopt a national population policy 'if necessary through legislative measures'. In the context of evolving a national policy of population control the CPI suggested the following: high priority to female literacy; people-oriented programmes without any discrimination against women; financial incentives for girl child, etc. The INC suggested the expansion of anti-natal and maternity services and educating the people about a small family norm and spacing.

Besides, the INC and BJP specifically suggested providing incentives for achieving the long-term demographic goals; effective integration of family planning programmes with health, nutrition, education and other community welfare programmes and through increased awareness and persuasive government policies and innovative communication campaign.

The NF, INC and BJP emphasized involving in a sustained manner the non-governmental and community organization. The whole thrust of this argument has been to make population planning not only a just a government programme, but it must become 'a movement of civil society as well'. The INC in particular emphasized the need for sustained political support in these programmes. In the context of rise in population, the INC in particular suggested the need for a 'more vigorous and determined effort in the 150 districts of the country where fertility decline is taking place very slowly'. The BJP also advocated a similar approach in these states which have lagged behind.

Public Distribution System

Public Distribution System (PDS) has been an important issue in the manifestos of national political parties since the First General Election 1952. In this context, the INC, SP and CPI suggested in the beginning controlled distribution of commodities in short supply. However, the BJS and PSP in this regard advocated the need for progressive decontrol.

Since the 1950s, holding the price line of essential commodities was another issue in which all the major political parties like INC, CPI, SP and BJS were in agreement. For this purpose, the INC suggested the establishment of consumer co-operatives to supply basic consumer goods at controlled prices; the BJS suggested regulating the price line through monetary and fiscal measures. The CPI suggested the need of the nationalization of banks and state trading in food grains, etc., while the PSP also suggested socializing the wholesale trade in food grains and other essential commodities and bringing foreign trade under state control. The SP and the INC suggested that producers of food grains must get a reasonable return.

In the 1980s, regarding the price-rise problem, a number of parties like INC, BJP, CPI(M), and NF, etc., voiced concern and suggested the need to check it by having a firm control on deficit finance, inflation, austerity in public expenditure, and progressive reduction in non-development expenditure as well as enforcement of Consumer Protection Act of 1986; expanding and strengthening of public distribution system and having preventive and punitive action against speculator, holder and black markerteers.

Since 2004, the emphasis is on strengthening public distribution system in the poorest and backward blocks of the country and through special schemes to reach food grains to the most vulnerable sections of society. The INC, the BJP and CPI(M) all suggested the need to ensure food security to such population.

In its 2009 manifesto, the INC suggested enacting a Right to Food Law that guarantees access to sufficient food, particularly to the most vulnerable sections of society. The INC pledges that every family living below the poverty line either in rural or urban areas will be entitled, by law to 25 kgs of rice or wheat per month at Rs 3 per kg. In the context of poverty CPI(M) emphasized the need to reintroduce of the universal PDS and abandon the targeted PDS based on flawed poverty estimates; and advocated for the expansion of the Antodaya scheme to cover wider sections of the rural and urban poor. The BJP also was in favour of providing the right to food; providing 35 kg of rice or wheat every month to BPL families at Rs 2 per kg under an improved and expanded Antyodaya Anna Yojana and universalizing and improving the functioning of the PDS.

The INC in its 2014 manifesto emphasized the need to expand the focus of the current food security schemes to include subsidized pulses and cooking oil for beneficiaries of the *Antyodaya Anna Yojna*.

Women

Since 1952, the INC, SP, BJS and CPI have been emphasizing the need for the removal of the social, educational and economic disabilities of women. All these parties also suggested the need for equal rights of women in every sphere, and the SP in particular pointed out that 'all social customs and practices that go counter to the principles of equality of women with men will be ended'. The SP in its manifesto of 1957 also suggested the need for a 'A civil code granting equal rights to women' and reservations in professions

The INC also pleaded for providing opportunities for women as legislators and in social activities. Similarly, the CPI suggested the need for the reservation of women in panchayats and other local bodies. The INC and the BJP suggested in one of its manifesto that 'the Constitution will be amended to provide for one-third reservations for women in Parliament and State Legislatures'. Similarly, the JD pleaded for the action of 30 percent of elected posts in Union and State Legislators, while the BJP suggested reservation of 33 percent seats in all elected bodies. The CPI(M) suggested one-third of the seats in legislature and Parliament for women. The INC pleaded in the late 1980s for reserving 30 percent in local self-government bodies for women.

The BJS, CPI, NF and INC suggested the need for strictly enforcing provisions relating to all laws providing for equal status for women and equal pay for similar work in all spheres. The NF in this context suggested a statutory All India Commission for Women to enforce all legislations for women rights and to monitor and accelerate the process of equal representation for women. The NF, INC and CPI (M) suggested the need to review 'all social legislations in concerning marriage, divorce, maintenance, custody, adoption, inheritance, etc.' It also suggested that the 'depiction of women in any form of obscenity and indignity will be banned through stringent legislator'. The BJP suggested to the need to appoint a commission to study problems of women

In a very generalized manner, reservation of jobs to women in various professions have been a part of the election manifesto of SP from the very beginning of the electoral system. The PSP similarly addressed this problem by advocating the need for reservation of jobs for women in the Gram Panchayats and municipalities. The CPI, and NF pleaded for 30 percent reservation for women in government jobs. The JD suggested the need to amend the Constitution give women preferential reservation in public employment. It also suggested the need for sensitization of the entire police force by extensive recruitment of women in judiciary and police force positions. The INC proposed in one of its manifestos to 'increase across the board, the number of women in government services'. It also suggested to launch a special drive to increase the representation of women in primary schools as teachers, as well as in the police force and judiciary at the all levels.

The BJS, CPI, CPI (M), JD and NF suggested to enlarge and make more substantial property rights of women including equal rights in parental property and land for women. The JD also supported the need to secure this aspect through proper legislation and actual implementation.

The CPI, the CPI (M) and the INC suggested atrocities on women such as sex determination test, child marriage, sati, dowry, bride-burning should be put down with a firm hand. The INC suggested the need to establish an Office of the Commissioner of Women's Rights for taking timely action in cases of atrocities on women. The INC also suggested to take 'stern measures to ensure the elimination of female foeticide and infanticide'.

The CPI(M) suggested the need for bringing a legislation against domestic violence and adoption of dowry eradication as a national mission. The BJP in the context of family-related disputes suggested to strengthen family courts to try all family-related cases. The CPI and INC suggested a special Act against atrocities on women

The CPI and NF suggested a comprehensive welfare programme with emphasis on mother and child care, provision of maternity homes and crèches at work centres.

A number of suggestions have been given exclusively for the development of women by different political parties:

- the CPI, CPI(M) and INC suggested a provision of social security for women agricultural workers and women in unorganized industry;
- the NF suggested creation of jobs on a massive scale for women and special vocational training institutions to encourage self-employment;
- the INC emphasized the need to make the Indira Mahila Yojana as a focal point for women's development programme. It also suggested that to strengthen Women's Development Corporations and vigorous implementation of Equal Remuneration Act;
- the JD in the context of the structural adjustments policies suggested promoting self-employment schemes, extension of minimum needs programmed including nutrition, drinking water, fuel etc.;
- the CPI suggested the need for special schemes for female-headed households in rural areas;
- the NDA suggested to set-up a Development Bank for Women Entrepreneurs;
- the INC suggested major expansion in schemes for micro-finance based on self-help groups, especially for tribal women, women belonging to scheduled castes, women below the poverty line, rural women and women in distress.

The following are some of the significant suggestions for women development in the manifestos of 2014 elections:

- INC: Pass Women's Reservation Bill; earmark 30 percent of all funds coming to local bodies for development of women and children; 'One – Stop Crisis Centres' for women; land rights for women, especially single women; launch programme to improve the child sex ratio.
- BJP: Pass Women's Reservation Bill; strict implementation of laws related to women, particularly those related to rape; provide a fund for the rehabilitation of rape victims; create an acid attacks

victims welfare fund; make police stations women friendly and increase the number of women in police at difference levels; enable women with training and skills; expand and improve working women's hostels; remove any remaining gender disparities in property rights.

- CPI(M): Pass Women's Reservation Bill; ensure equal pay for women workers; adopt social security measures for working women; have crèche facilities for all women workers; create a code of conduct for all elected representatives to adhere to standards of decency in public comments.

Youth

Since the Fifth General Election, the PSP, the SP, the CPI and the INC have had in their manifestos the issue regarding the voting right from twenty-one years to be reduced to eighteen years.

The second important aspect regarding youth related issues consist in 'saving them from the clutches of unemployment'. In this context, the SP in particular emphasized the need to launch a literacy army and a land army by starting a large number of public industries based on indigenous resources. The INC and NDA also had similar views involving youth in key tasks like literacy, rural development, legal awareness and social reforms. In this regard, the NDA was more specific by advocating the need for the creation of a National Reconstruction Corps, aimed at environmental protection. The SP also pleaded for the inclusion of right to work as a fundamental right. The JD emphasized the need to formulate, expand and strengthen self-employment schemes for youth by providing liberal credit facilities and entrepreneurial skills. The CPI also had suggested labour-intensive opportunities for providing employment to the youth in urban and rural areas. The CPI, the JD, BJP and the NDA and CPI(M) advocated the need for adopting a comprehensive policy for youth dealing with issues vitally affecting them. The BJP in this context pledged and also promised to set aside a substantial budgetary resource and setting up of a permanent National Youth Commission to monitor the implementation.

The CPI emphasized in the context of the youth the need to 'overhaul the educational system and to give it a secular and socialist content' while the NF and INC emphasized the need to strengthen and expand moral and physical education of the young and for this purpose encourage programmes of NCC, NSS, Bharat Scouts and Guides and promotion of sports and games.

In the 2014 manifesto, the CPI(M), INC and BJP provided the following approach for the development of youth:

1 CPI(M): The inclusion of the Right to Work as a constitutional right; provision of jobs or unemployment allowance; lift the ban on recruitment on Central Government and state government services; drastically amend the 'National Youth Policy 2014' to properly address the concerns of youth.
2 Congress: Focus on youth capacity building, education, leadership and development; commit to creating an enabling and rewarding environment to build the capacity of our youth to take on roles more actively in our country's future.
3 BJP: Initiate the 'Young Leaders programme' in all sectors to recognize, reward and involve these exceptionally talented youths to serve as role models and mentors for others; set up the National Youth Advisory Council; 'district level incubation and accelerator programme for encouraging innovation and entrepreneurship'.

Scheduled castes and scheduled tribes

Since the beginning, all the national political parties like the INC, CPI (M), BJS, SP and PSP emphasized the need in their manifestos for the implementation of the assurances given to SCs/STs in the Constitution. These national parties also suggested the need to provide larger funds for their upliftment and welfare. In this context, the CPI, the INC and the NDA suggested the need to amend the Constitution to extend the period of reservations to the SCs/STs. The INC, the CPI and the CPI (M) pursued affirmative active action for SCs/STs in the private sector also. The CPI suggested that these funds must be administered through popular agencies. The PSP, the BJS and the CPI advocated the need to provide on priority basis to the SCs/STs in the redistribution of land. The INC and the NF suggested the need that the plan allocation for the welfare of the SCs/STs shall correspond to their share in population. The CPI suggested 'to extend the policy of reservation to *Dalits* irrespective or religious obligations'.

The CPI, the PSP and the SP in the General Elections of 1952 and 1957 suggested the idea for providing regional autonomy for tribal compact areas and to amend suitably the Sixth Schedule of the Constitution.

The CPI, the PSP, the BJS and the BJP suggested the need to eradicate untouchability and casteism. The CPI in particular suggested 'a strong ideological campaign and education attacking and eradicating the very roots of casteist thinking in all layers of the society'. The PSP also had a similar view on this aspect. The CPI, the CPI(M) and the BJP suggested the need to take stringent measures to put an end to caste oppression and atrocities committed against dalits and tribals people.

A number of national parties like the BJP, the INC, the JD, the UF, the CPI and CPI (M) all suggested to need for a new forest policy based on partnership between the forest tribals and the forest authorities to protect tribals from exploitation. The UF suggested 'mak[ing] legislation for conferring ownership in respect of minor forest produce'. The JD suggested the need in this context to review all relevant laws and policies to guarantee the customary rights of tribals over land, water and forest resources.

The NF and the JD advocated that 'the tribal people will be removed from their habitat only in cases of compelling public interest and that, not without seeking their consent. When and if such displacement becomes unavoidable, full compensation, adequate rehabilitation, alternative employment shall be guaranteed'.

The INC, the CPI and the CPI (M) advocated for the need to protect the distinctive culture and way of life of the tribal communities as well as the need to foster the development of the languages of Adivasis. The CPI and the CPI(M) suggested that *Santhali* should be accorded national language status in the Eighth Schedule of the Constitution.

The BJS, the SP, the INC, the CPI (M) and the NF advocated for the need for the improvement of the functioning and the quality of their education. The INC advocated for 'Free education for the *Dalits* and Adivasis at primary, secondary and university levels as well as to increase national scholarships to these sections'. The BJP stressed the need to provide election to the Dalits and tribal people through the *Sarva Shiksha Abhiyan*. The CPI stressed the need to increase scholarships and hostel facilities and curb dropout rates among SCs.

In the manifesto of the 2014 election, the INC and CPI(M) favoured reservation in the private sector for SCs and STs. For this purpose the CPI(M) favoured a Central legislation while INC thought of creating of national consensus on this issue. The INC and the CPI(M) were also in favour of providing reservation to backward minorities (Christian and Muslim communities) through legislation. Both the INC and CPI(M) were in favour of bringing a comprehensive law against communal violence.

Besides, some of the other important provisions in the BJP manifesto relate to bring in a Uniform Civil Code, a national madrasa modernization programme and *Van Bandhu Kalyan Yojna* at the national level to empower tribals. The INC also provided the following in their manifesto: central legislation on the Scheduled Castes and Scheduled Tribes Sub Plans; ensure the passage of the Scheduled Castes and Scheduled Tribes (Prevention of Atrocities) Amendment Bill, 2013; encourage and support Scheduled Castes and Scheduled Tribe entrepreneurs etc.; focus on development activities for creating social and economic opportunities for Scheduled Tribes and ensure stringent implementation of PFSA, 1996, and the Forest Rights Act, 2006.

Minorities

By and large all national political parties – INC, CPI, SP, PSP and SWP – advocated the need to faithfully carry out the provisions in the Constitution for the protection of rights and interests of all minorities. The CPI also suggested that the Constitution should be amended 'to give more powers to Parliament and Union Government to ensure that minorities do get all necessary protection against discrimination and other communal encroachments on their rights and interests'. On this issue, the BJS believed in the equal rights of all Indian citizens irrespective of caste, creed or community. In this context, it further explained that minorities and majorities based on religion will not be recognized by this party. Equality of opportunity to all and special aid to the backward sections of the people will be its basic approach to the solution of the country's problems. Besides, special steps will be taken to promote minorities' educational and economic advancement.

The CPI (M) and INC suggested to form Equal Opportunity Commission to redress discrimination against minorities. The CPI, the PSP and the SWP advocated the need for the creation of permanent Minority Commissions at the All-India and the state levels with appropriate powers for the protection and safeguard of minority rights and interests besides examining their grievances and formulating concrete measures. The CPI, the JD and the INC and the NF suggested the need to give the Minority Commission a statutory status.

The CPI, the INC, the SWP and the SP pleaded for the need of taking effective steps at all levels against activities which are designed to rouse communal feelings. In this context, the SP in its manifesto requested that 'the Muslim community not to join political parties which encourage communal feelings and suggested that Hindus and Muslims should join hands on the basis of common citizenship to help in the development of the country'. The INC advocated the need 'to produce an atmosphere of unity and national integration in which caste or communal distinctions ceases to have any importance or relevance'. The CPI advocated the need for a 'ban on all anti-secular, communal propaganda as well as ban on para-military and similar other activities of the communal forces'. The INC suggested the need to 'enact a comprehensive law on social violence all its form and manifestations' The INC suggested that the National Human Right Commission (NHRC) monitor and investigate and make trial in cases of communal violence.

The CPI, the INC and CPI (M) specifically suggested the need to provide adequate facilities for instruction in the mother tongue at the primary stage of education to children belonging to linguistic minority groups. These parties also supported the need to provide Urdu its due place in states like Uttar Pradesh, Bihar, Madhaya Pradesh, Delhi, etc. These parties also favoured minorities' full freedom to establish, manage and run educational and other institutions as well as protect the autonomous character of educational institutions. The INC pleaded for 'amending the Constitution to establish a Commission for Minority Educational Institutions that will provide direct affiliation for minority professional institutions to central universities'. Besides, 'special steps will be taken to spread modern and technical education among women in minority communities particularly'. The BJP suggested a massive expansion of modern education among Muslims, particularly girls, through a network of schools in a public-private partnership programme. It also suggested providing capital assistance to new educational projects in low-income minority areas, cash incentives for the education of girls and computer centres in low-income urban areas and backward districts.

The CPI and the INC advocated the need for the adequate representation of the Muslim minority community in the police, civil and armed forces. The INC in this context also suggested for the 'development of entrepreneurship' in the minority groups. The CPI(M) suggested to include OBC Muslims in OBC quota with specific statewise allocations and provision of subsidized credit to Muslim youth.

The INC, the JD and the NF advocated for the need for legislation relating to *wakf* properties. However, the JD and the NF pleaded to bring *wakf* properties under Public Premises Eviction Act. The INC suggested to establish a Wakf Development Corporation.

Since the 1990s, in the General Elections, the emphasis in the manifestos of the political parties, like the NF, the INC and the JD, has been on effective check on enticement to communal passions. For this purpose, it has been suggested that the government should pursue appropriate recruitment policies in the police services by creating a mixed anti-riot force to ensure impartial conduct from them. The INC suggested to set up a High-Powered Commission to examine and give recommendations on how the representation of the minorities in public services could be enhanced. It was also suggested by the INC, the JD and the NF to provide full compensation to victims of communal and caste riots. The INC suggested the following: 'careful selection and placement of officers in communally sensitive districts; holding district-level officials responsible for preventing and containing riots; and severe punishment to government personnel found guilty of abetting communal offences'. The INC suggested ensuring a reservation for minorities in employment and education at the national level.

The CPI, the INC, the NF and the JD suggested the need to set up a Minority Development Authority to promote the economic development of minorities. The NF specifically pointed out 'reservations for the socially, educationally backward among the minorities'. The INC also suggested the need 'to include socially and educationally backward minorities in the list of beneficiary entitled to reservation and other special measures'. The INC pleaded for the need 'of special assistance on concessional terms to cooperatives organized by minorities groups'. The BJP suggested that it is against categorization of communities as it perpetuates 'notions of imagined discrimination and victim hood'. The CPI (M) suggested for the separation of religion and politics by legal means while the BJP suggested 'to set up a permanent inter-faith consultative mechanism to build harmony and trust among communities'.

On the issues relating to minorities, the manifestos of 2014 of INC, BJP and CPI(M), made the following observations:

1 Congress: Continue scholarships for children of the minority community; continue easy access to credit for minorities; bring the Prevention of Communal and Targeted Violence Bill, 2013, as a matter of priority; provide reservation for backward minorities in educational institutions and in government employment and ensure that the policy is implemented through proper legislation.
2 BJP: Strengthen minority educational systems and institutions; National Madrasa Modernisation programme will be initiated; empower *waqf* boards in consultation with religious bodies; take steps to remove encroachments from *waqf* properties; preserve and promote of Urdu; set up a permanent interfaith consultative mechanism to promote harmony and trust.

3 CPI(M): making the Minorities Commission a statutory body; formulating a sub-plan for the Muslim minorities on the lines of the tribal sub-plan; including all OBC Muslims in the OBC quota with specific state-wise allocations; earmarking 15 percent of priority sector lending by banks for the Muslims; laying a special emphasis on the education of Muslim girls.

Media and mass communication

Not much attention was focused regarding the issues relating to media and mass communication in the elections during the 1950s and 1960s. In the beginning only the SWP was raising suggestions for making All India Radio into an autonomous corporation. The media and mass communication issues became very prominent due to the internal emergency of 1974. During the 1977 General Election, the JP, CPI and CPI (M) in their manifestos strongly condemned and opposed the manner in which the All India Radio, the *Doordarshan* and the *Samachar* were used against democratic forces and the opposition was denied the opportunity to present its point of view to the people. The CPI and the JP by and large held identical views and suggestions regarding media and mass communication in the context of emergency of 1974. Some of the suggestions of CPI and JP relate to the following: censorship abolition, repealing the Prevention of Publication of Objectionable Matters Act, safeguarding freedom, converting All-India, Doordarshan and the Films Division into genuinely autonomous bodies and ensuring that news agencies are completely independent of the government.

All the national parties – BJP, NF and INC – favoured to make freedom of the press an explicit Fundamental Right. The BJP, National Front, CPI (M) and CPI also suggested to strengthen Prasar Bharati Corporation so as to become a genuine public broadcasting service. Almost all national parties suggested reviewing the Officials Secrets Act. The CPI and CPI (M) suggested the need to prevent the growth of monopolies in print and electronic media as well as no foreign ownership of print media. The JD suggested 'a suitable environment by helping in modernization of the language Press and the small and the medium newspaper'. It also suggested that governments advertising policy and rate structure should be rational and uniform. While the BJP also was of the opinion of 'discouraging monopolies', but, regarding private enterprise, suggested that (1) 'The uplinking of television programmes will be from India (2) Foreign equity investment in audio-visual media is restricted to 20 per cent (3) Management of all types of the media in Indian hands'. It also suggested establishing an 'independent autonomous public authority comprising representatives of all sections and interests'. It also suggested to evolve a strategic plan to strengthen India's National News Agency like PTI and UNI. The CPI and CPI(M) favoured the state to have 'a say in media policy and programme in public broadcasting service'. The CPI and CPI (M) favoured all national languages listed in the Eighth schedule of the Constitution should be equally encouraged and developed. The CPI and the BJP advocated the need for economic security and social welfare of journalist.

In the manifesto of 2014, on the issue relating to the mass media and communication, the BJP and INC did not emphasize any aspect. However, the CPI(M) advocated the following: all languages listed in the Eighth Schedule of the Constitution should be equally encouraged and developed; secular, progressive and democratic culture should be promoted; the glorification of violence and commodification of women and sex should be curbed; the Prasar Bharati Corporation should be strengthened to make it a genuine public broadcasting service for TV and radio; cross-media ownership should be prohibited to prevent monopolies; the entry of FDI in the print and electronic media should be reversed; a Media Council should be set up which can act as an independent regulatory authority for the media and internet governance should be taken out of US control to an appropriate international body.

Sports

The issues relating to sports have found occasional reference in the manifestos. The INC and the BJP addressed the problem of sports specifically by suggesting having in every school a playground; provide coaching, training, nutrition to promising sportsman, etc.; improve infrastructure for sports in every district; design specific sporting academies at the national and state level with world-class training facilities as well as tap natural talent particularly in tribal areas. The BJP in particular suggested initiating a National Sport Policy as well as moving sports from the State List to Concurrent List. The BJP on the issue of sports more specifically suggested the need to eliminate political interference from the National Sports Federations and National Olympic Councils.

In their 2014 manifestos, the BJP, INC and CPI(M) all highlighted the need to promote sports by ensuring that sports opportunities are expanded while the BJP proposed to inculcate a culture of sports at the school level and launching a National Sports Talent Search System. The INC promised to implement *Rajiv Gandhi Khel Abhiyan* to ensure high quality sporting facilities in every block of the country. The INC also proposed to set up a 'National Sports Education University' to educate students of exceptional talent.

Cinema

As far as the issues regarding popular cinema is concerned, the CPI was one of the first national parties to advocate the need 'for a policy of developing the cinema industry on progressive lines'. Later on the BJP also suggested certain steps for its better functioning:

> (a) allow movie-makers through suitable provisions in law to raise resources from financial institutions to curb the influence of underworld financiers (b) provide a 'green channel' clearance for the automatic certification (c) exempt quality movies from entertainment tax (d) encourage viewers to monitor the quality of movies (e) reserve 50 per cent of the places on the Censor Board and Censor Panels for women (f) create a special fund for promoting regional cinema (g) introduce legislation to ensure minimum wages and retirement benefits for movie artistes and crew.

Culture

In the context of culture, the CPI suggested the development of people's democratic culture as well as for generous and unbiased help to literary and cultural bodies and organizations and the establishment of national theatres and for drawing up people in the 'manifold fields of cultural activities'. It suggested 'rescuing culture from the grip of profiteers and foreign and Indian reactionary influences'. It pleaded for the economic rehabilitation of writers, artists and workers in the various cultural fields by providing them with the fullest opportunity in an atmosphere of freedom and joy, for the development of their talent and for the efflorescence of a popular and democratic culture.

The CPI, the JD, the CPI (M), INC and the BJP all suggested the need to conserve our ancient heritage and strengthening of secular, rational and scientific values in our society. The CPI in particular suggested the need to resist 'ideological and cultural invasion threatening our traditional cultural, moral and literacy values'. It also pleaded to rebuff 'spread of feudal and unscientific ideas of obscurantism, mysticism, superstitions, obscenity, glorification of crimes and violence'. The JD pleaded for 'a strong vibrant and people based reform movement inspired by teachings of our philosophers Saints, Sufis and Social Reformers to promote religious tolerance and intellectual dissent'.

The BJP in the context of performing and literary arts pledged for (1) 'preservation, propagation and popularization of our diverse cultural heritage (2) national integration through arts (3) taking arts to the people and bringing people's arts to national limelight (4) debureaucratization of arts and culture'.

Infrastructure

Science and technology

Almost all the national political parties – INC, BJP, CPI and CPI(M), etc. – in their manifestos emphasized the need for formulating a science and technology policy on the basis of rational outlook, scientific temper, creative work and development. These parties also advocated the need to prepare a national scientific and technological plan to be integrated with the economic plan. Another important provision in these manifestos relate to modernization of National laboratories and strengthening of existing centres of excellence and strengthening of Research and Development.

In the manifestos of 2014, the INC and the CPI(M) pointed out the need to enhance public funding in science and technology to atleast 2 percent of the GDP. The CPI(M) in this regard further mentioned the following: implementing new initiatives with adequate funding in emerging technologies such as solar; creating capability in electronics, including microelectronics; initiating programmes to break the monopoly of drug multinationals in critical areas and focusing on agricultural research to break monopolies of companies in seeds. On the other hand, in its manifesto of 2014, BJP emphasized the need for the following: using science and technology on a sustainable basis for ensuring food, agricultural, nutritional and environmental wealth, health and energy security of the people; creating a sustained effort on the alleviation of poverty; using scientific and technological capabilities along with our traditional knowledge pool and building world-class, regional centres of excellence of scientific research in the field of nanotechnology, material sciences, thorium technology and brain research.

Environment

In the 1950s and 1960s, the national political parties, like INC, BJS and PSP, pleaded in their manifestos to revise the forest policy to increase the welfare of the tribals with regard to the effective use of the forest wealth. The emphasis of these parties shifted in the 1980s both to check the depletion of our forest resources as well as to take effective steps for the protection of environment.

The national parties BJP, CPI, CPI(M), INC, NF and UF pleaded in their manifestos in the 1990s to frame an environmental policy integrating environment concerns with the needs of economic development. The INC manifesto in the early 1990s advocated the need for an integrated National Land Policy covering land use, its protection and rejuvenation. It was further mentioned that this holistic policy will integrate agricultural land, forest land, waste land, desert land, coastal land, land used for human habitat as well as land needed and used for industrial development, mining and irrigation. Two other considerations which have been constantly coming as part of the manifestos CPI, CPI(M), BJP, and JP relate to a uniform national rehabilitation policy or persons displaced by development projects. In most of the manifestos, mention has been made to check the pollution of rivers and other water bodies through effective regulation. Another important consideration in environment has been the problem of climate change. The INC, BJP, CPI and CPI(M) emphasized the need to initiate measures within the overall framework of higher economic growth.

The following are the views of major political parties on environment in their manifesto of 2014:

1 Congress: Bill to set up a national environmental appraisal and monitoring authority to conduct environmental appraisals; create empowered, well-funded agencies to clean up major rivers in the country; provide clean cooking fuel across the country; launch 'green national accounts' to ensure against environmental degradation; engage tribal and forest-dwelling communities in forest management; implement missions under National Action Plan on Climate Change; launch national mission on wind energy to harness the power of this clean and renewable source of energy.
2 BJP: Encourage cleaner production; ecological audits of projects and pollution indexing of cities and townships will be done on scientific basis; pollution control mechanisms to be set up on a priority basis; R&D and human resource development

in environmental technology to be promoted; set up foolproof mechanisms to protect and preserve wildlife; implement auction of precious resources through e-auction and other mechanisms; resource sharing, exploration and e-management will be undertaken through the use of technology.
3 CPI(M): Making the system and processes of Environmental Clearances effective, time bound, transparent, accountable and free of conflict of interests; taking steps to reduce emission of greenhouse gases; strengthening states to tackle natural and climate-related disasters; checking pollution of rivers and other water bodies through effective regulation and enforcement.

Energy

The five major problems emphasized in the manifestos of national political parties in the energy sector are (1) a need for a comprehensive national policy on energy, (2) a need to improve the working of power plants, (3) a need to develop a regulatory framework of energy sector, (4) a need to invest in power projects and (5) a need for alternative sources of energy.

One important area in this sector advocated by INC and JP as well as BJS relates to the development of alternative sources of energy and priorities to schemes for the utilization of solar energy, wind and tidal power and other non-conventional sources of energy and synthesize them in the national policy to cover all available sources of energy. Also, the INC as well as BJS emphasized the need for improving the working of power plants and the need for investment in power sector, etc.

In the post-2002 manifestos, emphasis was also placed on the development of a nuclear power programme. On the energy issue, the following were of the views of the BJP, INC and CPI(M) manifestos of the 2014 election:

1 BJP: come out with a responsible and comprehensive 'National Energy Policy'; focus on development of energy infrastructure, human resource development and upgradation of technology; take steps to maximize the potential of oil, gas, hydel power, ocean, wind, coal and nuclear sources. BJP considers energy efficiency and conservation crucial to energy security.
2 CPI(M): reviewing energy and telecom policies in tune with the interests of self-reliant national development; using the domestic market to develop power and telecom equipment manufacturing

in the country; reversing the trend towards private power producers, privatizing distribution companies; stopping the franchising of towns to private players; reviewing the Electricity Act 2003.

3 Congress: a clearly defined policy for fair, transparent equitable and time-bound development of natural resources; effectively implement the National Mission on Energy Efficiency to improve energy efficiency in all areas of the economy including power, transport, urban housing, consumer goods and in rural housing; work to ensure greater access to electricity; work to improve the quality and unit consumption of electricity in rural areas; create a new thrust to new and renewable energy, including hydel, solar and nuclear energy.

Transport

In the transport sector during the elections conducted from the1950s to 1960s, the emphasis of BJS and SP in their manifestos was on the coordinated development of road, rail, water and air transport. During this period the INC and SP favoured the nationalization of transport services while the BJS was opposed to this proposition. Another important aspect relates to the emphasis in the BJS manifestos since the very beginning on the development of inland water transport system.

During the 1980s, the INC manifesto highlighted the need to formulate a National Transport Policy which will look into the modernization and expansion of railways, ports, airports, road transport including urban transport with an emphasis on reorganizing all the transport means available in the country in a well-integrated perspective. The manifesto also emphasized the need for a mass transit system along with proper land use and control. The NF and the BJP also suggested the need for an integrated transport system with adequate emphasis on mass transist systems in urban areas. Both NF and BJP also emphasized the need to improve the inland water transport system.

The INC in their manifesto in the late 1990s advocated the need to four-lane national highways. The INC and the BJP emphasized the need for enhanced investment as well as technological modernization of the railways. The BJP, as in the earlier manifesto, again emphasized the need to develop inland waterways in the country because there is enormous potential, as well as the fact that water transport is much cheaper than surface transport. The BJP also emphasized the need for the development of coastal shipping as India has a long coastline. It also reemphasized the need for expansion in public investments in these sectors along with structural, organizational and pricing reforms

In 2014 election manifestos, the BJP, INC and CPI(M) emphasized the following:

1 BJP: create a public transport system, which can reduce the dependence on personal vehicles for transport, thereby reducing cost, time to travel as well as ecological cost; launch an Integrated Public Transport Project which will include roadways, railways and waterways; develop waterways for passenger and cargo transport; develop national logistics network for faster movement of goods.
2 Congress: launch a 'National Road Transport Safety Programme'. Road Accidents will be halved within five years by a strong-willed political commitment to this Programme, which will ensure that all million-plus cities are covered by High-Speed Rail.
3 CPI(M): increasing public investment in infrastructure; no further PPPs in domestic Airports already modernized by Airport Authority of India; no FDI in railways.

E-governance- information technology

The focus on information technology, as an issue, commenced in the manifestos of national political parties only since the late 1990s. While the INC emphasized the need to use the information technology revolution to improve governance by the computerization of key government departments, the opening up information kiosks, the use of internet to be expanded to old towns and villages and the continual efforts to create standard local language software. Some of the important issues taken up by the BJP and NDA manifestos relate to the initiation of national informatics policy.

In the context of contemporary relevance regarding information technology, an attempt has been made hereto provide some of the significant aspects of information technology as provided in the manifestos of CPI(M), BJP, INC of 2014 election:

(1) BJP: focus on increasing the penetration and usage of broadband across the country; leverage technology fore-Governance and engage proactively with the people through social media for participative governance; generate IT-based jobs in rural and semi-urban areas.
(2) CPI(M): taking Internet governance out of US control to an appropriate international body; promoting a people-centric Internet which builds social justice and free from control of global

corporations; promoting a global internet regime that protects the right to privacy and does not allow mass surveillance by governments.

(3) Congress: connect all 2.5 lakh Gram Panchayats with high-speed broadband connectivity with a view of improving public delivery mechanism; ensure the passage of the Electronic Delivery of Service Bill 2011 to effectively deliver all public services (like passports, ration cards and driving licences) electronically; work to establish a Rapidly Deployable Multi-Protocol Wireless Communication system interoperable across all the services engaged in disaster management.

Urban development

Urban Development as an issue did not find a place in a frequent manner in the manifestos of national political parties. This issue found place in the manifestos of INC of 1967 and 1984 and in the JD manifesto of 1996. In the 1967 and1984 manifestos of the INC, some of the issues were these: promote dispersal of industries; implement a national plan of urban development; set up fund to improve civic amenities in large metropolitan centres; establish new Housing Development Finance Corporations; develop viable infrastructure in small and medium towns; expand manifold slum improvement programme.

Some of the issues in the manifestos of JD of 1996 were these: reduce migration to urban areas; amend urban land ceiling; subsidize shelter to the poorer sections; create programme for sustainable cities.

In the 2014 elections manifestos of Congress, BJP and CPI(M) expressed the following issues regarding urban development:

1 Congress: ensure that Mayors and Municipal Chairpersons have fully functional powers, so that they can operate as Chief Executives Officers; continue to implement JNNURM-II with vigour and focus to ensure better sewage facilities, roads and multi-modal public transport.

2 BJP: initiate building 100 new cities; the approach to urban development will be based on integrated habitat development-building on concepts like Twin cities and Satellite towns; upgrade existing urban centres, transitioning focus from basic infrastructure to public utility services; giving priority to cleanliness and sanitation.

3 CPI(M): promoting planned urbanization; increasing public investment in public utilities and facilities in the cities to accommodate the growing migration by the working people; ensuring

affordable basic services like drinking water, sanitation, power, transportation, ration shops, health facilities, schools, street lighting, etc. for the urban poor; running adequately provisioned night shelters, homes and community kitchens for the most vulnerable and destitute; ensuring modern and affordable public transport and Mass Transit Systems.

Foreign policy and defence

Foreign policy

In the context of foreign policy, each party manifesto over a period of time (1952–2014) has dealt with issues like the following: pursuance of independent foreign policy; relations with Pakistan, Soviet Union, China, SriLanka, United States of America, Western Countries, Arab World and Israel; issues relating to nuclear capability; protection of the interest of People of Indian Origin in foreign countries; regional co-operation; foreign policy and new economic order and the institutional aspects of Indian Foreign Policy.

To develop friendly relations with all countries and pursue an independent foreign policy, without alignment with any blocs, has been an important component of the framework of India's foreign policy endorsed by all national political parties. As a matter of fact, this thinking became more manifest when all national political parties categorically suggested the need to build a third camp to keep away from the two power blocs. Later on, with the emergence of the Non-Aligned Movement (NAM), all the political parties suggested the need for the adherence to the principles and goals of NAM. However, in the context of non-alignment, the SWP was the only party which suggested that 'our foreign policy, needs to be reviewed and brought into closer relations to the realities of the international situation'.

The BJS has been pleading since the Third General Election (1962) to protect the interests of overseas Indians in matters such as citizenship, social assimilation, alleged discrimination, cultural identity, right of vote, etc. The BJP, in this context, emphasized the need to provide dual Citizenship to Indian citizens living abroad. Besides, the BJP also suggested to develop close relations with countries like Mauritius, Surinam, Guiana, Fiji and Trinidad.

The BJS, the SP, PSP and SWP, have been championing the cause to recognize the independence status of Tibet and support the Tibetan people's struggle for freedom against China's oppression.

In the context of friendly relations with the Arab World and Israel along with the question of Palestine, the BJS pleaded for establishing full-fledged diplomatic relations with Israel. The PSP was of the view to keep friendly relations both with the Arab World and Israel. The CPI(M) have been of the view to provide 'consistent support to the Arab people in their struggle against Israel aggression and right of the people of Palestine to have their own state'. On the other hand, the BJP emphasized the need 'to strengthen relations with Arab countries and pursue enhanced cooperation with Israel'.

Since the beginning, the issue of Indo-Pak relations has been mentioned in the manifesto of almost all national political parties. The approach of the INC, CPI, SP and PSP has been, by and large, to seek a peaceful solution to all outstanding problems with Pakistan. In the context of the Kashmir problem the national political parties had different views on this issue: the BJS advocated the need to follow a strict policy of reciprocity and not one of appeasement, and the reference made to the UNO should be withdrawn as a step for the settlement of the Kashmir problem. The CPI and the SP hold similar views regarding the withdrawal of the issue from the UN and the rejection of UN's arbitration.

Subsequently after the Indo-Pak war of 1965, the CPI manifesto emphasized the need to uphold the Tashkent declaration for further realization of normal relations between the two countries. In the 1970s, the SP, CPI and INC suggested the need to develop relations not only on a political level but also on economic and cultural fields and encourage the 'people to people contact'. The INC's approach related to meaningful bilateral dialogue with Pakistan within the framework of Shimla Agreement of 1972; the INC approached emphasized – bilateral dialogue with Pakistan within the framework of Shimla Agreement of 1972 and no third-party mediatory role and steps to ensure that nuclear weapons available with India and Pakistan are not used. The BJP's position regarding Pakistan consists of 'no comprehensive dialogue with Pakistan unless it dismantles the terrorist infrastructure and related activities'.

United Nations

The BJS, BJP, CPI, CPI(M) and INC emphasized the need for democratization of the United Nations to reflect the changes taking place in the world. Some parties like CPI and PSP advocated adequate representation of the New States of Asia and Africa in the various organs of the UN. The PSP, SP, INC and BJS supported the idea of providing full co-operation to the United Nations for world peace and fostering balanced economic development in the world. The BJS, BJP and CPI advocated the idea that India should be made a permanent member of the Security Council.

India–Soviet relations

The CPI and CPI(M), in a number of manifestos, advocated the need 'to expand and deepen India's friendship and economic and political relations with the Soviet Union'. The INC and NF also supported the idea in to have a close relationship with Russia, while the BJS emphasized the need to have friendly relations with the Soviet Union 'on the basis of mutual respect for sovereignty'.

India–China relations

In the context of foreign relations, the relationship with China has always been an important issue with national political parties. These parties hold different opinion on this problem specially after the India-China War of 1962. While the CPI, CPI (M) UF, JD and NF favoured exploring all avenues for a peaceful settlement with China; the INC approach has been to initiate, consolidate and expand 'confidence-building measure and to build closer economic trade, cultural, educational and political ties with China'. The BJP's approach relates to 'continuation in the dialogue process with China to achieve a mutually satisfactory resolution of the boundary issue'. The PSP and SWP regarded the communist China 'as the principle menace to freedom in Asia and calls for the building of a system of regional security by the countries of South and South Asia'. In this context, the SWP further pointed out that proper defence alliances with reliable powers are not only expedient but legitimate also.

Regional issues

The PSP from the very beginning supported the idea that 'India carries a special responsibility for developing associative life in South-East Asia'. The SWP and PSP also had the same view for building of a system of regional security by the countries of South and South-East Asia. The JP also favoured regional cooperation in South Asia. The NF, INC, CPI and CPI(M) emphasized the need to strengthen the role of SAARC while the BJP suggested the need for the establishment of regional common market by strengthening South Asian Regional Conference. The JD on the other hand pleaded for the establishment of the South Asian Free Trade Area (SAFTA) among the SAARC countries.

Nuclear capability

In the context of developing nuclear capability, since the 1980s, the INC have been occasionally talking about the need 'to safeguard India's sovereign right to use nuclear technology for her development on peaceful lines' and its commitment to 'time bound universal nuclear disarmament leading to general and complete disarmament'.

In the 1990s, both the CPI, CPI(M), JD and NF were forthright in their approach for India pursuing a policy of universal nuclear disarmament and not signing any discriminatory treaty like the Nuclear Non-proliferation Treaty and Comprehensive Nuclear-Test-Ban Treaty (CTBT) which permits the legitimization of weapons of mass destruction.

Foreign policy – new concerns

On the issue of foreign policy, some national political parties advocated for the need for fresh thinking as well as to have a close look at the institutional aspects of foreign policymaking. A number of political parties advocated the need to strengthen and expand our foreign policy from the perspective of Non-Aligned Movement (NAM). However, political parties like the SWP wanted the policy 'to be reviewed and brought into closer relation to the realities of the international situation'. While the SP advocated the need 'to end borrowed thinking and start thinking independently', the BJP suggested the need to set up a Policy Planning Committee to formulate a long-term foreign policy for India. The UF, JD, INC and NDA suggested the need to attune the country's foreign policy to promote India's international economic interest and appoint a Foreign Policy Advisory Council to periodically review India's relation with rest of the world. The INC emphasized the need to integrate our foreign policy with our economic priorities and advocated the need to refashion the foreign policy and foreign service 'to suit the contemporary world'.

Some of the significant issues which found mention in the manifesto of the INC, BJP and CPI(M) in 2014 election are given here:

1 Congress: improving relations with Pakistan while stressing on the need to work against the perpetrators of 26/11; continue to

extend all possible aid to rehabilitate Sri Lankan Tamils; time-bound inquiry into allegations of human rights violations committed by the Sri Lankan forces during the war; work with China to resolve differences of perception over Indian borders and the Line of Actual Control; mobilize support for India's permanent membership in the U.N. Security Council; protect overseas Indians from exploitation or threats; work to strengthen the South Asian Association for Regional Cooperation (SAARC) to meaningfully realize a South Asian economic community; protect overseas Indians from exploitation.

2 BJP: pursue friendly relations in the neighbourhood; work towards strengthening regional forums like SAARC and ASEAN; continue dialogue, engagement and cooperation, with global forums like BRICS, G20, IBSA, SCO and ASEM; expand and empower pool of diplomats; persecuted Hindus welcomed to seek refuge in India.

3 CPI(M): continued dialogue with Pakistan to resolve all outstanding issues; promote people-to-people contact; engage with the Sri Lankan government to devolve powers so that the Tamil-speaking people can have autonomy within a united Sri Lanka; work for an independent credible inquiry into the atrocities committed in the last phase of the war; extend full support to the cause of a Palestinian state; sever military and security ties with Israel; enact special efforts to build relations and ties with Bangladesh; approve the land boundary agreement and settle the Teesta waters agreements; revise the Indo-US nuclear agreement.

Defence

The following issues, over the years, have found mention in the manifestos of national political parties: defence preparedness and modernization, developing nuclear capability, defence policy, defence R&D and Indianization, emoluments and service-related matters, border surveillance and intelligence network and Defence Council and Disarmament.

The BJS from the very beginning highlighted the need for the building up of India's military strength through the provision of military training for young men and women, the nationalization of defence forces, the creation of a large territorial army and the speedy development of defence industries. The CPI was another party which emphasized the need to develop defence industries with a view to strengthen the security system and our national independence. The JP and INC also emphasized modernizing defence capabilities and improving and developing both higher technology and self-reliance in the Army, Navy and Air force.

In the context of self-sufficiency in defence preparedness, the BJP, PSP, NF, CPI, CPI(M), and INC, all emphasized the need for harnessing the atom both for peaceful development as well as manufacture nuclear weapons as deterrent. In the context of India's nuclear policy, the CPI(M) and NF and in particular were against signing any international treaty which is discriminatory. The CPI from the very beginning stood for disarmament and the banning of weapons of the mass destruction.

The BJS and PSP suggested from the very beginning the need for the establishment of a National Defence Council to evolve a National Defence Policy. The NF, BJP and INC also highlighted this aspect, the NF, BJP and INC also highlighted this aspect, by calling the set up as a National Security Council: to analyse security issues, as well as political and economic threats; to re-evaluate the country's nuclear policies; to expedite the development of the ballistic missiles and to enhance the capabilities of our external intelligence agencies.

The BJP suggested the need 'to evolve an overall security doctrine for India, which will be convincingly peace-oriented. The doctrine would take a total view of defence rather than a fractured service by service approach, which is a case at present and would give a central place to self-reliance in defence matters'.

The improvement of service conditions of the personnel of the armed forces, including ex-servicemen, has been an important issue in the manifestos of CPI, BJS, SWP, JP, BJP, NDA and INC.

Some of the issues, like maintaining vigilance regarding the defence of the country and penetration of foreign agencies, identification and elimination of foreign lobbies associated with defence weapons procurement and the enhancement of the capabilities of our intelligence agencies, have been voiced by the CPI(M) and the BJP.

The main issues highlighted by the INC, BJP and CPI (M) on defence-related matters in their manifestos of 2014 elections are the following:

1 Congress: continued and rapid modernization of our Defence Forces; ensure that the process of procuring the finest state-of-the-art equipment is carried out in an atmosphere of efficiency and full transparency; encourage indigenous manufacturing in every way; a 'National Commission for Ex-Servicemen' will be established to provide a further impetus to programmes designed for the welfare of their families and expand opportunities for them in

Nation-building and other productive activities; continue the missile programme to meet potential threats in the region.

2 BJP: set up four dedicated defence universities to meet the shortage of manpower; appoint a Veterans Commission to address the grievances of veterans; ensure greater participation of Armed Forces in the decision-making process of the Ministry of Defence; implement measures to improve the efficiency of Armed Forces Tribunals; initiate the process of digitization of defence land in cantonment and in other places; technology transfer in defence manufacturing will be encouraged to the maximum; encourage domestic industry to have a larger share in design and production of military hardware; revise and update India's nuclear doctrine; maintain a credible minimum deterrent that is in tune with changing geocentric realities.

3 CPI(M): revise the Indo-US nuclear agreement; have no importation of foreign nuclear reactors; pursue self-reliance in civilian nuclear energy based on domestic uranium and thorium reserves; pursue universal nuclear disarmament through the UN; pursue policies for the de-militarization of cyber space; protect Indian Internet and telecommunications networks from cyber attacks and surveillance by building indigenous capability; do not renew the Defence Framework Agreement with the US; create a national security apparatus, which will work within the framework of the parliamentary democratic system; have coordination between the Central Government and the state governments in tackling the Maoist violence.

Party manifestos – some observations

In the context of party manifestos, Rammanohar Lohia has made a distinct contribution by analysing their relevance as well as the need to make qualitative changes in their formulation.[28] He was closely associated with the preparation of party manifestos of the Socialist Party. He was one of the very few nationalist leaders who understood the deeper significance of party manifesto. From this perspective, his views which we propose to analyse have a lot of contemporary significance in terms of their application and usage in the present-day situation in India.

Lohia's first point relates to the 'political debate and propaganda' in India 'centered on final objectives to the comparative neglect of immediate programmes'. In the political debates and discussions in India, Lohia, while commenting the usage of the phrases like 'economic and social equality', 'casteless and classless society', 'end of exploitation and equal opportunities', 'peace and democracy', 'minimum standards in food, clothing and housing for all', 'freedom and values and goodness, lend themselves to flourishes and can be heard on all platforms have become a danger to the political mind of India'. In this context, Lohia was of the view that 'this debate and propaganda can and have become a danger to the political mind of India'. As a consequence, he observed that 'Radicalism in speech but conservatism in action on the one hand, and revolution in words but reaction in practice, become sanctified by daily usage'.[29] He advised the Indian people insist 'to political parties that they outline their roads of travel as distinctly as the end of their journey', otherwise 'the menace of inaction and threat to democracy will grow'.[30] For this purpose, he emphasized the need for providing political programme in a time-bound and concrete manner.

In the political debates in India, Lohia was also critical of the usage of 'generalized principles of equality, plenty, democracy and socialism'. Due to the lack of concrete meanings 'these principles neither mould the mind nor guide action'. Lohia was of the view that' They only serve to create a condition of general expropriation of phrases and of debates concerning tricks of language and manners of speech'. He suggested to the people to force political parties to put 'concrete meaning into their abstract generalizations'.[31]

Another issue which gained lot of prominence relates to the contents of party manifestos. This aspect came for judicial scrutiny in a case decided by the Supreme Court of India in July 2013. The case relates to the promise of freebies by the DMK and AIADMK in their election manifestos.[32] The Supreme Court observed 'that [the] distribution of freebies of any kind, undoubtedly, influences, all people. It shakes the root of free and fair elections to a large degree . . . such freebies at government cost disturbs the level playing field and vitiates the electoral process'.[33] The Supreme Court directed that the Election Commission 'to frame guidelines for the same in consultation with all the recognized political parties'. In February 2014, the Election Commission had introduced a new section on election manifestos in the Model Code of Conduct and prescribed the following three guidelines:

1 Election manifesto shall not be inconsistent with the ideals and principles of the Constitution and the letter and spirit of the Model Code of Conduct.
2 That, in the interest of free and fair elections, the political parties should . . . avoid making those promises which are likely to vitiate the purity of the election process or exert undue influence on the voters in the exercise of their franchise.

3 In the interest of transparency, level playing field and credibility of promises, it is expected that manifestoes also reflect the rationale for the promises and broadly indicate the ways and means to meet the financial requirements for it. Trust of voters should be sought only on those promises which are possible to the fulfilled.[34]

In the context of the Tamil Nadu State Assembly elections of May 2016, the Election Commission issued notices to AIADMK and DMK asking them to explain 'the rationale behind their promises and how they intend to fulfil them'. The Election Commission further pointed out that the 'trust of voters should be sought only on those promises which are possible to be fulfilled'.[35]

Notes

1 K. M. Munshi, *Constituent Assembly Debates: Official Report*, Vol. V, New Delhi: Lok Sabha Secretariat, Second Reprint, 1989, p. 340.
2 Ibid., p. 341.
3 Ibid.
4 Munshi, *Constituent Assembly Debates*, Vol. VII, p. 41.
5 For an analysis of the contradiction between the political and economic democracy of development approach see Francine R. Frankel, *India's Political Economy, 1947–1977: The Gradual Revolution*, New Delhi: Oxford University Press, 1978, pp. 71–112.
6 AICC Report of the Economic Programme Committee, 1947 in A.M. Zaidi and S.G. Zaidi, *Chief Editors The Foundations of Indian Economic Planning: An Attempt at Reshaping the Destiny of 600 Million Indians*, New Delhi: S. Chand & Co., 1979, pp. 597–612.
7 It consisted of Maulana Abul Kalam Azad, Jayaprakash Narayan, N.G. Ranga, Gulzarilal Nanda, J.C. Kumarappa, Achyut Patwardhan, and Shankarrao Deo.
8 Ibid., p. 611.
9 Ibid., p. 612.
10 Gene D. Overstreet and Marshall Windmiller, *Communism in India*, Berkeley, CA: University of California Press, 1959, p. 306 and M.R. Masani, *The Communist Party of India: A Short History*, London: Derek Verschoyle, 1954, pp. 115–118.
11 N.K. Krishnan, The Communist Party of India in Kashyap, ed., *Indian Political Parties*, pp. 73–74. See also P.C. Joshi, Reflections on Marxism and Social Revolution in India in K. N. Panikkar, ed., *National and Left Movements in India*, New Delhi: Vikas Publishing House Pvt. Ltd, 1980, pp. 179–212; Manoranjan Mohanty, Ideology and Strategy of the Communist Movement in India in Thomas Pantham and Kenneth L. Deutsch, eds., *Political Thought in Modern India*, New Delhi: Sage Publications, 1986, pp. 236–259 and Paul R. Brass and Marcus F. Franda, eds., *Radical Politics in South Asia*, Cambridge: The MIT Press, 1973, pp. 33–74.
12 Ibid., p. 74.

13 'Programme' Socialist Party, Bombay, 1947, pp. 12–13.
14 Prashanto Kumar Chatterji, *Dr Syama Prasad Mookerjee and Indian Politics 1938–1953: An Account of an Outstanding Political Leader*, New Delhi: Foundation Books, 2010, pp. 368–370 and see also Craig Baxter, *The Jana Sangh: A Biography of an Indian Political Party*, Philadelphia: University of Pennsylvania Press, 1969, p. 84; B.D. Graham, *Hindu Nationalism and Indian Politics: The Origins and Development of the Bharatiya Jana Sangh*, Cambridge: Cambridge University Press, 1990, pp. 158–195; Motilal A. Jhangiani, *Jana Sangh and Swatantra: A Profile of the Rightist Parties in India*, Bombay: Manaktalas, 1967, pp. 44–105; Sunder Singh Bhandari, Bharatiya Jana Sangh in Subhash C. Kashyap, ed., *Indian Political Parties: Programmes, Promises and Performance*, New Delhi: Research Publications, pp. 130–143.
15 B.R. Ambedkar, *States and Minorities: What Are Their Rights and How to Secure Them in the Constitution of Free India*, Bombay: Thacker & Co. Ltd, 1947, p. 35.
16 Hari Narke, eds., et al., Dr. Babasaheb Ambedkar *Writings and Speeches*, Dr. B.R. Ambedkar and his Egalitarian Revolution, Vol. 17, Part One: Struggle for Human Rights, New Delhi: Dr. Ambedkar Foundation, Ministry of Social Justice and Empowerment, Government of India, Reprinted 2014.
17 Ibid., p. 388.
18 Ibid., p. 393.
19 Ibid., p. 391.
20 Swatantra Party, *Preparatory Convention*, Bombay: Popular Book Depot, 1959, pp. 31–33 and see also M.R. Masani, *Why Swatantra*, Bombay: Popular Prakashan, n.d., and see also Howard L. Erdman, *The Swatantra Party and Indian Conservatism*, London: Cambridge University Press, 1967, pp. 188–211 and Motilal A. Jhangiani, *Jana Sangh and Swatantra: A Profile of the Rightist Parties in India*, Bombay: Manaktalas, 1967, pp. 106–132.
21 S. Gopal, ed., *Selected Works of Jawaharlal Nehru*, Vol.37, Second Series, *A Project of the Jawaharlal Nehru Memorial Fund*, New Delhi: Oxford University Press, 2006, p. 49.
22 Ibid., p. 54.
23 Broadcast to the nation (November 22, 1951), A.I.R. tapes, N.M.M.L. in Jawaharlal Nehru's Speeches 1949–1953. The Publication Division, Ministry of Information and Broadcasting, Government of India, Second Impression, 1957, p. 21.
24 Gopal, ed., *Selected Works of Jawaharlal Nehru*, Second Series, Vol. 16, Part-II (July 1st, 1951–October 31st, 1951), *A Project of the Jawaharlal Nehru Memorial Fund*, pp. 3–30.
25 Ibid, p. 13.
26 F.W.S. Craig, *British General Election Manifestos 1900–1974*, London: The Macmillan Press Ltd, 1975.
27 In comparing party manifestos, to provide a readable account, the year of the election has been avoided. However, exception has been made only when some significant change has occurred in the approach of an issue.
28 RammanoharLohia, *Marx, Gandhi and Socialism*, Hyderabad: Navahind, 1963, pp. 475–514.

29 Ibid., p. 398.
30 Ibid.
31 Ibid., pp. 478–479.
32 In the context of the Tamil Nadu State Assembly elections since 2001, the manifestos issued by DMK and AIADMK promised distribution of freebies to the electorates. As an illustration of the freebies, the AIADMK manifesto for the May 2016 elections promised to distribute the following: free cellphones for ration-card holders; free laptops with Internet connections for tenth and twelfth class students; maternity assistance of Rs 18,000; maternity leave increased from six to nine months; 100 free electricity units every two months; waiver of all farm loans (at a cost of Rs 40,000 crore); fisherfolk assistance to be hiked to Rs 5,000; women to get a 50 percent subsidy to buy mopeds or scooters; an eight-gram gold coin for women getting married. It has been estimated that approximately 70 percent of the state revenue will be spent on the implementation of these schemes. See Pulapre Balakrishnan, Public Policy, Private Gain, *The Hindu* (December17, 2015); Suresh Nambath, Voters in Search of a Party, *The Hindu* (April13, 2016); Arun Ram, Why Manifestos Mean So Much in TN, *The Times of India* (April13, 2016).
33 See S. Subramaniam Balaji versus The Government of Tamil Nadu & Ors., in the Supreme Court of India Civil Appellate Jurisdiction, Civil Appeal No, 5130 of 2013, http://indiankanoon.org/doc/106854428/.Though having a different connotation, it is interesting to point out a case in the context of Britain on a manifesto. In an election for Greater London Council (GLC) in May 1981, the Labour Party made a promise that, if they won, they would within in six months cut the fares on London's buses and tubes by 25 percent 'Because of its pre-election promise the G.L.C. believed that it had to abolish fares altogether or reduce them regardless of business principles. The G.L.C. did not consider the effect this decision may have on the ratepayers. The House of Lords held that a manifesto issued by a political party – In order to get votes – Is not to be taken as gospel. It is not to be regarded as a bond, signed sealed and delivered. It may contain – And often does contain – Promises or proposals that are quite unworkable or impossible of attainment'. Lord Diplock 'recognized that an elected member "ought" to give considerable weight, when deciding whether to implement policies put forward in a pre-election manifesto. However elected representatives must not treat themselves as irrevocably bound to carry out pre-announced policies contained in election manifesto'. Bromley London Borough Council versus Greater London Council, House of Lords [1983] 1 AC768.
34 S.Y. Quraishi, *An Undocumented Wonder: The Making of the Great Indian Election*, New Delhi: Rupa, 2014, p. 408.
35 Election Commission of India, *The Sunday Indian Express*, May 15, 2016, pp. 1–2.

CONCLUSION

Elections in India have been conducted for more than 100 years. The first election was conducted in 1909–1910. Since then, by and large, elections have been a continuing phenomenon. The historical analysis of political parties, elections and manifestos lends itself to some broad conclusions which are briefly discussed in this conclusion. While analysing, we treated these three constituents not as separate entities but as an interlinked composite phenomenon. In this phenomenon, the manifesto plays a pivotal role. It is the manifesto which on the one hand distinguishes parties from each other. On the other, the voters provide the mandate to the party which wins an election.

During the British period of Indian history, the political advance took place in a gradual manner. It commenced first when Lord Ripon made an Act in 1882 to make the local government structure democratic. At the provincial level, the right to exercise vote notionally was given by the Indian Councils Act of 1892. However, the right to vote was accorded a legal sanction only by the Act of 1909. This sanction was accorded on the basis of classes, interests and community. In the context of Act of 1909, it is true that very limited power was provided to the legislators – the power to ask questions and move resolutions on public questions, i.e. providing opportunities of criticizing the policy of the government without exercising any control. Under the Act of 1909, Bengal was the only province which was given the status of forming an executive council on the basis of elections. In the elections conducted under this Act, the Moderates (Banerjea Group) prepared a manifesto for the elections of 1912–1913. This is the first manifesto ever prepared by a political party in India. This manifesto highlighted the importance of good laws and also pleaded to the voters to exercise this right 'to return the best of our man'. It is a matter of common knowledge that, during the freedom movement, the political leadership was highly educated and very well conversant with the British political system and parliamentary practices. The British practices were followed in the literal sense of the term by all the political parties in India. In the successive years, the manifesto became a symbol of political parties' hopes, aspirations and desires to fulfill certain political, social and economic objectives.

The next political advance is related to the Act of 1919 which provided 'nation-building' subjects and administration under the dyarchy to the elected legislators. The period from 1919 to 1937 saw the operation of dyarchy in the British provinces. Due to the refusal of the Indian National Congress for the 'Council Entry', the Swaraj party, the Congress Democratic Party of India, the Responsivist Cooperation Party and the National Liberal Federation of India contested these elections under the Act of 1919 from a number of provinces.

Bal Gangadhar Tilak's Congress Democratic Party manifesto of 1920 has been one of the most significant documents containing some highly progressive ideas on the reconstruction of Indian society. In one sense of the term, Tilak was much ahead of his times. Tilak's manifesto on the one hand identified the basic problems of the country: sanitation, compulsory education, industrial and technical education, medical relief and encouragement to indigenous medicine, village control over reserved and protected forests, etc. And, on the other hand, it emphasized the need for the development of industries by all recognized methods, a minimum wage to the labouring classes, the relationship between capital and labour on equitable basis and taxation according to the capacity of the various classes, the readjustments of provinces on linguistic basis and the unity of Hindus and Muslims. Tilak's manifesto, though formulated in the backdrop of a colonial set-up for the first time, showed what progressive ideas can bring about.

These reforms also saw the emergence of political parties at the provincial level: the National Unionist Party (Punjab) and Justice Party (Madras). In the context of the Justice Party, it is important to emphasize that this party launched in 1916 the first-ever regional movement in India. One of the high points of this party was its 'non-Brahmin Manifesto' which expressed desires for advancement in education, job reservation for the social and economic betterment of the non-Brahmins. It is significant to mention that the 'non-Brahmin Manifesto' remained for the Justice Party their main plank in the elections of 1920, 1923, 1926 and 1930.

The period from the1928–1937 saw the emergence of the most intense debate on the ideology of the Indian National Congress. This debate was between the Gandhities and the Socialists represented by Mahatma Gandhi and Jawaharlal Nehru respectively. It is true that, till the 1920s, there was not much thinking on the ideology or political programme within the Congress Party. Upto this period, there was only the Gandhi Programme consisting of production and use of khadi, communal unity, prohibition, etc. It was more a programme of social reform than an ideological creed of a party. It was Jawaharlal Nehru more than anyone else who was keen that the party formulate an ideology to serve as a guiding spirit for the social and economic reconstruction of the country after independence. With this broad objective, he initiated, through his addresses, pamphlets, debate and discussion with Mahatma Gandhi, some important resolutions in the party. The first such resolution was made in 1929 known as the Economic Objective of the Congress which pleaded to make revolutionary changes in the existing structure. This was followed by adoption of Fundamental Rights and Duties and Economic Programme at Karachi in 1931. It was a result of the joint effort of Mahatma Gandhi and Jawaharlal Nehru.

The emergence of Congress Socialist Party within the Indian National Congress in 1934 with their very radical objectives, activities and plan created a deep rift between the Gandhites and the Socialists. Mahatma Gandhi was the first to react and express serious reservations on their assumptions on antagonism between the classes and the masses and between the labourers and capitalists. He was also critical of their methods which were based on coercion. Jawaharlal Nehru's socialistic outlook was questioned by the Congress right-wing leaders. Due to the initiative of Gandhi, this debate finally ended at the time of the drafting of an election manifesto for the 1937 elections.

The debate on forming the ideology of the party between the Gandhities and Socialists has been the most intense debate during India's freedom movement. Since this debate, we have not witnessed in the INC a debate of such a dimension. Due to the initiative of Gandhi, in a way, the manifesto for the 1937 elections formalized the attitude and approach of the Congress on a large number of social and economic issues. The first manifesto of the Congress Party for the elections of 1937 mainly consisted of the revised Gandhi Constructive Programme as well as the Fundamental Rights and Economic Programme of 1933. It was devoid of all the radical plans of action of the Congress Socialist Party.

The 1937 elections brought both the Indian National Congress and the Muslim League to contest the election for the first time. Both these parties contested the elections in all the British Provinces. The 1937 elections also saw the emergence of National Unionist Party (Punjab), Krishak Praja Party (Bengal) and National Agriculturist Party (United

Provinces). By and large, all these parties had a common frame of approach to many social and economic problems. However, their approach on the question of land relations differed in a significant manner. The National Unionist Party (Punjab) emphasized the need for the development of agriculture and related occupations without touching the land relations. The Krishak Praja Party (Bengal) emphasized the need for the abolition of zamindari without compensation; on the other hand, the National Agriculturalist Party (United Provinces) manifesto was silent on the question of land relationship.

The high point of Congress manifesto 1945 was to provide for some constitutional rights which later on were incorporated as Fundamental Rights in the Constitution of India. It emphasized the various measures for the removal of poverty, unemployment by modernization of industry and agriculture. It also provided for social control of the mineral resources and means of transport. Another point of the manifesto was the removal of intermediaries between the peasant and the states by payment of 'equitable compensation'. This was an advance over the 1937 manifesto of the Congress Party. The manifesto for the first time also provided the necessity to develop friendly relations with all nations, particularly with neighbours in Far-East, South-East, Asia and Western Asia.

In the context of the 1945 election, it is interesting to point out that the Communist Party, also for the first time, issued its election manifesto. On the question of agrarian policy the manifesto pleaded for the abolition of landlordism, the nationalization of all key industries and the control of all basic industries and capital resources. Another important aspect was its advocacy for the need to develop cottage industries as well as large-scale industries to achieve maximum growth.

Immediately after gaining independence, all the political parties, particularly the INC, SP, the CPI, Jan Sangh and the All India Scheduled Castes Federation, got engaged in the preparation of the political programme for the social and economic reconstruction of the country. For the Congress, it was the time to redeem its pledges. The Economic Programme Committee (1947) under the Chairmanship of Jawaharlal Nehru was constituted to draw a programme based on 'Social Justice and Equality'. The Committee favoured basically co-operative functioning in agriculture and in the sphere of industry and pleaded for the dominant role of the state and the public sector. On the other hand, the SP in its 'Programme' (1947) suggested the abolition of zamindari and pleaded that the economy must be brought under social control and subordinated to the overall plan of development. The Jan Sangh in October 1951 emphasized in its draft manifesto 'the rebuilding of

Bharat on the basis of *Bhartiya Sanskriti* and *Maryada*, as a political and social democracy granting equality of opportunity and liberty to individuals'. While the CPI in its 'Statement of Policy' (October 1951) underlined 'the need for India evolving its own path of revolution', it took into consideration the specific conditions of the country. The All India Scheduled Castes Federation in its draft manifesto prepared by Dr B R Ambedkar in October 1951 spelled out its approach as radically different from other national political parties. The document emphasized that the party will be ready to adopt any plan of social and economic betterment of its people irrespective of its origin and provided it is consistent with its principle. Besides the rapid industrialization of the country and 'reconstruction of Indian agriculture' the manifesto also stressed the need of 'controlling the excessive growth of population'.

In the context of the Congress, it is interesting to point out the first Industrial Policy Resolution of the Government of India 1948, which came out just after the approval of the Economic Programme by the AICC in February 1948 nearly negated all the major recommendations made by the Economic Programme Committee (1947). Since Independence, it has been some kind of a practice in the party to make resolutions radical in tone and conservative in action.

In India, after independence, manifestos have not remained simply a parliamentary practice and a tradition to follow during election time. In this context, the Constitution of India carries 'Instruments of Instructions' in the form of Directive Principles of State Policy to serve as a guide in the formulation of legislations and policies for making social change.

One of the most dominant features in the context of political parties and elections in India has been the growth of state or regional parties. This growth has been to a large extent due to the diversities – religious, ethnic, linguistic, social and cultural. Besides, since the Second General Elections (1957) it was realized that there is a need to all progressive people to unite against the Congress. As a result, alliances were formed in more than eight states on the basis of a mutually agreed minimum programme. Another high point of this election relates to the fact that the Congress lost the right to rule in eight states. In almost all the states, since no party commanded a majority, coalition governments were formed. Subsequently, due to the spilt in the Congress Party, Fifth General Elections were announced. The Congress fought the election on a 'radical programme of economic and social development'. It resulted in two-thirds majority for the Congress Party.

The period from 1977 to 1984 relate to the beginning of coalition politics at the Centre, the political alliance among the Socialist Party,

Swatantra Party, Jana Sangh and the Congress (O), which resulted in the formation of a new political party – the Janata Party – just before the Sixth General Elections. The emergence of the Janata Party was made possible with the common programme on economic, social and political issues. The imposition of the emergency and the incumbency factor contributed in a significant manner the success of Janata Party in the 1977 elections. The Janata Party manifesto suggested a number of changes in the Constitution and proposed to bring a different approach to the social and economic problems of the country. The Janata Party's failure has been due to contradictions within the alliance partners. This phase also saw the coming back of the Congress Party to power in the elections of 1980 and 1984 on the basis of providing stability in the country.

The period from 1989 saw the emergence of coalition and minority governments at the Centre – a trend which continued till May 2014. A significant outcome of electoral alliance has been a striking similarity of views and approach in the alliance partners on a large number of issues facing the country. The coalition governments have drawn state and regional parties in the mainstream of the national politics. These parties no longer confined their vision and ideas at the state level alone but hold the views on all national problems and issues of significance. Increasingly due to their vote power, these parties come in a position to dictate terms. In the working of the UPA I and II, between 2004 and May 2014, there were many instances where the alliance partners started playing some role in the policymaking domain of the Union Government, especially in the area of foreign affairs and security issues.

The comparative analysis has provided a remarkable degree of similarities in approach to most of the social, economic and political problems by the national political parties. In the context of political issues, all the parties expressed their commitment to uphold the constitutional provisions relating to secularism, characterizing it as the basic character of the Indian state. Similarly, on electoral reforms, most of the national parties agree to bring reform on issues like right to recall, defection, funding of elections, prohibiting criminal persons, contesting elections and institutional aspect of the electoral system. All the parties advocated the need to check corruption by setting up an independent, impartial commission at the Centre and the states. In Jammu and Kashmir national parties differed in their approach. All the major parties emphasized the need to set up a National Judicial Commission for the appointment of judges in higher judiciary.

On economic issues, all national parties favoured planning as an approach to the various aspect of national life. It was only the

Swantantra Party which advocated abolishing planning and the Planning Commission As far as tenancy reform, all the political parties were in favour of the abolition of the zamindari system. However, there were differences in the means to be adopted. Regarding the industrial policy in the post liberalization phase, the various parties differed in their approach. However, all the major national parties pleaded for redefining the role of the public sector. However, the CPI and CPI(M) were against wholesale privatization of public sector. These parties also favoured their strengthening in core areas and promoting autonomy and efficiency.

The other significant trend relates to the emergence of issues since the 1970s, which earlier did not form the part of the manifestos: environment, climate change, consumer protection, human rights, crimes against women, black money, drainage and sanitation, national highways, etc. Besides, in the content of manifestos since the late 1980s, there is a more pronounced emphasis on issues relating to gender, terrorism, corruption in public life, judicial reforms, inflation, foreign policy and security concerns, etc.

Since the beginning, the elections and elections-related issues have been gaining considerable importance and coverage both in reporting and discussion in the print media. However, since early 1990s, due to its wider coverage in the electronic media, the reach and spread effect has gone far and wide. This has become possible due to the availability of television channels available in Hindi, English and regional languages. However, it is disheartening to note that the debate, discussion and coverage mostly centres around personality, caste, communal divide and incumbency factors. There is almost negligible discussion on the comparative aspects of the manifestos of contesting political parties. This aspect is more important and meaningful to make the electorate aware of the stand of political parties on the major issues. The electronic media can play a very significant role in educating the electorate and making them aware about the finer points of party manifestos of political parties on major issues and, thereby, sensitizing the voters and raising the level of debate and discussion. This type of understanding of the manifesto by the electorates, it is hoped, will impact the election results in a positive manner.

NOTE ON THE BIBLIOGRAPHY

A study dealing with political parties, elections and manifestos need to connect and look into very many areas: the history of freedom movement, constitutional development, system of representation, electoral system, political parties, party manifestos and elections. Besides, party manifesto(s) is an outcome of ideas on nation-building and modernization both before and after independence. To this extent, this study looks primarily before independence into the social, economic and political views of prominent nationalist leaders along with the resolutions of the Indian National Congress and some important committee reports. These aspects, to a large extent, impacted the party manifestos. After independence the party manifestos of national political parties, provide the most authoritative views on all aspects: political, social, economic, as well as foreign and defence-related issues. Emphasis has also been given on comparative aspects of manifestos as well as elections conducted during 1952–2014.

Introduction

An understanding of political party manifesto requires some comprehension of the concept of ideology. The following monographs provide a fairly comprehensive understanding of this term: Daniel Bell, *The End of Ideology: On the Exhaustion of Political Ideas in the Fifties* (New York: Free Press of Glencoe, 1961); David E. Apter, ed., *Ideology and Discontent* (New York: Free Press of Glencoe, 1964); David L. Sills, ed.,'*Ideology' International Encyclopedia of the Social Sciences*, Vol. 7 (New York: Macmillan & Free Press, 1968) and Giovanni Sartori, Politics, Ideology, and Belief Systems, *The American Political Science Review*, Vol. LXIII, No. 2 (1969). Paul E. Sigmund, ed., *The Ideologies of the Developing Nations* (Second Revised Edition, New York: Praeger,

1972) provide an overview on the ideologies of the developing nations in the formative period of their development.

It will not be out of place to mention the following works which represent two important sources which impacted to a considerable extent the ideologies of the developing world: Karl Marx, Friedrich Engels, *The Communist Manifesto*, With an Introduction by A.J.P. Taylor (Middlesex, England: Penguin Books Ltd., 1967); and see also the discussion between Theodor Adorno & Max Horkheimer (dated between March 12–April 2, 1956) on 'a contemporary version of the Communist Manifesto'. *Towards A New Manifesto*, *New Left Review* 65 (September–October 2010) and W.W. Rostow, *The Stages of Economic Growth: A Non-Communist Manifesto* (Cambridge: Cambridge University Press, 1960); In the Indian context, M.N. Roy's, *New Humanism: A Manifesto* (Calcutta: Renaissance Publishers Private Ltd., 1947) provides an outline of 'Radical Democracy'. Besides, D.G. Dalton's, M.N. Roy and Radical Humanism, The Ideology of an Indian Intellectual Elite in Edmund Leach and S.N. Mukherjee, eds., *Elites in South Asia* (Cambridge: Cambridge University Press, 1970), examines certain ideas of M.N. Roy as they evolved from Marxist to radical humanist phase.

Cecil S. Emden, *The People and the Constitution: Being a History of the Development of the People's Influence in British Government* (Second Edition, London: Clarendon Press, 1962), traces the history of 'people's part in English Government' and in a way traces the evolution of the practice of modern manifesto. Richard Rose, *Do Parties Make a Difference?* (London: The Macmillan Press Ltd, 1980); Dennis Kavanagh, The Politics of Manifestos, *Parliamentary Affairs*, Vol. 34 (1981); and S.E. Finer, Manifesto Moonshine, *New Society* (November 1975) analyses the importance of manifesto in the British politics. Richard Crossman, *Inside View: Three Lectures on Prime Ministerial Government* (London: Jonanath Cape, 1972) not only analyses the importance of party manifestos in the context of British Labour party but also characterize it as 'the Battering Ram of Change'. The term 'programmatic' has been in use instead of 'ideological or 'doctrinal' since last more than four decades, Leon D. Epstein, *Political Parties in Western Democracies* (London: Pall Mall, 1967) deals with many aspects of manifestos in the context of western democracies.

Since early 1970s in the western democracies, the study of party manifestos has become important: F.W.S. Craig, ed., *British General Election Manifestos 1900–1974* (London: Palgrave Macmillan, 1970) provides the text of British Labour and Conservative party manifestos. Ian Budge, David Robertson and Derek Hearl, eds., *Ideology, Strategy and Party Change: Spatial Analyses of Post-War Election Programmes in 19 Democracies* (Cambridge: Cambridge University Press, 1987) is an important contribution in the growing literature on ideology within a common framework. Ian Budge, Strategies, Issues and Votes: British General Elections, 1950–1979, *Comparative Political Studies*, Vol. 15, No. 2 (July 1982) is an interesting study on the electoral issues and their impact on voting behaviour; Richard

I. Hofferbert and Hans- Dieter Klingemann, The Policy Impact of Party Programmes and Government Declarations in the Federal Republic of Germany, *European Journal of Political Research*, Vol. 18 (1990) is an important contribution from the perspective of impact of manifestos on public policies.

Chapter 1: evolution of ideas on nation-building and modernization

This chapter traces the evolution of political and economic thought of the prominent nationalist leaders. It commenced with Raja Rammohun Roy who is regarded as the Father of Modern India. Some important publications dealing with Renaissance are these: R.C. Majumdar, ed., *The History and Culture of India: British Paramountcy and Indian Renaissance*, Part II (Bombay: Bharitya Vidya Bhavan, 1965); R.C. Majumdar, H.C. Raychaudhari and Kalikinkar Darra. *An Advanced History of India* (London: The Macmillan Press Ltd, 1950); Partha Chatterjee, *Nationalist Thought and the Colonial World: A Derivative Discourse?* (New Delhi: Zed Books Ltd., 1986). Two important publications which give an overview of Raja Rammohun Roy's thinking are V.C. Joshi, *Rammohun Roy: And the process of modernization in India* (New Delhi: Vikas Publishing House Pvt Ltd, 1975); and Bruce Carlisle Robertson, *The Essential Writings of Raja Rammohan Roy* (New Delhi: Oxford University Press, 1999).

Some of the publications which in the form of compendium provide an overview of political thinking of the prominent nationalist leaders are these: Wm. Theodore de Bary, et al. (complied by) *Sources of Indian Tradition* (New York: Columbia University Press, Third Printing 1960); A. Appadorai, *Documents on Political Thought in Modern India*, Vol. 2 (Bombay: Oxford University Press, 1973–76); Ramachandra Guha, ed., *Makers of Modern India* (New Delhi: Allen Lane Penguin Books, 2010) Theodore L. Shay, *The Legacy of the Lokamanya: The Political Philosophy of Bal Gangadhar Tilak* (London: Oxford University Press, 1956); and A. Appadorai, *Indian Political Thinking: In The Twentieth Century From Naoroji to Nehru- An Introductory Survey* (London, 1971); D. Mackenzie Brown, *The Nationalist Movement: Indian Political Thought from Ranade to Bhave* (Berkeley, CA: University of California Press, 1961); G.N. Sharma and Moin Shakir, *Politics & Society: Ram Mohan Roy to Nehru* (Aurangabad: Parimal, 1976); Benjamin Zachariah, *Developing India: An Intellectual and Social History* c 1930–50 (New Delhi: Oxford University Press, 2005); Ananya Vajpayi, *Righteous Republic: The Foundation of Modern India* (Cambridge, MA: Harvard University Press, 2012).

A large number of studies have come on economic thought during the period of the freedom movement. Some of the important monographs dealing with Indian economic thought are these: B.N. Ganguli, *Indian Economic Thought: Nineteenth Century Perspectives* (New Delhi: Tata McGraw-Hill

Publishing Co. Ltd., 1977); V.B. Singh, *From Naoroji to Nehru: Six Essays in Indian Economic Thought* (New Delhi: MacmillanIndia Limited, n.d.); B.N. Ganguli Dadabhai, *Naoroji and the Drain Theory* (Bombay: Asia Publishing House, 1965); Mahadev Govind Ranade, *Essays on Indian Economics: A Collection of Essays and Speeches* (Second Edition, Madras: G.A. Natesan, 1906); Romesh Dutt, *The Economic History of India in the Victorian Age*, Vol. 2 (Seventh Edition, London: Routledge & Kegan Paul Ltd, 1950); Meenakshi Mukherjee, *An Indian for All Seasons: The Many Lives of R.C. Dutt* (New Delhi: Allen Lane Penguin Books, 2009).

In India, planning consciousness came after the setting up of the National Planning Committee by the INC in 1938. The Reports on National Planning under different political organizations became available between (1944–1949): K.T. Shah, ed., *Report of the National Planning Committee* (Bombay: Vora & Co., 1949); B.N. Banerjee, G.D. Parikh and V.M. Tarkunde, *People's Plan for Economic Development of India, being the Report of the Post-War Reconstruction Committee of the Indian Federation of Labour* (New Delhi: A.K. Mukerjee, 1944); S.N. Agarwal. *The Gandhian Plan* (Bombay: Padma Publications Ltd., 1944). This document is now reproduced in Shriman Narayan, *Principles of Gandhian Planning* (Allahabad: Kitab Mahal, 1960); Purshotamdas Thakurdas, J.R.D. Tata, G.D. Birla, Sir Shri Ram, Kasturbhai Lalbhaj, A.D. Shroff and John Matthai, *A Plan of Economic Development for India*, Part I and Part II (Bombay: Penguin, 1944).

In the evolution of modern political thought in India, the contribution of Mahatma Gandhi is very significant. Mahatma Gandhi's *Hind Swaraj* constitutes his most important writing. Raghavan Iyer, ed., *The Moral and Political Writings of Mahatma Gandhi*, Vol. I, *Civilization, Politics, and Religion* (Oxford: Clarendon Press, 1986) contains not only the text of Hind Swaraj but also Mahatma Gandhi's observations on this booklet mainly in the form of letters, Preface to various editions of the booklet from March 1910 to October 1945; see also Anthony J. Parel, ed., M.K. Gandhi, *Hind Swaraj and Other Writings* (Cambridge: Cambridge University Press, 1997); Nageshwar Prasad, ed., *Hind Swaraj: A Fresh Look* (New Delhi: Gandhi Peace Foundation, 1985); and Bikhu Parekh, *Colonialism, Tradition and Reform: An Analysis of Gandhi's Political Discourse* (New Delhi: Sage Publications, 1999); Jawaharlal Nehru's, *The Discovery of India* (Seventeenth Impression, New Delhi: Oxford University Press, 1997); gives the essence of his thinking on changes necessary in India with reference to political, social and economic issues. See also Sarvepalli Gopal, *Jawaharlal Nehru: A Biography*, Vol. 3 (Bombay: Oxford University Press, 1976–84); Michael Brecher's, *Jawaharlal Nehru: A Political Biography* (London: Oxford University Press, 1958).

The following monographs provide a broader understanding of the national movement: Bipan Chandra, *The Rise and Growth of Economic Nationalism in India* (New Delhi: People's Publishing House, Reprint 1984); A.R.

Desai, *Social Background of Indian Nationalism* (Third Edition, Bombay: Popular Book, 1959); Madhu Limaye, *Indian National Movement: Its Ideological and Socio-Economic Dimensions* (New Delhi: Radiant Publishers, 1989); Sumit Sarkar, *Modern India 1885–1947* (Madras: Macmillan India Limited, Reprint 1985); Mike Shepperdson and Colin Simmons, eds., *The Indian National Congress and the Political Economy of India 1885–1985* (England: Dartmouth Publishing Co. Ltd., 1988); Bipan Chandra, *Nationalisation and Colonialism in Modern India* (New Delhi: Orient Longman, 1979).

The following monographs deal with the Indian National Congress, its struggle for freedom and its contribution to the evolution of political and economic thought: B. Pattabhi Sitaramayya, *The History of the Indian National Congress*, Vol. 2 (Bombay: Padma Publications Ltd, 1946–7); A. Moin Zaidi, ed., *A Tryst with Destiny: A study of economic policy resolutions of INC passed during the last 100 years* (New Delhi: Indian Institute of Applied Political Research, 1985); A.M. Zaidi, ed., *Congress Presidential Addresses*, Vol. 5 (New Delhi: Publication Department, Indian Institute of Applied Political Research, 1885–1985); B.N. Pandey, ed., *A Centenary History of the Indian National Congress (1885–1985)*, Vol. 5 (New Delhi: Vikas Publishing House Pvt Ltd, 1985). See also some of the INC reports like, Nehru, *Report: An Anti- Separatist Manifesto* (New Delhi: Michiko & Panjathan, Reprinted 1975) and *The Resolution on the Fundamental Rights and Economic Programme* 1931.

Chapter 2: constitutional reforms, electoral system, political parties and elections before independence

Historically the period between 1885 and 1947 saw the emergence of two broad initiatives in the political life of the country: the emergence of the Indian National Congress and the struggle for freedom. This struggle carried with it the demand for representation. The grant of limited franchise and representation on communal basis led to the emergence of political parties on sectarian lines, party manifestos and electoral system and elections. All this gave a new momentum, to the political life of the country.

The focus of this chapter is on the development of representation and electoral system since the Minto-Morley Reforms of 1909. The following publications provide insights into the politics pertaining to the question of representation. Countess Mary Minto, *India Minto and Morley, 1905–1910* (London. The Macmillan Press Ltd, Reprinted 1935); Stanley A. Wolpert, *Morley and India: 1906–1910* (Berkeley, CA: University of California Press, 1967); Herbert Risley, *The People of India* (Second Edition, New Delhi: Oriental Books Reprint Corporation, 1969); Dietmar Rothermund, Emancipation

Or Re-Integration: The Politics of Gopal Krishna Gokhale and Herbert Hope Risley in D.A. Low, ed., *Soundings in Modern South Asian History* (London: Weindenfeld & Nicolson, 1968). Regarding the electoral system envisaged in the Act of 1909, the publication by A. Rangaswami Iyengar, *The Indian Constitution: An Introductory Study* (Second Edition, Madras: G.C. Loganadham Bros, 1913) provides a clause-by-clause account of the electoral processes and procedures.

The second important development in the system of representation and electoral system came with the Montagu-Chelmsford Reforms and the Act of 1919. In this context the *Report on Indian Constitutional Reforms* (Calcutta: Superintendent Government Printing India, 1918) not only made important observations on the working of the Act of 1909 but suggested many changes in the Legislative system and the electoral system by providing separate representation for Sikhs, Indian Christians, Anglo-Indians and Europeans. Besides, it also suggested a Franchise Committee under the Chairmanship of Lord Southborough to look into the question of extension of franchise. Debendra Nath Banerjee, *The Indian Constitution and its Actual Working* (Bombay: Orient Longmans Limited, Green & Co., 1926) provides a good account of the Act of 1919 primarily with reference to the system of representation and the electoral machinery. *Report of the Reforms Enquiry Committee* 1924, under the Chairmanship of Muddiman (Calcutta: Central Publication Branch, Government of India, 1929) examined the system of dyarchy. This Report gave many suggestions regarding representation, franchise, etc. These aspects have also been examined in the publication by Kerala Putra, *The Working of Dyarchy in India 1919–1928* (Bombay: D. B. Taraporevala Sons & Company, 1928).

The third phase in the development of the system of representation and electoral system came with the Indian Statutory Commission, *Report of the Indian Statutory Commission*, Vol. 2 (Calcutta: Government of India Central Publication Branch, 1930). This Report made some significant suggestions: termination of dyarchy, provincial Cabinet with joint responsibility, wide franchise, enlarged financial resources, constitution of Legislative Assembly, continuation of the Council of State, etc. N Rajagopala Aiyangar, *The Government of India Act, 1935: With a Commentary, Critical and Explanatory* (Madras: The Madras Law Journal Office, 1937) gives a detailed account changes in brought out under the Act of 1935 with special reference to representation and the electoral system.

The Act of 1909 gave rise to the emergence of political parties, party manifestos and elections. Elections were conducted in 1909–1910, 1912–1913 and 1916: J.H. Broomfield, *Elite Conflict in a Plural Society: Twentieth Century Bengal* (Berkeley, CA: University of California Press, 1968) and J.H. Broomfield, The Vote and the Transfer of Power: A study of the Bengal General Election, 1912–1913, *Journal of Asian Studies*, Vol. 21, No. 2 (1962), provide in the context of Bengal very rich insights about shortcomings in the electoral system and party organization, etc. Eugene F. Irschick,

Politics and Social Conflict in South India: The Non-Brahman Movement and Tamil Separatism, 1916–1929 (Berkeley, CA: University of California Press, 1969); Robert L. Hardgrave, *The Dravidian Movement* (Bombay: Popular Prakashan, 1965); D.A. Washbrook, *The Emergence of Provincial Politics: The Madras Presidency, 1870–1920* (New Delhi: Vikas Publishing House, 1977) provide a detailed analysis of the emergence of provincial politics along with non-Brahman movement.

Under the Act of 1919, general elections were conducted in 1920, 1923, 1926 and 1930. In the context of Punjab, the following monographs and articles dealt with Punjab politics with emphasis on electoral politics Raghuvendra Tanwar, *Politics of Sharing Power: The Punjab Unionist Party 1923–1947* (New Delhi: Manohar Book Service, 1999); I.A. Talbot, Deserted Collaborators: The Political Background to the Rise and Fall of the Punjab Unionist Party, 1923–1947, *The Journal of Imperial and Commonwealth History*, Vol. XI, No. 1 (October 1982). The following publications brought out by the Indian Council of Historical Research contain analysis on elections and Provincial Legislatures: Amit Kumar Gupta, *North West Frontier Province Legislature and Freedom Struggle 1932–47* (New Delhi: Indian Council of Historical Research, 1976); Amalendu Guha, *Planter Raj to Swaraj: Freedom Struggle and Electorate Politics in Assam 1826–1947* (New Delhi: Indian Council of Historical Research, 1977); K.M. Patra, *Orissa State Legislature and Freedom Struggle 1912–1947* (New Delhi: Indian Council of Historical Research, 1979); Satya M. Rai, *Legislative Politics and the Freedom Struggle in the Panjab 1897–1947* (New Delhi: Indian Council of Historical Research, 1984); Gautam Chattopadhyay, *Bengal Electoral Politics and Freedom Struggle 1862–1947* (New Delhi: People's Publishing House, 1984); S. Krishnaswamy, *The Role of Madras Legislature in the Freedom Struggle 1861–1947* (New Delhi, 1989). Manoranjan Jha, *The Role of Central Legislature in the Freedom Struggle* (New Delhi: National Book Trust, 1972) deals with the issues relating to electoral politics.

Under the 1935 Act, elections were held in 1937 and 1946. R. Coupland, *The Constitutional Problem in India* (London: Oxford University Press, Reprinted 1945), analyses elections of 1937 in all the provinces and the working of the provincial governments in the context of their electoral programme. Two other important publications regarding 1937 elections in the context of Bombay and Bihar are these: Rani Dhavan Shankardass, *The First Congress Raj: Provincial Autonomy in Bombay* (New Delhi: Macmillan India Limited, 1982) and Vinita Damodaran, *Broken Promises: Popular Protest, Indian Nationalism and the Congress Party in Bihar, 1935–1946* (New Delhi: Oxford University Press, 1992). B.B. Misra, *The Indian Political Parties: An Historical Analysis of Political Behaviour up to 1947* (New Delhi: Oxford University Press, 1976) provides an analysis of parties and their political behaviour as well as elections of 1937 and 1946. V.P. Menon, *The Transfer of Power in India* (Bombay: Sangam Books Ltd, 1957) also provides an insightful account of general election of 1946.

The following publications provide different facets regarding elections of 1937 and 1946 in the context of Muslim League: Z.H. Zaidi, Aspects of the Development of Muslim League Policy, 1937–47 in C.H. Philips and Mary Doreen Wainwright, eds., *The Partition of India: Policies and Perspectives 1935–1947* (London: George Allen & Unwin, 1970); K.K. Aziz, ed., *Muslims Under Congress Rule 1937–1939: A Documentary Record*, Vol. 2 (New Delhi: Renaissance Publishing House, Reprint 1986); Ayesha Jalal, *The Sole Spokesman: Jinnah, the Muslim League and the Demand for Pakistan* (Cambridge: Cambridge University Press, 1985).

The following publications provide election related issues regarding the Agriculturist Party (Uttar Pradesh) and Krishak Praja Party (Bengal) respectively: the Agriculturalist Party has been dealt in P.D. Reeves, Landlords and Party Politics in the United Provinces, 1936–7 in Low, ed., *Soundings in Modern South Asian History* (London: Weidenfeld and Nicolson, 1968); Shila Sen's, monograph on *Muslim Politics in Bengal 1937–1947* (New Delhi: Impex India, 1976) deals with the elections of 1937 and 1946 in the context of Krishak Praja Party.

The following compendiums are of significance in providing a good deal of information on many aspects of Indian Constitutional Development, National Movement and partition: Anil Chandra Banerjee, ed., *Indian Constitutional Documents, 1757–1939*, Vol. 3 (Second Edition, Calcutta: A. Mukherjee, 1948); B.N. Pandey, ed., *The Indian Nationalist Movement, 1885–1947: Select Documents* (London: The Macmillan Press Ltd, 1979); Sir Maurice Gwyer and A. Appadorai, *Speeches and Documents on the Indian Constitution 1921–47*, Vol. 2 (Bombay: Oxford University Press, 1957); C.H. Philips and Mary Doreen Wainwright, eds., *The Partition of India: Policies and Perspectives 1935–1947* (London: George Allen and Unwin Ltd, 1970).

Chapter 3: electoral system, political parties and Lok Sabha elections

The first aspect in part three provides the Constitutional provisions on the electoral system. K.M. Munshi, *Constituent Assembly Debates: Official Report*, Vol. VII (New Delhi: Lok Sabha Secretariat, Reprint 1989) provide clause by clause debate and discussion on the Draft Constitution dealing with the electoral system. In the context of adult suffrage, the following publications highlight the significance of the transformation from 'a passive subject to a voter'. Valerian Rodrigues, ed., *The Essential Writings of B.R. Ambedkar* (Fifth Impression, New Delhi: Oxford University Press, 2008) Granville Austin, *The Indian Constitution: Cornerstone of a Nation* (Bombay: Oxford University Press, 1966); David Gilmartin, Election Law and the 'People' in Colonial and Post-colonial India in Dipesh Chakrabarty, Rochana Majumdar and Andrew Sartori, *From the Colonial to the*

Postcolonial: India and Pakistan in Transition (New Delhi: Oxford University Press, 2007); A.H. Somjee, *Political Capacity in Developing Societies* (London: The Macmillan Press Ltd, 1982).

Some of the important issues relating to election laws and electoral system and party recognition rules are discussed in the following publications/articles: V. S. Rama Devi and S. K. Mendiratta, *How India Votes: Election Laws, Practice and Procedure* (New Delhi: Butterworths, 2000), gives a comprehensive account of election laws and procedure. E. Sridharan, The Origins of the Electoral System Rules, Representation, and Power-sharing in India's Democracy in Zoya Hasan, E. Sridharan and R. Sudarshan, eds., *India's Living Constitution* (Third Impression, New Delhi: Permanent Black, 2011); Csaba Nikolenyi, Recognition Rules, Party Labels and the Number of Parties in India: A Research Note, *Party Politics*, Vol. 14, No. 2 (2008), deals with the legal aspects of the party recognition system in India.

The following monographs are concerned with the political parties in India and also address some of the emerging issues: Zoya Hasan, ed., *Parties and Party Politics in India* (New Delhi: Oxford University Press, 2002); E. Sridharan, The Party System in Niraja Gopal Jayal and Pratap Bhanu Mehta, eds., *The Oxford Companion to Politics in India* (New Delhi: Oxford University Press, 2010); Douglas V. Verney, How Has the Proliferation of Parties Affected the Indian Federation? A Comparative Approach in Zoya Hasan, E. Sridharan and R. Sudarshan, eds., *India's Living Constitution* (Third Impression, New Delhi: Permanent Black, 2011); Peter Ronald deSouza and E. Sridharan, eds., *India's Political Parties* (New Delhi: Sage Publications, 2006); Mahendra Prasad Singh, Rekha Saxena, eds., *India's Political Agenda: Perspectives on the Party System* (New Delhi: Kalinga Publications, 1996).

The following monographs are concerned with the coalition politics in the context of elections of 1998, 1999, 2004 and 2009: Csaba Nikolenyi, *Minority Governments in India: The Puzzle of Elusive Majorities* (London: Routledge, 2010); Bidyut Chakarabarty, *Forgoing Power: Coalition Politics in India* (New Delhi: Oxford University Press, 2006); Subhendu Ranjan Raj, *Coalition Politics in India: Dimensions of Federal Power Sharing* (New Delhi: Manak Publications, 2009). The following articles though written in the context of coalition politics and elections at the state level in the 1960s and 1970s, however, do provide an understanding on the need for ideological basis for coalition alliance: Pran Chopra, Ideology as Basis and Power as Functions in K.P. Karunakaran, ed., *Coalition Governments in India: Problems and Prospects* (Simla: Indian Institute of Advanced Study, 1975); A.R. Desai, Need for a Definite Programme in K.P. Karunakaran, ed., *Coalition Governments in India. Problems and Prospects* (Simla: Indian Institute of Advanced Study, 1975); V.M. Sirsikar, Repercussion on Democratic Experiment in K.P. Karunakaran, ed., *Coalition Governments in India: Problems and Prospects* (Simla: Indian Institute of Advanced Study, 1975).

The following publications provide a good background of the processes of elections: W.J. M. Mackenzie, *Free Elections: An Elementary Textbook* (London: George Allen & Unwin Ltd, 1958); T.E. Smith, *Elections in Developing Countries* (London: The Macmillan Press Ltd, 1960); Shri Ram Maheshwari, *The General Elections in India* (Allahabad: Chaitanya Publishing House, 1963); Special Issue on Administering Elections in India, *The Indian Journal of Public Administration*, Vol. XXXVII, No. 3 (July–September 1991); P. D. Reeves, B. D. Graham and J. M. Goodman, *A Handbook To Elections In Uttar Pradesh 1920–1951* (New Delhi: Manohar Book Service, 1975) is a good collection of election related information and statistics from 1920 to 1951; Mukulika Banerjee, *Why India Votes?* (New Delhi: Routledge, 2014) deals with the question, 'Why are Indian voters enthusiastic about elections'?

The following section provides references for the last sixteen elections 1952–2014:

First General Election, 1951–1952: *Report on the First General Elections in India*, 1951–52*, Election Commission of India, Vol. 1 (New Delhi: Government of India Press, 1955) Asoka Mehta, *The Political Mind of India: An Analysis of the Results of the General Elections* (Bombay: A Socialist Party Publication, 1952); Ramachandra Guha, Democracy's Biggest Gamble: India's First Free Elections in 1952, *World Policy Journal* (Spring 2002); Irene Tinker and Mil Walker, The First General Elections in India and Indonesia, *Far Eastern Survey*, Vol. XXV, No.7 (July 1956); Pranab Mukherjee, *Challenges Before the Nation* (New Delhi: Vikas Publishing Hosue Pvt Ltd, 1993).

Second General Election, 1957: *Report on the Second General Elections in India*, 1957, Election Commission of India, Vol. 1 (New Delhi: Routledge) S.L. Poplai, ed., *National Politics and 1957 Elections in India* (New Delhi: Metropolitan Book Co. Private Ltd, 1957); Selig S. Harrison, Hindu Society and the State: The Indian Union in K.H. Silvert, ed., *Expectant Peoples: Nationalism and Development* (New Delhi: Vintage Books, 1963); Margaret W. Fisher and Joan D. Bondurant and Tinker H., *Indian Experience with Democratic Elections*, Monograph Series, No.3 (Berkeley, CA: Indian Press Digests, December 1956); Richard D. Lambert, Hindu Communal Groups in Indian Politics in Richard L. Park and Irene Tinker, eds., *Leadership in Political Institutions in India* (Princeton, NJ: Princeton University Press, 1959).

Third General Election, 1962: *Report on the Third General Elections in India*, 1962 Election Commission of India, Vol. 1 (New Delhi: Election Commission); Rajni Kothari, The Congress 'System' in India, *Asian Survey*, Vol. 4 (1964) and Surindar Suri, Towards a Theory of Indian Politics: Some Implications of the Results of the General Election, *The Economic Weekly*, December, 1962 and see also for the development of the party system after independence as well as dominance of the Congress Party and a detailed analysis of the results of1962 elections – Gopal Krishan, One Party Dominance – Development and Trends, *Perspectives*, supplement to the *Indian Journal of Public Administration*, Vol. XII, No. 1 (January–March 1966).

Fourth General Election, 1967: *Report on the Fourth General Election in India*, 1967, Election Commission of India, Vol. 1 (New Delhi: Government of India Press); M. Pattabhiram, ed., *General Election in India 1967: An Exhaustive Study of Main Political Trends* (Bombay: Allied Publishers, 1967); Sulekh C. Gupta, Fourth General Elections: Its Dimension and Dialectics, *Mainstream* (March 1967); Norman D. Palmer, India's Fourth General Elections, *Asian Survey*, Vol. VII, No. 5 (May 1967) and S.P. Varma and Iqbal Narain, eds., *Fourth General Election in India, Volume One Political Surveys* (Bombay: Orient Longmans Limited, 1968).

Fifth General Election, 1971*: *Report on the Fifth General Election in India*, 1971, Election Commission of India, Vol. 1 (New Delhi: Government of India Press); W.H. Morris-Jones, India Elects For Change and Stability, *Asian Survey*, Vol. XI, No. 8 (July 1971); Myron Weiner, The 1971 Elections and the Indian Party System, *Asian Survey*, Vol. XI, No. 12 (December 1971).

Sixth General Election, 1977: *Statistical Report on General Election, 1977 to the Sixth Lok Sabha*, Election Commission of India, Vol. 1 (New Delhi: Election Commission, 1978); S. Devadas Pillai, ed., *The Incredible Elections: 1977: A blow-by-Blow Document as reported in the Indian Express* (Bombay: Popular Prakashan, 1977); Stanley A. Kochanek, Mrs. Gandhi's pyramid: The New Congress in Henry C. Hart, ed., *Indira Gandhi's India: A political System Reappraised* (Boulder, CO: Westview Press, 1976); Ram Joshi and Kirtidev Desai, Towards a More Competitive Party System in India, *Asian Survey*, Vol. XVIII, No. 1 (November 1978); Oliver Mendelsohn, The Collapse of the Indian National Congress, *Pacific Affairs*, Vol. 51, No.1 (Spring 1978); Myron Weiner: The 1977 Parliamentary Elections in India, *Asian Survey*, Vol. XVII, No. 7 (July 1977); Norman D. Palmer, The Two Elections: A Comparative Analysis, *Asian Survey*, Vol. XVII, No.7 (July 1977); Harry W. Blair, Mrs. Gandhi's Emergency, The Indian Elections of 1977, Pluralism and Marxism: Problems with Paradigms Modern, *Asian Studies*, Vol. 14, No. 2 (1980); D.A. Low, *Eclipse of Empire* (Cambridge: Cambridge University Press, 1991); Jyotirindra Das Gupta, India 1979: The Prize Chair and the People's Share – Electoral Diversion and Economic Reversal, *Asian Survey*, Vol. XX, No. 2 (February 1980); Kuldip Nayar, *The Judgement* (New Delhi: Vikas Publishing House Pvt Ltd, 1977); Norman D. Palmer, India in 1976: The Politics of Depoliticization, *Asian Survey*, Vol. XVII, No.2 (February 1977).

Seventh General Election, 1980: *Statistical Report on General Election, 1980 to the Seventh Lok Sabha*, Election Commission of India, Vol. 1 (New Delhi: Election Commission, 1981); S.K. Chaturvedi, *The Seventh Lok Sabha Election: An Analysis of Peoples' Verdict* (Kanpur: Grantham, 1981); Javeed Alam, The Vote for 'Political Stability' and the Implication:

An Analysis of 1980 Election Results, *Political Science Review*, Vol. 21, No. 4 (October–December 1982); Y.C. Bhatnagar and Moin Shakir, The Seventh Lok Sabha Elections, *Indian Journal of Political Science*, Vol. 41 (1980) and N.D. Arora, Analysis of 7th Lok Sabha Elections in the State of Punjab, Haryana and J & K, The *Indian Political Science Review*, Election Issue (July 1980); Henry C. Hart, The Indian Constitution: Political Development and Decay, *Asian Survey*, Vol. XX, No. 4 (April 1980).

* It is important to mention that the Election Commission Reports from 1952 to 1971, i.e. the first four general elections, used however to contain analysis of election-related issues in volume 1 of each Report. This practice was discontinued after 1971. As such, the Election Commission Reports from 1971 onwards contain in volume 1 national and state abstracts and detailed results and, in Vol. 2, constituency data-summary related to that period.

Eighth General Election, 1984: *Statistical Report on General Election, 1984 to the Eighth Lok Sabha*, Election Commission of India, Vol. 1 (New Delhi: Election Commission, 1985); V. Bhaskara Rao, ed., *General Elections in India: Some Issues of Eighth Lok Sabha Elections* (New Delhi: Uppal Publishing House, 1987); J.R. Siwach, Eighth Lok Sabha Elections, *The Indian Journal of Political Studies*, Vol. 9 (December 1985); Walter Hauser and Wendy Singer, The Democratic Rite: Celebration and Participation in the Indian Elections, *Asian Survey*, Vol. XXVI, No.9 (September 1986); Iqbal Narain, India in 1985: Triumph of Democracy, *Asian Survey*, Vol. XXVI, No.2 (February 1986); Harold A. Gould, A Sociological Perspective on the Eighth General Election in India, *Asian Survey*, Vol. XXVI, No. 6 (June 1986); David Butler, The Winter's Election, *Representation*, Vol. 25, No. 98 (March 1985).

Ninth General Election, 1989: *Statistical Report on General Election, 1989 to the Ninth Lok Sabha*, Election Commission of India, Vol. 1 (New Delhi: Election Commission, 1990); Harold A. Gould and Sumit Ganguly, eds., *India Votes: Alliance Politics and Minority Governments in the Ninth and Tenth General Elections* (Boulder, CO: Westview Press, 1993); Mahendra Prasad Singh, ed., *Lok Sabha Elections 1989: Indian Politics in 1990's* (New Delhi: Kalinga Publications, 1992); Mahendra Prasad Singh, Ideological Spectrum in Mahendra Prasad Singh and Rekha Saxena, eds., *India's Political Agenda: Perspectives on the Party System* (New Delhi: Kalinga Publications, 1996); *The 'People's Verdict', Seminar* No. 368 (April 1990); Dennis Austin and Anirudha Gupta, India's Ninth General Election, *Round Table*, No. 314 (1990); Walter K. Anderson, Election 1989 in India: The Dawn of Coalition Politics? *Asian Survey*, Vol. XXX, No. 6 (June 1990); Atul Kohli, From Majority to Minority Rule: Making Sense of the 'New' Indian Politics in Marshall M. Bouton and Philip Oldenburg, eds., *India Briefing, 1990* (Boulder, CO: Westview Press, 1990).

Tenth General Election, 1991: *Statistical Report on General Election, 1991 to the Tenth Lok Sabha*, Election Commission of India, Vol. 1 (New Delhi: Election Commission, 1992); Robert L. Hardgrave, After the Dynasty: Politics in India, *Current History* (March 1992); Walter K. Andersen, India's 1991 Elections: The Uncertain Verdict, *Asian Survey*, Vol. 31, No. 10 (October 1991); Mitu Sengupta, How the State Changed Its Mind: Power, Politics and the Origins of India's Market Reforms, *Economic & Political Weekly* (Special Article) (May 2008); A.G. Noorani, Ayodhya Again: The BJP's Unconstitutional Project, *Frontline* (July 1991); Pranab Mukherjee, *Challenges Before the Nation* (New Delhi: Vikas Publishing House Pvt Ltd, 1993).

Eleventh General Election, 1996: *Statistical Report on General Election, 1996 to the Eleventh Lok Sabha*, Election Commission of India, Vol. 1 (New Delhi: Election Commission); Pramod K Kantha, General Elections, 1996: BJP Politics: Looking beyond the Impasse, *Economic and Political Weekly* (November 1997); Walter Andersen, India in 1995: Year of the Long Campaign, *Asian Survey*, Vol. XXXVI, No.2 (February 1996); Aditya Nigam, India After the 1996 Elections: Nation, Locality and Representation, *Asian Survey*, Vol. XXXVI, No. 12 (December 1996); Sudha Pai, Transformation of the Indian Party System: The 1996 Lok Sabha Elections, *Asian Survey*, Vol. XXXVI, No.12 (December 1996); BM, UF Government Emerging in True Colours, *Economic and Political Weekly* (June 1996); Paul Wallace, General Elections, 1996: Regional Parties Dominant in Punjab and Haryana, *Economic and Political Weekly* (November 1997); Sudipta Kaviraj, The General Elections in India, *Government and Opposition*, Vol. 32 (1997); E. Sridharan, Coalition Politics, *Seminar* No. 437 (January 1996); Prannoy Roy and Dorab Sopariwala, Political Alliances: Fatal Attraction, *India Today* (April 15, 1996).

Twelfth General Election, 1998: *Statistical Report on General Election, 1998 to the Twelfth Lok Sabha*, Election Commission of India, Vol. 1 (New Delhi: Election Commission); Ramashray Roy and Paul Wallace, eds., *Indian Politics and 1998 Election: Regionalism, Hindutva and State Politics* (New Delhi: Sage Publications, 1999); Sudha Pai, *State Politics New Dimension: Party System, Liberalisation and Politics of Identity* (New Delhi: Shipra Publications, 2000).

Thirteenth General Election, 1999: *Statistical Report on General Election, 1999 to the Thirteenth Lok Sabha*, Election Commission of India, Vol. 1 (New Delhi: Election Commission); Cruel Choices *Seminar* No. 480 (August 1999); Aditya Nigam and Yogendra Yadav, Electoral Politics in Indian States, 1989–99, *Economic and Political Weekly* (August1999); Rob Jenkins, Appearance and Reality in Indian Politics: Making Sense of the 1999 General Election, *Government and Opposition*, Vol. 35, No.1 (2000); Nagindas Sanghavi and Usha Thakkar, Regionalisation of Indian Politics, *Economic and Political Weekly* (February 2000); Yogendra Yadav and Suhas Palshikar, From Hegemony to Convergence Party System and Electoral Politics in the Indian States, 1952–2002, *Journal of Indian School of Political Thought*, Vol. 13, No. 1 and 2 (January–June 2000).

Fourteenth General Election, 2004: *Statistical Report on General Election, 2004 to the Fourteen Lok Sabha*, Election Commission of India, Vol. 1 (New Delhi: Election Commission); R Sthanumoorthy and Leena Mary Eapen, Election Issues in Election: Recent Trends, *Economic and Political Weekly* (March 2004); Christophe Jaffrelt, The BJP and the 2004 General Election: Dimensions, Causes and Implications of an Unexpected Defeat in Katharine Adeney and Lawrence Saez, *Coalition Politics and Hindu Nationalism* (New York: Routledge, 2005); *'A Mandate For Change' Seminar* No. 539 (July 2004); Kanchan Chandra, *Why Ethnic Parties Succeed, Patronage and Ethnic Head Counts in India* (New York: Cambridge University Press, 2004).

Fifteenth General Election, 2009: *Statistical Report on General Election, 2009 to the Fifteenth Lok Sabha*, Election Commission of India, Vol. 1 (New Delhi: Election Commission); Paul Wallace and Ramashray Roy, eds., *India's 2009 Elections: Coalition Politics, Party Competition, and Congress Continuity* (London: Sage Publications, 2011); Ajay K. Mehra, ed., *Emerging Trends in Indian Politics: The 15th General Election* (London: Routledge, 2010); Verdict 2009: Myths and Hypotheses, *Economic and Political Weekly* (May 2009); National Election Study 2009, *Economic and Political Weekly* (October 2009).

Sixteenth General Election, 2014: Venkitesh Ramakrishan, Right at the Centre, *Frontline*, Vol. 31, No. 11 (May 31–June 13, 2014), pp. 6–10; Election Commission of India, http://eciresults.nic.in/; Ravinder Kaur, The' Emerging' Middle Class: Role in the 2014 General Elections, *Economic and Political Weekly*, Vol. 49, No. 26–27 (June 28, 2014); Badri Narayan, Modi's Modus Operandi in the 2014 Elections, *Economic and Political Weekly*, Vol. 49, No. 20 (May 17, 2014); Editorial, Behind Modi-led BJP's Spectacular Performance, *Mainstream*, Vol. LII, No. 22 (May 24, 2014), p. 2; Bharat Dogra, Elections Give BJP Historic Victory, But Some Disturbing Trends Can't Be Ignored, *Mainstream*, Vol. LII, No. 22 (May 24, 2014), pp. 7–8; Abhijit Ghosh, No Paradigm Shift in Sixteenth Lok Sabha Elections, *Mainstream*, Vol. LII, No. 19 (May 3, 2014), pp. 15–16; Pratip Chattopadhyay, Towards Lok Sabha Elections 2014: Politics, Parties in West Bengal, *Mainstream*, Vol. LII, No. 19 (May 3, 2014), pp. 17–22; Bharat Dogra, Crucial Questions for Left Forces, *Mainstream*, Vol. LII, No. 19 (May 3, 2014), pp. 23–26; Editorial, Modi Wins Massive Anti-Congress Mandate, *Mainstream*, Vol. LII, No. 21 (May 17, 2014), p. 2; Badri Raina, The Modi Whirlwind, *Mainstream*, Vol. LII, No. 21 (May 17, 2014), pp. 3–4; Arun Srivastava, Muslim Voters and BJP's Secularist Attempt, *Mainstream*, Vol. LII, No. 21 (May 17, 2014), pp. 7–8; Diptendra Raychaudhuri, Election 2014: RSS Swallows the Great Indian Media! *Mainstream*, Vol. LII, No. 21 (May 17, 2014), pp. 19–26.

Chapter 4: a comparative analysis of party manifestos of national political parties

The following publications provide an overview on the working of democracy: Upendra Baxi, 'The Little Done, The Vast Undone' – Some Reflections on Reading Granville Austin's, The Indian Constitution, *Journal of the Indian Law Institute*, Vol. 9 (Penguin Books, 1967); Sunil Khilnani, *The Idea of India* (New Delhi, Reprinted 2004, 2011); Ramachandra Guha, *India After Gandhi: The History of the World's Largest Democracy* (London: Macmillan, 2007); and Jean Dreze and Amartya Sen, *An Uncertain Glory: India and its Contradictions* (New Delhi: Allen Lane, 2013).

In the Indian context, there has been an important contribution by Perry Anderson, *The Indian Ideology* (New Delhi: Three Essays Collective, 2012) criticizing the idea of India, its democratic stability, multicultural unity and impartial secularism of the Indian state. The following two publications broadly deal with policy and performance of the Congress Party and the Janata Party respectively: B.B. Misra, *The Congress Party and Government: Policy and Programmes* (New Delhi: Concept Publishing Company, 1988); Madhu Limaye, *Janata Party Experiment: An Insider's Account of Opposition Politics*, Vol. 2 (New Delhi: B. R. Publishing Corporation, 1994).

The problem of inequality and democracy in the context of India has been discussed and analysed in the following publications: Gunnar Myrdal, *Asian Drama: An Inquiry Into the Poverty of Nations*, Vol. 3 (New York: Twentieth Century Fund, 1968); Myron Weiner, The Struggle for Equality in India, *Foreign Affairs*, Vol. 40, No.4 (July 1962); Pratap Banu Mehta, Breaking the Silence: Why We Don't Talk about Inequality – And How to Start Again, *The Carvan*, Vol. 4, No. 10 (October 2012); Joseph E. Stiglitz, *The Price of Inequality* (London: Penguin, 2012) also dealt with this problem, however, in the context of United States of America.

The following articles and monographs provide a perspective on the ideology of the major political parties in India.

INC: AICC Report of the Economic Programme Committee, 1947 in A.M. Zaidi and S.G. Zaidi, *Chief Editors, The Foundations of Indian Economic Planning: An Attempt at Reshaping the Destiny of 600 Million Indians* (New Delhi: S. Chand and Company, 1979); Ram Joshi, R.K. Hebsur, eds., *Congress in Indian Politics: A Centenary Perspective* (Bombay: Popular Prakashan, 1987); Shriram Maheshwari, Ideological Vision and Reality in B.N. Pandey, ed., *A Centenary History of the Indian National Congress* (1885–1985), Vol. 5 (New Delhi: Jointly Published by All India Congress Committee and Vikas Publishing House Pvt Ltd, 1985).

Communist Party of India: Gene D. Overstreet and Marshall Windmiller, *Communism in India* (Berkeley, CA: University of California Press, 1959) and N.K. Krishnan, The Communist Party of India in Subhash C. Kashyap, ed., *Indian Political Parties: Programmes, Promises and Performance* (New

Delhi: Research Publications, 1971); see also P.C. Joshi, Reflections on Marxism and Social Revolution in India in K. N. Panikkar, ed., *National and Left Movements in India* (New Delhi: Vikas Publishing House Pvt Ltd, 1980); and Paul R. Brass and Marcus F. Franda, eds., *Radical Politics in South Asia* (Cambridge: The MIT Press, 1973); Manoranjan Mohanty, Ideology and Strategy of the Communist Movement in India in Thomas Pantham and Kenneth L. Deutsch, eds., *Political Thought in Modern India* (New Delhi: Sage Publications, 1986).

Jana Sangh/BJP and Swatantra Party: M.R. Masani, *Why Swatantra* (Bombay: Popular Prakashan, n.d.), Howard L. Erdman, *The Swatantra Party and Indian Conservatism* (London: Cambridge University Press, 1967); Motilal A. Jhangiani, *Jana Sangh and Swatantra: A Profile of the Rightist Parties in India* (Bombay: Manaktalas, 1967); B.D. Graham, *Hindu Nationalism and Indian Politics: The Origins and Development of the Bharatiya Jana Sangh* (Cambridge: Cambridge University Press, 1990); Gurdas M. Ahuja, *BJP and the Indian Politics: Policies and Programmes of the Bharatiya Janata Party* (New Delhi: Ram Company, 1994); Christophe Jaffrelot, ed., *The Sangh Parivar: A Reader* (New Delhi: Oxford University Press, 2005); Craig Baxter, *The Jana Sangh: A Biography of an Indian Political Party* (Philadelphia: University of Pennsylvania Press, 1969); Baldev Raj Nayar, *Globalization and Nationalism: The Changing Balance in India's Economic Policy*, 1950–2000 (New Delhi: Sage Publications, 2001) for a good account of economic reforms under the United Front 1996–1998 and BJP led government 1998–1999; Thomas Blom Hansen, *The Saffron Wave, Democracy and Hindu Nationalism in Modern India* (New Delhi: Oxford University Press, 1999); Walter Anderson and Shridhar D. Damle, *The Brotherhood in Saffron* (New Delhi: Vistaar Publications, 1987); Thomas Blom Hansen, and Christophe Jaffrelot, eds., The *BJP and the Compulsions of Politics in India* (New Delhi: Oxford University Press, 1998); Christophe Jaffrelot, *The Hindu Nationalist Movement and Indian Politics 1925 to the 1990s* (New York: Columbia University Press, 1996); Barbara R. Joshi, *Democracy in Search of Equality: Untouchable Politics and Indian Social Change* (New Delhi: Hindustan Publication Corporation, 1982).

Socialist Party: Jaya Prakash Naryan, ed., Yusuf Meherally, *Towards Struggle: Selected Manifestos, Speeches and Writings* (Bombay: Padma Publications Ltd, 1946); *Programme-Socialist Party* (Bombay: Socialist Party, 1947); Hari Kishore Singh, *A History of the Praja Socialist Party [1934–59]* (Lucknow: Narendra Prakashan, 1959); N. C. Mehrotra, *The Socialist Movement in India* (New Delhi: Radiant Publishers, 1995); N.G. Goray and Surendranath Dwivedy, *Why Praja Socialist?* (Bombay: Popular Prakashan); Madhu Limaye, *Why Samyukta Socialist?* (Bombay: Popular Prakashan, 1967); Girja Shankar, *Socialist Trends in Indian National Movement: Being a Study of the Congress Socialist Party* (Meerut: Twenty-First Century Publishers, 1987); *We Build For Socialism* (Bombay: Socialist Party, Reprinted November 1951).

INDEX

For Product Safety Concerns and Information please contact our EU representative GPSR@taylorandfrancis.com Taylor & Francis Verlag GmbH, Kaufingerstraße 24, 80331 München, Germany

Batch number: 10725981

Printed by Printforce, the Netherlands